*The Left Hand of God*

# The

# Left

# Hand

# of God

A Biography of the

# Holy Spirit

## Adolf Holl

Translated from the German by John Cullen

Doubleday   New York London Toronto Sydney Auckland

The display type in this book has been set in the font "RuachPlain."

The composition of this work was begun in December 1993 and completed in December 1996. The epigraph on page viii is taken from Adolf Holl, *Wie ich ein Priester wurde, warum Jesus dagegen war und was dabei herausgekommen ist* (Reinbek: Rowohlt, 1992), p. 59.

PUBLISHED BY DOUBLEDAY
*a division of Bantam Doubleday Dell Publishing Group, Inc.*
*1540 Broadway, New York, New York 10036*

DOUBLEDAY *and the portrayal of an anchor with a dolphin are trademarks of Doubleday, a division of Bantam Doubleday Dell Publishing Group, Inc.*

BOOK DESIGN BY TERRY KARYDES

*Library of Congress Cataloging-in-Publication Data*
*Holl, Adolf.*
    *[Linke Hand Gottes. English]*
    *The left hand of God: a biography of the Holy Spirit /*
*by Adolf Holl; translated from the German by John Cullen.*
        *p.        cm.*
    *Includes bibliographical references and index.*
    *1. Holy Spirit—Controversial literature. I. Title.*
*BT123.H6513        1998*
*231'.3—dc21        98-17994        CIP*

*ISBN 0-385-49284-7*
*Copyright © 1997 by Adolf Holl;*
*first published in the German language by List Verlag, Munich, Germany*
*English translation copyright © 1998 by John Cullen*
*All Rights Reserved*
*Printed in the United States of America*
*November 1998*
*First Edition in the United States of America*
*10   9   8   7   6   5   4   3   2   1*

# Translator's Note

Anyone who lays hands on a work written in one language and wrests from it a version written in another is glad of an opportunity to annotate, to explain, to compensate for inadequacies, to hedge his bets. *The Left Hand of God*, a densely packed and wide-ranging book, offers ample grounds for expatiation, but I shall mention only a couple of essential points.

The first of these is linguistic. In German, the Holy Spirit is called *der Heilige Geist*. As one might suspect, *Geist* is akin to the English word "ghost," but neither "spirit" nor "ghost," though possible translations, adequately reflects the spectrum of meanings that *Geist* has in German. These include "mind," "intellect," and "wit," and thus the French *esprit* is a better rendering of *Geist* than any single word that English supplies. *Geist* has dispirited many translators from the German—Hegel's *Phänomenologie des Geistes*, for example, has been Englished as both *Phenomenology of Mind* and *Phenomenology of Spirit*—and one can but ask the reader to bear in mind the broader range of the original German word that is here generally rendered as "spirit."

The second point concerns sources, attributions, and notes. Though his documentation is quite meticulous, Adolf Holl, like many European writers, makes very sparing use of quotation marks, and the reader must often guess which words are the author's own and which are those of the source he's quoting. Furthermore, Dr. Holl frequently follows a practice common in Catholic writings: he telescopes or conflates passages from his sources, sometimes making what he refers to in his notes as a "montage," and he paraphrases many authors, including biblical ones. I have tried to indicate all directly quoted, unaltered citations by putting them within quotation marks or (less often) italicizing or indenting them; but all montages, conflations, rearrangements, paraphrases, and the like have been allowed to stand without indication in the body of the text, as they do in the original. While there is no separate bibliography, complete bibliographical information on each of the works cited appears in the Source Notes.

—*John Cullen, May 3, 1998*

# Contents

But when it calls,

there's only one thing to do.

In such cases

an answer is always expected.

for P.S.

# *Preface*

FOR ANY HALFWAY SIGNIFICANT GOD,

a thousand years pass in a trice. And therefore accounts of

the lives of particular divinities—examples of a forgotten

literary genre—must necessarily range over longer periods of time

than what is required for biographies of historical figures.

The aretalogists, as those who wrote descriptions of the gods used to be called, did not wish to organize their material in a sequence of events passing from birth to death; they favored a thematic arrangement that followed the various well-known manifestations of the mighty divinity in whose honor they were writing.

Admittedly this pattern overlooks the fact that the world of the gods, too, is subject to the law of mortality. A walk into the nearest museum will show the dead gods whom nobody worships anymore. No one, therefore, can describe gods successfully without taking into account their origin and their passing.

It was granted to few divinities to move beyond the narrow provincialism of their beginnings and into a broad, polyglot cosmopolitanism. The Egyptian Osiris is one example; there were temples dedicated to him throughout the Roman Empire. Eventually he was driven out by the Hebrew Yahweh, whom Jews, Christians, and Muslims worship to this day as the absolute champion of all divine history.

Out of this same field proceeds the Spirit who, according to Christian belief, unites with the Father and the Son to form the Most Holy Trinity. It was he who seized the man Jesus and opened his mouth to announce the good news of the Gospel to the Jews. It was owing to the Holy Spirit that a few Galilean fishermen found the courage, after the Nazarene's death, to preach a world religion. Moreover, the Holy Spirit granted Christians sensational experiences, ecstasies and inspirations, which were then talked about and helped bring the evangel to the people.

The Holy Spirit is portrayed most often in animal form, in the shape of a dove, which places him beyond any human resemblance, in contrast to the Father and the Son and their familiar facial features.

The iconographic reticence concerning the depiction of the third divine Person corresponds to the distinct restraint exercised by the established Christian churches in their liturgical dealings with the Holy Spirit. Only very seldom are prayers directed to him personally, and but one feast a year, Pentecost, is celebrated in his name.

This god's traces are quite visible, however, in the history of heresies and wrongheadedness: among Syrian hermits, French *perfecti*, German mystics, English freethinkers, American Negro slaves, among artists and communists, eccentrics, feminists, and inventors. Again and again in such realms of experience, the spark of an effusive joy flashes out, momentary and fleeting. These are the moments when the divine in man makes itself manifest. According to an old tradition, the harp that is played at such times has ten strings.

*The Left Hand of God*

# *Easter*

# *Joy*

I T WAS HIGH TIME FOR A NEW GOD. TO BE

*sure, the priests of Jupiter were busy as of old, maintaining good relations with the higher*

*powers, and all around the Mediterranean the Divine Wife had her altars, where pilgrims*

*submitted their petitions and the sick hoped for a miracle.*

*But more and more foreign cults from the eastern parts of the Roman Empire* were appearing alongside the traditional gods. Noblemen's sons, dissatisfied with the faith of their fathers, were traveling from the Tiber to the Nile to be initiated into esoteric mysteries.

Now and again an imported deity even managed to acquire a temple in Rome. None, however, got so far as to reign supreme in the sacred sphere from Spain to Syria, from Africa to Britain.

This is how things stood when the followers of a certain Chrestos began to cause a stir. This remarkable sect agitated among the lower working classes and the slaves, shunned the public baths, the chariot races, and the gladiatorial combats, and preached contempt for the gods. No one was very disturbed when the authorities took severe measures against these opponents of religion.

What was known about them was scanty enough. They prayed to a Jew who had been crucified as a criminal; they met in secret, never failed to support one another, had congregations in every large city, and were tightly organized.

And they believed in God—not the conventional, generic designation used for the plural gods of Mount Olympus, but the absolute, singular entity in the otherworldly realm, next to whom the familiar multiplicity of celestial beings shrank down to a demonic deception.

Against all expectations, this God, of Jewish origin (like the man who died on the cross), rose to become the central religio-political authority in the Roman Empire, with well-known consequences for Europe and the rest of the world.

Behind this amazing sequence of events was a hidden force that the Christians, right from the beginning, called the Holy Spirit.

Further reports about the workings of this force are quite fragmentary. It hides between the lines of the basic Christian texts and gives itself away only through hints that seem encoded, as though it wanted to deny its decisive role in the salvation process.

*Whoever can crack the code and read the signs will see the beginnings of Christianity in a different light. Considered in this light, those beginnings suggest a condition that in our narrow-minded times would probably be seen as a psychiatric disorder.*

*Then Jesus becomes a man possessed; the only question is by whom or what.*

*For thoughtful people, the answer to this question is almost certainly not to be found in the Bible.*

# A Dove
# from Heaven

THE FIRST DECENTLY RELIABLE NEWS about the intervention of a "Holy Spirit" in the course of earthly events comes from the second decade of our era. In those days, it is written in the Gospel according to Mark, Jesus came from Nazareth in Galilee and was baptized in the Jordan by John. And at once, as he was coming up out of the water, he saw the heavens torn apart and the Spirit, like a dove, descending on him. And a voice came from heaven, "You are my Son, the Beloved; my favor rests on you." In Matthew's Gospel, the apparition that Jesus saw is called "Spirit of God." Luke is the clearest of all. The Holy Spirit, with the definite article, descended on Jesus out of the opened heavens "in a physical form, like a dove." Finally, in the fourth Gospel, John the Baptist is presented as a witness: "I saw the Spirit come down on him like a dove from heaven and rest on him."

Therefore, only Jesus and his baptist discerned the manifestation of the deity in dovish form. So the question suggests itself: How did they both know that the heavenly bird embodied, of all things, the Holy Spirit? Not a single passage in the Hebrew Bible mentions the Spirit of God in connection with a dove.

.   .   .

In the stories, as they circulated among the followers of both Jesus and John and were later included in the Christian Gospels, one can still notice the original tension between the two men. They appear as a pair of rivals, like Romulus and Remus or Cain and Abel. One of them must die, and in this case it is John, for whom the executioner is already waiting; the decision, however, is first made in the visionary space that envelops the two ecstatics. In this space, other certainties hold sway than those of the humdrum world. The thing that takes shape out of the cascading light of the opened heavens, descends as a dove, and finally stops, hovering above the chosen one—this must have its origin in the divine sphere, must, for devout Jews, come from Yahu (Yahweh), the Most High (praised be His Name), whose exhalations have always quickened the prophets: God's Spirit, *ruach yahu*. And there's another, simultaneous decision, concerning which baptism the heralds of God's oncoming Kingdom will ordain in the future—not the baptism in water, but the baptism "with the Holy Spirit."

And at once, Mark goes on, the Spirit drove him into the desert. That makes it clear how the new baptism works, first of all for Jesus, the Nazarene, whom the dove has marked as the favorite of heaven. John, the baptizer with water, must exit. Hereafter the spiritual dove is never sighted again.

And the Jordan flows on into the Dead Sea, the lowest point on earth, where Lot's wife stiffened into a pillar of salt because she was too curious. There, surrounded by inhospitable desolation, Jesus is to encounter another spirit, not a holy one this time, but the dastardly adversary called Shaitan. In this flat stretch of desert land he commands the numberless djinns, a tumultuous, twittering retinue of half-demons that bear the mantle of the Prince of Darkness. Spirits are everywhere, partly incarnate, not gods, not beasts, not human, sexless, with claws, beaks, goggle eyes, scales, tails.

But Jesus, as Luke emphasizes, is "filled" with the Holy Spirit, and his victory in the power struggle is assured from the outset. Into the madhouse of the spirits bursts God's command: *Hear ye! No others before me! All homage to me alone!*

At once the fiends disperse in every direction, desisting until the next attack. Already the flame-faced messengers are approaching from Yahweh's throne in order to boost the exhausted man's failing energy. Angels looked after him, Mark comments. Then, he continues, Jesus went into Galilee, proclaiming the good news of God. Current conditions will soon change, All Things Will Be Made New, Abraham's table is already laid for the hungry, heaven on earth, Thy Kingdom come.

The people who hear the new sound most clearly are those who are possessed. Already, with the Nazarene's first entrance into the splendid temple in Capernaum, the action begins, as though on the stage. A man begins to bellow. The "unclean spirit" (Mark) that has taken possession of him speaks in the first-person plural; he's not the only one who's nervous: "What do you want with us, Jesus of Nazareth? Have you come to destroy us? I know who you are: the Holy One of God!"

So the demons know what's going on. Now the man from Nazareth must show what he's capable of. The preacher has already turned into an exorcist. Two harsh commands are aimed at the center of the disturbance: "Be quiet! Come out!" Immediately the body of the possessed man goes into convulsions. The occupying force is not ready to withdraw so abruptly. Finally comes a long-drawn-out shriek, the signal for departure. Then silence. Mutterings in the crowd: "He gives orders even to unclean spirits and they obey him."

Matthew and Luke have information about the exorcised spirit's next moves. When it comes out of a man, it goes through waterless country looking for a place to rest, but cannot find one and returns thereupon to its former home, finds it vacant, swept clean, chilly. Takes seven more spirits, craftier than itself, and together they go back into the deserted house and live there.

That sounds fairly dangerous. The world of the evangelists is filled with spirits, much as the island of Bali is for its present-day inhabitants.

Thus the evangelists insist all the more energetically upon the uniqueness of the Spirit that has taken possession of the Nazarene. Only this Spirit "from above," as John's Gospel describes him, may bear the attribute of holiness. It must be he who has chosen Jesus as Israel's Redeemer, as the *māshīah* (that is, the Messiah, literally "the anointed one," in Greek, *christos*). Without this Holy Spirit, Jesus would never have become Christ, and the religion that traces itself to Jesus Christ would have had to look for another name.

# *Huff  and  Puff*

*N*O, CHRISTIANITY IS NOT A RELIGION of the book, at least not originally. The Nazarene left no writings behind. Do not cling to me, the Jesus of John's Gospel admonishes his loving friend, Mary of Magdala. Thus does he fend off as well any attempt to pin him down in written words. Apparently Jesus had no time to bother with paper and writing tools. From the start, therefore, the holy scriptures that were written about the Nazarene after his death incurred the suspicion of having distorted his original intentions. And this is why surreptitious traces of a profound self-irony sometimes emerge—perhaps unintentionally—as they do, for example, in the apostle Paul's second epistle to the Corinthians, where he says that written letters kill, but the Spirit gives life.

Here, in the middle of Paul's text, the divine principle of origin, under the name "Spirit," without whose intervention the Nazarene would have remained a carpenter, balks at the written word's tendency to fix its subject.

*G*eist ("spirit"): with this word the Germanic peoples, when they came to be baptized, translated the Greek word *pneuma* (*spiritus* in Latin) in the Bible. *Pneuma* was in turn a translation of the Semitic root *rwh*, feminine in gender, pronounced *ruach* in Hebrew and *rucho* in Syriac; its original meaning was "air in movement."

Indeed, the Germanic Geist did have in common with the Semitic ruach incorporeality, as well as a certain liveliness; but the scorching wind from the Arabian desert, likewise called ruach in the Hebrew Bible, could mean nothing to the men of the north.

In John's Gospel, on the other hand, the original sensuousness of the ruach is still there: the pneuma blows wherever it pleases. You hear its huff, but you cannot tell where it's coming from or whither it's puffing. So it is with everyone born of the pneuma.

The pneuma in the Greek original of this passage quite clearly betrays the feeling for language characteristic of the Semitic tongue from which it was translated. The quotation lets the ruach blow like a violent storm, but soon uses it as a metaphor for a sudden, transforming force that makes a new person of whomever it strikes.

Accordingly, the process indicated here would be quite stormy, and this, again, must remain as foreign to the essentially sedate German spirit (holy or not) as an Oriental market.

On the other hand, the 378 passages in the Hebrew Bible that mention the ruach readily associate it with everything that runs athwart the monotonous course of things, whether it has to do with the creation of the world or an outburst of rage, with Yahweh's condescension to the man Moses, with the resuscitation of dead bones, the guarantee of Samson's unprecedented physical strength, ecstatic runners racing for God, the metamorphosis of a guerrilla such as David into a respectable king. As soon as the ruach comes blowing down, the sons and daughters of Israel begin prophesying, young men have visions, councillors are haunted by dreams of the future, and God makes a new testament.

So also in the case of Jesus, the carpenter Joseph's son. How the ruach exercised this man, whose earlier life remains obscure, is betrayed by a little word that the evangelist Mark, to no particular purpose, lets slip some forty-one times: *euthys*. This word is a mere filler, easily overlooked, occurring at the beginning of many a sentence, connecting one episode to the next: *right away, just then, immediately, at once.*

This little word gives a driving tempo to the Nazarene's life. For something like a year he must rush breathlessly from one appointment to the next, until it's all over for him. In Mark's Gospel, the staccato pulse of the ruach starts the moment Jesus climbs out of the waters of the Jordan after his baptism. *At once* heaven is torn open, the dove descends, the imperious voice rings out. And *at once* the ruach casts its man into the desert. Jesus beckons to Simon and his brother, and *immediately* they leave their nets lying on the shore of the Sea of Galilee and run after him. And *as soon as* the Sabbath comes, Jesus goes into the synagogue in Capernaum. *Right away* the possessed man cries out.

And so forth, all through Galilee, then on to Tyre and Sidon, down to Jericho, and finally up to Jerusalem for the Passover, where Jesus is arrested, and where the last *euthys* hastens his delivery to Pilate, early in the morning of Good Friday, the day that will bring him to the cross.

Jesus is allowed to take his time only after his death, during the course of his deification, his enthronement at the right hand of the Father, and for this no further *euthys* is necessary in the Gospel according to Mark.

# *Soon!*

A HEBREW INHERITANCE IS EVIDENT, therefore, in this spiritual acceleration of the ruach, of the One whose name pious people in Jesus' time no longer pronounced for fear of offending God. On this account the ruach of God was provided with the definite article and the attribute of holiness by those who, under the impression of their Master's divine power, were together with Jesus from his baptism in the Jordan until his crucifixion on Golgotha.

As mentioned, this Holy Spirit was in something of a hurry, and news of such urgency had been announced for some time in certain tracts that constituted a new kind of disaster literature. It flourished between 200 B.C. and 100 A.D., and it was written by impatient Jews for whom the old era couldn't run its course fast enough. One of them called himself John and his little book "Apocalypse of Jesus Christ." *Apocalypse* means "revelation," and the book later gave its name to the entire genre.

It is highly unlikely that this author had ever looked the living Jesus in the eye, despite the fact that he gave himself the name of one of the Nazarene's disciples. For the writer of the Apocalypse, the earthly Jesus had been a terrifying figure whose voice sounded like the rushing of a mighty waterfall, whose eyes were like a burning flame, and whose feet seemed to be made of white-hot iron.

The author affirms, right at the beginning of his work, that he heard this figure's voice while "in the Spirit" one Sunday on the island of Patmos, and thus he claims for himself the same heightened awareness that was granted to Jesus and John when they caught sight of the dove at the end of the twenties (A.D.), in the fifteenth year of the Emperor Tiberius' reign, as Luke tells us. Since then a few more world rulers had traveled on to Hades, among them the arch-enemy and persecutor of Christianity, Nero, who died in the year 68 after the birth of Christ. On the other hand, according to the evidence of John's Apocalypse, which was written down in the last years of the Emperor Domitian's reign—the date can be worked out to around the year 95—the Holy Spirit was still very much alive.

The addressees of the Apocalypse, seven Christian societies in as many cities, all mentioned by name and lying in the western portion of what is today Turkey, apparently knew the meaning of "in the Spirit" as well as the author did—otherwise he would surely have explained it to them. They were likewise informed about the speech habits of dragons and about the significance of the number 666, as well as other arcana that were to cost later exegetes many a brooding hour. So esotericism was rampant in the Christian circles of Ephesus and Pergamum, where the faithful bent to study copies of the Apocalypse. He who has an ear, let him listen to what the Spirit is saying to the churches. Seven times the author repeats the instructions from on high that were the cause of his writing, so that there can be no doubt that his pen was guided, not by writer's vanity, but by the holy pneuma, the ruach of the Lord Jesus, the faithful witness, the first-born from the dead, the highest of earthly kings.

Those to whom John's Apocalypse is addressed are not invited to make any common textual study or enjoy any reading pleasure, but to swerve into a sphere of spiritual experience that embraces both the Lord Jesus and the author and even includes his readers, who are apostrophized in his work as seized by the Spirit and whose ears hear only if they have become inspired ears. The Holy Spirit, whatever he may have to say in detail, has become the sole medium for those he favors, and this medium is the message as well.

The nonfavored—that is to say, "dogs, fortune-tellers, and the sexually immoral, murderers, idolaters, and everyone of false speech and false life"—remain "outside," locked out by the Spirit-Medium. In the apocalyptic scenario, the sphere of spiritual experience is that of the sects.

In the inspired space that the author of John's Apocalypse spreads open "in the Spirit," fierce energies are mobilized—fear and trembling, vengeful thoughts, pleasurable anxiety, certainty of victory. From the fifth chapter on, Jesus Christ as sacrificed Lamb, fitted out with seven horns and seven eyes, steps onto the visionary stage; he appears in a total of twenty-eight passages in the text, a monstrous central figure disinclined to put up with any nonsense. Emphasis is laid upon the Lamb's mighty wrath. He has scarcely opened the first four seals of the scroll wherein is written the fate of all mankind when the steeds of the apocalyptic riders break into a trot, and they aren't bringing anything pleasant. And they were given authority over a quarter of the earth to kill by the sword, by famine, and by plague, and through wild beasts. The psychoanalyst Carl Gustav Jung certified that the author of the Apocalypse spun an extensive web of resentments, that a veritable orgy of hatred, wrath, and blind destructive fury worked itself out in fantastic, terrifying images perhaps comparable with the outward manifestations of deep psychosis. Of course, this leaves open the question of whether the Holy Spirit or the unknown writer on Patmos bears responsibility for the furious galloping of the Apocalypse.

Maybe they both do. By way of exoneration of the Holy Spirit, it turns out that his mouthpiece cheated a little with regard to the originality of the visions he described. The four remarkable beings who appear in his fourth chapter, for instance, didn't originate in a vision, as the author claimed, but were copied out word for word from the book of the prophet

Ezekiel. Little effort is required to pick out examples of other borrowings from the apocalyptic literature. These demonstrate that the author of John's Apocalypse was well-read, but do not unconditionally attest to his qualifications as a virtuoso ecstatic. Perhaps his situation resembled that of the Swedish mining engineer and visionary Emanuel Swedenborg, who now and again, while merely reading a sacred text, suddenly found himself "in the Spirit," chatted with angels, and even encountered various apocalyptic dragons. Sixteen hundred years lie between Swedenborg and the drafting of the Apocalypse, but such a length of time is apparently of no consequence when the next world comes to life.

A key word of great significance has just been dropped: psychosis. This word occurred to Jung as he was reading the Apocalypse, but he was far from equating ecstatic religiosity with madness. He knew it was unlikely that a world religion was based on the jabbering of lunatics. Jung thought of himself as a physician. While Christians wrangle about the proper perception of the truth, the renowned psychologist wrote, the doctor is busy with an emergency. Whoever has investigated schizophrenic delusions knows about the appearance of archetypal motifs in the psyches of people who have never heard of mythology.

In the course of his own therapy sessions, one of Jung's colleagues, the Prague psychiatrist Stanislav Grof, came across those same collective, prototypical images that Jung called archetypes. At first Grof worked with LSD, then with hyperventilation or accelerated breathing. By these means participants are able to reach an altered state of consciousness and to experience once again the trauma of their birth, with all the anxiety and trepidation that accompany the unborn child as it makes its way into the light of the world. Grof expressly mentions apocalyptic visions in his account of the various images that are sighted on such a journey. Dragons, for example, may appear, or angels and devils in deadly combat, right up to the final release from all anxiety, with a great deal of light and radiant colors, as in the last two chapters of John's Apocalypse, where the bride of the Lamb comes down from heaven in the form of a golden city with twelve pearly, glittering gates.

Grof makes no sharp distinction between psychotic disturbance and mystical ecstasy. He simply accepts the ability to integrate one's experiences into everyday life as the boundary line between a clinical and a religious episode. According to Grof, the "transpersonal" sphere includes both saints and madmen. This conclusion is theologically acceptable too.

For the devout in Ephesus, where the monumental temple of many-breasted Artemis stood, or for those in Pergamum, where the colossal statue of Zeus loomed above the city, everyday life was determined by powers that they as Christians rejected out of hand. The Apocalypse inculcated in them, "in the Spirit," the belief that soon all heathenish abominations would turn into a wasteland in the course of a single hour and become a landscape of ruins, fit only for archaeologists.

This notion wasn't completely false, as the intervening time has proved. Of course, it took a few hundred years for the Apocalypse's visions of doom to become reality. Right at the outset, the Secret Revelation emphasizes that the time is near, and shortly before the end the imperious divine voice says, *I am indeed coming soon.* What was meant by that, neither the author nor the addressees of the Apocalypse could know. They took the Holy Spirit literally, which was a mistake.

Admittedly, without this mistake they would have been forgotten long ago.

# *After  Easter*

THE WORK OF THE HOLY SPIRIT DURING the sixty-five years between the baptism of the carpenter's son and the dictation of John's Apocalypse reached its absolute high point in the weeks that followed Christ's death on the cross. The executed man's comrades, both men and women, must have experienced what happened during that period in distinctly different ways, if the Gospels, which were put in writing several decades after the events, are to be trusted.

Sometimes it is a stranger who, at the crucial moment, lets himself be recognized as the man heretofore believed dead. Another time the corpse itself, with the stigmata of its wounds still fresh, joins the distraught apostles through closed doors and accepts their hospitality. Or a young man, clad in white and stationed in the empty tomb, gives the frightened women a lecture on the enormity that has taken place: "He has risen, he is not here." For another witness, the sight of the grave cloths lying in the tomb is sufficient to make him believe. Even a representative of skeptical reserve, the doubtful Thomas, puts in an appearance, as though the text wanted to make an ironic allusion to the traps that scientific thought can fall into. Blessed are those who have not seen and yet believe, the doubter is told. Thereafter comes Christ's ascension, before the eyes of the faithful, with the promise that the exalted one will soon return. Seven weeks after Easter, in the firestorm of Pentecost morning, the Holy Spirit at last manifests himself definitively. He is the unremittingly effective gift of grace, bringing the new Israel a supremely reinvigorated prophetic power among the peoples.

Now, all this happened a good while ago, and the generations following the Christian Big Bang must consider themselves latecomers, superficially baptized as they are. In the Easter stories that are read to them, what is most important remains unsaid. A change in each individual consciousness took place among those who bore their Jesus to the grave and then made ready to go back to their fishing boats and cooking pots, and nowhere is it revealed how such a change was brought about.

At first, the apparition of the living corpse in their midst spreads horror among them, and the ghost's comforting words—that he isn't one—merely indicate the abyss that had to be bridged over before terror could transform into jubilation. Did this jubilation among an inner circle of the Jesus Group, which comprised a dozen people at most, then spread to the rest of his followers? If so, a riddle still remains: How did such a congregation of jubilators mutate into the energetic divine messenger service that set off along the roads of Palestine, Syria, Arabia, and Asia Minor in order to spread the news that an executed Jew had snapped his fingers at death?

All that has been preserved is a couple of obscure allusions (for the latecomers to decipher) to the manifestations of the Spirit that occurred between Easter and Pentecost in the year of Christ's death. We are told that the Master, returned from the kingdom of the dead, breathed on his disciples and said, "Receive the Holy Spirit." Another passage asserts: "We are well aware that we have passed over from death to life." Peter tells of how the Holy Spirit came down on him and the other apostles; it was a kind of outpouring, and they were filled with mighty eloquence and rhetorical power.

Sleep deprivation may have played a certain role in all of this. We're informed that the men and women who had been especially close to Jesus occupied an "upper room" in Jerusalem after their Master's ascension, so that "with one heart" they might stay together there "constantly in prayer." This snapshot, if it happens to be correctly lighted, shows a primary group of an exceptional kind, jolted by God. It's hard to imagine that these people attached much importance to an undisturbed night's sleep during their wanderings with the nervous Nazarene. Then came the anxiety of the last few days after Palm Sunday in Jerusalem, a time filled with forebodings of inevitable disaster. So you had not the strength to stay awake with me for one hour, says the Master on the night of his arrest to the exhausted, drowsy disciples. At the first cock crow early on Easter morning, after the petrified bewilderment of Holy Saturday, a few women run out to the tomb and are immediately surprised by some exceedingly vivid manifestations of the other world. At first the men maintain their reserve, but they are quickly swept up in the events that turn the slain man into a victor, until he dissolves in air and leaves an empty place at the table where they were wont to break bread with him, in that upper room that is mentioned only once, without any further explanation.

That's because there is no explanation. The unique, unrepeatable group dynamic that developed in the days before the Pentecostal explosion and pulsated among persons of Jewish descent—they are called by their names—cannot be observed through the keyhole. All we can see are a few overexcited men and women who have little time for personal hygiene, who, when hunger makes itself felt, distractedly chew one or two bites of food, who sleep little, and who have only one thing in mind: to fill the new void at the center of their community with the presence of him whom they so sorely miss. *Maranatha.* "O Lord, come!" Normally such a droning as this leads to nothing whatsoever, even if it lasts for hours, unless God the Holy Spirit should feel moved to occupy the power vacuum and take over this already fairly flipped-out bunch of analphabetic housewives and fishermen, who will shortly be convinced that they have a permanent connection to the enthroned glory wherein Father and Son live eternally, as it was in the beginning, is now, and ever shall be, world without end.

Amen. After nine o'clock in the morning of Pentecost Sunday, the permanent connection is live, the Spirit machine has begun its work with a firestorm, it's anno Domini 30 if the details are correct. The latecomers would be happy to learn how the Holy Spirit picked out his four evangelists during the course of the next forty years and would be particularly interested in everything worth knowing about how the Christian Bible came into existence, but unfortunately they must content themselves with a couple of the apostle Paul's Epistles, dictated during the fifties A.D., and with the first twelve chapters of the Acts of the Apostles, which were written down in about 70 A.D. Neither the Epistles nor the Acts offer useful particulars about the Holy Spirit's methods of insinuation, the so-called inspiration responsible for the stern, gentle prose that later, throughout the Christian era, queens and shoemaker's apprentices, popes and nuns, conquistadors and colonized peoples would read on their knees.

For a hundred years, Bible scholars among the latecomers have been tormented by the question of which of Jesus' Gospel sayings actually could have originated with him, and which were formulated only after his death in the religious circles of those who believed in his resurrection and hoped he would return soon to judge the world. These included Jews and Greeks, Egyptians and Syrians and Romans, for the Good News traveled fast.

As academic teachers, biblical commentators cannot allow any confidence in the workings of the Holy Spirit to influence their scholarly prose;

they must remain objective as they conduct their researches. If they are reasonably sure that one of the Nazarene's important sayings was coined only twenty or thirty years after his death, they speak of "communal formulation," as though familiar biblical quotations could be summarily ascribed to the self-importance of religiously inflamed loiterers. Such foolishness doesn't begin to account for the fact that the Bible was for so long the most popular of all books.

It was for this reason that the philosopher Ernst Bloch (d. 1977), that fascinating messianic Marxist, thought little of such parade-exegetes as Rudolf Bultmann. His "de-mythologizing," according to Bloch, calls all cats black, all fairy tales old wives' tales, and fails to hear Prometheus' voice in the murmuring of the myths.

Biblical scholars, therefore, cannot be expected to provide answers to the latecomers' questions about the origin of Western book culture. Erudition is capable, at best, only of indicating the basic political, social, and economic conditions in which the fundamental writings of Christianity were composed.

Such an overview permits the discovery that in the Holy Land, just at the time of the Holy Spirit's most intense inspirational activity, a war broke out that was to have disastrous consequences for the people of Israel.

N*ot a single stone will be left on another.* That, according to Mark, is what Jesus said as he gazed on the temple in Jerusalem, which was regarded as one of the wonders of the world. No other of the Nazarene's prophecies was fulfilled so precisely. Of the whole magnificent edifice only a single wall remains, which King Herod's workers had taken ten years to erect and which was not even fifty years old at the time of Christ. The work of mass destruction that went on in the summer of the year 70 A.D., the Romans' answer to four years of insurrection in Judea, deprived Abraham's descendants of their political and religious center. It would not be recovered until the State of Israel's victory in the 1967 Yom Kippur War.

But, strangely enough, the writings of the Christian Bible make no direct mention of either the Jewish War or its gruesome end. Only indirectly, in one of Jesus' threatening speeches, is there a reference to the armies that will surround Jerusalem and lay the holy city desolate.

Considering the obvious hostility that all four evangelists felt toward "the Jews" (see the Gospel of John), this silence seems astonishing. Today there is a nearly unanimous assumption that the Gospels were written after the destruction of Jerusalem in 70 A.D. If this is true, we might well ask why the evangelists passed up this opportunity to rub the Jews' noses in the destruction of their temple as a divine punishment for their disbelief.

Did the Holy Spirit refuse to allow such nastiness? After Auschwitz, it would be nice to be able to imagine such a thing. But, unfortunately, it's well known that God generally prefers to duck unpleasant questions.

# *Bibble, Bubble, Babble*

IT TOOK THREE HUNDRED YEARS FOR Christian believers to agree upon which Gospels were inspired by the Holy Spirit and which were not. The rejected Gospels, and there were many of them, were withdrawn from circulation. That some of them have nevertheless survived is a fact known only to specialists. In keeping with official ecclesiastical regulation, the Holy Scriptures of the "New Testament," as available in bookstores, comprise the Gospels according to Matthew, Mark, Luke, and John, plus fourteen Epistles attributed to Paul, a couple of other letters, the Acts of the Apostles, and the Apocalypse of John, for a total of twenty-seven different Scriptures.

These have frequently been too few for people who were vigorously seeking God. Despite the fact that the canon of divine revelation had been authoritatively fixed, such people couldn't really believe that the Holy Spirit had ceased all activity around the year 100 A.D. The most meteoric proponent of this sort of spirituality was Thomas Müntzer, who was beheaded in 1525 for his part in the German Peasants' War. If a person all his life has neither heard nor seen the Bible, Müntzer announced, he could still, like all those who wrote the Holy Scriptures without the aid of any books at all, have an undeluded Christian faith through the righteous teaching of the Holy Spirit. Thus did Müntzer assert, cheekily enough, the essential contemporaneity of all those who came afterward with the writers of the Holy Scriptures, provided the latter-day faithful stood under the afflatus of the Holy Spirit. Martin Luther then reacted to his radical colleague with appropriate severity, accusing him of having mocked the entire Bible by calling it "bibble, bubble, babble." Müntzer had, in fact, used language just as strong as Luther's. A person who knows nothing about God's inward word in the depths of his soul, Müntzer wrote, must remain ignorant, even if he's gobbled up a hundred thousand Bibles.

It's not readily possible to reconcile the written principle, as represented by Luther, with Müntzer's spiritual principle. In the one case there is an appeal to established writings, in the other to their eternally present source. Ernst Bloch found that the figure of the solitary, spiritual person, which appears very early in the history of Christianity, can be understood as the prototype of creative people in the modern age.

This is a lovely compliment for the Holy Spirit, and it comes from an atheist to boot.

# *Pentecostal*

# *Shouts*

Among western intellectuals, the ru-

mor persists that God died sometime after the French Revolution. This same period marks

the birth of the so-called Pentecostal movement, whose members are currently estimated at

more than one hundred million.

# *Jerusalem, U.S.A.*

WAS THAT GOD? ON APRIL 9, 1906, according to the memoirs of a certain Georgia Bond, the fire came down among the saints in Bonnie Brae Street.

She meant the Holy Spirit, as reported in the Acts of the Apostles: "When Pentecost day came round, they had all met together, when suddenly there came from heaven a sound as of a violent wind which filled the entire house in which they were sitting; and there appeared to them tongues as of fire; these separated and came to rest on the head of each of them. They were all filled with the Holy Spirit and began to speak different languages."

"Among colored saints," wrote Mrs. Bond, the Pentecostal fire had been ignited once more, during an Easter service led by Pastor W. J. Seymour, a guest preacher and likewise, as they said in those days, a colored man.

And upon this occasion tongues began to speak in different ways, as had happened once in Jerusalem.

First, we're told, an eight-year-old boy was seized, and then the other brothers and sisters. Word spread quickly, so Pastor Seymour hired an old church at 312 Azusa Street for prayer meetings. The story goes that the saints jubilated there for three days and three nights, and a great crowd came and made it almost impossible to enter the hall. Anyone who managed to get in, however, soon fell under God's power. They all rejoiced so hard that the foundations of the building began to shake. It is said that women kissed strange men.

It happened thus, in Los Angeles, between Easter and Pentecost in the

Year of Our Lord 1906. As far as the white press was concerned, the whole commotion was nothing but the antics of crazy Negroes.

On the letterhead of the new congregation in Azusa Street, Seymour's name stood next to that of his teacher, Charles F. Parham, who had set up a little Bible school in the small town of Topeka, Kansas.

Parham wrestled with a problem that had already been a topic of discussion among fourth-century Christians in Anatolia. How can the Holy Spirit be induced to take up permanent residence?

As Parham realized, the Bible had always held the answer. If anyone began to speak "in tongues," that person was and remained filled with the Holy Spirit. It is written in the Gospel of Mark that these signs will be associated with believers: they will cast out devils, have the gift of tongues, pick up snakes, and if they drink some deadly poison, it will not harm them. They will lay their hands on the sick, who will recover.

Parham didn't fancy experimenting with poisonous snakes. But what was the meaning of the new tongues that the first Christians were able to speak in?

In the original Greek of the New Testament, the word *glōssa* could mean both "tongue" (the organ of speech) and "language," just as the word *tongue* does in English. Paul bears witness that quite a few Christians in Corinth actually spoke "in tongues"; moreover, the Acts of the Apostles leaves no doubt that the chief apostles, through preaching and laying on of hands, brought about in at least a good many cases the immediate descent of the Holy Spirit upon the newly converted, whereupon these people, baptized in the Spirit, began to speak in tongues, praising God.

The Bible gives no definite information about the nature of this new linguistic competence. The narrative of the Pentecost miracle merely states that those who were filled with the Spirit began to speak in "different" tongues (or languages), "as the Spirit gave them power to express themselves," and Jews from other countries understood them as though they had expressed themselves in each visitor's native language, in Latin, Greek, Syrian, Persian.

Despite such obscurities, Parham was convinced that the Holy Spirit could be persuaded to perform the miracle of tongues anew, and this time in God's own country.

The floors of the rooms in Azusa Street were strewn with sawdust. The pews consisted of planks laid on top of packing crates. And the saints jubilated. Their lives otherwise provided them with few occasions for rejoicing.

The American Pentecosts were prepared well in advance. In England, the popular preacher John Wesley (d. 1791), the founder of the Methodist Church, had made a distinction between ordinary and perfected Christians. The latter lived, as it were, like angels, exempt from the danger of falling into sin and error, and the outpouring of grace that made possible their steadfast perseverance in goodness was called "the second blessing" or "baptism in the Spirit." Charles Grandison Finney, a native of Connecticut who earned his living in a law office, underwent such an experience in the year 1821. "As I was about to take a seat by the fire," Finney wrote in his memoirs,

> I received *a mighty baptism of the Holy Ghost.* Without expecting it, without ever having the thought in my mind that there was any such thing for me, without any recollection that I had ever heard the thing mentioned by any person in the world, at a moment entirely unexpected by me, the Holy Spirit descended upon me in a manner that seemed *to go through me,* body and soul. I could feel the impression, *like a wave of electricity,* going through and through me. Indeed it seemed to come *in waves,* and *waves of liquid love;*—for I could not express it in any other way. And yet it did not seem like water, but rather as *the breath of God.* I can recollect distinctly that it seemed to *fan* me, like immense wings; and it seemed to me, as these waves passed over me, that they literally *moved my hair like a passing breeze.*

Three years later, Finney began his first campaign to sanctify America. This was the time of the countryside "awakenings," which were a feature of elaborate mass events held outdoors, in the open air. Preachers of Finney's type would speak so urgently to the consciences of farmers and their wives that they would keel over by the dozen, and afterward, when they got back on their feet, they were certain that their lives had made a new beginning; they had been "born again."

This kind of revival, however, provided only the first blessing, not the second. The many thousands of conversions did indeed rouse frozen Christians from sin's icy slumbers; but this was by no means a guarantee that they were thereby established in the sanctified state. In the New World, too, the devil was walking about like a roaring lion, seeking whom he might devour. Hadn't sheer excess of joy in the born-again life produced a passel of squalling brats begotten out of wedlock during so many open-air exercises in the blessedness of the Lord?

Very wisely, therefore, Finney distinguished between the emergence of grace in a hardened sinner's heart and the overwhelming baptism in the Spirit which presupposed a way of life already cleansed of stain, as in Bonnie Brae Street in 1906, where the Spirit—at least according to the official version—had suddenly flashed into sanctified souls.

But Finney didn't live to see this. He died in 1876 at Oberlin College, where he had built up the department of theology.

Jean Frédéric Oberlin (d. 1826), after whom the college was named, was a clergyman from Alsace who endeavored to improve the physical as well as the spiritual welfare of the souls entrusted to his care. In 1789 he had enthusiastically welcomed the French Revolution, seeing in it the small stone that would crush the kingdom of the Antichrist, as is written in the second chapter of the Book of Daniel. Nevertheless, the pastor was no wild-eyed revolutionary. In Georg Büchner's prose fragment *Lenz*, a bewildered poet finds temporary refuge with the benevolent Oberlin. The guest is soothed by the older man's "noble, serious face," in which he discerns the immense peace "that comes upon us in moonlit, melting summer nights."

"The vein of sensitivity is alike in nearly all human beings," Büchner wrote. "All that varies is the thickness of the crust through which it must break. One need only have eyes and ears for it."

The crust around the sensitivity vein was apparently thinner in America than it was in Europe, especially among black people, and generally among people of limited means rather than among the well-to-do. "Blessed are you who are weeping now: you shall laugh."

The nearer the end of the nineteenth century loomed, the more urgent grew the longing for a new Pentecost. American revivalists spread the tidings of a worldwide movement of the Holy Spirit as far as Germany. For ten years the servant of God Richard G. Spurling prayed, wept, and preached among the backwoodsmen of the Appalachian Mountains, on the Tennessee-North Carolina border, until in 1896 a mighty revival broke out, complete with baptisms of the Spirit and speaking in tongues. All this pious tumult got on the nerves of some uncouth fellows who set fire to the houses of their newly sanctified erstwhile drinking companions; there were even reports of gunfights between hardened and converted sinners. Several fanatics for whom the baptism of the Spirit was not enough experimented with gunpowder and oxygen, in hopes of introducing the baptism of "holy dynamite." And in Sale Creek, Tennessee, in 1901, a certain George Hensley began handling rattlesnakes during divine services, a practice that would later become a fixed custom which persists to this day in Poor Valley, near Cumberland Gap, where Virginia shoves a bit of itself westward between Kentucky and Tennessee.

Sociologists, eternally curious, have considered the matter more closely. In a total of two hundred prayer meetings of the snake-handling congregations, three people were bitten, none fatally. A young man who had been bitten on the hand immediately began to run in circles around the altar and the pulpit while the poisonous snakes were being shut up again in their plywood crates. The congregation started dancing wildly, hands were laid on the victim. One hour later the boy wiped the blood off his hand and returned to his place as the sermon continued: *They will drive out demons, speak in new tongues, pick up snakes. Whoever believes will be saved, whoever does not believe will be condemned.* The snake test, nevertheless, was unable to gain general acceptance as proof of a person's having received the baptism in the Spirit. The future belonged to "speaking in tongues."

Like this, for example: *Aria, ariari isa, akia akiari isa.*

And like this: *Ka sia sia.*

Also like this: *Siai siriai siriai, ai siriai siriai, si siriai siriai siai sisi ai.*

Or like this: *Ulalalala galala, takan dalalalala, undei dalalalala, kani kadilalalala, taka, dalala, ukei dalalala.*

And so forth. Tape recordings of the speaking "in tongues," the repetition of the Pentecost miracle in the twentieth century, showed that the Holy Spirit, to all appearances, attached no importance to intelligibility. The syllables gushing forth from the mouths of those whom the Spirit had moved made no sense in any language on earth. These sounds lacked all the peculiarities that make a human language comprehensible to those who speak it and foreign to those who have cultivated different linguistic peculiarities. Such spiritual gabbling came from a time that predated the Tower of Babel.

And therefore the Pentecostal fluency recognized no racial barriers either. What had broken out among the colored saints in Azusa Street quickly spread among white believers too. Black Pentecostal bishops ordained white preachers. A Norwegian minister named T. B. Barratt, on a journey to America in 1906, came under the fire that was falling in Azusa Street, and his tongue was loosened. After his return he held heavily attended Pentecostal meetings in Oslo, began to dance for joy before the congregation, and got written up in the *Social Democrat* newspaper, which called what was happening an "idiot factory." In 1909 Daniel Berg, a Swedish worker who had emigrated to the United States, visited his homeland and there experienced the baptism of the Spirit. On his return to the U.S., he and his friend Gunnar Vingren joined a Pentecostal congregation in Chicago. Vingren was shown in a dream that he and Berg were to bring the fire of the Holy Spirit to Pará. Neither of them had ever heard this name before. They betook themselves to the city library in Chicago and learned that they had been called to go to Catholic Brazil. At first, after they arrived in Belém in 1910, only a few Brazilian tongues broke into Pentecostal jubilation; but by 1940 the "Assembléias de Deus" numbered 400,000 members in 1,600 congregations.

In North and South America, in Europe, in Africa, and in Asia, millions of people learned to abandon their acquired speech habits for a few ecstatic moments and revert to baby talk, because, as the Scriptures tell us, God has ordained praise from the mouths of babes. Unless you become like little children, you shall never enter the kingdom of Heaven.

# *Daily   Pentecost*

*T*HE MAYAN VILLAGE WHERE THE CULTURAL anthropologist Felicitas D. Goodman wanted to observe the workings of the Holy Spirit lies on the Yucatán peninsula in Mexico, about sixty miles east of Mérida and twenty-five miles north of the famous ruins of Chichén Itzá. In her publications, Mrs. Goodman gives the village a fictitious name: Utzpak. She went there for the first time in the summer of 1969, equipped with a tape recorder and a notebook. There was no vacancy in the only hotel, which was filled with engineers from a road construction company engaged in putting an expressway through some nearby cornfields. At last the researcher found lodging with a woman who belonged to Utzpak's Pentecostal congregation. Settling down into her new environment presented Mrs. Goodman with certain difficulties, among them the impressive cockroaches that were running around everywhere—that is, around the only room in the house, the setting for all aspects of family life. Divine services were held four times weekly—for two to three hours on Tuesday, Thursday, and Saturday evenings, and on Sundays from six in the morning until around noon, followed by religious instruction for the adults and then, toward evening, by another prayer service that often lasted until ten or eleven o'clock at night. At first only seven men and five women were present in the clay hut that served as the congregation's church. There was a new pastor, whom Mrs. Goodman calls Lorenzo. Thus everything was ready, the story of Jesus and the Twelve could be enacted again, but this time a cultural anthropologist was in the room.

.   .   .

Unlike Jesus, Brother Lorenzo is married. In addition to Spanish, he speaks Mayan, which is an advantage in his missionary activity. Moreover, he has at his command, through divine grace, the gift of speaking in tongues, which he is to bring to Utzpak. This is the reason why his bishop has sent him here. Lorenzo belongs to the "apostolic" branch of the Pentecostal movement; this branch started bearing fruit in other parts of Mexico in 1914 and developed offshoots in the Yucatán in 1959, though with meager success. Utzpak's five thousand inhabitants, almost all of them baptized Catholics, view the Pentecostals' strenuous efforts with suspicion.

Lorenzo begins his ministry in the spring of 1969. Only two members of his congregation, both males, have mastered the secret of rejoicing in tongues. By the end of August of this year, there are already twenty-two people of both sexes who fall into a trance during divine service and burst into the high-pitched, ear-splitting sacred shouts:

*Bubububububububu.*

Whenever a brother or sister in the Pentecostal congregation has exulted in this way for the first time, Lorenzo makes an entry in the church register: "Baptized with the Holy Spirit."

The decibel count during church services rises accordingly, especially on Sundays. Time after time the noise attracts curious neighbors, who stare in amazement at the goings-on. Every now and then one child or another falls so completely under the spell of the general excitement that he or she arrives, spontaneously and, as it were, playfully, at what is granted to the grown-up brothers and sisters only after some effort, namely the shift into Pentecostal ecstasy.

On June 29, 1969, a Sunday, two men, aided by Lorenzo, successfully synchronize their tongues with the rhythm of the Holy Spirit. The cultural anthropologist is present, her tape machine is running, and she's busily taking notes.

Lorenzo has insisted that all the candidates for Spirit baptism come to church fasting that morning. The service begins with the usual hymns. *Santo Espíritu descende.* "Come down, Holy Spirit." A guitar accompanies the singing. When the people are not standing up or kneeling down, as they frequently do, they sit on folding chairs. A few festoons of brightly colored paper flowers decorate the room. Forty feet by twenty feet. Men on the right, women on the left. In front, a raised podium with a rostrum. Lorenzo gives a talk. He speaks with youthful verve and even makes the occasional joke: Without the help of the Holy Spirit, I'd surely fall asleep in church. Before I received the Holy Spirit, I was an undecided, fickle man. Now I feel I'm up to the challenge of life. For now, I want you to forget all the thoughts that usually go through your heads. The men must stop thinking about tomorrow's work, the women must stop thinking about cooking the midday meal. The Holy Spirit feels disturbed by such thoughts. When he really comes, many people want to shout out loud or jump up and down. You mustn't suppress these impulses. Other people, as soon as they start to feel something, are afraid that something strange is happening to them. All the same, they should just let it happen and not put up any resistance. Now, all those who haven't yet received the Holy Spirit, come up front by me and kneel down. I'll tell you what you must pray: *Séllame, séllame.* Seal me.

The congregation kneels and sings zestily: *Fuego, fuego, fuego es que quiero. Dámelo, dámelo, dámelo, Señor.* It's fire that I want. Give it to me, Lord. Then the rapid prayer for the Spirit's seal begins, faster and faster. *Séllame, séllame, séllame.* And soon Lorenzo starts: *Aria ariari isa. Akia akiari isa.* He bends down to one of the kneeling candidates and shouts into his ear, exulting in tongues, thrusting his fists up and down in time with the stressed syllables. He grabs the man's head and shakes it. Three other men, already familiar with the switching process, are now jabbering away too, their eyes closed. As yet none of the women has been seized by the Holy Spirit. *Séllame, séllame.*

Lorenzo has a little bell that he rings to signal the end of each trance episode. He wipes the sweat from his forehead and speaks in a calm voice. If there's anyone who prefers to pray for the Spirit at home, he says, that's not a problem. The important thing is to feel something. Two men say yes, indeed, something or other did happen to them just now. Good, let's try it one more time.

It's been a long while since falling into what the cultural anthropologist calls a "trance" has been an extraordinary event for Lorenzo. Like someone turning a light on and off, he switches effortlessly between his usual tone of voice and the altered register he uses for Spirit-jabbering. Sometimes it comes over him spontaneously, when he uses the word *poder* ("power") in his preaching, or *misericordia* ("mercy"), or *aleluya*. Then his face takes on a pensive expression, he seems to be lost in thought, and he must, as it were, fetch himself back. There were times when the Lord Jesus' eyes, too, grew dark, so that the world disappeared for him—and for his twelve apostles as well. Did he himself speak at such times, or another through him? How can we know? (*What I say to you I do not speak of my own accord. The Holy Spirit will remind you of all I have said to you.*)

At the end of the service, two men step forward and give thanks to God for *el gozo*, for the joy.

O ne week later, to her complete surprise, the joy comes over Mrs. Goodman as well. She makes notes:

July 6, 1969. The Sunday morning services start at six. I am up early, and I'm already dressed. Before I can light my gasoline stove, my informant is already knocking on the door. I quickly swallow a raw egg, grab my tape recorder, and we're on our way. In the church, Eusebia goes to kneel at the altar. The last conscious memory I have of the episode to follow is that of thinking about my childhood, when we had to say a brief prayer before we were allowed to sit down in church.

Then, I do not remember where, I leaned against something, I do not know what. I saw light, but then again I was surrounded by light, or perhaps not, because the light was in me, and I was the light. In this light I saw words or letters standing on their heads, descending upside down as if on a waterfall of light. At the same time I was full of a gaiety, as if my entire being were resounding with silver bells. Never before had I ever felt this kind of luminous, ethereal, delightful happiness. I recovered with the thought that now I finally know what joy is.

The twelve aren't enough, the congregation wants to grow. The Lord Jesus has become invisible to the world. But you will see me. No one can enter the kingdom of God without being born through water and the Spirit. For August 4, 1969, Lorenzo has got hold of a flatbed truck to drive the congregation to the baptism with water. The correct order of the baptisms can't always be maintained. Sometimes the Spirit comes sooner than the water. Sometimes he keeps people waiting even after they've been baptized.

In Utzpak there are two kinds of people, *los ricos* (the rich) and *los demás* (everybody else). None of those who clamber into the truck are rich. *(Alas for you who are rich: you are having your consolation now. And Jesus, filled with joy by the Holy Spirit, said, I bless you, Father, Lord of heaven and earth, for hiding these things from the learned and clever and revealing them to little children.)* The faithful drive north, to the sea.

A young woman with her baby at her breast speaks little. Her husband has threatened to beat her if she gets baptized. Another mother has brought her child along, too. He's crippled.

The sky is overcast, there's a shower of rain. The sea is warm. Those who are to be baptized wade out into the water, first the women, and then the men. The crippled child is also carried along and immersed. The Mayan language has no word for sin. The Indios do indeed know the Spanish word that expresses the idea, *pecado,* but it means nothing to them. They prefer, therefore, to list the things that are forbidden after baptism: *cine, baile, tomar, fumar.* No movies, no dancing, no alcohol, no cigarettes. Adultery is forbidden, too. Of course, the Bible says nothing about movies and cigarettes, but the devil is notably inventive.

*Bububububu.* After her baptism, the crippled child's mother stands knee-deep in the water with tears running down her cheeks. Water and the Spirit have come over her. Now she's in the heavenly kingdom. When the child was immersed, he moved his little legs.

The cultural anthropologist has work to do at her university and returns to the U.S. After her departure, Lorenzo's Pentecostal congregation increases by about three dozen brothers and sisters. A loudspeaker system, a gift from their co-religionists in the United States, is installed in the assembly room. Several young women between fourteen and sixteen years old learn the Holy Spirit's language and are proud of their sanctity. Pentecost takes place every day now, for the established times of prayer in the church are no longer enough for the faithful. They even meet in their houses to delight together in the joyous feeling of rapture that comes when the Holy Spirit takes command. The men of the congregation work many volunteer hours to build a wall around the church grounds, and the pastor's residence is renovated as well.

The cultural anthropologist returns to Utzpak in the beginning of July 1970. By now the congregation numbers nearly eighty, and a further dozen have enrolled for the next group baptism. The only topic of conversation, writes Felicitas Goodman, is Anselmo's visions.

Anselmo (not his real name), twenty-six years old, an agricultural worker and a barber's apprentice, has had an animated religious career. Baptized as a Catholic, then a Presbyterian, a Baptist, a Jehovah's Witness, a Pentecostal. The previous year he received the spiritual gift of tongues from Lorenzo. If he doesn't pray for his wife's conversion ten times daily, all is not well with him. His wife has several male friends who give her money. In the beginning of May, the devils came. Suddenly, while he was praying, Anselmo couldn't feel his head anymore. This went on for a few minutes, and there was no use touching and pressing it. Thereupon he fell into a faint, and since then he feels that he's being persecuted by the forces of evil. Then, a few days later, he saw them for the first time, gathered around his hammock at four o'clock in the morning, and he had to run from them, but he didn't get far before he collapsed to the ground with foam on his mouth. Lorenzo was called and, together with several other brothers, prayed over Anselmo; and some hours later the fit was over.

At services on Sunday, May 17, Anselmo saw several candles, although there weren't any in the room. They were guttering, about to go out. It is high time, said a voice. The end of the world is nigh.

Two weeks later there was a meeting of the pastors of all the Pentecostal congregations in the Yucatán, together with their assistants, in the town of Villahermosa, and on this occasion Anselmo was given a new blessing of grace. He saw a bright shield shining on the foreheads of some brothers, while the faces of others appeared gloomy and dark.

Anselmo's last vision came to him on June 20. He spent the night with Lorenzo. Both men had hung their hammocks in the church. Around three o'clock in the morning, Anselmo was awakened; he saw two ribbons, one bearing the image of a woman, the other blank, and a pair of scissors. Lorenzo explained the ribbon with the woman's image as a reference to the temptation of adultery, which one must struggle against, and the other ribbon as a call to preaching and missionary activity. Lorenzo too seemed to be undergoing a crisis.

The congregation notices that Lorenzo is making trips to Campeche, his hometown, more and more frequently. It's said that what he really wants to do is move there. Further word has it that he dips into church funds whenever he feels like it. All wit and animation have disappeared from the pastor's sermons. He often speaks against *las suciedades del mundo*, against sex, against diversions, against scientific theories, nothing but filthy things. He describes in great detail the torments of the damned in the quagmire of hell, and more and more frequently he calls upon the congregation to remain standing during assemblies, even when they last for hours, to give honor to God.

On July 12, Lorenzo explains that the devil has very little time left to finish his work, and therefore he's concentrating his efforts on the sanctified in the Pentecostal congregation.

This time the cultural anthropologist has brought along a film camera, so she's in a position to document a little apocalypse here in Utzpak. (*I, Jesus, have sent my angel to you to attest these things to you for the sake of the churches. And the Spirit and the Bride say, "Come!" Let everyone who listens answer, "Come!" I am indeed coming soon. Amen; come, Lord Jesus.*)

On July 30, 1970, the time is at hand.

On the previous evening, July 29, the church is closed to the sisters. Lorenzo has convened a meeting in which only the brothers may participate. Two other pastors from out of town have arrived. The topic of the debate is a vision that came to one of the brothers. He saw a great many Pentecostal churches, and the rooms where the faithful assembled were dirty and covered with cobwebs. The time has come to announce to the congregations that Christ's second coming is imminent, and that they must cleanse themselves.

The women have been told to pass the night in prayer. They do so in their houses. The linguistic performers among them have gone off into frequent trances, sometimes for as long as ten minutes—*agonizando*, as the women call it. Naturally prayers are also said for the little crippled boy, who is still not completely well.

In the early morning the women hear that the men have reached a decision. Six brothers, among them Anselmo, have been chosen to announce the imminent end of the world to the surrounding villages. As an emblem of his preacherly dignity, Anselmo has a fountain pen in the breast pocket of his shirt. Toward morning the demon attacked him so fiercely that he tried to kill himself. The two brothers who prevented him from doing so saw two angels standing behind him; one carried a sword, the other a whip.

U p to this point everything has gone according to a script that one can look up in the last book of the Christian Bible, the Apocalypse, or Book of Revelation. The author fears that the zeal of the congregations he's writing to has begun to wane. If they do not return to the "first" love that characterized their charismatic beginnings, divine punishments threaten them.

In fact, the cultural anthropologist has already noticed that the trance behavior of some brothers and sisters in Utzpak has become feebler than it was last year, that the speaking in tongues has slowed down (Lorenzo is an example of this) and occurs less often. In certain respects, this is a threatening situation. If the baptism of the Spirit and its effects pass, then a person is in danger of falling back into his old anxieties and vices. In the American professor's opinion, that's the reason for the urgency of Anselmo's visions, that's why the devil is trying him. But even she is surprised by the eruption that starts in the evening of July 30 and will continue into September, like a state of lawlessness in which previously established norms have been abolished.

F or more than twenty-four hours, the brothers and sisters of Utzpak's Pentecostal congregation have hardly slept. All the same, at least forty men and women, together with many children, come to the evening prayer service. July 30 is a Thursday. A baptismal journey to the sea is announced for the following Sunday; this will be the last opportunity to reserve a seat, as it were, on the correct side at the Last Judgment. There are still some hesitant souls, among them the cultural anthropologist. She's already baptized, she says. Perhaps this evening will bring success in breaking down such resistance. One of the brothers hardly has time to inaugurate the service with an invitation to pray for all those who would like to open themselves to grace, when another brother, panting heavily, his eyes bulging, breaks into the Pentecostal jubilation. Immediately they all leap from their seats, shouting prayers as though with a single voice. From this point on, there's no such thing as an orderly course of events. Lorenzo rings his bell, again and again, in vain. The glossolalia has gone out of control; about twenty brothers and sisters with reddened faces and foam-flecked lips are vociferously bawling out their spiritual joy to high heaven, weeping and sweating, exulting by turns. Meanwhile the children are wailing; a few isolated men and women try to start singing a hymn. Lorenzo picks up a Bible and attempts to read aloud from it, but a brother is whirling his arms in the air so violently that concentration is out of the question. The cultural anthropologist can't take notes fast enough, too many things are happening simultaneously, and suddenly Lorenzo is at the microphone. And you, sister Felicitas, he shouts at her with trembling lips, if you don't surrender to God, you will die. Then Anselmo takes up the charge, this is the very last chance to request baptism, and bends over the professor as she writes; his saliva drips on her notebook. Does she at least feel remorse for her sins? Yes, indeed. Well, good, that's something at least, alleluia. Enraged neighbors hammer on the door—it's nearing eleven o'clock at night; a mother tries in vain to bring her teenage daughter out of her trance, she fans her, offers her a glass of water. Eight women and nine men have come to the podium; they wish to be baptized as soon as possible. Jehovah is with us, Anselmo yells into the microphone, everyone must come to the church at six tomorrow morning.

Was that God?
No, say the cultural anthropologist's two most important in-formants. Mrs. Goodman, who calls them Eusebia and Nina, is bound to Eusebia by ties of friendship; Nina is Eusebia's daughter. The professor

has had to return to the U.S. When she comes back to Utzpak in January 1971, she'll speak with the two women in detail, and they'll tell her that Satan began his attack on their congregation on July 30. Meanwhile they correspond. Nina writes to Felicitas Goodman on September 16: Satan has driven our congregation mad. Terrible things happened in the church in August.

At first, the month of August seemed to be blessed by favorable signs. Sixteen men and women were baptized in the sea, and the next day nine men left Utzpak to go preaching in the neighboring villages. There were prayer meetings in the church every evening, frequently lasting until eleven o'clock. They prayed for an unbelievably long time, according to Eusebia. They didn't do anything in tongues, all they did was shout. Afterward the brothers had to assist the sisters because they couldn't walk properly, it was as though they were drunk.

By the second week of August it was clear that the nine missionaries had failed. They came back one after another, close to starvation because no one had given them anything to eat. Meanwhile their women had made themselves at home inside the church, cooking together and running a single large household. Of course, one of the sisters consumed all the meat by herself, leaving the others nothing but beans. No one gave a thought to cleaning up. The children peed on the floor, dirt accumulated in the corners.

Lorenzo, when he wasn't visiting a neighboring congregation, of all things, sat around apathetically and stared into space. He didn't even comb his hair, Eusebia reports.

Around August 20 the young glossolalia stars go berserk. Suddenly one of them orders that from now on Eusebia, her husband, and Nina must fast from six in the morning until six in the evening, because they continue to harbor doubts concerning the imminent end of the world. Nina and Eusebia obey this command for a few days, but the next blow falls quickly. One of the girls orders that everything red in color must disappear from the church at once, including the Bibles, because their pages are edged in red. Another girl commands that anything that has any color at all must be put out. The devil has appeared to her. He looked like an eagle, high up in the sky. Then she sits down on the altar, spreads her thighs, and screams, *puta,* whore. Mrs. Goodman writes that she was unfortunately unable to find out anything about the connection between sexuality and religious ecstasy in Utzpak.

The congregation obeys the girls' orders. Eusebia relates how they threw everything out, the Bibles, the flower vases, even the guitar. During the early morning service on August 30, a Sunday, it is announced that there has been a revelation. The Holy Spirit gives the congregation two weeks' time to burn everything that isn't white. My husband had a red handkerchief, Eusebia remembers. But she didn't burn it; she hid it. Other sisters burned their colorful clothes, along with bedsheets and even a radio. That evening almost all the women appear in white clothing. They form a large circle to keep the devil outside. They must burn their shoes, too, announces one of the girls. Many of them are *agonizando,* as though in childbirth, and the brothers must hold them tightly to keep them from falling off their chairs.

Finally one of the most respected women, a member of Utzpak's Pentecostal congregation since 1960, travels in desperation to Villahermosa in order to report this muddle to the bishop. Shortly thereafter, on September 10, an emissary from the church authorities arrives in Utzpak and proclaims that the congregation there has unfortunately been possessed, not by the Holy Spirit, but by the devil. In the future, there must be no outcries during divine services. God is not hard of hearing. Eusebia adds that it was obviously the devil who made them go so far as to toss the Bibles out of the church. By that point, if not before, Nina observes, the brothers should have realized whose influence they were acting under. But they were blind. Later they wept bitterly when they recognized how sorely they had been deceived.


One year later. Lorenzo and Anselmo have left Utzpak. The gift of tongues has almost completely disappeared. As for the end of the world, it has apparently been postponed. The devil, too, has seen his strength diminish.

The period of time covered by the story of Jesus and the Twelve, however often it may be repeated, rarely extends beyond two years. Then comes the sobering up, the calming down, the routine, the rules—in short, the Church. Over its main door hovers the dove, like a dangerous memory.

Basically, Mrs. Goodman thinks, the Holy Spirit was only toying with the people in Utzpak. He didn't communicate anything to them. He has no character. Although the Pentecostals spoke of him constantly, they could not agree on how they had experienced him. He sprayed water on one person's shoulders, he came in through another's stomach, he climbed up a third one's spine. He seemed to be a decidedly inconsistent fellow, hardly suitable as a partner in a scientific investigation.

# *Unutterable Groans*

*T*HE VERY FIRST PENTECOSTAL CONGREGA-tion, about which a few fragmentary reports have been preserved, was founded by the apostle Paul in the city of Corinth, where, around the year 50 A.D., that strange man lived for a while as a tentmaker. "I thank God that I speak with tongues more than any of you," Paul later wrote to the Corinthians. He doesn't reveal how he was granted this divine gift.

Paul hadn't learned the polyglot Pentecostal speech from the Naza-rene, nor yet from any of the Twelve. On the contrary. When the first martyr from the ranks of the Jesus Group was stoned to death in Jerusa-lem, a young man named Saul was sighted at the execution, full of zeal against Stephen, who had forfeited his life. But an intervention from the divine sphere turned Saul, persecutor of Christians, into Paul, apostle of the people, as every child knows. On the road to Damascus, the light from heaven. *Saul, Saul, why are you persecuting me?*

*Who are you, Lord?*

*I am Jesus, whom you are persecuting.*

"I went off to Arabia," Paul reports, "and later I came back to Da-mascus. Only after three years did I go up to Jerusalem to meet Cephas. I stayed fifteen days with him but did not set eyes on any of the rest of the apostles, only James, the Lord's brother."

No information has been handed down to us, therefore, about when and on what occasion Paul first fell under the spell of rejoicing in tongues. In any case, the tentmaker Aquila and his wife Priscilla, with whom Paul lived in Corinth, must have passed some exciting moments when the pious man lost his composure within their small circle and disclosed his secret: Jesus was buried, but on the third day he was raised to life. Appeared to Cephas; and later to the Twelve. And next he appeared to more than five hundred of the brothers at the same time, and last of all to me too, the child untimely born. No eye has seen, no ear has heard, what God has prepared for those who love him. *Ai siriai si siriai sisi ai.* Not in the words of human wisdom, but in words taught by the Spirit. Heard words said that cannot and may not be spoken by any human being. Whether in the body, or out of the body, I do not know, caught up into the third heaven, into Paradise. *Aria isa akia isa ka sia.*

Was that the angels' language?

When Paul turned up in Corinth, a fifty-year-old Jew on an exalted mission, trained both as a rabbi and as a tentmaker (marital status: single), at first sight one might have thought him a preacher for some sect or taken him for one of the threadbare itinerant philosophers who were roaming around Corinth and droning out their wise sayings on street corners. But the man had the right password ready when he appeared in Aquila's shop in the rug bazaar and asked for work. Aquila had been baptized in the name of the Lord Jesus. Although the Jesus movement was only twenty years old, it had already recruited several brothers and sisters among the Jews of Rome, including Aquila and his wife. Some time later they had gone to live in Corinth, because religious groups were subjected to less strict surveillance there than they were in the capital city of the empire.

Before long it turned out that a high-ranking master of esoteric insights, a passionate ideologue, a charismatic with energy to burn, was hiding behind the inconspicuous journeyman. When Paul was in the right mood, he would lay his hands quite gently on a person's head, and all at once the chosen one would begin jabbering away, possessed by the Holy Spirit. Word of this spread. It wasn't exactly the best company that gathered on the upper floor of the dwelling where Priscilla and Aquila greeted the guests who had come to hear Paul's evening talks. There were ordinary tradespeople and craftsmen from the bazaar, slaves, casual workers and market women, loiterers, people of no substance, street merchants, perhaps one or two loose women disgusted by their own trade, and the inevitable wealthy widow searching for meaning. Later these were joined by a few respectable gentlemen and their families, for example, the president of the synagogue.

It's not hard to reconstruct what these diverse audiences got to hear; we need only look at the seven Epistles personally dictated by Paul. If we do so, we'll notice at once that the apostle had scarcely an inkling of what would later be written in the four canonical Gospels of the Christians. Only once does Paul quote a saying of any weight from the mouth of the Lord Jesus, but Paul's source for this remains unclear. Otherwise there's no sort of hint that Paul knew a single one of the stories recounting the Nazarene's miracles as they were preserved in the memories of the twelve apostles, starting with the baptism in the Jordan and going up to Christ's ascension. The Savior's birth in a stable, the wedding at Cana, the Sermon on the Mount, the raising of Lazarus from the dead, the miraculous feeding of the four thousand, the Transfiguration on Mount Tabor, the story of the suffering and death of the carpenter's son, are all missing from Paul's writings; they contain none of the key events that people who are steeped in Christianity today keep lodged in the back of their minds from childhood on.

In spite of this incredible absence of color in Paul's discourses, the people of Corinth got their money's worth, for he hammered into their heads a word that the Gospels lack: freedom.

The glaring word stood out against a somber background: Before long, soon, very soon, God's wrath will break in upon mankind, upon all the whoremongers, perverts, pederasts, blasphemers, misers, ruffians, calumniators, show-offs. No matter whether you're a Jew, equipped with the law of Moses, or a Greek, furnished with the light of reason, you are in any case inexcusable, my friend, because you are in a state of sin. As it is written. Paul trots out a few Psalm verses that he knows by heart. All have turned away. There is not one who does right. Viper's venom behind their lips. Not a single one of them is upright. So every mouth is to be silenced, and the whole world brought under the judgment of God.

No hope of rescue?

On the contrary. In the immeasurable shard heap of the Last Judgment, a few pitchers and vases remain intact, as though by a miracle. These are you, my brothers and sisters. Abraham had two sons, one by the slave girl and one by the freewoman. These two women stand for the two covenants. One was given on Mount Sinai; the other shines down from above on you, the children of the freewoman.

The slaves in Paul's audience had surely never heard of Abraham. The news that they were called to freedom, however, was most congenial to their desires. This man made it abundantly clear that social ranks, hierarchies, and disparities meant absolutely nothing to him. Jews, Greeks, rich, poor, men, women, slave, free—under the water of baptism, under the fire of the Spirit, they were indistinguishable, freed from the burden of inequality, jubilating with one voice, exulting in the happiness of their deliverance from the general ruin.

Practice follows theory. A person can attain the privileges connected with being a Christian only by giving himself in faith to the Lord Jesus and by receiving the waters of baptism. The sea was only a mile or two away, and perhaps the Corinthian Pentecostals, like their twentieth-century descendants, stood in water up to their bellies. Threefold immersions, supervised by Paul in person. Just at this moment, in at least some cases, occurs the outbreak of what Paul calls *pneumatikos,* and it brings various forms of spiritual ability, which are collectively known as "charismatic gifts." Whether the Corinthian's rejoicing in tongues sounded like Felicitas Goodman's tapes must remain an unanswerable question.

That's not a serious problem. The Holy Spirit, whose frequency Paul was tuned in to, apparently had several programs in his broadcast schedule, not just the Pentecostal linguistic show. As soon as the Christian crowd in Corinth began receiving the signal, washerwomen were transformed into preachers, master cobblers into theologians, while the community was praising God. The text of a new prayer was declaimed in one corner, from another came an improvised hymn. Some people suddenly felt within themselves the power of healing, prophecies were spoken aloud, and there was even some success in the interpretation of strictly private ecstasies. As soon as the proceedings became too lively for him, Paul intervened. Rather five words with sense than ten thousand spoken in a frenzy. Everybody wait their turn. Just suppose guests burst in while everybody's jabbering at once. These outsiders would have to believe that we're out of our minds. . . .

Distinction between the sexes remained a delicate point. Because the Holy Spirit bestowed proofs of his powers on both men and women indiscriminately, the women's head covering became a matter of dispute in Corinth. Did the new freedom go so far that a prophetess might appear with her head bare? No, the apostle decided, giving his decision a super-natural basis. "Because of the angels," the woman must wear "a sign of authority" on her head. Female charismatics had to realize that they couldn't go beyond certain limits.

Moreover, the contrast between well-to-do and impoverished children of God caused further problems. A wealthy man named Gaius, whom Paul had baptized with his own hands, made his spacious house available to the Corinthian congregation for their gatherings. On such occasions people liked to sit down and share a light meal, just as is customary today in clubs and other associations. The host evidently found nothing wrong with offering ample refreshments, both solid and liquid, to the dignitaries among the brothers and sisters while the have-nots were fobbed off with meager fare. So the former made their way home full and tipsy, while the latter had to go to bed with growling stomachs.

To counter his flock's tendency to indulge in the banal meannesses typical of small-group dynamics, Paul mobilized the Holy Spirit's noblest gift. And even though I should have the gift of prophecy, the apostle declared, though I could penetrate all mysteries and know all knowledge, yes, though my faith were so powerful it could move mountains—if I am without love, I am nothing. Even though I command the language of the angels, if I speak without love, I am no more than a booming gong or a tinkling bell. The gift of prophecy disappears, jubilation in tongues falls silent, esoteric knowledge grows stale. Love, however, never comes to an end.

It is remarkable how often the Pauline Epistles speak of this *agapē*— the Greek word for love—as though it were some sort of novelty. (*Caritas* is its Latin translation.) Agapē was not to be confused with sexual appetite, nor with the erotic aspect of the emotional life. Agapē is always patient and kind, Paul writes. It is never jealous, nor boastful or conceited, never acts tactlessly, never seeks its own advantage, does not take offense or store up grievances, rejoices not at wrongdoing but in the truth. It is always ready to make allowances, to trust, to hope, to endure whatever comes.

In comparison with agapē, conspicuous signs of grace—all the Pentecostal exaltations of the Christian beginnings in Corinth—seemed like fleeting whims incapable of long life, fragments of a whole whose nature remained obscure. These signs owed their existence, at least in the Apostle's view, to a purely positive energy field pulsing deep inside the deity. In exceptional cases, it became possible to experience that force, as was happening, for example, in Corinth, amid shivering and shouting. But if anyone equated such manifestations as these with the spiritual principle from which they were transmitted, that person was like a baby that can't yet digest solid food.

Agapē, on the other hand, was for grown-ups, something "poured into our hearts by the Holy Spirit," as Paul wrote in his letter to the Christian community in Rome. Paul had anticipated the trap that Pentecostalism can easily fall into when raving mouths and trembling lips are childishly prized beyond their worth. It cannot be denied that agapē's features, at least as Paul describes them, had turned a bit matronly, not to say old-maidish, as though the wild Spirit had put on a nun's habit. Therefore, as soon as the Apostle felt that the first enthusiasm was beginning to wane, he issued warnings: Do not stifle the Spirit. Do not despise the gift of prophecy with contempt. The brothers and sisters, baptized in the Spirit, were to keep burning, glowing, seething, boiling, like the iron in the fire, like the soup on the stove. If the Holy Spirit withdrew completely, the cold boredom of everyday life threatened to take his place.

This danger had not yet come to pass in Corinth when the divine Spirit that was driving Paul onward caused him to leave the city. In the twenty years of his missionary travels, the apostle covered at least ten thousand miles, usually on foot, walking along country roads, and occasionally by ship. Through letters and messengers, he remained in constant contact with the congregations he had called into being. To his Corinthians he wrote two Epistles, the earliest examples of the nervous prose dictated by that Spirit who would later advance to membership in the Trinity. In one of these, Paul told the Corinthians, "Where the Spirit of the Lord is, there is freedom."

But the slaves among the Corinthian Pentecostals did not by any means have their freedom purchased for them on this account, nor did the Holy Spirit conjure a single chicken into any poor person's pot. The women even had to go on keeping their heads covered. Nevertheless, the Spirit "of the Lord" (Jesus), as Paul calls him, had brought a new tone to the long history of masters and servants, a tone cheekier than anything usually heard in religion until then. Distinctions between people, in former times always based on speech, sex, skin color, possessions, and use of weapons, would no longer be the chief consideration. From now on, the subjunctive mood would color perceptions of reality. The scheme of things was incomplete. Inside it were dark wishes, like moans in a dream. The whole creation has been groaning, Paul wrote to the Romans; it is lying in labor, and we are groaning with it. Then, a few verses further on, an unprecedented theological audacity occurs: God, too, is made to groan. According to Paul, the Spirit himself intercedes for us in groans that cannot be put into words. Paul underlines his point with a word that he uses only in this one passage: *alalētos,* "unutterable." That is, the Holy Spirit, the *ruach,* the *pneuma,* groans inarticulately as he comes to the aid of human weakness, which doesn't know how to pray.

He had heard it himself, this remarkable man. Caught up into the third heaven, he had heard God's language, which must remain untranslatable, but which sometimes becomes a stammering in tongues—when the fuses blow, when a person loses self-control, as was the case in Corinth and elsewhere, and in other times, in 312 Azusa Street, for example, "among colored saints," or with the Indios of the Yucatán in the year 1970.

Seen in this way, the miracle of Pentecost remains a groan, God's groan, which cannot be put into words.

# *Third*

# *Person*

THE TRIUMPH OF CHRISTIANITY IN THE

*fourth century after Christ transformed the Holy Spirit into a divine Person. The heavenly*

*dove became a dully gleaming mosaic over the main portal of the colossal church of Hagia*

*Sophia in Constantinople, and the memory of the agitated beginnings of the new religion*

*passed into oblivion.*

# Constantine's Dream

IN THE SILENCE OF THE NIGHT, A
rushing of wings. The emperor receives the directive in a dream. A fresco
in the church of Saint Francis in Arezzo shows the sleeper, guarded by two
armored men. At his feet sits a courtier, open-eyed, but blind to the
higher power above him as it swoops down upon the emperor.

In the gray dawn of October 28, 312 A.D., the emperor will issue an
outrageous command. The monogram of Christ is to be painted on his
bodyguards' shields. Then the battle of the Milvian Bridge, a few miles
outside of Rome, can begin. Constantine's opponent is his rival for control of the western empire, a certain Maxentius.

The new sign emerges victorious. While the imperial troops are making their magnificent entrance into the Eternal City, the priests of Jupiter
on the Capitoline hill await the emperor himself, so that the rituals of
thanksgiving may begin. The priests wait in vain. His Majesty has other
vows to fulfill.

The Senate discusses the wording of the inscription to be carved on
Constantine's triumphal arch. His success, the finished inscription informs
the reader, is due to the "instigation of divinity." This pallid formulation
suits the awkward situation the senators find themselves in. They cannot
yet guess that they have been demoted to heathens overnight. The emperor, too, knows the Christian religion only through hearsay. But he
learns fast.

. . .

Had Constantine been inserted into the equations of a plan conceived on high long before? In the town of Split on the Dalmatian coast, a retired emperor wandered in amazement through his palace. Diocletian, like Constantine a military man, considered the Christians subversive elements and enemies of order. He'd had a few thousand of them executed. Now, all at once, their secret practices were receiving the grace of official favor; indeed, there were even reports of bishops entering and leaving the imperial court. The old man on the covered walkway overlooking the sea kept his thoughts to himself. The dice had been thrown, and he'd gambled everything away.

Constantine was the winner. (Father: general; mother: innkeeper's daughter; served under Diocletian and Galerius; in 306, after the death of his father in York, proclaimed emperor by his troops; after 312, sole ruler in the western half of the Roman Imperium; after 324, in the eastern half as well; in 330, dedication of Constantinople as the second capital of the empire, equal in status to Rome.) Such luck could come only to one who had received a nod from heaven. That was the official version of the imperial court, represented by Constantine's biographer, one Eusebius, a bishop and writer of the early Church. According to Eusebius, Constantine assured him, under oath, that a cross, towering above the sun in the noonday sky, had appeared to him and his troops, and next to the cross these words: "By this, conquer." At first, the text goes on, the significance of the miracle was hidden from the emperor, but that night in a dream he saw God, carrying the same symbol in his hand and commanding him to use it in the battle.

Another Christian author, Lactantius, to whom the emperor entrusted the education of his son, Crispus, contented himself with a more succinct version. While sleeping, Constantine had been told to depict the "heavenly sign of God" on his soldiers' shields and then venture out to fight. Accordingly, the letter X had been turned into Christ's monogram. This very X (the Greek letter chi, the first letter of the name of Christ) showed up soon afterward on the imperial coinage, combined with the letter P (which is, in Greek, the letter rho, the second letter of the divine name). Constantine's helmet and his standards were also adorned with the new sign.

Not much more can be learned about this supernatural intervention in the course of things.

There is, one should note, a confusing aspect to all this: heavenly interventions had been set in motion against the Christian cause, too, as in the case of another, later emperor, Julian, a nephew of Constantine the Great. After Julian's early and sudden death, he became known as "the Apostate." This man was granted a mere twenty months to restore the venerable old gods to their former brilliance and thwart "the Galileans," as he called his uncle's co-religionists.

From his childhood on, Julian, though raised as a Christian, felt himself beloved by glorious Helius, the divine essence of the radiant sun. Julian learned that this same Helius had been held in reverence by Constantine, too, at first under the god's own name, and later in the figure of Christ. The priests of the old gods, now deprived of their power, would whisper to the imperial nephew when his search for esoteric knowledge brought him to Pergamum or Ephesus: his uncle's betrayal, they said, was a threat to the Empire. There was also the occasional oracular pronouncement, delivered in secret, that confirmed Julian's view of his own destiny; he would restore the religion of his ancestors, the Flavian family, which had provided the Empire with a number of illustrious rulers. In addition, there was the fact that the young pretender to the throne, in the course of his studies, had acquired a growing passion for the thousand-year-old culture of the Greeks. In comparison with Plato's dialogues, the Gospels seemed to him more and more like badly written mountebanks' tales.

In Ephesus, Julian signed on to attend the lectures of the neo-Platonist philosopher Maximus, a mystagogue of the first rank, learned in the art of eliciting speech from the godhead. The prince received his initiation in a crypt dedicated to Mithras, twin brother of Helius, and whatever it was that he heard and saw during the course of that night, Julian kept it to himself. Later, as emperor, the convert dropped hints, but only in veiled imperial language, about what had been said to him: Bear in mind that, if you follow us, you shall become a god.

Therefore, after Julian became ruler of the Empire at the end of 361, he set a multiplicity of divinities against the theological singularity of the

Christian religion. The imperial couriers, carrying edicts from Constantinople designed to bring new life to the gods' old shrines, started appearing in governors' palaces all over the Imperium. Christian bishops were put on notice that in future they must tolerate the traditional cults, give back the treasures confiscated or stolen from the temples, and pay for whatever damages had been done to them. The worship of Hermes and Demeter, Calliope and Apollo, Zeus and Athena, was to be reinstated everywhere, with sacrifices and processions, with the fragrance of incense and the music of flutes.

Soon favorable inscriptions in Julian's honor began to appear, carved into the milestones that lined the traffic routes from Syria to the Alpine passes, and dedicated to the redresser of past sacrilege, the restorer of the temples. The emperor had a shrine to the sun erected on the grounds of his residence in Constantinople so that he could celebrate the Mysteries personally. Everyone knew that the young monarch had lived a celibate life since the death of his wife, a life marked by martial simplicity and piety. The Christians were still in the minority, and they had no choice but to swallow their bitterness over this about-face in the religio-political sphere.

But not for long. On June 26, 363, at the age of thirty-one, Julian, campaigning against the Persians, fell in battle. The night before he died, the genius of the Empire appeared to him. The apparition's head was covered, and it spoke not a word.

Julian had been called onto the stage before he grasped what the director wanted from him. The Imperium required a new god; Helius had already begun to metamorphose into Christ.

Both emperors, Constantine and Julian, had been deemed worthy to receive supernatural manifestations. The Christian historians solved this problem in their own way. They took the view that Julian had let himself be led astray by demons. Anyone who did not believe this was henceforth to be considered a heathen.

This version of things proved fatal to the philosopher and mystagogue Maximus, Julian's tutor. After the passing of his imperial patron, the old gentleman was unceremoniously turned over to the executioner and put to death.

Thus did Constantine's dream prove true.

# *Farewell to the*
# *God-filled Women*

AROUND THE YEAR 60, AT DELPHI IN Greece, a disquieting incident occurred. Warned by portentous auspices, the prophetess had reconciled herself unwillingly to the performance of her office. When she began to prophesy, her voice was hoarse, and she appeared deeply distraught; but before long an evil spirit seemed to take hold of her, and she ran screaming to the entrance of the shrine, where she sank unconscious to the ground. All those who were present fled in panic. Later the woman was found, more or less restored to her senses; however, she died after a few days.

Three hundred years later, the Emperor Julian visited Delphi. Although it was rich in tradition, the place had suffered a diminution of prestige under his uncle Constantine. In his endeavor to put an end to the Galilean nightmare and to induce the old oracle to speak once again, Julian requested a pronouncement. To His Imperial Highness's dismay, Apollo had his priestess inform him that this was absolutely the last time that any oracle would come forth. Henceforward, all communication would cease. And with that the god fell silent forever.

Between these two incidents occurred the decline of an institution that the wise Heraclitus, long before, had described as follows: The lord whose oracle is in Delphi neither indicates clearly nor conceals, but gives a sign.

Apollo was the lord in question; his directives issued from the mouth of his priestess, the sibyl or Pythia, a farm girl with a talent for divine service. After a bath of purification, she would betake herself to the prescribed place, there to answer, spontaneously, fluently, and without reflection, the questions presented to her. She did so "with raving mouth," as Heraclitus expressed it, and always in the first-person singular, the "I" of Apollo. This is the way decisions were made about what place the Greeks should choose for the site of a new city, which foreign peoples ought to be considered friends and which foes, what laws were to be passed. The Pythia distributed grades among the gentlemen, letting them know which of them were pleasing to the god; she named the best trade routes and announced which artistic style, which music or divine image deserved preference; she gave information about the causes of epidemics and famine.

For a thousand years, Greeks and barbarians made decisions based on these responses, and so many a city still standing today owes its origins to a saying uttered by one of those women, who had never left the village she was born in.

For the sibyls were regarded as "filled with the god," that is, imbued with an authority not subject to the usual coordinates of time and space. As long as the prophetesses could fulfill their duty of responding to the queries put to them, they were divinely inspired. After that, they were only tired.

Plato, no less, has provided us with a theory concerning this phenomenon. He has Socrates lecture on the subject. "The greatest benefits come to us through madness when it is bestowed on us as a gift of the gods. The prophetess at Delphi and the priestesses at Dodona have conferred many splendid benefits on Greece for both private citizens and whole states through their madness; while in their right minds they have done little or nothing." Socrates goes on to say that a distinction should be made between madness "brought on by mortal maladies" and the madness that arises "from a supernatural release from the conventions of life." The philosopher divides heaven-sent madness into four types: "To Apollo we ascribed prophetic inspiration, to Dionysus mystic madness, to the Muses poetic afflatus; while to Aphrodite and Eros we gave the fourth, love-madness, declaring it to be the best."

The town mentioned in the text, Dodona (today Dhodhoni, about sixteen miles southwest of Ioannina, near the Greek-Albanian border), lies in ruins. Some lead plaques have survived, inscribed with questions and answers from the days when the oracle was active; it ceased to exist only after the Christian era began.

Delphi and Dodona were by no means the only centers of pilgrimage where people came with questions for the god-filled women. In Calabria, for example, near what is today Naples, the Greek colony Cumae was home to a sibyl of wide renown, whose cave overlooking the sea was the goal of many a pilgrim. The Emperor Augustus ordered that her pronouncements, which had been preserved in writing, be brought to the newly built temple of Apollo on the Palatine hill; later many other oracular books were added to the collection. It remained under lock and key, and senators were permitted to consult it only if the state was in danger.

In the period following Augustus' reign, there were many places where men educated in philosophy were operating an oracle service. This did not improve matters unconditionally. The responses of these priest-prophets, formulated in elegant hexameters or iambics, read like excerpts from Platonizing theologians. They praised Him to Whom no name can do justice, Who dwells in the fire, imperturbable, born of no mother, all-knowing: God.

Those in need of such counsel had to take elaborate precautions, as was the case in the shrine of the oracle of Claros, which lay a day's journey from old Ephesus. Consultations took place at night, and not every night was suitable. While the pilgrims waited, they told the temple staff what was on their minds. The priest of the oracle was thus not wholly unprepared as he was subjecting himself to the prescribed fasting in a place apart. At the designated hour, he awaited the pilgrims before the Doric columns of the temple dedicated to Apollo. The god's statue, more than ten feet tall, stood beside the colossal altar where sacrificial victims were slaughtered. Torches were lighted, and the descent began into a low, narrow corridor roofed with slabs of blue marble. After thirty yards the company reached a chamber, where they took their seats on the stone benches that were ranged along the walls. A block of blue marble, the Earth Mother's navel, marked the entrance to the underworld. Then the priest of the oracle disappeared, all alone, into an inner chamber, where there was a spring. The man drank from it, fell straightway into a state of divine madness, and began to prophesy. Whatever he gasped out was simultaneously cast in verse by an officiant in the outer chamber and recorded in writing by the secretary, who had come along for this purpose. Then the troop of pilgrims, deeply stirred, passed through another corridor and emerged into the open. For hours they sang the old hymns in Apollo's praise, standing in the night-shrouded little wood that surrounded the temple, until the stars grew pale and it became time to bow toward the east in anticipation of the first rays of daylight.

Similar ceremonies were on the Emperor Julian's mind as he set about pushing his uncle's Chi-Rho back into the corner with the other sects and placing Greek culture, the culture of the gods, at the center of things. But he had come too late, as certain events in Antioch, where he stopped in the summer of 362, were to show.

Antioch (today Antakya in southern Turkey), a lively city with half a million inhabitants, next to Alexandria the most important trading center in the east, notorious for its lax morals, was already largely Christianized and had only recently been endowed with a magnificent church, whose cupola dominated the skyline. This did nothing at all to prevent the people from celebrating in July the festival of Aphrodite's beloved, Adonis, who had to die at this time, like the cropped grain. Julian, clad only in a loincloth, insisted on appearing before the public as a priest, as the central figure in the traditional procession, in which the municipal prostitutes also took part.

Two hours' walk from the city lay Daphne, a place of pilgrimage complete with an oracle of Apollo in a wooded vale, idyllically situated between sheer cliffs and waterfalls, with shady paths, temples, and theaters. The chief attraction was a colossal statue of Apollo, seven hundred years old, fashioned out of ivory by the master Bryaxis, with hyacinths for eyes.

When Julian inspected Daphne, he was appalled. No one had thought about making the necessary preparations for a sacrifice. As the emperor's irritation began to show, a goose was quickly taken from the temple custodian's house, slaughtered, and burned on an altar. Julian found neither incense nor baked offerings for the gods in Apollo's temple, which was, moreover, quite dilapidated. The emperor's retinue included a philosopher, who immediately performed the rites necessary to mollify the insulted and agitated gods. As he was doing so, it became clear that there was a Christian sarcophagus in the temple precincts, polluting the air.

Naturally a long time was required to load the stone casket on a wagon so that it could be transferred to the cemetery in Antioch. Meanwhile an angry group of Christians had gathered at the scene, and they accompanied the casket with shouts of protest.

Then, during the night of October 22, the temple of Apollo burned down; Bryaxis' work of art was likewise incinerated in the blaze. In the streets of Antioch, insulting songs were sung against Julian, mocking him as the grouch who sleeps alone at night and can think of nothing but fanning altar fires.

The emperor was thoroughly convinced that the Christians had had something to do with the cremation of Daphne. Before departing on his Persian campaign, he avenged himself on them by appointing a particularly nasty official governor of all Syria, including the city of Antioch.

In March 363, Julian and his troops crossed the Euphrates and made a rapid march to Carrhae (Harran in modern Turkey), where several days' rest was declared. The night before the march resumed, the emperor was troubled by dismal dreams.

Later it was learned that on that very same night, on the Palatine hill in the Eternal City, the temple of Apollo, where the sibylline books were kept, had been destroyed by fire.

# *Official Faith*

BUT WHAT HAD HAPPENED TO THAT "MAD-ness arising from a supernatural release from the conventions of life," the madness which, according to Socrates, fell under the jurisdiction of Apollo, whose prophetic afflatus had caused the sibyls to speak with raving mouths? Was the god's decision to fall silent forever tantamount to the end of all prophecy, or did it signify something else, namely the conclusion of a process in the divine world whereby the Aryan Apollo had been deprived of his power and the Semitic Yahweh moved into the foreground?

We have an early hint that something of the sort was going on. Around the year 260, the oracle of Apollo at Didyma (nine miles from modern Akkoy in southwest Turkey) spoke in praise of the "enviable Hebrews," who worshiped one, single god. The aforementioned oracle of Claros also knew the God of the Jews and even called him by his name: Iao. Apollo's pronouncement stated that this most high god was to be worshiped as Hades in winter, as Zeus in spring, as Helius the sun in summer, and in autumn as the delicate Iacchus, who was linked to the corn goddess as husband and son.

This was certainly not what the Hebrews had in mind, but it betrayed a certain tendency to let the divine multiplicity merge into a single god so distinct from the human world that it was forbidden to make an image of him. Indeed, the Jews were not even allowed to speak his name. The Galilean from Nazareth whose initials were emblazoned on Constantine's helmet had addressed this god as "Father," and therefore the Christians believed that the Nazarene was the Son of God.

Of course, if Christ's sonship was to be taken literally, this meant that the Godhead was now doubled. And, since all good things come in threes, there emerged very early in Christian societies the formula that was to revolutionize religious practice all around the Mediterranean Sea: *In the name of the Father, and of the Son, and of the Holy Spirit.*

Three gods? Definitely not that. When Constantine put his trust in the Chi-Rho—we should note that he was in a military encampment, where quick decisions are essential to survival—he had got himself mixed up with a thoroughly unusual religion. Who was this Chi-Rho?

A few months after Constantine's victory at the Milvian Bridge, a name emerges like a gray eminence in his edicts: Hosius, Christian bishop of Córdoba in Spain, spiritual spokesman for the emperor, and soon to be his emissary in matters regarding state policy toward the Church. Hosius knew what he was about.

First of all, Constantine had to learn that his new divine patron did not figure merely as a god among other gods, like Apollo or Helius in the assembly of the Olympians. This Chrestos or Christus laid claim to exclusive rights that were unthinkable in the amiable divine world familiar to Constantine. The Chi-Rho's attitude toward the gods was the same as Constantine's toward his rivals in the struggle for absolute imperial power: me or them.

In addition, the emperor must understand that his new heavenly Lord thoroughly despised any representation of the divine by idols, statues, or earth-navel-stones, along with the burning of sacrificial victims on altars and the whole business of sacred slaughter. That could cost a lot of jobs, and people would complain about having to give up the inexpensive meat that the temples provided to the poor.

Moreover, the emperor had to be prepared for people to consider him a godless man, one who, like the Christians, was utterly lacking in piety, whether toward the familial godlings of the household shrines dedicated to the Lares, or toward the Manes, the spirits of the departed, or toward the heavenly ones themselves. Their images were to be found everywhere, in magnificent sculptures, and passers-by blew kisses to them.

In all these matters, the emperor could count on only a tiny minority for support. Of the fifty million inhabitants of the Roman Empire, two or three percent, at most, were Christians. If, in the area of relations between Church and State, Constantine moved forward with extreme caution, the Chi-Rho would have to understand his plight.

Another reason for slow progress was that the Christians, observed at close quarters, had the same effect on the emperor as a swarm of hornets. Their savagery in questions of faith brought into politics a new factor, which Constantine faced, at first, with perfect incomprehension. He would soon have occasion to test his strategic and tactical knowledge on theological battlefields.

As soon as Constantine publicly tolerated the Christian communities, they plunged with great vehemence into a debate over the divine nature of the Chi-Rho. The dispute had begun on the Nile, in the land of priestly officialdom and preoccupation with the afterlife, of mummy science and tomb tourism. There, starting in 313, a Libyan named Arius served as presbyter and catechist in the parish church of Baucalis in Alexandria, much to the satisfaction of the celibate women who delighted in his preaching. Austere in the conduct of his life, with a melancholy, Christlike countenance, Arius was a deeply learned dialectician and man of letters, whose good connections to influential bishops were well known. He had reached the age of fifty and stood at the pinnacle of his eloquence.

What he had to say accorded with a long tradition in Egyptian theology, originating in pre-Christian times, that had considered in detail the problem of uniting divine personalities into trinities, as well as the question of a divine son's relationship to his father. In the century before Constantine, Origen, the Christian star of such speculations, had left behind hundreds, indeed thousands of writings, composed in the chiaroscuro of a prose style whose originality was unrivaled. He saw the trinity of God the Father, God the Son, and the Holy Spirit as a unity of the divine will, but only the Father was entitled to adoration, because Son and Spirit remained subordinate to him.

Arius, too, preached that the Son was a god of the second rank. The idea of attributing to the Christ, to the Savior incarnate, a divine, eternally existent nature seemed to him blasphemous. Hadn't Jesus himself said that the Father was greater than he?

When confronted with such subtleties in the beginning of 325, after his final, decisive victory over Licinius, his only remaining rival for the imperial crown, the emperor naturally failed to show any understanding for them. Hosius reported to him that all the Egyptian and Syrian bishops were in a complete uproar over the teachings of a certain Arius concerning the relationship between God the Father and God the Son. Constantine's mind was apparently on something else. He ordered Hosius to draft a letter and to travel to Alexandria with a message, written in the emperor's name, that would put an end to the theological quarrel. Arius' views, the letter said, were not at all new, and they concerned a rather minor point in the interpretation of a biblical passage from the book of Proverbs regarding the creation of divine wisdom. It was imprudent to deal with such questions of detail in public, even though people might have different opinions about them in private.

When Hosius arrived in Alexandria, the rival fronts had already stiffened. The bishop of Alexandria would not hear of lifting the ban of excommunication he had placed on Arius, who had moreover turned to bishops from other localities for help. Meanwhile, the bishop of Rome had also been informed of the situation, letters, pamphlets, rectifications, and acts of faith were circulating among ecclesiastics in the eastern half of the Empire, and in the theaters the first jokes about the clergymen's quarrel were being cracked.

In the beginning of May, 325, Constantine set the apparatus of the imperial chancellery in motion. It sent out hundreds of letters of invitation, in which the bishops of the Empire were requested to attend a solemn conference to be held in Nicaea (modern Iznik in northwestern Turkey). The date that had been fixed was of great urgency, the emperor wrote, and he had chosen the meeting place because of its pleasant climate. He himself would be present. The bishops would travel by imperial post, and, in order to spare their excellencies needless expense, all the costs of their sojourn would be paid out of public funds.

Constantine had calculated correctly. On June 19, the emperor, attired in his purple mantle and adorned with the bejeweled insignia of his office, entered the great conference hall in the palace he had reserved for the council. The church leaders rose from their places; the monarch requested permission to sit, which was granted by a gesture. Three hundred and eighteen churchmen had come, among them several old gentlemen who had endured torture under Diocletian. In a brief address, the emperor bade them all to consider peace and concord as the most important goals of this illustrious assemblage. Then, under the discreet direction of Hosius, the discussions began. It soon became clear to Arius and his followers that the emperor was quite prepared to sign harsh decrees of banishment against dissenters.

The outcome was correspondingly unanimous. Only Arius and two of his comrades-in-arms refused to sign the creed approved by the assembly. This creed stated that the Son was born of the Father, God of God, light of light, consubstantial with the Father. The document went on to say that anyone who asserted that there was a time when the Son was not, or that the Son was created out of nothing, would be committed to the devil.

At the end of August, as a reward for their laudable decision, the council fathers were invited to take part in the ceremonial banquet that the emperor held for them in celebration of the felicitous result of the conference. It was like being in heaven, noted Bishop Eusebius, who as the official chronicler wrote a description of the events. Past the guards, who were standing watch with drawn swords, the clerics proceeded to the inner chambers of the palace, where the emperor was awaiting them with a personal gift for each guest.

Arius wasn't invited. The emperor exiled him to northern Illyria, and three years passed before he was allowed to return.

From then on, the Nicene Creed was regarded as dogma. However, it turned out that the text still required certain corrections. The council had avoided referring to the Holy Spirit as God.

# The Eternal Triangle

*T*HIS EMBARRASSMENT WAS RELATED TO the question of what sort of influence on the faithful the leaders of the Church were willing to attribute to the divinely inspired madness that Socrates had described. From the very beginning, divine inspiriting had been the decisive experience for Christians, and for this reason they had even invented a name for the power by which they felt themselves seized: holy *pneuma*.

They called it "holy" because, when human breath issued in fervent prophecies, it did so thanks to that peculiarly exalted state that lent authority to inspired utterance, in distinct contrast to ordinary speech.

Joy, peace, truth, life, love: the key words of salvation that the Christians listened to in their gatherings were a constant reminder of the trembling lips, the quavering voices of those by whom they had first been spoken—their apostles and prophets and martyrs and confessors.

Blood had been shed, because God-filled men and women, during the time of the persecutions, had refused to show reverence to the mute idols of the heathens or burn incense to deified emperors. They had been brought into the arena in chains and committed to the beasts, given as prey to the African panthers who were starved for a week and then released from their cages. Singing and praying, each saint awaited the fangs of the animals, but these, terrified by the howling crowd in the stadium, took their time before pouncing. Since the violent end of the first martyrs in Jerusalem, six or seven years after the execution of Jesus Christ, Christians had believed that the courageous deaths of their heroes bore witness to the superior spiritual power of their God. (Filled with the Holy Spirit, Stephen saw the heavens thrown open and the Son of man standing at the right hand of God. Immediately they thrust him out of the city and stoned him.)

So now let us turn to this question: Was the Holy Spirit to be understood as an impersonal divine force, or was he, if possible, to be conceived as an independent God, distinct from Father and Son? In the summer of 325, the imperial prince, Julian, at the time still a student in Athens, was astonished to hear about this problem when he made the acquaintance of Gregory Nazianzen, also known as Gregory Theologus. Together with a certain Basil and his brother, Gregory was promoting the deification of the Holy Spirit. These three men were the celebrated "Cappadocian fathers," so called because of their common homeland in central Anatolia. In matters of faith, they were deadly serious. "His dastardliness," Gregory later wrote of Julian, "became apparent to the world only when he came to power and could act at his own discretion; but I had already seen what he was when I met him in Athens. I based my perception on the imbalance of his character and the excess of his constant flood of emotions. When I looked at him, I was filled with foreboding."

One can discover, in the careers of the Cappadocians, a characteristic turning point to which they owed their standing among the self-confident bishops in the Imperium's new elite. Born into well-to-do Christian families, the young men first completed the sort of education that would smooth their passage into the upper ranks of the state bureaucracy— philosophy, rhetoric, literature. However, the idea of such an ascent soon appeared empty to all three of them. Basil and his friend Gregory opted for the asceticism of the monkish life. When they were both thirty years old, they established a remote cloister together in order to devote their lives to prayer and theological science. Basil's younger brother soon joined them, and the three Cappadocians spent several long years bent over their books. This was during the time when the Emperor Julian, embarked on the ship of religion, was attempting to regain control of the helm. The Cappadocian fathers had nothing but scorn for him. In one of his discourses, Gregory addressed the apostate. "Just open it," he wrote, "open your theater! For what other name can your temple have? May the people come streaming in when your heralds call them! Show them the interpreters of your inspired oracles! Explain to your loyal followers your theological books, complete with their divine wars, their titans, giants, and hydras, their hellhounds, chimeras, and gorgons. . . ."

Shortly after Julian's death, Basil was ordained a priest in Caesarea (modern Kayseri, Turkey), the chief city of Cappadocia, where in 370 he was promoted to archbishop and metropolitan. One year later he appointed his brother bishop of Nyssa, a small town in his diocese, and in the year 372 he ordained Gregory as well. Shortly thereafter Basil produced his treatise *On the Holy Spirit.*

Up to that time, lack of clarity concerning the third name of God had predominated among theologians. "Some of them," Gregory observed, "have assumed that the Holy Spirit is a force; others, that he is a creature; still others, that he is God; and finally there are several who have accepted none of these views."

The way out that the Cappadocians discovered owed a great deal to the theater and its personae, whose masks were familiar to everyone. They took as their starting point the assumption that God's inner essence was beyond all description. But God apparently had an affinity for the stage, and so sometimes he appeared in terrestrial events as the Father principle, sometimes in the shape of the Son, and on still other occasions in pneumatic form.

God: one essence, three actors.

Unfortunately, neither Hebrew nor Greek, the two languages used in the books of the Bible, included an unequivocal word for what the Cappadocian fathers had in mind. The most apt choice was the Latin word *persona* (its original meaning was "mask" or "role"), which likewise came from the theater, but which seemed better suited to take on a denotation of personal distinctiveness. All sorts of letters regarding this matter went back and forth between Greek and Latin theologians, until a formula was adopted that clarified the question of the divine triangle reasonably well: one God in three Persons.

This formula completed the construction of the speculative pyramid whose geometrical rigor would, in future, be directed at the teeming heathen brood of gorgons and herms, nymphs and chimeras, satyrs and centaurs, titans and sphinxes, corn goddesses and demigods, at that hybrid muddle that mixed together—menacingly, obscenely, capriciously—heaven, earth, and underworld, human faces and animal shapes.

"I have not yet conceived of the One," wrote Gregory, "and already I am illuminated by the Three. I have not yet distinguished among the Three, and yet again I am led back to the One." Whatever circulated outside this metaphysics of light was of the devil.

With commensurate energy, the bishops of the Catholic Church endeavored to convey the multifarious gods of traditional piety down to the site of all their future romps—the Christian hell.

Obviously, the fathers of the Church needed powerful allies in this difficult undertaking. For this reason they derived their authority from those predecessors who were now reigning on heavenly thrones with the Lord Jesus, the twelve holy apostles.

# *Acts of the Apostles*

THE APOSTLES WERE ALSO ON CONSTANTINE'S mind when he placed the order for the construction of the church that was to serve as his mausoleum in Constantinople, as the last resting place for his imperial bones. His sarcophagus, flanked by two groups of six columns in honor of the twelve apostles, was to occupy the center of the cruciform building.

And so it was done. The emperor's chronicler, Eusebius, wrote that Constantine hoped his dead body would be deemed worthy of the same prayers that were due to the apostles.

There was a good reason for this impudence. The twelve apostles had ended their days in various cities, but Byzantium, also known as Constantinople, the emperor's second Rome, was sadly not among them. The emperor sought to remedy this deficiency with the creation of his mausoleum. In the event, twenty years after Constantine's death the relics of the apostle Andrew were transferred from northern Greece to Constantinople, as well as the remains of the evangelist Luke (from Boeotia) and of Paul's disciple Timothy (from Ephesus). The status of Byzantium was thereby enhanced in its open rivalry with old Rome, which derived its primacy from the torments of the apostolic princes Peter and Paul. Constantine had learned that of all the bishops of Christendom, those who enjoyed the most prestige were the successors of those men who had been installed in office personally by one of the apostles. Rome was not the only place where proper lists were kept that traced the spiritual lineage of incumbents back to an apostle and thus to the very person of the Chi-Rho himself, who had sent his apostles out into the world with divine authority.

Authority was the whole point in referring to the Jewish fishermen and traveling preachers whose work was so sacred to Christians. If anyone could show that he derived his office from the intention of one of the apostles, from the laying on of hands in an unbroken succession of ceremonies first celebrated by Peter, or Paul, or Andrew, or John, etc., whose purpose was to vest their successors with the power of the Holy Spirit, then such a person belonged to the oldest nobility of Christianity and might indeed call his rank apostolic.

That was quite important, because from the very beginning Christians had been influenced by all sorts of teachers, who for their part had also appealed to the Holy Spirit, and who not infrequently had taught opinions contrary to those of their superiors, with dissatisfaction and strife as consequences. In such cases the decrees of the apostolic fathers could be ranged against the contestable and uncertain results of personal inspiration. This tactic was all the more effective when carried out simultaneously and in unison, that is, with the concurrence, for example, of the bishops of Jerusalem, Rome, Antioch, and Ephesus, each of whom owed his prestige to one of the apostles.


For all that, the Christian bishops (from Greek *episkopos*, "overseer") had a certain problem with the Holy Spirit. Would he descend upon each of them with the same violence he had used in the days of the apostles?

In the Acts of the Apostles, which circulated among the Christian communities, the Holy Spirit fell, as it were, automatically upon any person on whom an apostle had laid his hands. Then the cheeks of the chosen one grew red, his tongue was loosened in divine speech, and his eyeballs turned upward, where they could see the Lord Jesus, seated on high on his eternal throne, in the glory of God the Father.

The hysteria of the apostolic Spirit-mediation must have disconcerted the staid, middle-aged men whose activities were mainly confined to organizing relief for the poor in Christian communities and to the everyday chores of their office, such as performing weddings, settling disputes, executing wills, laying construction plans, and similar matters. A divinely guaranteed monopoly on preaching during congregational prayer meetings was sufficient to enable the bishops to stop the mouths of the less stable members of their flocks.

The bishops' preaching monopoly came under the jurisdiction of the Third Person of God. In order to ensure that future preachers would be able to count on a reliable measure of grace, particular precautions were taken at every bishop's consecration. The presence of at least three, but preferably seven or twelve bishops from neighboring congregations was required when a new man was to receive the laying-on of hands. Before that happened, all praying aloud ceased for a while, and in the growing silence everyone present concentrated on the Holy Spirit, whom they desired to call down upon their future colleague.

It could not always be determined unequivocally whether the Holy Spirit was fully involved in every case. Christian bishops often formed factions that underwent various metamorphoses and fought one another furiously, especially in the eastern half of the Empire. The disputing parties kept their anathemas handy, ready to consign their enemies to the devil, and in many cases the question of whose side the Holy Spirit was on got resolved only after a Christian emperor had intervened in the quarrel, as Constantine had done with the Council of Nicaea.

At the same time, there was no denying how powerfully the Holy Spirit was at work among clerics, too, especially during the golden century of Christian theology that began after the death of Constantine. In Antioch, that John whom people called Chrysostom ("Golden Mouth") because of his great eloquence was preaching, and in Nisibis

(Nusaybin, Turkey) the Syrian deacon Ephraem was earning his name as a "zither of the Holy Spirit" because his hymns and songs made people so happy. The profundity of the Cappadocian fathers was as renowned as the erudition of Jerome, who translated the Bible into Latin. In the west, Ambrose and Augustine were teaching; their names would resound through the centuries. Other bishops, such as Saint Martin of Tours and Saint Nicholas of Myra, whose bones were later transferred to Bari, delighted the people with miraculous works. Furthermore, it could not be overlooked how sure-handedly the fathers of the Church were making distinctions in Christian writings between the reliable word of God and lesser texts and thus cementing the biblical foundation for a structure of sound teaching, unadulterated since apostolic times.

Seen in this way, the leading lights of the Christian episcopate were obviously more than a match for the priests of the heathen oracles, whose responses were becoming more and more schematic. In the fullness of his rank, the bishop appeared before the faithful as their spiritual father—ascetic, grave, in direct contact with God. Whoever wanted to learn how to organize a new religion could not overlook the bishops. The Emperor Julian knew that when he admonished the priests of Jupiter to emulate their Christian colleagues in caring for the poor.

After the end of their golden century, the figures of the most outstanding bishops and fathers of the Church migrated to the mosaics and icons of the Christian basilicas. The rank they assumed there made them equal to the apostles, crowned like them with the halo of divine authentication.

Unfortunately there remained some unsolved problems.

# *The Gift of Tears*

THE DEMONS HAD BY NO MEANS RE-
mained inactive. When you saw them, what was the use of whistling
through your teeth? Apparently not even the water of baptism was of any
help, no matter that it was administered in the name of the Father, the
Son, and the Holy Spirit. Even after receiving the sacrament, many Christians fell into the Adversary's clutches.

When that happened, the radiance of the Elect faded from the
wretch's forehead, his heart hardened in lust for possessions, his flesh
coveted his neighbor's wife, his mouth grew accustomed to lying and his
hand to violence. It was especially among the pious that the enemy, the
Evil One of old, sought his prey, like a stalking lion, hungry to swallow
some wriggling life forever.

Faced with this extreme threat to their very existence, the Christian
hermits in the deserts of Egypt, Palestine, and Syria exercised themselves
in a constant struggle against the demons. Hour after hour they would
touch their foreheads to the floor and raise their arms to heaven: *Have
mercy!*

At the same time they were accumulating experiences that didn't seem
altogether harmless. Gregory, the Doctor of the Church, had a cousin, a
friend of all the Cappadocian fathers, who was called Amphilochius. He
was consecrated bishop of Iconium (today Konya, Turkey) in 373.
Amphilochius found himself compelled to take measures against a practice
that was developing a lively following, especially among the monks and
hermits of Anatolia. Through the use of a particular breathing technique,
they endeavored to be rid of demonic temptations once and for all and to
win over the Holy Spirit to long-term indwelling. Much to Amphilochius'

dismay, a follower of these Enthusiasts, as they were called, was heard to say something to the effect that baptism was useless, and that only intensive, permanent prayer brought about the definitive exit of the devil, whereupon the Holy Spirit made his entrance in perceptible fashion.

The Enthusiasts didn't think very highly of the bishops' instructions. They preferred to be taught by women who were familiar with the workings of the Spirit through their own experience.

As far as Amphilochius and his counterparts were concerned, these prophetesses were a plague upon the land. They wore their hair short, dressed like men, neglected to observe the periods of fasting ordained by the Church, and despised the notion of commitment to the family. When the Spirit penetrated them, the sensation was more intense than any joy they felt in the act of love. The latter led to lying-in and to the squalling of children, and so the god-filled women had rather be possessed by their beloved Spirit than by a man. The sibyls had surfaced again; it wasn't Apollo who spoke through them now, but the third divine Person of Christendom.

The bishops had their doubts about that. At several synods, they solemnly committed the Enthusiasts to the devil for disparaging baptism, but these proceedings did little good; the Spirit wouldn't let himself be extinguished in the ladies so easily. In the heresy indices of the Byzantine judicial archives, a firm belief in the physically perceptible indwelling of the Holy Spirit appeared for centuries as one of the thousand falsehoods that the devil had sown in the field of sound teaching.

Amid all this condemnation, the guardians of the faith overlooked two valuable hints that the Holy Spirit had dropped during the time of his activity in Anatolia and Syria. These hints, meant for the instruction of all those who strove for perfection, highlighted the significance of breathing and of weeping for human well-being.

There was a corresponding training program for those who had sought their freedom in the cloisters of the East. Its goal was to slow down breathing in a permanent and controlled way. The so-called monologion was used, a brief cry of prayer adapted to the rhythm of breathing, in and out, again and again, until one's heart, no longer disturbed by thoughts, found rest. Then it could happen that the Spirit appeared before the inner eye as light and as fire, accompanied by the precious gift of tears that washed any hardness away.

The monologion is still cultivated today, for example on the Athos peninsula, also called the "Holy Mountain," east of Thessalonike. Entrance to this enclave is of course forbidden to women.

The sacred Mount Athos (about 6670 feet high) gives its name to a monastic community that has been in existence there for a very long time, consisting of monasteries, hermitages, and small farms, widely scattered over an austere landscape of woods, undergrowth, and rock. The traditions of the monks of Mount Athos relate that the Mother of Our Lord Jesus Christ, shortly after the Holy Spirit's descent during the feast of Pentecost in Jerusalem, was sent to Athos as a missionary. When she landed there, a massive statue of Zeus burst into a thousand fragments. Later the Emperor Constantine was contemplating the notion of founding his new Rome on the Athos peninsula. The Mother of God, they say, appeared to him in a dream and dissuaded him from his plan, whereupon Constantine endowed a chapel on the spot where Mary had come ashore.

Since that time, Christian inspiration has been perpetuated on Athos, laid up in the grave features of the old icons on the walls of the monastery churches, untouched by progress or modernity. Inspiration is present in the liturgy of songs and hymns, of invocations and rituals whose subject is a story that begins with the annunciation of the Angel Gabriel and comes to an end with Mary's death. The story of salvation is not subject to the passage of the years. The Savior's birth in a stable, his work among men, his miracles, his suffering and death, his resurrection and ascension—all the mysteries of divine love proceed incessantly from the depths of the Most Holy Triad. And the highest privilege of all consists in being able to give honor, together with the angels, to the uncreated Light.

The passage of the years means something to the outside world, however, and the Athos monks have had somehow to come to terms with it—with the Ottomans (1430–1912), with Adolf Hitler (1941–1944), with the European Community (since 1981). At such times they have referred to their rights, which are attested in documents, to their artistic treasures, which are worthy of protection, and to the long history of their traditions.

For centuries the Islamic world adopted a lenient attitude toward the men of Athos, who shared its reservations about *Evropi*, about the West beyond the Danube and the Adriatic, where papacy, enlightenment, industry, socialism, and godlessness all had their beginnings. These were the monstrous products of arrogance, unlovely and short-lived, like the undertakings of that very Julian who had ordered the desecration of Constantine's chapel on Athos—in vain, of course.

From a monologuist's point of view, the world needs no further renewal. It has already happened: under Constantine, who transferred his residence to the East, and under the saintly fathers Basil and Gregory, whose instructions still give life on Athos its rhythm today, as it did in their time.

And the treasure-house of the Vatopedion monastery preserves the Virgin's girdle, which the Mother of God left behind as a memento for the apostles before she was assumed into heaven.

# *Ave Maria*

IN CHURCHES AND MUSEUMS, IMAGES of the archangel's visit to the Virgin Mary are enduring reminders of a notable divine intervention in wordly affairs. The Holy Spirit will come upon you, Gabriel announced to the frightened girl, and the power of the Most High will cover you with its shadow.

Will take possession of you as of the prophetesses and prophets from the depths of time, will penetrate into you as a man into a woman.

Ever since the Italian Trecento, the Virgin—as depicted on painted panels above the altars of Europe—has looked like a young, expensively dressed noblewoman, ready, so to speak, for a high-level visitor. The angel, for his part, enters her private chamber in the shape of a man, which makes for a certain amount of erotic tension. His greeting to the young lady has remained fixed in the memory of the Christian peoples: *Ave Maria.*

The angel of the Lord declared unto Mary, and she conceived by the Holy Ghost. From the very beginning, she was supposed to think of this conception as the result of a divine act of procreation—though this doesn't exactly jibe with another biblical quotation, according to which the divine bride's consort engendered the fruit of her womb: Joseph begot Jesus, who is called the Christ.

Those who don't confuse reality with truth will be able to accept both assertions.

In reality, Joseph was the father of Jesus, who is called the Christ. But it remains true that God had a hand in the matter.

The pictures of the Flemish, Italian, and Spanish masters sometimes portray the Most High as a dove hovering over Mary's head or as a beam of light from above, or indeed as absolutely nothing, which is surely the shrewdest choice. The divine sphere should never be represented at all, as a reading of the Ten Commandments will show.

In the liturgical calendars of the Christian churches, Gabriel comes back every year on the twenty-fifth of March to make the Annunciation to Mary. A country saying remarks that the swallows, too, return around this time. Nine months later, as always, the child Jesus will lie in his manger. Swallows and divine worship take their bearings from conditions that cannot be ascertained in history classes.

History classes ignore beginnings and concentrate solely on dates. They describe sequences of events, analyze causes and effects. Time's arrow is on its way into the future. Divine worship, on the other hand, takes the beginnings that history classes must remain blind to—for example, the beginning of the Christian era through Gabriel's visit to Mary—and makes them present. The stories that are told in the churches, the tales whose unalterable texts are repeated again and again, commence with a formula that transports the pious congregation into the events of an eternal beginning: *At that time.*

"At that time the angel Gabriel was sent by God to a town in Galilee

called Nazareth, to a virgin." Thus begins the Gospel that's read on
March 25. When March 25 falls on a weekday, there are usually only a
few old women in the church. Worldly events fade away for them while
the sacred ceremony is going on, and time's arrow comes to a standstill, as
it were, in the middle of the air.

# *Heavenly Light*

SCARCELY HAD EMPEROR CONSTANTINE AD-

*justed his politics to the Christian monogram when a heavenly voice made itself*

*heard in upper Egypt. Its addressee was a hermit named Pachomius, and at first*

*he hesitated to translate into action the command he had received, because it was*

*unheard of. Only after a second admonition did he dare to begin the construc-*

*tion of the first Christian monastery in the Roman Empire.*

*This development signaled the installation of an escape principle that divided humanity into "carnal" and "spiritual." From now on, with express reference to the Third Person of God, the monasteries offered a program of spiritual life characterized by its stark contrast to the usual bustling of the children of the world.*

*The price of admission to peace of mind had to be paid with renunciation of possessions and descendants, of mobility and laughter, of the thirst for knowledge and the sense of beauty. The thing worked outstandingly well, as if according to a plan. In the time of Charlemagne, when Europe was a backward, barbarous part of the world, poor and sparsely settled, monks and nuns were copying the verses of Ovid and the orations of Cicero, singing the Psalms of David, distilling medicaments, and letting machines work for them, as in a factory. No one would have thought that these pious figures were busy preparing the Industrial Revolution.*

# *Where Have We Been Thrown?*

"ONLY A GOD CAN RESCUE US NOW. The only possibility that remains for us is to make preparations, in our thoughts and in our writings, for the appearance of the god, or for the absence of the god if we go down to ruin; so that we go down in the face of the absent god."

Thus spoke the philosopher Martin Heidegger, in September 1966, to the magazine *Der Spiegel.* It was not until ten years later, after the thinker's death, that the interview was allowed to appear in print.

Heidegger is considered the most profound German thinker of the twentieth century. From 1933 to 1945 he was a member of the National Socialist German Workers' Party; because of this, he was forbidden to teach for several years after the war.

In 1936, in the town of Frascati, near Rome, a conversation took place between Heidegger and his student, Karl Löwith, in which Heidegger acknowledged that the reasons for his support of National Socialism were rooted in the nature of his philosophy. Löwith had fled to Italy because of his Jewish descent. When he arrived for the meeting with Löwith, Heidegger was wearing his party badge.

Despite various pleas, especially from Jews who knew and admired his work, Heidegger couldn't bring himself to utter a word of remorse for his belief in the "inner truth and greatness" of National Socialism. It appears that oracular pronouncements, even in our technological age, are irrevocable.

Another Jewish student of Heidegger's, Hans Jonas, discovered in 1934 a "peculiar analogy" between his master's teachings and those of the "Gnosis" in late antiquity. At the time of Jonas's discovery, there were only a few theologians and classical philologists who were interested in the Gnostics. In his treatise *Being and Time,* which first appeared in 1927, Heidegger had stipulated as a fundamental category of human existence the concept of "thrown-ness" (*Geworfenheit*). This matched, right down to the word choice, the ideas of the Theosophists who flourished in the beginning of the Christian Era and who were the subjects of Jonas's monograph. More than forty years were to pass before the value of his work began to be recognized.

Jonas's study focused on the early history of the Christian Era, on those first centuries that had turned the page to a new chapter in world history. Jonas declared that Jesus and Paul did not hold the sole copyrights on this text. His detailed examination of the subject led to the conclusion that the Jewish Savior and his apostle were at best the first and second fiddles in an orchestra that made music with many instruments, playing notes whose composer remained anonymous. A way of feeling about the world was spreading among people for the first time, from the eastern rim of the Mediterranean to deep inside Asia. To betoken the unknown Master who was the author (words and music) of this new song, Jonas chose an old German word: *Geist,* spirit.

By this he did not mean the panting breath of sibylline, prophetic, or possessed utterance, but rather a silent principle that particularly liked to work its effects on the solitary contemplative, like a dawning light.

This process began with several questions. Who were we? What have we become? Where were we? Whither have we been cast? Whither do we hasten? From what have we been set free?

Knowledge in such a questionable field is called "gnosis."

Jonas named his work, which he never completed, *Gnosis und spätantiker Geist,* literally "Gnosis and the Spirit of Late Antiquity." In it he expressly stated that his research topic had been given a living language by Heidegger's analysis of existence. In Heidegger's analysis, human life is called "being unto death," and the response to it is anxiety.

The Second World War cost the lives of fifty million human beings. What they had paid for remained an open question.

And look. In December 1945, immediately after the end of the most strenuous sacrificial slaughter in all human history, the earth in upper Egypt, as though by a miracle, disclosed a message that had been buried for 1,600 years. The site of the discovery was the upper Nile, sixty miles downstream from old Thebes. One morning the brothers Muhammad and Khalifah Ali left the village of Al-Qasr with their camels to go and dig humus soil at the foot of Djebel el-Tarif, a limestone cliff on the edge of the desert. As they were digging, they struck something hard. It was a sealed clay urn more than three feet tall. Inside were a great many closely written pages, packed in envelopes made of goat's leather and partially damaged. The two fellahin and their relatives correctly guessed that such a find was worth money. Little by little, the manuscripts began to surface in Cairo. One installment, smuggled out of the country by the Belgian antiquarian Eid, changed hands for 35,000 Swiss francs and was given to the famous psychoanalyst Carl Gustav Jung as a present for his eightieth birthday.

The old gentleman's fondness for the patrimony of heretical Christianity was well known.

For this extraordinary cache of manuscripts—named after the town of Nag Hammadi, near which it was found—brought to light a library of heretical teachings: left-handed tractates, gospels, secret writings, all of them quite far from what the imperial Church in the reign of Constantine considered orthodox.

The Spirit of an oddball, cross-grained Christianity, pushed underground by stern bishops, heretic-persecutors, heresiologists, had climbed up out of the earth. The guardians of the faith would not accept that the Spirit blows where it pleases, as it is written in the Gospel of Saint John. As far as they were concerned, anything that smacked of gnosis came not from the Holy Spirit, but from the devil.

There was a simple reason for such abhorrence. In the papyrus pages (1,153 in all) from Nag Hammadi, which wound up in the Coptic Museum in Cairo, the God of the Bible, the Creator, was from time to time openly derided as a bungler and a botcher who, operating behind the mask of almighty power and goodness, had cobbled together a disastrously shoddy business, a wretched world full of suffering, injustice, violence. The true God of the Gnostics, inaccessible in the eternal light, might have no inkling of the disgusting mess made by the undergod.

The early Christian Theosophists deviated from one another in the details of how they depicted the cosmic misfortune that had resulted in the unholiness of earthly conditions. They were unanimous, on the other hand, in rejecting the joys of parenthood, because reproductive activity presupposed a certain agreement with what exists. If it weren't for children, the beasts and monsters that were creeping about the earth in human form would quickly disappear, forever, and the last of the light particles that had been imprisoned inside human bodies could finally be fetched home, or, to put it better, restored to their proper place in the original state of things, when there was a clear separation between the positive pole and the negative pole.

For the Atomic Age, such conceptions provide a fascinating perspective.

. . .

But the Ethiopian slave girl's sweet little bottom, was that supposed to be abhorrent, too? But of course, responded the Gnostic men's choir. Just look at what comes out of that posterior part. Ordure and stench.

The orthodox believers who hammered heretics had a hard time taking a stand against this kind of contempt for the flesh, because they themselves were filled with it. The Spirit (the *ruach*, the *pneuma*) allowed himself to be conceived in any number of ways, even as an occurrence in the brain's electricity, but surely not as a manifest incarnation of the particularly fleshly kind so clearly expressed, from the male point of view, in the physical charms of women. The Spirit stood in theological and philosophical opposition to swelling curves, almond eyes, stroking hands, upper and lower lips, kissing tongues. Female flesh had irritated male thinking since long before the birth of Christ. One could trace the origin of spiritual enlightenment back to the centuries that had given the world Greek money, democratic order, and Socratic acumen. There was no place for feminine charms in the spiritual world.

Nevertheless, Greek civilization had always admired the comeliness of the scheme of things. The Greeks called it "cosmos," which comes from their word *kosmein*, "to adorn." Their friendly gaze willingly took time to contemplate the female form, carved out of marble, as an embodiment of spiritual beauty.

In contrast, the Nag Hammadi texts read as though they were written on the run. In the Gnostic library, the goal of the hero who has been cast adrift in foreign lands is not, as in the case of Odysseus, the domestic hearth and the faithful spouse, but an immaterial hereafter flooded with uncreated light. Only rarely does the heavenly light let itself be perceived on earth, and in such cases it seems at best a small, capricious, unpredictable spark in the depths of the soul. But to anyone who has seen that light, even if only once, all earthly light seems dim.

If nothing else, a more cheerful form of loathing for the world was the order of the day for the Christian cliques—Jewish, Greek, Egyptian, Syrian, Anatolian, and Roman—among whose members Gnostic esoterica circulated during the second and third centuries. It was cheerful because people in those circles were convinced that they knew the Logos, the Word, which placed the individual and the world in a meaningful context. Already, in the Garden of Paradise, the clever serpent in the Tree of the Knowledge of Good and Evil had offered Eve the key to this mystery, whereupon the Lord of the Garden had flown into a rage. The investigators of hidden knowledge particularly loved reading the Bible against the grain like this, because it gave them the sensation of being a few steps ahead of ordinary Christians.

Besides that, the esoteric Christians clung to their Holy Spirit. They were the spiritual ones, the *pneumatikoi,* while the rest of mankind remained encumbered by fleshly cravings. The spirit is willing, but the flesh is weak. The Pneumatics were the strong ones. That made them, like the philosopher Martin Heidegger, both interesting and dangerous.

# Female Voices

WITHIN THE CIRCLES DEDICATED TO esoteric studies, it is only very seldom that the male voices, filled with hostility toward life, are interrupted by a woman. When she speaks, it is with the voice of Mary Magdalene, to whom Jesus, who is her lover, has imparted knowledge about which the twelve apostles haven't a clue. This in turn angers Simon Rock (*Petrus*), the man with the keys to the kingdom of heaven, and he forbids the woman to open her mouth. I'm afraid of him, the Magdalene confesses, because he hates the female race.

The fundamental disturbance in relations between the two sexes cannot be more clearly expressed than in this isolated third-century request for the right to speak. The trouble had turned the Nazarene into a mama's boy, an eternal bachelor who couldn't let any woman near him once he'd ascended into heaven. In vain had the Holy Spirit distributed his charismata indiscriminately among both men and women during the first fifty years, when the Pentecostal jubilation was still fresh. Yes, in those days women—prophetesses, preachers, soothsayers, evangelists, theologians—weren't ashamed to declare publicly the inspirations that had come to them. It is even conceivable that one or another of the Nazarene's female companions might have claimed the same rank as Simon Rock and the other apostles in the earliest Jewish Christian societies—perhaps that same Mary of Magdala who had accompanied her friend to his execution while Jesus' troop of male disciples was conspicuously absent. Or the other Mary, the one from the village of Bethany, whom Jesus had expressly praised by saying that she had chosen the best part.

It wasn't long, however, before a few men, agitated and upset by the self-assurance of Christian women, began to make their voices heard. We can read, in the various Epistles that they disseminated under the name of Paul, that preaching was the province of men only, and naturally that men alone were fit to perform all the executive duties in the Christian congregations. "For Adam was formed first and Eve afterward, and it was not Adam who was led astray but the woman who was led astray and fell into sin."

During the second and third centuries, the gentlemen who thought this way gradually took command of most Christian communities. But not all of them.

Around the year 200, a man named Aberkius, from the province of Asia (western Turkey), ordered a tomb inscription that was to stress the most important events of his life. According to Aberkius, a divine shepherd, who pastures his flock with wide-open eyes and possesses reliable knowledge, sent him to Rome that he might look upon a people charged with protecting a gleaming seal and ruled by a queen garmented in gold. The dear Paul and the lady Pistis had accompanied him on his journey. He had traveled through Syria as well; everywhere he had found fellow believers, who entertained him with bread and mixed wine. Let whoever understands this pray for Aberkius.

The encoded text (*pistis* means "faith"), which only initiates could understand, alludes to the Christian celebration of the Lord's Supper, and indeed to Jesus himself, with his radiant gaze. It is obviously no accident that the apostle Paul appears in the company of a woman. The reference to the Roman queen likewise adds a feminine accent, as does the immaculate virgin mentioned elsewhere in the inscription in connection with the ritual meal.

The pious mystification of expressing in code the leading role that women played in the life of a Christian community seems like part of a trail that was carefully covered up later. It's only from some spiteful remarks made by members of Simon Rock's faction that we can infer what things were like before the Constantinian turning point. How impudent and audacious they are, these heretical women, fumed the ecclesiastical writer Tertullian. They are bold enough to teach, to engage in argument, to enact exorcisms, to undertake cures, and, it may be, even to baptize! The imputations of heresy that spewed from this man's pen were contemporaneous with the formulation of Aberkius' inscription. Tertullian, a jurist from North Africa, never called the female leader of a Christian congregation in his hometown by any name other than "this viper."

This kind of insult was no isolated case. Precisely those Christian circles in which women were still allowed to have some say found themselves branded by their opponents with the stigma of moral and ideological perversion. Before the discovery at Nag Hammadi, what these disparaged souls truly thought and how they really lived had to be painstakingly reconstructed from the polemical writings of those who made it their business to spy on other people's faith and morals. These writings mention the bizarre names given to some heretical sects, names that the worthy authors shuddered to pronounce: Carpocratians, Barbelognostics, Ophites, Phibionites, Stratiotici. The disputatious Bishop Epiphanius reported on all manner of scandalous behavior in his "Medicine Chest" (*Panarion*) of antidotes to the crypto-Christians' poison. It is customary among them, he says, to appear at prayer stark naked; after a sumptuous meal, such as roast meats and wine, the amorous mingling takes place. Another connoisseur of the scene, one Irenaeus, attacked the deviants with similar ferocity, enraged that they should think of themselves as perfected and pneumatic. Around the year 180, Irenaeus was bishop of Lyons, and he relates that a seducer named Marcus turned the heads of the Christian women there. He started with clever magic tricks. Then, using prayerlike conjurations, he succeeded in making the chalice with the sacred wine appear purple and red. He encouraged the women to speak the words of transformation over the wine, and then to pour their chalices into his until it overflowed. He would declare a woman a prophetess with the words, "Grace has come upon you; open your mouth, and prophesy." Whereupon the deluded victim impudently uttered the most arrant nonsense. In all of this, Irenaeus implies, we should not exclude the possibility that the deceiver enticed his female disciples with an invitation to enter the perfection of the sacred bridal chamber and take up the seed of light.

In contrast, not a single passage in the Gnostic library of Nag Hammadi favors a dissipated way of life or dissolute morals. Instead there emerges conspicuously often in the theosophical constructs of this exclusive clergy a female principle, ranked equally with the male, even unto divinity, addressed by different names, made mythographically dynamic, and interwoven with numerical symbols.

These cogitations surely didn't come from the Bible.

The young ladies in Rome or Alexandria who perused Gnostic treatises frequently demonstrated a certain weakness for reading matter seasoned with philosophy. As a rule, they owed their acquaintance with the Christian faith to the chambermaids who massaged their tummies. It was a marvelous religion, with a youthful shepherd as its god, and he offered eternal life. Women were a decided majority in Christian gatherings. Well-to-do ladies in the prime of life who had been widowed young or had never married, or who found married life not to their taste, were held in especially high esteem. They sponsored the poor, visited the sick, and received orators from out of town as guests in their villas—highly cultured, ascetic men, with visionary eyes, whose spiritual quest had found an inspiration that sounded like a call from the upper spheres bidding them to come home at last.

The leaders of the schools of pneumatic Christendom—they were later assigned prominent positions in the heretic catalogs—were men of such caliber: Basilides, Marcion, Valentinus. They sprang, so to speak, out of nowhere onto the stage of world history, a hundred years after Christ's death, and they found an attentive public among educated female admirers of Jesus.

The Greek word for wisdom (*sophia*), feminine in gender, appears in the teachings of these Theosophists like a recurring theme, subject to innumerable variations. In one of them, this divine Sophia sits on a mountain, lusts after herself, fulfills her desire, and becomes pregnant from her desire. Throughout this creative process, in which the world has its origin, no male figure is anywhere to be seen. In other versions the goddess flows out of another female being, Pistis, or she suffers a miscarriage that develops into a monster with nothing better to do than to create the world.

The Gnostic Sophia makes no secret of the fact that she is lusty by nature. She gets lost in all sorts of heavy seas; she'd like to go to bed with her father, preferably, but also with her son. Innocence and whorishness combine in her as in Frank Wedekind's Lulu. And to cap it all, she's even equated with the Holy Spirit, the Semitic *ruach,* whose serpentine wiles in Paradise get the better of the Lord of the Garden.

The writings from Nag Hammadi include a short text in which this female self-assurance goes so far as to speak in the first person, with a voice of thunder. The poem boldly addresses the reader: "Look upon me, you who reflect upon me. Be careful. I am the first and the last, the honored and the despised, the whore and the saint, woman and virgin, mother and daughter. I am silence, I am voice, I am modesty and seductiveness, I am bold and distraught, everywhere hated, everywhere beloved. I am Sophia."

Unfortunately, we cannot discover whether, before these verses were written down, they were first recited by a man or a woman, perhaps before a small circle of like-minded devotees of both sexes during some long afternoon of animated conversation that took place, for example, on an estate in the Roman Campagna.

It can be assumed that a discreet erotic charge hung in the air at such gatherings. And why not? Such groups were surely uninterested in reproductive activity. The women, not burdened by pregnancies, labor pains, or nursing, remained youthful and trim. The men had sown their wild oats long since, as was frequently the case by the age of forty in those days.

Only rarely is there a slight lifting of the veil that lies over this elegant piety, which didn't yet require women to play the role of Cinderella. Occasionally a feminine name is dropped in connection with preaching activity and the duties of a congregational leader, as in the case of a certain Marcellina, for example, who turned up in Rome around 150.

Then there was a woman named Flora, but all we know about her is that she received a theological lesson by correspondence. Otherwise they remain anonymous, all the cultivated female God-seekers of an esoteric Christendom that was to perish during the dark centuries, the time of the migration of peoples. A tomb inscription from Rome calls those women to mind; it was dedicated by an affectionate husband to his wife, Flavia Sophia, in the third century. "Anointed in the baths of Christ"—the deceased is addressed in this fashion—"you hastened to look upon the Great Angel, you entered the bridal chamber and ascended immortal to the bosom of the Father."

This is the first word on the broken tombstone: *Light.*

# *That  Other  Disciple*

THE OLDEST, MOST GOD-FILLED TEXT of the new spirituality that arose after the birth of Christ was called the Gospel of Saint John; according to Church tradition, the person who seems to be meant here is the apostle of the same name. In the Gospel itself, though, another version is offered. A brief note written by someone else at the very end of the Gospel states that the disciple whom Jesus loved was the author of the little book; he was a witness of the things he wrote about, and he speaks the truth.

What he had written entered the Christian Bible as the fourth Gospel. Its opening verses are as follows: *In the beginning was the Word, and the Word was with God, and the Word was God.*

It is improbable that a fisherman from Palestine named John, a certain Zebedee's son and one of the Twelve who followed Jesus, had such eloquence at his command. It's even doubtful whether the apostle John could read and write at all. His name was meant to lend the necessary authority to the writing of this nameless disciple of Christ. The book, at first without a title, was put into circulation around the year 100, possibly in

Ephesus, and within a very short time it became popular among Christians. However, critical voices were raised in opposition, and perhaps this caused admirers of the wondrous text to hit upon the idea of giving it out as the Gospel of the apostle John. Attributions of this sort were by no means uncommon at that time.

The real author, on the other hand, the disciple whom Jesus had particularly taken into his heart, deliberately remained anonymous; he hid himself, so to speak, between the lines.

During a meal that took place before the feast of the Passover that was to prove so fateful for Jesus, the beloved disciple slips into the text for the first time. He is reclining on the couch so close to the Master that he can lean his head on his chest. Later, the only man to stand together with Christ's mother and the beautiful Mary of Magdala under the cross, he watches as a soldier thrusts a lance into his teacher's breast. On Easter morning he runs ahead of the apostle Peter to Christ's tomb, finds it empty, and a wave of happiness washes over him. Finally, at the end he is sitting with Peter and some other disciples, among them John the fisherman, in a boat on the Lake of Gennesaret. He sees a figure on the shore and he knows: that's him. In another hidden allusion, we learn that "the other disciple" is on familiar terms with the Jewish high priest, which makes matters even more mysterious.

The beginning of the last book of the Christian Bible, the Apocalypse of Saint John, causes additional confusion. I, John, writes the author, your brother and partner in hardships, was on the island of Patmos, I was in ecstasy in the Spirit, and I heard behind me a mighty voice.

Tradition identifies the lone visionary as the apostle who was also the author of the fourth Gospel. Modern experts, mistrustful as they are, no longer believe this. Thorough analyses of style and word choice in both books have demonstrated the unlikelihood that the Apocalypse of Saint John and the Gospel of Saint John could have come from the same hand.

Thus, behind the figure of John, other figures emerge out of the depths of time. They are indistinct, as though seen through fog, and among them is that very same "other" disciple who had known Jesus personally and was reclining near him at supper when the apostle Judas left the room to notify the chief priests and their henchmen.

At that time this disciple must have been rather young, if fifty or sixty years after Christ's death he was still in a position to put his memories in order and make of them the book whose opening verse reveals a first-class theologian: *In the beginning was the Word.* He may also have written those three epistles that have been preserved in the Christian Bible under the name of the apostle John. In them an old man speaks with the kind of mildness that has long since turned its back on earthly affairs. "We are writing this to you so that our joy may be complete. This is what we have heard from him and are declaring to you: God is light, and there is no darkness in him at all."

A nd so, after the destruction of Jerusalem by the Romans, and in the shadow, as it were, of the great goddess Artemis, whose world-famous temple stood in Ephesus, an old Jew, a member of an intimate circle, was bringing into religion a range of new tones: The hour is coming—indeed is already here—when you will call upon the Father neither in Jerusalem nor elsewhere; your prayers will have to be said in the spirit. God is spirit. What is born of flesh remains flesh; what is born of the Spirit becomes spirit. It is the Spirit that gives life, the flesh has nothing to offer. The Holy Spirit will teach you everything.

The old man, as he was respectfully called by the Christians in Ephesus, introduced an unusual name for the Holy Spirit—*paraklētos*. Literally translated this word means "he who has been summoned," and in Greek it was used to denote a legal adviser in court, an intercessor, an advocate, a defender. The correct Latin translation of the word is *advocatus*. The juridical coldness of this rendering isn't at all compatible with the warm stream of Johannine prose. The sense preferred by the eastern fathers of the Church seems more authentic and lends an amicable tone to the workings of the Spirit: comforter. Centuries later, Luther also translated the word in this way.

"I shall ask the Father," says the Jesus of Saint John's Gospel, "and he will give you another Comforter to be with you forever, the Spirit of truth whom the world can never accept since it neither sees nor knows him." In the recollection of the old man in Ephesus, the memory of his beloved Master's voice mingled with such thoughts as may arise during the course of an eventful life: "Old man, just write down what you've told us so often, that way we'll always have it."

"I'm supposed to write? Dictating would be less strenuous."

The result of his efforts, especially in Jesus' last discourses in the Gospel of Saint John, is not surpassed in tenderness by any other text in the whole thick Bible. Children, I shall be with you only a little longer. You will look for me. I am going now to prepare a place for you. Then I shall return to take you to myself. Do not let your hearts be afraid. Remain in my love. My peace I bequeath to you. You will be weeping and wailing while the world will rejoice. In my Father's house there are many places to live in. It is for your own good that I am going, because unless I go, the Comforter will not come to you. However, when the Spirit of truth comes, he will lead you to the complete truth.

The old man knew that the person who spoke in this way had kept his promise. In the evening of the first day of the week after his execution, when the doors were locked, he had come, the dead man, into the midst of his disciples, not like a ghost, but in flesh and blood, had greeted them with "Shalom" and showed them his wounds. The old man narrates that the disciples were filled with joy at seeing the Master again. Then the apparition breathed on them with the words: "Receive the Holy Spirit. If you forgive anyone's sins, they are forgiven."

And then? But the old man had no further memory of this occurrence, or he was tired of talking.

According to the biblical narrative in the Acts of the Apostles, Paul too had sojourned in Ephesus. Right at the start of his work there, he had laid hands on several men in order to bring the Spirit down upon them, whereupon those who had been thus confirmed immediately broke into the jubilation in tongues.

This sort of sudden fit was rather foreign to the Spirit of Christ as it was known to that other, well-beloved disciple. The old man thought about flowing water, about mighty rivers, when the Holy Spirit came to his mind, and, strangely enough, this force burst forth from the depths of the Master's heart, quenching eternal thirst. It may be that the memory of the lance-thrust on Golgotha played some part in this. *And there came out blood and water.*

In any case, something unbelievable had taken place between Good Friday and Easter Sunday. The Master's death had brought about the outpouring of the Holy Spirit, whereby the disciple became an Evangelist, a bearer of the good news of eternal life. Whoever believes in me, the Master had said, will never die. The "other" disciple had grasped the meaning of this in the moment when he entered the empty tomb in which the Master's corpse had been laid. It is the Spirit that gives life. The comforting Spirit had succeeded in making the light of the Master's divine nature shine in the well-beloved disciple. The light shines in darkness. The real light, which gives light to everyone.

The Gospel "according to Saint John," as it was called, owed its existence to an inspiration that was able to forgo salivation, rolling eyes, and chattering tongues. The Spirit in which it was written addressed itself to educated people, not to analphabetics. The Comforter of the fourth Gospel did not activate clairvoyant power or prophetic stammering, but rather granted insight into the deepest of connections. *Whoever does the truth comes out into the light.*


Unfortunately, the old Jew declared to the intimate circle of wisdom seekers in Ephesus, people prefer darkness to light, for their deeds, as a rule, are evil. Whoever does wrong hates the light and avoids it, that his dastardliness may not be uncovered.

The old man from Ephesus, who was perhaps identical with the young man who had nestled so close to the Master, told the story of an unending love. In his narrative, the concept of God and the principle of love are one and the same—the positive pole in the fundamental relationship of tension that inheres in every event. The negative pole, known as "the world," does not present a particularly pleasant image. It is ruled by greed, hatred, and blindness. Only a few decades previously, the love principle had tried one last time to make itself clear to the world. In Palestine, the Spirit had descended upon the man Jesus in the form of a dove, as a sign that the chosen one had appeared. He would bring the world the news that God loved it exceedingly, although in vain. In spite of the signs and miracles that the chosen one performed, the world gave no credence to its shining light. On the contrary. Jewish priests and Roman soldiers hauled the Son of God before Pontius Pilate's judgment seat. When asked what crime he had committed, Jesus replied, "My kingdom is not of this world."

The old man of Ephesus kept coming back to this central distinction. He related how the Master, at the end of the Last Supper, before he was taken prisoner, had raised his eyes to heaven and used such words as only a God could utter: Father, the hour has come. Glorify your Son so that your Son may glorify you. I have revealed your name to those whom you took from the world to give me. I am not praying for the world, but for those you have given me. I am no longer in the world, but they are in the world. I passed your word on to them, and the world hated them, for they are not of the world any more than I am of the world.

In the world, not of the world.

The formula was extraordinary because it established a distance between I and not-I that had previously been unthinkable. To Greek sensibilities, the world was neatly ordered and all-embracing; to Jewish piety, it was a creation of God. And God saw all he had made, and indeed it was very good.

The Gospel according to Saint John, on the other hand, displayed a total negation of everything that exists, couched in a language of dissatisfaction whose effect is not particularly charming. When it came to the prevailing conditions, the Johannine Spirit, the Comforter, behaved toward them like a district attorney for whom the entire cosmos was the accused. Before the court stood the "prince of this world," and he was obviously the devil.

To move from the diabolization of the world to the radically spiritual life required but a single step. That step was to be taken in Persia.

# Mani

THE BRIDGE BETWEEN JESUS AND BUDDHA was built around the year 250 A.D., in the land of the Tigris and Euphrates rivers, by a remarkable man named Mani. He referred his teaching expressly to the inspiration of the Spirit-Comforter whose efficacy had been announced by the old man of Ephesus.

The Paraclete revealed to me, Mani asserted, all that has been and all that will be. He revealed to me the mystery of light and darkness, the mystery of Adam's creation, the mystery of the Tree of Knowledge, whose fruit Adam ate and through which his eyes were opened, as well as the mystery of the apostles who are sent into the world, and moreover the mystery of the chosen ones and the sinners. Everything that the eye sees and the ear hears and thought thinks have I perceived through the Paraclete.

The Holy Spirit's new ambassador called himself "the Apostle of Light" and saw himself, in a line with Buddha, Zoroaster, and Jesus, as the final, definitive, and perfect witness to eternal truth. Mani obviously didn't suffer from an inferiority complex, but that was not surprising; his mother sprang from the upper nobility. Deeply read in Old Persian, Indian, Hebrew, Greek, and Christian sacred literature, Mani was also well-versed in medicine, art, and music. Since he was handicapped from birth by a lame leg, he had to endure being abused as a cripple by his enemies.

Those enemies were the priests of the ancient fire temples, whose flames were not allowed to go out. As far as they were concerned, Mani was a heretic and a demon. In the end they caught him, accused him before King Bahram I, and managed to have him incarcerated. Mani died in prison at the age of sixty.

He left behind a world religion, fitted out with holy scriptures, moving ceremonies, untiring missionaries. A half century after the death of its founder, the Manichaean Church had affiliates throughout the Roman Empire; Diocletian signed the first imperial edict against the Manichaeans in the year 297. Manichaeism became the state religion in the Turkish Uigurian empire in 762, penetrated into China, and, exhausted by the merciless hostility of its Zoroastrian, Christian, Islamic, Buddhist, and Confucian rivals, disappeared from religious history only in the high Middle Ages. Apparently the Paraclete's Spirit-Church included in its agenda such basic contrariness that it couldn't survive for long as a health resort for the masses.

In fact, what the Comforter had said to Mani offered a radical solution to all the distresses of life—by virtue of the principled, organized, and irrevocable renunciation of progeny. Through the mystery of the chosen (*electi* in Latin), who formed the inner circle of the Spirit-Church, men and women were put into the world like retorts in order to distill the precious light-matter from it; the means of doing so was a rigorous minimalization of all vital functions, whether oral, manual, or genital. Once a day the perfected (as they were also called) sat down to a sacred meal, which was solemnly served to them by their less-gifted listeners (*auditores*). This meal consisted of bread and water, along with a little garden produce, chiefly cucumbers and melons, which were believed to contain a particularly high percentage of light. When the perfected, the chosen ones, consumed food, photons were collected together in each of them as in a distillation device. Later, when they sighed at prayer, those little particles of God would escape from their mouths and find their way back to the positive pole.

This elaborate procedure had to be followed because earthly affairs were beclouded, characterized by that unholy dimness that the esoteric theosophies of the Near East lamented again and again. Mani's system expressed the situation in military terms, portraying it as a struggle between the empire of light and the land of shadow, which were in a permanent state of war with one another. Half an eternity ago, long before the creation of the world, the forces of darkness had managed to get in their power a prototypical soul. Thereafter the only way the world could be contrived was through a mixture of light and darkness, of spirit and matter.

In the ensuing cosmological war, the sole objective was the definitive reestablishment of the original state of the universe, when there was division between positive and negative, God and devil, light and darkness, spirit and flesh. Finally, whatever particles could not be brought back to the realm of light would be formed into a shapeless clod for all eternity. A conflagration of cosmic dimensions would rage for exactly 1,468 years, until the waste dump of evil was permanently sealed.

In the meantime, the saints of the Spirit-Church confidently raised their eyes to the moon. As it waxed, it collected the scattered particles of light; then, when it was on the wane, it passed them on to the sun, which for its part radiated light particles still farther upward as it coursed through the twelve signs of the zodiac. In the crescent moon there was still room for the souls of the chosen, as soon as they had shed their earthly crusts. And for the unperfected there was always the solace of knowing that after several reincarnations they too would escape this terrestrial vale of tears and set off on the ultimate journey.

For this is the case: to be alive is to suffer.

The formula was first coined by the Lord Gautama, by him who had become the Buddha, the "Enlightened One" from whose eyes the scales had fallen. In the India of King Asoka (reigned c. 273–c. 232 B.C.), many of those who were seeking escape from suffering, both men and women, trod the Buddha's noble eightfold path. It was considered the most recommendable rule for living, much as Christianity was to be six hundred years later in the Imperium of the Emperor Constantine.

The king had become a Buddhist after a bloody campaign of conquest. He was famous for having his edicts carved into rock and stone. When an independent country is subjugated, one such edict declares, the one beloved of the gods is extraordinarily distressed by the murder, death, or deportation of his fellow human beings, and such acts weigh heavily on his soul. Subsequently the king is said to have sacrificed the hair of his head and beard and to have put on monk's clothing until the business of government called to him once more. Shortly thereafter the ochre robes of the Buddhist monks began to appear everywhere on the subcontinent. A

ruler with pangs of conscience had become the patron of a new culture—
the cloistered life.

The men in the yellow robes avoided not only women, but also all
needless questions about the meaning of life, the existence of God, and
survival after death. They held themselves aloof from the traditional practice of religion, with its litanies, libations, and slaughtered goats. They
wandered around the country as their Master had done, carrying only the
Eight Needful Things: three robes, a cup for alms, scissors, needle, belt
cord, water filter. During the rainy season, from June to September, they
retreated to a base, where they learned the sayings of the Buddha by heart
and gained precise knowledge about their own bodies by means of intense
concentration on its various fluids, its muscles and bones, its slow decline
into death through rot and decay.

Mani may have met these naysayers when he visited the Indus valley
after the Paraclete awakened him. Mani seems not to have thought much
of the color yellow. He himself wore two-toned leg coverings—leek green
and red—along with a sky-blue cape. Later the priests of his religion in
Persia favored clothes of gleaming white, accessorized with the towering
tiaras they wore on their heads.

But clothes don't make the monk. Mani was convinced that he embodied in his person the *Maitreya* that had been foretold, the Coming
Buddha, the favorably disposed. He was thus free to use what he had
learned from the Indian religious cloisters to regulate the lifestyle of the
new Spirit-Church's inner circle. In any case, this was how Mani understood the mission given him by the Spirit-Paraclete. The way between
India and the Mediterranean goes through Iran, and so it was appropriate
that it was a Persian who acted as the intermediary in the meeting between
Jesus and Buddha, which took place under the roofs of monastic culture.

While Mani was still alive, according to Persian Fragment M², a
certain Addas was active in Egypt, preaching the doctrine of light
and founding numerous monasteries. At a similarly early date—the latter
half of the third century—a Christian pastoral letter was sent out against
the Manichaean missionaries, who were accused of being opposed to

marriage. Special warnings were issued against the women who went from house to house stirring up people in the name of the Persian prophet.

The scanty references in this document are surprising, because they do not make the usual connection between the beginnings of monastic life in the Near East and the influence of the Christian hermit Saint Anthony, who went into the desert around the year 275. Instead, this new way of life is characterized as an import from Persia, inspired by Buddhism and Theosophism and wafted over into Egypt, and therefore there can be no question of its biblical origin.

And in fact: nowhere in the writings of the first Christian generation (Paul's Epistles and the four Gospels) is that fundamental revulsion for the world without which there can be no monastic life ever made into a program of renunciation. Indeed, it is even reported that the Nazarene took great pleasure in the occasional glass of wine, and that he spent a mere forty days in the desert before he was tempted by the devil. To the Jewish mentality from which the Jesus story came, contempt for female flesh was as alien as doing without a brood of happy children. To be sure, the gaunt figure of John the Baptist might be claimed as the prototype of the ascetic celibate, but over against him stood the portrayal of Jesus himself, who let a notorious prostitute massage his feet in public. Moreover, the warmheartedness of the feelings attributed to the Master—in the house of Lazarus and his two sisters, for example—found no place in the image of a monkish father, and it was even more certain that a person dedicated to abstinence would never have stood for the close proximity of the loving youth whom the old man of Ephesus wrote about so vividly.

No, it wasn't Jesus who came up with the idea of throttling love for life, but the Spirit-Paraclete, the Comforter, who was waiting with the right answer to the existential despair felt by many people between Persia and Egypt. Where have we been thrown? The call from the light-flooded hereafter, as it was sounded among sensitive women who belonged to ladies' circles within certain Christian groups, counseled its hearers to flee from the flesh, to shun the vulgar pleasures of the gladiatorial games, to study Theosophical tractates in silence, to eat vegetarian food, to retreat from economics and politics, to do without descendants. At first, all this took place within the framework of ordinary domesticity that had obtained since the second century after Jesus' death—that is, since Christian hopes for Christ's quick return and the end of all things had come to naught. Moreover, a great many Christians had become acquainted with dungeons, or had been condemned to drudgery in the quarries, and that had a bad effect on their outlook. The world presented itself as enemy territory.

The Comforter will lead you to the complete truth, says Jesus in the Gospel of Saint John, and apparently the complete truth lay in always saying no, in renunciation, in abstention from the joys of the senses; it lay in the "angelic life," as the business was called.

During the hundred years before he caused the complete truth to flash like lightning in the spirit of the Persian Mani, the Comforter had by no means remained idle. Here and there, especially in Syria and Anatolia, and as far as the Tigris—on whose banks the young Mani grew up, in a rural religious society that had strict rules about purification and required frequent ablutions—the Paraclete had found a dedicated following among young people of both sexes. These were twenty-year-olds with a sense of mission. They came from various Christian congregations, and they thought that the soft bridal bed offered no prospects for a daring life. So they ran away from home, like the wild Thecla in a novel whose episodes were on people's lips around the year 200. (The chief character was a passionate maiden who, in the amphitheater at Antioch, leaped naked into a pool filled with sharks and remained unharmed.) To the astonishment of settled Christians, these young, happy wanderers rambled from village to village, singing their religious hymns, chanting exorcisms, begging their way through the countryside, and cultivating their otherness.

Jesus had died young; Mani began preaching when he was twenty-five years old. Soon he was accompanied by two dozen elect disciples, all of them young men and women. The new Spirit-Church began as a youth movement. It was cosmopolitan in makeup, unattached to a hometown or a fatherland or a mother tongue, and on the way to a future when the sexes would be equal. It had the zest of naïveté and the freshness of new beginnings, but its achievements were more potential than actual. The first disciples of Mani had appeared in Egypt by 244, and therefore several decades before Saint Anthony, the first Near Eastern desert father whose name we know. The Manichaeans set up houses where the chosen ones could live in community, monastically separated from the world of brute force, greed, and sexuality. If this information is correct, then Christian monastic life owes its beginnings to that same Mani whom the Catholic Church later denigrated as a trickster and an unstable character. Further support for the Manichaean origins of monasticism is given by the fact that Mani's adherents, at the time of the First Council at Constantinople (381 A.D.), included most Egyptian metropolitans and bishops, as well as a great many hermits. And the urn found at Nag Hammadi, which came to light in 1945—only a few kilometers, we should note, from the site of the first Christian monastery known to us by name—contained many writings affiliated with the very same spiritual movement that had informed the religious thought of Mani, but no trace of the Epistles of Saint Paul or the canonical Gospels according to Matthew, Mark, Luke, and John. There had been no need to hide these latter works in the middle of the fourth century; Constantine's imperial Catholicism was the established faith.

By contrast, the writings that had been buried were radical documents produced by a mentality whose force fields lay between the Ganges and the Nile, and they were the formulations of the profound hopelessness to which all world religions owe their existence. Mani's young Spirit-Church, though it found solace in the words of the Comforter, formed a congregation which gave that hopelessness its most comprehensive and logically consistent expression.

Mani had permitted and even encouraged his chosen ones to use perfumes, but their scents very quickly faded into oblivion in the Egyptian cloisters.

# *The Best Part*

*I*N FORMER TIMES, THE PHILOSOPHER Wittgenstein reflected, people went into monasteries. Were they stupid or insensitive people? Well, if people like that found they needed to take such measures in order to be able to go on living, the problem cannot have been an easy one.

Wittgenstein's own experience had made him familiar with the problem. Two of his four brothers had committed suicide; a third had fled to America, where one day he jumped from a boat and never surfaced again. Wittgenstein was utterly familiar with the thought of ending his own life. The solution of the problem of life, he asserted at the end of his famous *Tractatus Logico-Philosophicus*, can be seen in the disappearance of the problem. During the summer of 1920, after a year of deep despair, he worked as an assistant gardener at the Klosterneuburg monastery, just outside Vienna. But the problem of life, nevertheless, would not disappear. For despair of existence seizes upon the most gifted like a sickness unto death, and remedies against it cannot be found in pharmacies.

For the Egyptian Saint Anthony, the prototypical Christian loner, the means of grace offered by the Church obviously proved too weak to make life's torments disappear. "If you wish to be perfect, go and sell your possessions and give the money to the poor; then come, follow me." That's the challenge to live the life of the elect, to break with mediocrity, and the young farmer who heard it in his village chapel took it altogether literally. He gave away the farmland he had inherited and moved into an old hermit's shack, withdrawn from the world, far removed from banal needs and pleasures. Later he shut himself up in a burial chamber; provided by a friend with the barest necessities, he maintained a deathly silence for fifteen long years.

Thus begins the biography of Saint Anthony, written around 356 by the ecclesiastical politician Athanasius, bishop of Alexandria, in the midst of the debate over the correct interpretation of the divine nature of Christ and of the Holy Spirit. Resolutely taking sides, Athanasius had his desert father speak out against Mani's messengers. At the same time, he kept quiet about the supernatural disagreement between God the Son and God the Holy Spirit regarding the whole truth about the proper way for people to live their lives; the view opposed to that of Father and Son was advocated by the Paraclete and Comforter, who lacked all family feeling.

Clearly it was the Paraclete who ultimately shooed Anthony out of his tomb and drove him still farther away from other people, into an abandoned fortress at the edge of the Nile valley, and then at last completely into the desert, where survival becomes an art. How else could Anthony have known that God reveals himself best in a wasteland? The Bible, at any rate, contains no sort of recommendation for the life of the hermitage or the monastery. It can scarcely be denied that the Paraclete shows a certain inclination toward Indian notions about the divine world.

Saint Anthony became famous because of the multifarious ways in which the demons tormented his person. According to Athanasius, boredom is one torment our hermit was not subjected to. The stalwart man was besieged by denizens of the infernal regions in droves; they came in the shapes of lions, bears, leopards, bulls, wolves, adders, and scorpions, ready to attack, dreadful, loud with bellowing and hissing and howling. Athanasius portrayed his godly hero as an outpost in the wilderness, in the dwelling place of departed souls and evil spirits. These latter felt severely disturbed by the hermit's presence.

This scenario cried out for a conqueror whose inner strength could withstand the onslaught of the infernal powers. The biographer wasn't interested in depicting a chronologically ordered sequence of incidents in the course of a life; his style was determined by a preexisting literary model, as was usual at the time in portrayals of holiness. This genre was called aretalogy, that is, the word (*logos*) about the glorious deeds (*aretai*) of the supernatural world.

After twenty years the hermit decided to open the barricaded gates of his citadel by the Nile and show himself to the people who had laid siege to its walls, hoping—in vain up to now—to beg a blessing from the extraordinary man. Athanasius' description of his hero at this moment is appropriately overpowering. Anthony was in the best of health as he stood before the crowd, writes Athanasius, neither wasted away by fasting nor limp from lack of movement; he looked contented and cheerful and not in the least somber, despite his long struggle with the Prince of Darkness. Athanasius tells us that the great number of visitors didn't cause Anthony any noticeable dismay, nor did he appear even slightly affected by the flattery and admiration that he encountered. Soon several men took up residence in the surrounding countryside, intent on following the example of this athlete of Christ.

Later in the text we are told that Anthony lived to be more than a hundred years old, and that he still had every one of his teeth when he died.

After the year 300 A.D., more and more fearful souls heeded the call of the desert: *Prepare a way for the Lord.* The training program that confronted them was vastly more difficult than Mani's instructions for his chosen ones. About sixty miles southeast of Alexandria, in the Wadi al-Natrūn—where four Coptic monasteries still stand today—the anchorites strove to better themselves according to principles that not only aimed at starving the sexual urge to death, but also led to the obliteration of all traces of the individual ego, in a manner reminiscent of the world-renouncing Indian sages. Sleeplessness played an important role, and the most popular position for prayer trained the hermit to remain motionless with his arms outstretched for hours on end in the blazing sun. Spiritual exercises were interrupted only by the weaving of palm leaves into the baskets and rope that were the hermits' livelihood. There was but one daily meal, taken after sunset. It consisted mostly of bread, which could be kept a long time, along with wild chicory and salt (necessary to prevent dehydration)—hardly much more than a thousand calories per day. Those who were advanced could get by on three or four meals a week.

Such a one, Palamon by name, lived in upper Egypt, a day's march from the Valley of the Kings and in the same region as what is today the village of Nag Hammadi. He was not at all pleased one day when a knock on his door disturbed his rest. The young visitor was named Pachomius, and at length he persuaded Palamon to teach him the proper rhythm of life. After Pachomius had been there for seven years, the old man died, and Pachomius obeyed the supernatural voice that had ordered him to build a monastery at the end of the passable world.

In the future, efforts to obliterate the problem of life were no longer to be made in isolation, but in private institutions run according to precise rules and under the command of a superior whose authority permitted no contradiction.

In the space of twenty-five years, Pachomius established and organized nine monasteries for men and two convents for women between present-day Al-Uqsur (Luxor) and Akhmim, one hundred miles down the Nile. Nag Hammadi was the center of this activity. Pachomius worked according to a detailed plan that left nothing to chance and committed each person to a serious geometry of spatial order, with every day broken up into blocks of time for sleep, work, and prayer. Each institution offered places for 1,440 men or women, divided into ten units of 144 each; these were in turn assigned to four workhouses, each containing thirty-six persons living in twelve cells, three to a cell. The workhouses were specialized for different crafts and headed by a master who answered to the abbot or by a mistress responsible to the abbess. Only the superior knew the code, composed of the twenty-four letters of the Greek alphabet, which registered each monk or nun according to his or her characteristics—a sort of refined grading system.

Vitality and obstinacy are hard to break, as Pachomius knew from his own experience. Naked women, youthful and merry, rose up out of nothing before him again and again. This tended to happen, of all times, at the very hours when meals were served. One had to shut one's eyes and keep them closed at such sights, until finally they dissolved into thin air. Then suddenly the surge of a crowd of people could be heard, and above it all a cry: Make way for the incomparable man of God. The phantoms also tried to provoke the monastic founder to laughter by grimacing and groaning as they labored to shift a palm frond as though it were a great boulder.

A monk who laughs is lost, decreed Pachomius. Silence is golden. Monastics were allowed to sleep only in a seated position, leaning against a wall, and never longer than three or four hours. Any physical contact among the devotees was rigorously prohibited, because the flesh under the habit was always lying in wait for the slightest stimulus.

In compensation, the reading of edifying writings was not forbidden. Their contents, as the find from Nag Hammadi shows, corresponded to the left-handed inclinations of the old man of Ephesus, and to Mani's as well. Sleep-deprived people who are constantly hungry have little cause for casting a cheerful eye on the world.

The fellahin who bought the brothers' baskets and cords had just as little to laugh about. Their daily ration hardly differed from that of the monks. Furthermore, their labor had to provide for wife and children, and the whims of the Nile made for many a hungry year, when families had to resort to choking down meals of hyena meat. The monasteries, on the other hand, could afford to run their households while storing some provisions, and working in their fields wasn't drudgery to benefit a hard-hearted landowner, but service to a community. Securing new recruits for Pachomius' spiritual barracks presented no problem whatsoever.

So the church writer and theologian Saint Jerome had good reason to cheat a bit in his translation of the Greek Bible into Latin. The passage in question occurs in the Gospel of Saint Luke, where Jesus appears as a guest in the home of Lazarus and his two sisters, Martha and Mary. Mary sat down at the Lord's feet, the text tells us, and listened to his words. Martha, however, was distracted by various chores. She came in and said, "Lord, do you not care that my sister is leaving me to do the serving all by myself? Please tell her to help me." But the Lord answered her, "Martha, Martha, you worry and fret about so many things, and yet few are needed, indeed only one. It is Mary who has chosen the better part, and it is not to be taken from her."

In his version, Saint Jerome transformed the better part into the best (*optimam partem*), for already, forty years after Pachomius' death, the Lord's words were considered the fundamental authorization of the monastic life. Jerome himself, born in a small town north of modern Trieste, had completed his studies in Rome. Soon afterward, passing through Trier on a trip to Gaul, he encountered hermitism for the first time. Later he was promoted to papal secretary. In 386 he settled in Bethlehem as founder and abbot of four monasteries. The words *unum necessarium*, as used in his translation of Jesus' remarks to Mary, became a familiar quotation in all the monasteries of Christendom for the next thousand years: Only one thing is necessary. Mary has chosen the best part.

The best part, the one necessary thing, the *vita contemplativa* behind monastery walls, the call to contemplativeness issuing from a defensive attitude to life, stood in opposition to the many varieties of worse parts, to the *vita activa* of the bustling world, to chasing after the wind.

Such differences were at work in the arrogance of Mani's chosen ones, in the elitism of the Buddha. The Gospels, too, contained traces of this way of thinking. Many are called, few are chosen.

But how could the masses be spoken to, the people who began to stream into Christian basilicas during Constantine's reign, these but superficially baptized heathens with their delight in chariot races, loose girls, taverns, hare hunting, steam baths, and gladiatorial games?

The Buddha and Mani treated the common faithful with great forbearance, like little children. What those children were up to lacked all sense, but they couldn't help it because they had looked upon the light of the world with too much dust in their eyes. The fathers of the Catholic Church, however, when it was in the process of coming into existence, followed a different policy. Two ways, wrote Constantine's court theologian and historian Eusebius, two ways have therefore been bequeathed by our Lord to his Church. One way excludes marriage and children, along with wealth and possessions, and exceeds the natural powers of men and women. More congenial to them, on the other hand, is the second, simpler way. It leads to the respectable nuptial chamber, to caring for offspring, to the business of government, to the military profession for the conduct of just wars, to agriculture and trade, and also to the endowment and administration of Church property. Both ways, although differing in nobility—about this there could be no doubt—led to heaven. Mani's Spirit-Church, therefore, whose attitude toward the sexual urge was on principle contemptuous, should be persecuted without mercy.

Which in fact happened, for a thousand years.

In return, radically spiritual members of both sexes, insofar as they followed the instructions of the Catholic Church, were allowed to live monastically regulated lives. They functioned as a constant reproach to the carnal men and women who were too weak for the angelic life but nevertheless heeded the command of their creator, God, who had ordered them to "be fruitful and multiply" in the first chapter of the Bible.

The question of whether the priests and pastors of the Catholic Church had also been enjoined to follow the rule of celibacy remained controversial through many long centuries. As a rule, clerics and popes lived at the intersection between spirituality and carnality, sometimes even with wives and children, yet all were branded with the seal of the elect. With this compromise, the missionaries of the Catholic Church proselytized the entire Roman Empire and the German and Slavic peoples in the vicinity of the triangle formed by Rome, Byzantium, and Moscow.

From the Atlantic Ocean to the Pacific, with monasteries flourishing from Ireland to Japan, world history seemed to be preparing itself for a Paraclete era. No one could know that the next person to found a religion would be a family man. The Holy Spirit apparently spoke in different voices, allowing Muhammad to keep a harem after having comforted Mani with the rule of abstinence.

# And Cast
# into the Fire

ON AUGUST 4, 1234, THE FRIARS BELONGING to the Order of Preachers in Toulouse passed an enjoyable day. They celebrated the founder of their order, Saint Dominic, who had been canonized in July, with a morning festival service, and then, as they were preparing to consume a holiday meal in the refectory of their monastery, an informer appeared with the news that a mortally ill heretic had just received the comfort of her religion. Up and at her. Raimond de Fauga, a Dominican monk and the bishop of the city, after ordering his comrades to wait in front of the moribund old woman's house, presented himself to her as a fellow initiate and elicited from her an unequivocal formulation of her heresy. Thereupon the offender was given a summary trial, convicted of holding heretical beliefs, condemned to death, carried together with her deathbed to a hastily erected pile of wood, and immediately burned at the stake. Then all the brothers washed their hands thoroughly, returned to the refectory, and partook "joyfully of what had been prepared for them."

The comfort (*consolamentum*) mentioned in this episode, just one in the endless campaign of terror conducted against the Spirit-Church, could be bestowed only by the chosen ones, the "perfects" (*perfecti*), the strange messengers of a radical Christianity in whom the Manichaean *electi* had returned, right under the noses of the Roman Catholic clergy. In 1143 they appeared, as though from nowhere, in Cologne, where they aroused suspicion. Everwin von Steinfeld, a provost, could not get over the fact that the ranks of the perfects included women who stepped forward and preached. The religious gentleman was yet more astonished when two men who were members of this remarkable group, showing great calmness—indeed, acting positively cheerful—mounted the woodpile that an infuriated mob had collected in order to burn them at the stake. The worried provost wrote a letter to Bernard, abbot of Clairvaux, founder of many religious houses of the reforming order known as the Cistercians. The letter asked how it was possible that heretics were capable of the very same cheerfulness in the face of death that had distinguished the illustrious martyrs of early Christianity. Bernard reassured his colleague. Such courage, the learned monk pointed out, in conjunction with the chaste and lowly way of life that people attributed to the heretics, merely went to show the utter insidiousness and playacting ability of the devil, the secret master of this dangerous lot.

Was this another youth movement, as fresh as it had been in the days of the Persian Mani, that succeeded in winning over so many noble misses and miller's lads from the Rhine delta to the Pyrenees and over to the Po within a few decades? Most assuredly, the new/old spiritual trend discomfited the serenity of the seniors while appealing to the selectivity of young eyes, for which dull half-tones have little significance. As clear as the light in the mountains, as ardent as the southern sun, the doctrine "Of the Two Principles" allowed no middle course, no live-and-let-live in the struggle between light and darkness, good and evil. In the cosmic conflict, whoever was ready to take a stand on the battlefield of his own body—by eating only vegetarian food, abstaining from sex, and renouncing all acts of violence—was allowed to receive the Comforter's consecration and join the ranks of the perfects. After those in the solemn assembly who were to be initiated had said an Our Father, they made the vow of triple renunciation, confessed their sins, and then knelt before the consecrator. He laid upon their heads the book of the Gospels, opened to the first passage in the Johannine prologue: *In the beginning was the Word.*

The ritual summoned down the Paraclete, the Comforter, the Spirit announced in Saint John's Gospel. Thus the act of consolidation served also as a baptism, not with water, but in the fire of the Spirit, which would later be taken quite literally by the papal Inquisition. A certain Ekbert, theologian and abbot of the double monastery of Schönau (southwest of Bonn), recommended burning at the stake as the most appropriate fire baptism for all heretics.

Ekbert, author of eighteen sermons against the "Cathars" from the year 1163, stigmatized the new Spirit movement with that appellation, effectively branding the heretics as far as the authorities were concerned. The ancient heresy lists, which included a report on the *catharoi* (the "Pure"), had provided Ekbert with the name. In the third century, they constituted a rigorous Christian sect, but later they fell on hard times because of their deviation from the paved middle road of the imperial Church. Ekbert detected in those Cathars the forerunners of this new false doctrine, which was closely related to Mani's teachings about the chosen ones. In addition, the Cathars' name resembled another designation, which Nicholas, bishop of Cambrai, was investigating at about the same time: "Katter." This word was reminiscent of cats, and in the popular imagination of the time, the cat was the quintessentially diabolical animal. There was a rumor among the people that the miscreants made it a practice at their gatherings to kiss a black cat under its tail. In the vernacular, the cat-kissing "cat people" and the dastardly Cathars from Manichaean times blended to form the word for heretics (*Ketzer* in German, *gazzari* in Italian). This was a menacing insult, combining repugnance and fear, horror and curiosity, hatred and murderousness.

The perfects, whose numbers were rapidly increasing, had few illusions about the risks they ran when they traveled through the countryside, conspicuous in their black garments, and publicly criticizing the wealthy Church. It was only in the cultivated south of France that they were able to find aristocratic patrons and a growing following made up of men and women from all levels of the population, which treated them with respect and referred to them as *bonshommes*, "good people."

Thus, during the calm (a scant fifty years) that preceded the papal storm, two clergies stood opposed to each other in the triangle between Agen, Albi, and Carcassone, the domains of the counts of Toulouse. On the one side was the defenseless bonhomie of the perfects, men and women who had cheerfully turned their backs on the world, a subculture with its roots in the hidden network of the Paraclete's congregations. The other side, embodied by the Catholic clergy, had likewise abjured the pleasures of the flesh—at least theoretically—but they nevertheless remained inextricably bound up with earthly things (two thirds of European soil was the property of the Church) and harnessed to the business of politics, whose bloody enterprises they left up to the sword arms of the kings and barons who were their accomplices in dominion over Christendom. The clerics themselves wielded the spiritual sword, as it was called in the interpretation of a Bible passage in which the apostles refer to two swords. One was meant to subdue people's bodies, and the other their souls.

Thereby it became clear what the dispute between the two clergies was all about. Both of them appealed to the Holy Spirit for their validity. The papal side enjoyed a monopoly on brute force, and the questions addressed to the perfects in the monotonous hearings before the tribunals of the Inquisition, whether they dealt with attitudes toward the Bible, the sacraments, marriage, or eternal life, always centered around a single issue: willingness to submit to the authority of the Church. The Catholic Holy Spirit set great store by professions of faith, by formulas and dogmas, and had thereby renounced his divine freedom, his tempestuous ways, his unpredictability. The Catholic Holy Spirit was like a bird in a cage.

By contrast, the Spirit of the heretical Christians of southern France, the Comforter, brought the word *no* to the people, brought a divine negation of the failed creation, an invitation to liquidate every solid thing. The Holy Spirit of the perfects also admitted comparison with a bird; he sat, however, not in a cage, but in the top of a tall tree, and he hooted at the world.

In May 1167, the perfects in the south of France made a mistake. They set about preparing a great reception for Nicetas, a Greek Orthodox priest from Constantinople. He had traveled across Lombardy in the company of a delegation of perfects from northern Italy. Nicetas was acting as an intermediary with the Balkans, where, since the days of Mani, the doctrine "Of the Two Principles" had persisted among the Bulgarian Christians who were followers of the priest Bogomil, as well as among the monks of the capital of the Byzantine Empire.

In the castle of Saint Félix de Caraman, near Toulouse, Nicetas had the privilege of greeting Messrs. Robert d'Épernon from the north of France, Sicard Cellerier from Albi, and Bernard Cathala from Carcassonne. They were appearing as the leaders of their congregations, together with a goodly number of men and women from Languedoc who wished to be consecrated as perfects by the guest from the East.

As far as the Catholics were concerned, the public nature of these events was a provocation, a heretical council held by a counter-church. Was there not in Saint John's Gospel, which these renegade Christians held in such high esteem, a passage precisely recording the fate of all heretics? They are swept together and cast into the fire.

Heretics everywhere. It was not the earldom of Toulouse alone that was teeming with them, but also the towns of Nevers, Vézelay, Auxerre, Troyes, Besançon, Metz, Reims, Soissons, Rouen, and Arras, and the archdioceses of Narbonne, Bordeaux, and Bourges. News of their successes was arriving from the German bishoprics on the Rhine as well as from Passau and Vienna, but especially, of course, from busy northern Italy, from Milan to Udine and from Como to Viterbo. A general conspiracy against the Roman Catholic Church. That was the sentiment of the papal Curia, where all pieces of information were brought together. Since 1198, an energetic young lord from the family of the noble Counts of Segni had ruled there, under the name of Innocent III. He never had any illusions about the grand mess whose management he'd taken over. He considered himself the Vicar of Christ, the representative of the Lord God, and he caused the new title to be inscribed in his papal bulls. This blasphemous claim gave him a free hand to eradicate the weeds in the Lord's vineyard. By decree, he defined all heresies whatsoever as crimes against the crown. In March 1208, after the murder of a certain Pierre de Castelnau from the Cistercian monastery of Fontfroide, who as papal legate had excommunicated the Count of Toulouse, Innocent had the decisive inspiration of calling for a crusade against a Christian land: "Rise up, ye soldiers of Christ, rise up, ye Christian princes, gird on your swords, avert the ruin of the Church, come to her aid, destroy these heretics by force of arms, for they are far more dangerous than the Saracens!"

The appeal from Rome had its effect. One year later, the French knights were polishing their weapons. Mercenaries were recruited from Spain, Flanders, Bavaria, and Saxony. Then, in the summer, five hundred nobles, veteran campaigners, accompanied by their squires and footmen, moved down the Rhône valley. Abbot Arnaud-Amaury of the monastery of Cîteaux lent the undertaking an aura of spiritual consecration. It was he who ordered the massacre of Béziers, where the entire population was slaughtered on July 20, 1209.

Since that day, the Holy Spirit hasn't liked to be seen in Rome.

During the next hundred years, wood was continually being gathered for the piles on which perfects were burned, as many at one time as possible. In the year of our Lord 1239, noted the monk Aubry de Trois-Fontaines, a welcome offering was made unto the Lord on the Friday before Pentecost: 183 heretics were burned at the stake, in the presence of the King of Navarre and the Baroness of Champagne.

The question of whether the perfects were truly comforted was answered when they were awaiting execution, during the hours of their ultimate personal trial. At such times it becomes apparent whether the consciousness has learned to silence the endless interior monologue and to let the ego kernel be absorbed into the positive energy fields that pervade the world: *Do not be afraid of those who kill the body and after that can do no more. Anyone who wants to save his life will lose it. No one can take away your joy.*


"At the present time," wrote the poet Nikolaus Lenau to the theologian Martensen on April 24, 1838, "I'm working on a long epic poem, *The Albigensians*. The crusades sent against the heretics by Pope Innocent III constituted the greatest tragedy in Church history and deserve poetic treatment." The poet, writing in the restorative period known as the Age of Metternich (1815–1848), wanted to strike from the defeat of the Cathars the spark of unconquerable freedom. The light of heaven does not let itself be put to rout.

Which is to say that there can be no defeat in the struggle between the positive pole and the negative pole. Lenau also left the end of his heretic tale in verse appropriately open. Its last words are these:

*And so forth.*

# Mouth
# of Truth

To THE AMAZEMENT OF CHRISTIANITY,

*which expected no further surprises from the Holy Spirit, there arose in Mecca a prophet*

*who recited continually from a divine book that had sunk into his heart. Thirty years after*

*Muhammad's death, the Muslims ruled over an area stretching from Yemen to the Caspian*

*Sea and taking in Egypt, Syria, and Persia. Apparently Constantine's dream of a*

*victorious Christendom had been but an evanescent sign.*

# *The Night*
# *of Determination*

 *I*N THE SILENCE OF THE NIGHT, A COMMAND:
*Read!*

But the man thus addressed has no book to recite from.

Then the voice, once again: *Read!*

In the course of that night, the book he is to read from sinks down into the Prophet's heart. It will rest there for three years, until the Prophet has overcome his doubts and begins to recite from the Koran in his heart.

In the gray light of dawn, the Prophet emerges from his cave in the solitude of the mountains and catches sight of the gigantic figure. Terrified, he turns to gaze in another direction, sees the angel of God again. Gabriel is looking at the Prophet from every side. There he stood on high—the Prophet attests—in the distance. Then drew near until the space of two bow-lengths remained. Gave his servant the revelation. Who will dispute something so apparent?

We sent down the Koran in the Night of Determination, recited the Prophet. But how can you know what the Night of Determination is? Better than a thousand months is the Night of Determination. The angels and the Spirit come down on that night, by God's leave, until the flush of dawn.

The Prophet: Muhammad. Forty years old, married, a trader in Mecca. The year of his break with the Meccan sheikhs marks the beginning of the Islamic calendar. In the year 622 A.D., the Prophet emigrated to Medina. Later there was no one capable of explaining why this incidental occurrence, which concerned perhaps seventy people, was the origin of a world religion.

Was the Holy Spirit dissatisfied with the Christian emperors? Would the soothsaying of the prophet Jesus be fulfilled, who promised a Comforter to the rightly guided?

You believers, recited the Prophet, do not make friends of Jews and Christians. Unbelievers are those who say that God is one of three.

When the Prophet felt a recitation coming on, he shivered and asked for a covering. From under the covering, his groans and cries could still be heard. In the year of the Prophet's death, his very last recitation proved so heavy that his camel was driven to its knees.

We have whispered unto you, recited the Prophet, as we whispered to Noah and to the Prophets after him, to Abraham, Ishmael, Isaac, Jacob and their lineage, to Jesus, Job, Jonah, Aaron, and Solomon. To David we gave a psalter. Those are they to whom we gave the book, the power to judge, and the prophethood.

You people of the book, recited the Prophet, why do you quarrel about Abraham, when the Torah and the Gospel were sent down only after him? Abraham was neither a Jew nor a Christian.

No recitation of the Prophet concerning the Spirit that had descended upon him has been handed down.

After walking around the sacred Ka'ba during the yearly pilgrimage for the last time, the Prophet recited: Today I have perfected religion for you, and I have granted you a full measure of my grace. Now I am satisfied that you have Islam as your religion.

At first, Islam presented no particular problem for the Christians in Egypt, Palestine, and Syria. The religious policies of Constantine's successors had given Christians little cause for rejoicing. Again and again the Byzantine emperors had acted as theologians, issuing decrees of banishment for venerable men of God, and this behavior enraged the oldest Christian communities in Jerusalem, Alexandria, and Antioch. Since the Council of Nicaea, these had found themselves increasingly pushed into the corner of the old believers, surprised by their faith's new requirements, which went against the grain of their convictions. Finally the break between the old Church and Constantinople had come in the year 451, at the Council of Chalcedon (Kadiköy in modern Turkey). All at once, because there was a question concerning the relationship between Christ's human and divine natures, the Egyptian, Syrian, and Armenian Christians were obliged to consider themselves enemies of the official faith. Subsequently the imperial Curia meddled more and more outrageously in the affairs of those patriarchates that were richest in tradition, deposed insubordinate bishops, threw refractory monks into prison.

Thus, to many Christians in the Near East, the arrival of the Muslims meant freedom from the yoke of Constantinople. In 636, in the battle of the Yarmuk river (today the boundary between Syria and Jordan), hadn't the Arabic Allah been victorious over the Byzantine Trinity? At any rate, the Muslims in Damascus secured themselves a corner in the Christian basilica so that they might direct their prayers toward Mecca. There was little objection to their doing so.

After all, the Christian credo noted that the Holy Spirit spoke through the prophets. The Muslims unequivocally honored the memory of Jesus (his name in Arabic is Isa) as an outstanding prophet. After him, however, Muhammad had come, like a final seal on the charter of God's plans for the family of mankind. For many Christian souls between Jerusalem and Córdoba, these were reasonable arguments, and the mosques began to fill.

By contrast, in France, Italy, and Germany, where the cross of Christ reigned, spiteful stories began to circulate in which Muslims were portrayed as swindlers. In the most entertaining example of such tales, a wicked priest, who had striven in vain to obtain a cushy benefice from the Roman Curia and was thirsty for revenge, sailed to Arabia and made the acquaintance of Muhammad. The priest tamed a dove and taught it to sit on the Prophet's shoulder and pick birdseed from his ear. Then this cleric called the people together into Muhammad's presence and secretly released the dove. At once the bird flew to Muhammad's shoulder and put its beak to his ear. The people watched in amazement and believed that the Holy Spirit had come to whisper the word of God unto the Prophet.

There was also the story of a heretical monk and archdeacon from Antioch named Sergius, who had been expelled from his monastery. Sergius, it was said, journeyed to Arabia, where he related to Muhammad a great many biblical tales; later the Prophet passed them off as having been revealed to him by the angel Gabriel. Naturally, the many beautiful women in Muhammad's harem were the subject of much discussion, as was the story that he suffered from epilepsy, which the Saracens were said to have interpreted as prophetic ecstasy. Thus, early on, the Christians of Europe looked upon Muhammad as a swindler who had led the Saracens down the garden path. The pope called for a war against the Muslims, and the knights obeyed.

To be sure, this lack of respect toward the Holy Spirit was avenged. At the court of Frederick II of Hohenstaufen, a joke about the three swindlers of mankind made the rounds; they were Moses, Jesus, and Muhammad. Around this same time, disappointment over the warring truths of Jews, Christians, and Muslims found expression in the Parable of the Rings that Lessing was later to use in his play *Nathan the Wise*: the right ring cannot be proved. In Paris, liberal arts students with no respect for the seriousness of religion poked fun at the fairy tales of their theology professors. The modern age had begun.

It is an age that has had its fair share of prophets and prophetesses, but these latecomers have lacked the power to set a world religion in motion. After Muhammad, the Holy Spirit apparently lost his enthusiasm for such undertakings.

# *Speak, Lord, Your Servant Is Listening*

*T*HE SPIRITUAL POWER OF ALLAH, THE one true God—which, accompanied by the angel, had descended upon the man from Mecca—is called *ruch* in the rhyming Arabic prose of the Koran and therefore makes no attempt to disguise its origin in the Semitic root *rwh* (feminine gender, signifying "air in movement," pronounced *ruach* in Hebrew). At least one thousand years before Muhammad, in the Promised Land of the tribes of Israel, this word was already in use to indicate any sort of prophetic message-bearing. Among those tribes were the couriers and messengers of God, both men and women, who were the first to speak out, with hitherto unheard-of recklessness, against the pride of kings and the duplicity of priests.

The Spirit who spoke through their mouths had absolutely no interest in the workings of religion as they had become established since the end of the last Ice Age. Quite the opposite. He (or rather she, since the raging *ruach* was feminine) attacked the most dubious aspect of all conventional divine worship: the holocaust of victims on all the sacrificial altars, the incinerated flesh of all the bulls and rams whose stench was offered as a precious fragrance and wafted up into the nostrils of heavenly powers wherever in the world agriculture and livestock provided nourishment for mankind.

The *ruach* didn't want to have anything to do with these sanctified atrocities. She had her herald Amos announce her message: I take no pleasure in your burnt offerings. Further details are given in the very first chapter of the Book of Isaiah: "What are your endless sacrifices to me? I am sick of burnt offerings of rams and the fat of calves. I take no pleasure in the blood of bulls and lambs and goats. Bring no more futile cereal offerings; the smoke from them fills me with disgust. Your New Moon and your meetings I utterly detest; to me they are a burden . . . You may multiply your prayers, I shall not be listening."

So the criticism of religion is manifest in the prophetic texts of Jewry. It can be found in concentrated form, like a thunderbolt, in the Book of Hosea: "Mercy is what pleases me, not sacrifice." And indeed this pronouncement is to be found in the Gospel of Saint Matthew, as a quotation from the mouth of the prophet Jesus, whose coldness toward the temple factory is so palpable you can feel it.

It's no wonder that Christians were identified with atheists by Roman officials between the reigns of Nero and Constantine.

Seen in this way, the Holy Spirit's first thousand years extend from the emergence of Jewish prophecy to its culmination by Muhammad, with Jesus Christ in between. The criticism of religion wasn't the only thing that this energetic epoch set in motion. For the first time, and to the amazement of kings, a call had been sounded demanding justice for the poor. In addition, a principle of hope was instituted, which promised mankind a new heaven and a new earth—contrary to every priestly service throughout the cycle of the seasons, whether in honor of Shiva or Zeus, Baal or Osiris, Cybele or Vitzliputzli. The prophets had their eyes on the omega-God of the Last Judgment; their sense of time looked forward, into the future. That gave their gaze a certain rigidity, as is the case with all visionaries, and they surely heard voices.

All prophets—a total of 124,000, according to an Islamic estimate—are completely unanimous on one point: it is not they who speak, but God who speaks through them.

Before things get that far, the individual must go through a thorough shake-up, which is known as the "calling." This process is described in an especially detailed manner in an old Bible story set in Shiloh, a rundown place of pilgrimage north of Jerusalem. The priest Eli is grieving over his two wayward sons, also priests, because of the impious way they perform services at the shrine. The mother of Samuel, the chief character in the story, has dedicated her son to the service of Yahweh. Hardly more than a boy, Samuel sleeps in the sanctuary, close by the ark of the Lord, where the tablets inscribed with the Ten Commandments are kept. One night he hears a voice calling, Samuel, Samuel!

He must get up and run to the priest's room: Here I am. You called me.

No, go back and lie down.

Then the voice once more. Eli shakes his head. Perhaps you were dreaming.

Then a third time: Samuel, Samuel!

Now the old man is getting suspicious. If there's another call, then say, "Speak, Lord, your servant is listening."

Samuel obeys, and at once the connection works. The text continues: Yahweh then came and stood by, calling as he had done before. Now Samuel knows how he must answer, and Yahweh begins to speak. His first communication is a dangerous threat: *I am going to do something in Israel which will make the ears of all who hear of it ring.*

From that point, Samuel must take on the role of a prophet. Frequently the messages that he has to pass on will be disagreeable to the people around him. Again and again Yahweh will stand before him and give out warnings, issue orders, adduce proofs of his mercy. The report closes by stating that Samuel's words were acknowledged throughout Israel.

Samuel probably lived around 1000 B.C., during the Late Iron Age in Palestine, when the Israelite confederation was getting ready to establish a monarchy. Its first representatives, Saul and David, caused the stories that were told about Samuel among the people to be committed to writing. In these stories, the stern man of God appears as the head of a whole host of ecstatics who had their huts at Ramah, two hours by foot from Jerusalem. What went on there can be gathered from an episode that makes King Saul into a proverbial figure. He has sent his soldiers to Ramah, where David, his rival for the throne, is staying. These warriors burst in upon a dance practice in the prophet school, are promptly seized by the Spirit of Yahweh, and fall into ecstasies. Saul sends two more commandos, with the same result, until finally the king in person sets out to take David into custody. Saul isn't in Ramah very long before the *ruach* seizes him too; he falls into a prophetic frenzy, strips the clothes from his body, and ends by lying naked on the ground for a day and a night. Hence the saying: Is Saul one of the prophets too?

This remarkable story moves on a curve between the primeval frenzies of shamans and the dervishes of a later age, and the prophetic element remains wordless. The border beyond which possession lies is not even clearly drawn, for in another version of Saul's entrancement the Yahweh-Spirit leaps on him like a predator on its prey and transforms him into another person.

One hundred and fifty years later, the *ruach*, the precursor of the Holy Spirit, is still pretty wild. This time it has sought out Elijah, who has 450 prophets of Baal put to death at the foot of Mount Carmel (near modern Haifa). One striking aspect of this is that Elijah's competitors are likewise designated prophets, albeit in the service of a different power. They cut themselves, inflicting heavily bleeding wounds on their own bodies, and in the process fall into a trance. Against Elijah, devoted servant of the tempestuous Yahweh, they have no possibility of success. In stark contrast to the excessive violence practiced against the cooperative of the god Baal, an episode in the Elijah cycle brings the man of God to Horeb, God's mountain, better known as Mount Sinai, where Yahweh gave Moses the Ten Commandments. And in the mountain stillness Elijah describes the situation to this same Yahweh: They have torn down your altars. They have put your prophets to the sword. I am the only one left, and now they want to kill me.

The tale goes on: Elijah is to stand in front of the cave where he has spent the night; however, before he can do so, a mighty hurricane comes up, but Yahweh is not in the hurricane. After the hurricane, an earthquake, but Yahweh is not in the earthquake. After the earthquake, fire, but Yahweh is not in the fire. Last of all, a light, soft murmuring lets itself be heard, and immediately Elijah covers his face with his cloak, to protect himself from God, and steps into the open.

The point could hardly be made more clearly. The Spirit of God is more likely to materialize when the moving air, the *ruach* from which it takes its name, is calm.

Elijah left no written messages behind. In keeping with standard prophetic practice from time immemorial—along with dancing, leaping, and twitching—he wore a shaggy animal skin. The king of Israel, with whom Elijah was locked in combat, was named Ahab. His wife, a Phoenician princess, promoted the worship of Baal, which was widespread over the entire Near East, extending as far as Carthage, where twenty thousand infants were sacrificed to Baal every year. The servants and worshipers of Yahweh, like their representative Elijah, found themselves ranged with the progressive forces in world history, and therefore in opposition to the sacrifice syndrome. From the contemporary view of things, this is a point in Elijah's favor.

A nd so forth. What more shall I say? asks the author of the Christian Epistle to the Hebrews. There is not time for me to give an account of Gideon, Barak, Samson, Jephthah, David, Samuel, and the prophets, who through faith conquered kingdoms, did what was upright, and earned the promises. Others were put to the torture, still others had to bear being pilloried and flogged, or even chained up in prison; they were stoned, or sawn in half, or killed by the sword; they wore only the skins of sheep and goats; they were starving, frightened, mistreated; they wandered around in deserts and mountains, in the caves and chasms of the earth.

This portrayal of the prophetic career doesn't sound very inviting. Actually, now and then a candidate for prophetic status *did* refuse to comply with the divine call, we are told, because of the gloomy prospects such a choice entailed. The best known of these narratives is the story of Jonah, who is called to go to the city of Nineveh and preach repentance, but who prefers to take a ship and flee from Yahweh. Jonah winds up in the belly of a fish, and only then does he realize that he must obey. He is promptly spat up onto dry land and fulfills his mission.

As for Jeremiah, son of the priest Hilkiah in the territory of Benjamin, he tries to get off the hook by pleading his tender age: Ah, Lord Yahweh, I do not know how to speak, I am only a child. He gets a brusque answer:

*Do not say, "I am only a child," for you must go to all to whom I send you and say whatever I command.*

Jeremiah is ranked among the prophets of Scripture. He belongs to the literarily active messengers in the Holy Land, whose masterpieces were produced between the years 750 and 500 before Christ. His is a fierce prose, vibrant with otherworldly experience. Jeremiah undergoes his relationship with God like one who has been seduced, indeed raped. In vain, he resolves to forget the insistent voice, "but then there seemed to be a fire burning in my heart, imprisoned in my bones. A curse on the day when I was born!"

# The Sin Against the Holy Spirit

*W*HEN THE CARPENTER'S SON WAS IMMERSED in the waters of the Jordan, the laws of Moses and the sayings of the prophets had long since become Holy Scripture, fixed on papyrus leaves for Jews to learn by heart, and no iota of the text might be changed. Whether the man from Nazareth had read all these Scriptures, along with the devotional literature of his time, with its visions of the imminent end of the world—this cannot be determined. Whatever he may have done in the years between his childhood and his entry upon the scene as a messenger sent from God, the Gospels are silent about it.

But at once, when the Nazarene had hardly begun to drive out devils, heal the sick, raise the dead, people began to say: A great prophet has risen up among us, God has visited his people, Elijah is come back again.

Or perhaps not. Saint Mark's Gospel has a theological committee from Jerusalem make a journey to test the Galilean miracle man's orthodoxy. Their verdict is notably curt. It is through the prince of devils that he drives devils out, the scribes decide; the exorcist from Nazareth is himself possessed.

A maxim was mobilized against this infamy, a pronouncement whose black rage presents a riddle even to Christians who believe firmly in the Bible. All blasphemies will be forgiven, except for one alone: anyone who blasphemes against the Holy Spirit will never be forgiven.

This severe decree exposes a nerve that must remain intact. The Nazarene's authority is the same that loosed the tongues of Moses and Elijah, as well as David and the other prophets, all of whom owed their words to that unique inspiriting which tolerates no skepticism in its regard. Not even then, when the Spirit's man hangs in his final ignominy on the cross and thoroughly disappoints his public. *Wait! And see if Elijah will come to save him.*

It's common knowledge that Elijah failed to show up.

But the Nazarene had made his provisions. Saint Mark tells us that Jesus led his three most intimate companions—namely Simon, who was called Rock, and the brothers James and John, the sons of Zebedee, who were called the Sons of Thunder—up a mountain. Having arrived at the top, Jesus takes the three fishermen with him into the blissful timelessness of meditation. While their sense organs keep quiet, Jesus appears, suffused with light, in deep and sacred conversation with Moses and Elijah. Oh, yes. Let us make three shelters, one for you, Rabbi, one for Moses, and one for Elijah. Then the cloud, and out of it the voice: *This is my Son, my Beloved. Listen to him.*

Such a night is not easily forgotten. But the Nazarene warns his comrades to tell no one what they have seen until after the Son of Man has risen from the dead. He doesn't reveal to them what that means.

For contemporary Bible scholarship, which listens to such stories with the courteous reserve of a psychiatrist whose patient is recounting his experiences, Christ's transfiguration must be fitted into a literary genre, an art form exploited by the author in order to illustrate a dogmatizable truth. How could a European or American theologian—his fingernails neatly trimmed, his walls lined with books—entertain the loony notion that the founder of Christianity might have been an ecstatic, a person like any medium in Salvador da Bahia or Haiti, where even children know how the world can be made to disappear?

The Gospels make it thoroughly clear (to initiates with their own experiences of this special kind) that the Nazarene now and again fell open-eyed into the vivid slumber of the visionary. If Jesus requires strength for a miraculous deed, he turns his eyes to heaven and draws a deep breath, so heavily that it sounds like a sigh (*stenagmos*), or like a snorting noise (*enebrimēsato*) linked to profound distress (*etaraxen eauton*). When he feels the Holy Spirit coming, the same thing happens, and then he says some strong words that will not be suppressed. And sometimes he exults (*ēgalliasato*) in the Holy Spirit (*to pneumati to hagiō*). Anyone who knows the code can easily figure out when the text wishes to indicate the exceptional spiritual state that brings inspired revelations; the signals are such expressions as "in the Spirit," "in the power of the Spirit." They refer to the singularity of the vibrations that get the prophet going.

His disciples too?

The Gospels tell us that they shall drive out devils, heal the sick, raise the dead.

Unfortunately, how one learns to do that has not been handed down to us. In any case, thirty years after Jesus' death, Saint Paul characterizes the gift of prophecy as a gift that the Holy Spirit gives with some frequency and that serves to build up the community. And several prophets mentioned by name are said to have arisen in the first Christian congregation in Antioch. Apparently the Nazarene had passed along his extraordinary talents.

# *A Question*
# *of Selectivity*

*T*HE MORE PROPHETS THERE ARE, THE more difficult it becomes to filter out the correct program from the jumbled, competing signals of the divine broadcasting system. In the Greek-influenced everyday culture of the cities on the shores of the Mediterranean Sea, *prophētes* was a current word before and after Christ. For a small tip, the *prophētai*, both men and women, would foretell any client's future on street corners and in market halls. If while doing so they managed to roll their eyes and speak in altered voices, so much the better. For this reason they were popularly known as *engastrimuthoi*; that is, belly speakers, ventriloquists. Many people believed that well-formed, bright young boys, since their innate premonitory powers had not yet been corrupted, were particularly suited to enlistment as a sort of divine wind instrument. Each lad was given a freshly washed shirt to wear, and, after he was perfumed, flute music put him in the proper frame of mind. Then all it took was a light touch on the forehead, and a *daimon* began to speak through him; not an evil *daimon*, but rather a disharmony of the immaterial cause-and-effect networks, the correlations, interdependencies, and matrices of the great expanse of destiny, which links everything to everything else and in which the flutter of a butterfly's wing can cause a typhoon.

From such an otherworldly sphere as this, only equivocal messages penetrated human ears. Then aunts and grandmothers would put their heads together, but frequently they remained at a loss to know what to do with these boys. Further difficulties occurred when a medium used his wits to help along his dwindling inspiration and disgorged Spiritualistic nonsense instead of supernaturally instigated prophecies. None of this was new; already in his time, the Emperor Augustus had found it necessary to gather together more than two thousand copies of anonymous prophetic writings and consign them to the flames.

The times were prophetically inflationary, and it wasn't exactly easy for the Holy Spirit to assert himself against such strong competition. From the very beginning, the fundamental Christian writings warned their readers to beware of cheap tricksters, zealots, and lying orators.

Hadn't an Egyptian miracle man and self-styled prophet gathered four thousand fools around him in the fifties (A.D.) and marched on Jerusalem, only to be hacked to pieces by the soldiers of the procurator Felix on the Mount of Olives?

Therefore, when cries are heard proclaiming that the Messiah is here or the Messiah is there, mistrust is the appropriate reaction. This warning was perfectly relevant in the explosive Palestine of the Nazarene's day, where rebels made big speeches, quarreled among themselves, and were quick to reach for their knives. "You will be able to tell them by their fruits," Jesus admonished his companions. While several prophets were running around Palestine with daggers hidden in their clothes, those in Corinth were pouring out words in floods. They prophesied in wild confusion, all at the same time, and brought chaos into the Christians' gatherings. So Paul cautioned the prophets in writing that they should not interrupt one another: Two or, at most, three prophets at a divine service are enough. If a prophet who has not yet spoken feels a revelation coming on, the previous speakers should stop speaking. Women are to hold their tongues in any case.

By denying women the right to witness, those who were charged with "distinguishing among spirits" eliminated one of their problems. At least in Corinth, whatever members of the female sex produced by way of prophetic speech could be shunted aside as unseemly from the start. Surely this was not entirely correct.

For the sisters could appeal forthwith to the prophet Joel, who had expressly included "daughters" in the outpouring of the Spirit; Simon Rock also liked to quote this passage, but he added, "In the last days."

Whether in Palestine and Syria, Anatolia or Greece, the extemporary witnessing of the Christian faithful constantly brought to their lips that odd demonstration of power, the essential good news: The kingdom is coming soon. The trumpet is going to sound, and then the dead will be raised imperishable. In an instant, we, the living, shall be changed.

From this arose a simple rule for selecting the right station from the airwaves of prophetic transmission: anyone who showed no interest in the Last Judgment could not be a true prophet.

One must therefore be careful. Ventriloquism isn't enough; everything depends on content. Not every spirit is to be trusted, as Christians of the second generation read in the epistles that served to edify the congregations. "But test the spirits to see whether they are from God! For many false prophets are at large. This is the proof of the spirit of God: any spirit which acknowledges Jesus as the Messiah, come in human nature, is from God; every spirit which denies Jesus is not from God, is the spirit of the Antichrist, of whom you have heard."

It was a terrible suspicion: a spawn of Satan could be hiding under the prophet's cloak. And weren't the inveterate anti-Christian liars capable of the most refined dissembling, of simulating acts of faith in order to lure unsuspecting souls into their snares?

It was this very question that split Christian groups into two camps in the middle of the second century.

The crisis of faith was set off by a Christian named Montanus, who came from a remote, mountainous region in the Phrygian countryside, south of Eskişehir in modern Turkey. The voice that Montanus was deemed worthy to hear spoke in the first-person singular: I am awake, while mankind lies in slumber. I play upon him like a musician striking his lyre.

Montanus, who apparently had read the Gospel of Saint John, said to himself that this was the voice of the Comforter promised by Jesus. The Comforter also announced his presence to two women of Montanus' acquaintance, Priscilla and Maximilla, through whose mouths the Holy Spirit made himself heard as in the days of old. Thereupon the news that a third Testament was about to emerge began spreading among the mountain villages.

The outrageous message ran as follows: The New Jerusalem will descend from heaven upon the earth, not in the Holy Land, but in Pepuza. This spot was so small that archaeologists have always searched for it in vain. In Pepuza, therefore, Christ's millennial reign would soon begin, according to the prophecies of Montanus and his two prophetesses. Pilgrims came from far and near to hear the prophesying women, whose pronouncements spared no one, including, for example, the lax bishops who permitted Christian virgins to wear short scarves on their heads.

This new advent from the Phrygian uplands had definite feminist leanings. Eve, the mother of the human race, was praised for her wisdom; Moses' sister was considered a prophetess in her own right and stood not at all in her brother's shadow. Girls dressed all in white and carrying torches lent the gatherings of the mountain Christians an element of proud femininity, whose influence spread quickly and even traveled by ship as far as Carthage, where it won the prominent theologian Tertullian as a spokesman.

It goes without saying that most of the fathers of the Church put up a bitter fight against equality of prophetic rights for women. This opposition movement gained a succès d'estime in Lyons. They smuggled several of the mountain faction's tracts into the prison, where a throng of Christians were awaiting execution. The condemned prisoners, who as future martyrs enjoyed the highest prestige, rejected the Phrygian teachings. A report on this matter reached the bishop of Rome and caused him some consternation.

The cleverest move to make against the Phrygian tendencies was based on philology. Without ecstatic depersonalization, the argument ran, Montanus and his prophetesses would never have been able to function as the Holy Spirit's lyres. But a man might search the Greek Bible in vain for a passage in which the word *ekstasis* was linked with the concept of inspiration by the Holy Spirit. Therefore, the raptures of the Phrygian prophet and his two helpmeets could come only from demonic possession.

Anathema, to the devil with them. The defenders of orthodoxy declared that these mountain farmers from the hinterlands of Asia Minor were a fanatical sect that had no legitimate place in the Catholic faith. Montanism was put on the list of heresies and thereby pushed aside, out of the way of a Church that was looking for broad-based support. In principle, after the Montanist prophecy, virtually every instance whatsoever of possession by the Spirit was stigmatized and rejected for the next thousand years of the Sacrum Imperium that Constantine had molded. The couriers and messengers of God, both men and women, disappeared into the underground, the Holy Spirit became a theological abstraction, and the liturgy in the basilicas proceeded without further interruption.

Neither emperor nor pope could guess that the next concerted disturbance would come out of Mecca and lure half the world away from them.

# The Figurative Sense

FOR MUHAMMAD, JEWS AND CHRISTIANS were believers in the Bible and therefore definitely worthy of a place on the stage of world history. "Do not argue with the people of the Book [ahl al-kitab] unless in a fair way," the Prophet admonishes the rightly guided. "And say, Our God and your God are one." The Muslims also had their ultimate, definitive Book. Everything that the Holy Spirit had spoken into the ears of his messengers had been established for all time in the texts of the Torah, the Gospels, and the Koran. The three religions of the Book preserved their divine dictations like unique, irreplaceable treasures. Anyone who possessed a copy of the venerable text was considered worthy of respect.

The guardians of the prophetic inheritance, all the rabbis, exegetes, theologians, imams, philologists, muftis, and religious scholars, were and are lucky people in their way, screened off from the noise of the world in their libraries and studies, alone with the voices of the dead, reading and writing, only infrequently disturbed by students eager for knowledge. Such people lived their lives according to a program hardly different from that of modern literary figures, writers, or journalists, as Jean-Paul Sartre recognized. "Withdrawn from Catholicism, the sacred settled into literature, and the man of letters appeared, the *ersatz* of the Christian I couldn't be. . . . The Other remained, the Invisible, the Holy Spirit, the one who guaranteed my mandate and regulated my life according to great, anonymous, sacred forces. . . . I was happy."

The trustees of the divine word also need the Holy Spirit. They know that they aren't prophets, that—since revelation has come to an end—authentic prophesying isn't possible anymore. Their task must consist in interpretation, explication, application. Therefore they require the Holy Spirit, the special power that came rushing down upon the prophets. How else, if not under the guidance of the original creator of Holy Scripture, could they understand what its occasionally obscure, ambiguous, profound words and sentences are supposed to express?

Henceforward the Holy Spirit would no longer rumble about in the open country, in the deserts and the mountains; instead he would operate in a subtler manner, through understanding, Spirit-guided understanding: *intelligentia spiritualis.* The Holy Spirit had become an author who wanted to be read, to be read again and again, until the moment when a new comprehension dawned and the exegete reached for his pen to insert one more gloss in the margin of the inviolable text. Libraries from Persia to Ireland began to fill with commentaries, glossaries, catecheses, collections of aphorisms, and in those libraries sat the scribes, augmenting the existing glosses with further commentary. The longer the undertaking, the more ponderous and witless it became. Those employed in it were busily at work on a construction that must never be finished.

"I have changed," Sartre noted at the age of fifty. "I caught the Holy Spirit in the cellars and I evicted him; atheism is a cruel, long-drawn-out enterprise; I believe I've conducted it to the end. . . . For almost ten years, I've been a man who wakes up cured from a long, bittersweet madness and who can't get over it and who's unable to remember his former transgressions without laughing and who no longer knows what to do with his life. . . . I've disinvested, but I haven't taken off the habit: I still write. What else can I do?"

.   .   .

The "Other," as Sartre called his Holy Spirit, the invisible sovereign of his own living program, had also looked over the shoulder of an author and master thinker to whom the Christian notion of service to the word of God owes its fundamental orientation. His name was Origen (d. 254), and he was called Adamantius (adamantine, diamond-hard). The hardness of this remarkable man showed itself early on; in his younger years he castrated himself so that he could work undistracted. His father, an elementary-school teacher in Alexandria, was executed as an incorrigible Christian. By the age of eighteen, the son was teaching and eking out a living for the family. Origen was active as a catechete in the underground church of his native city and soon joined the disciples of the esoteric master Ammonius Sakkas, who taught a kind of Platonic theology, though admittedly without reference to the Bible. In compensation, Origen tackled a mammoth project, the production of a reliable edition of the entire Jewish Bible in six parallel columns: one for the Hebrew text in the Hebrew alphabet, another for the Hebrew text in the Greek alphabet, and the rest for four different Greek translations.

Word of Origen's undertaking spread. He found a patron, who put at his disposal a team of speed writers and copyists; they took down what Origen dictated to them and duplicated it, working (it would seem) day and night, for the tireless man published at least two thousand works, if not more. There was hardly a verse in the Jewish and Christian Bibles that Origen left unconsidered, whether in brief explanations of difficult passages (*scholia*), lectures (*homilai*), or learned commentaries (*tomoi*). Even on his extensive travels, which took him as far as Arabia, Origen dictated to his stenographers whatever came into his head—letters, polemics, expert's reports. When he had time, he got himself ordained as a priest, fell out with the bishop of Alexandria, and founded a theological college in the port city of Caesarea (today Horbat Qesari in Israel), where he taught a five-year curriculum that moved from logic and dialectics, through physics, geometry, arithmetic, and astronomy, to ethics and philosophy, before finally culminating in biblical interpretation. Origen passed the last test of his hardness at the age of sixty-five, when he was tortured in prison during a raid against the Christians. He died a few years later, renowned as the most prominent representative of Christian intellectuality.

A century and a half later, several audacities turned up in his theology, and because of them Origen was never declared a saint or a doctor of the Church. But the thoughts of the adamantine man continued to exercise influence even without official recognition; more than those of Ambrose of Milan or Augustine of Hippo, they entered the bloodstream of Western theology and biblical scholarship. The theologian Urs von Balthasar (d. 1988) held the opinion that none of the Church's thinkers has remained so invisible and omnipresent as Origen.

His secret: he was as little interested in history as he was in women.

As an Egyptian, Origen (which means "son of Horus") was naturally oriented toward the divine world. In comparison with attendance at the sovereign court of the life hereafter, the events of the human world paled to a trivial alternation of war and peace, well-being and starvation, rising and falling like the Nile. Only the Empire was permanent. The pharaohs came and went, or, to say it better, the pharaohs, having made their fleeting appearance, left their palace and were carried over the Nile to the west, where eternity began.

What was a citizen of Alexandria, even if only moderately well-read, supposed to make of the banal nomads' tales of the Hebrew Bible, the Greek version of which was couched in a style of great clumsiness, filled with Semitisms on top of that, and larded with copying errors and editorial inconsistencies? Anyone who had read but a single line of Plato would give the Bible—that muddled collection of anecdotes about David and Goliath, Esau and Jacob—a brief glance, get bored, and lay it aside. Educated elites all around the Mediterranean gradually began to wonder how any intelligent contemporary could bear to associate with Christians; even a traveling journeyman found it difficult to suppress a yawn during the stories that were told to the faithful at Christian gatherings: Away with all this rubbish! That's what sensitive Christian souls were already demanding a hundred years before Origen, people like Marcion, who expected his followers to read only the Gospel of Saint Luke and a few of the Epistles of Saint Paul.

Then came Origen. His stroke of genius, which saved the Bible from becoming ridiculous, was to declare that the literal meaning of its stories was inconsequential. God and his Holy Spirit could not possibly have

intended to communicate tales of ghastly butcheries or adulterous pec-
cadillos; what they whispered to their messengers was meant to be written
down for a human race sorely in need of salvation. There must be a
hidden meaning, a figurative sense to be discovered in the old legends of
Palestine, right down to their smallest details.

One of Origen's homilies, for example, dealt with a passage in the
Book of Genesis. There it is said that Isaac caused various wells previously
blocked up by the Philistines to be reopened. Only after several tries did
he succeed in finding a reliable source of water without causing friction
with other tribes of herdsmen. He called this well "Expansion," because
God had given him an open space where he might spread out.

The brief story was quickly told. The audience apparently wanted to
hear more, for Origen immediately turned to the "secrets" that could be
pulled up out of the well story like a refreshing drink for thirsty mouths.
Look upon our Isaac, the Lord Jesus, he said. This was the decisive leap
out of the land of the Jews and into the Roman Empire, where the
Christian Church was seeking its "expansion," out of the past and into the
present and future, past the literal sense of an ephemeral episode and into
the spiritual dimension of a figurative sense. The latter, as Origen emphasized, could be recognized only by those in whom the Holy Spirit had
lighted a lamp "deep inside." Without such enlightenment we remain
quibblers, thickheads, creatures of the flesh, Philistines who block up the
bubbling waters with earth. Therefore may our Lord and Savior enlighten
our hearts, for his is the power and the glory forever and ever. Amen.

The "Jewish fables," as our steel-hard preacher called them, were no
longer to be taken into consideration, at least not as regards the question
of how things really happened long ago in Jerusalem and its environs,
when Abraham sent his flocks out to pasture or Solomon chatted with the
Queen of Sheba. Instead of this, the reading of the Holy Scriptures had to
happen "in the Spirit" in order to coax from them every significance the
divine author had concealed in the history of the Jews, particularly regarding the fulfillment of his plan for salvation in Christ and his Church.

Origen was arrogant enough to believe that only the comparatively
intelligent believers in Christ, the "spiritual" ones (*pneumatikoi*), were capable of grasping the sense of Scripture in this way. Of course, he desired
even these to lead austere lives. Simpler souls, for whom the deeper mean-

ing of the Bible remained hidden, had to be content with professions of faith. A hundred years later, they would fill the basilicas of the Catholic faith under the Emperor Constantine. Anyone still looking for the Holy Spirit by then had to betake himself to an Egyptian monastery.

# *Changes*
# *in the Brain*

ORIGEN'S INTERPRETATIVE ART, WHICH enabled him to track down a hidden meaning in any prophecy from the distant past, had not just come to him out of the blue. In ancient Hellas, several hundred years before the birth of Christ, the job title *exēgētēs* (interpreter, expounder) was already a familiar term, indicating the official interpreters of sacred law, oracular pronouncements, and stories about the gods. Exegetes had a great deal to do, and their divine patron was the nimble Hermes, no less, who acted as a mediator between gods and men. Quite often, the stories of the Olympian gods narrated in the admirable writings of Homer and Hesiod contained unedifying details; the numerous amours of lofty Zeus, for example, did not necessarily provide a proper model for the younger generation.

The Jewish scribes, too, had long since developed the rules they used for interpreting Moses and the prophets. Already in the first century after Christ, one of these scribes, Philo of Alexandria, was the first to blend Greek exegetical methods with the rabbinical tradition. Then his published writings, in their turn, stimulated Origen's thinking.

Thinking. Without a high intelligence quotient, all of them—the Greek, Jewish, Egyptian, Christian, and (later) Muslim exegetes—would have been unfit for their work. The Spirit to whom they owed their ideas was no longer exactly the same as the tempest-God of the Pentecost miracle, no longer raged like the wild *ruach* whose attacks had overtaken

Samuel, and resembled only distantly the divinely inspired madness that had set the sibylline prophetesses raving. His sphere of activity in the central nervous system had changed.

Not from one day to the next, of course, and not everywhere at the same time. The clearest indications that a spiritualization process was slowly getting under way among humankind can be found in Greece, where the Homeric poems were sung for a few hundred years before finally being written down in the eighth century before Christ. Since then, many generations of teachers of Greek have labored to drum the *Iliad* and the *Odyssey* into youthful heads. But it is only recently that scholarly research has discovered a fundamental deficiency symptom in the Homeric epics. What they are lacking is self-awareness in the modern sense of the term. In the thinking of the Homeric heroes, there's no verb that means "to decide," no word for "mind" or "soul" in the sense of personal, individualized faculties. Instead there are expressions such as "my heart," in which we can see the dark beginnings of a notion of the ego, of personal identity, gathering strength but not yet so far advanced as to reflect upon itself. One may search the Homeric epics in vain for a sign of the distinction, self-evident to modern eyes, between subject and object, between the stream of consciousness and the outside world. Nor can one find the sober, planning, calculating mind at work, the capacity for abstract thought functioning together with the logical operators of rational speech and writing. Neither the blond Achilles nor the cunning Odysseus had at his disposal a self.

In compensation, they heard voices.

For example, just in the touchiest moment of a harsh quarrel between Agamemnon and Achilles—the valiant sword has already been drawn— the raging warrior feels himself seized by the hair. Achilles turns around and sees, he alone, the fearsome eyes of the goddess, hears her clear order to calm down, and obeys.

An even more detailed scene describes how the deeply disturbed Achilles listens to reason, as spoken to him by his dead mother. Wild with grief over the loss of a friend slain in battle by Trojan Hector, Achilles has killed his enemy, abused his corpse, and left it to rot unburied. This in turn has disturbed the gods, who were watching from their convention center on Olympus while Achilles tied Hector's body, the body of a king's son, to his chariot and dragged it along the ground.

Some time passes, and then one day Achilles suddenly sees his mother, who sits down next to him in his tent and gives him a good talking-to: Dear son, how long will you eat out your heart, lamenting and sighing for grief? As soon as the apparition fades, Achilles obeys the command the gods have given him through his mother's mouth and turns over to Hector's father the body of his son.

In short, the gods play the role of the consciousness. This is the finding of Julian Jaynes, the Princeton psychologist who has made what is thus far the boldest proposal for explaining the slow emergence of the "I" that is at the center of the modern consciousness.

The basic assumption of Jaynes's theory is that Achilles should be considered representative of a mentality that was widespread four thousand years ago from Egypt to Mesopotamia and, with the appropriate adjustments in time, in all the other advanced cultures that we know of—in the Indus valley, along the Yangtze river, in Central America and the Andean highlands—in all the places where there were large cities and a sacral kingship, with temples and statues of the gods. In these civilizations, according to Jaynes, the brains of the subjects had two centers of speech at their disposal: the left (or, more precisely, the dominant) side was, as it is today, in charge of everyday speech, and the right (nondominant) side was for the speech of the gods. In stressful situations this part of the brain verbalized the empirical wisdom of forefathers, the commands of dead chieftains or deified queens and kings.

That something of the sort is possible will be confirmed by any psychiatrist who has ever had anything to do with schizophrenics.

It is beyond dispute that the three speech areas, without which no one could utter a word, are located in the left hemisphere of the brain. At the time of the old pharaohs, Jaynes believes, a "hallucinatory area" had been localized in the right hemisphere. This area produced the royal or divine commands, which were then registered by the left hemisphere as voices. Jaynes has determined that the cable running between these two electrochemical complexes is a band of fibers little more than an eighth of an inch in diameter, the so-called anterior commissure. "Here then, I suggest," writes the professor, "is the tiny bridge across which came the directions which built our civilizations and founded the world's religions, where gods spoke to men and were obeyed because they were human volition."

Strictly speaking, there is no way of proving this forceful assertion, because the brains of our forefathers have long since fallen to dust. Professor Jaynes, therefore, had to inspect the silent relics of the vanished civilizations whose dealings and doings are reconstructed by archaeologists. On one of his excursions into cultural history, Jaynes visited the remains of a village in Palestine located about twelve miles north of the Sea of Galilee and dating from about 9000 B.C. According to the level of knowledge that had been attained by that time, Jaynes suggests, it was here that "the first god" lay buried. The god in question was a skeleton. "I am suggesting," Jaynes writes, "that the dead king, thus propped up on his pillow of stones, was in the hallucinations of his people still giving forth his commands. . . . This was a paradigm of what was to happen in the next eight millennia. The king dead is a living god."

With that, any metaphysics, all transcendence or supernature, is reduced to electrical processes in the brain to which nothing "out there," where the divine spins its web, corresponds. According to Jaynes, religion turns out to be a nostalgic longing for the voices once produced in the right hemisphere of the brain. In the course of time these became weaker and weaker, until finally they fell silent altogether.

Jaynes traces the gathering silence in the right hemisphere of the brain back to (among other things) natural catastrophes, such as the devastating volcanic eruption in the Aegean Sea. In the course of the second millennium before Christ, these disasters provoked a period of social chaos, and the divine world's reaction to it was silence—for the simple reason that the authorities of tradition had no answer ready for the new conditions. Better prepared were people whose unsettled lives had taught them to listen less to otherworldly voices and more to themselves: traders and soldiers. Archilochus, the first Greek poet whose verses use the first person, was a mercenary. He lived around 650 B.C. and therefore not so long after the deeds of Achilles were fixed in writing. Nonetheless, the difference between these two soldiers is considerable. One of them could read and write, and the other couldn't.

Moreover, Archilochus, in contrast to Achilles, carried his soldier's pay in the form of little bars of precious metal, and soon after his death the first minted coins began to circulate. With the spread of literate culture and money transactions, the oracular institution began to decline; prophets became ventriloquists, sibyls became hysterics.

Whether people without self-consciousness, as Jaynes describes them, but with their right-hemispherical voices of command, were ever present in such numbers as would have been necessary for the social organization of entire civilizations must of course remain doubtful, as must Achilles' "kinship" with contemporary schizophrenics. At the end of his thick book, Professor Jaynes, not without self-irony, admits that he's produced a somewhat flamboyant theory. By responding in the negative to the question of whether there's something divine at work "out there," he has catapulted himself into the frigid cosmos, and from there he looks down, rather displeased, upon the cultural history of the last four thousand years. We have made a mistake, the professor thinks.

Research into schizophrenic hallucinations remains untouched by such reflections. Patients who hear voices are requested, for example, to press a button whenever the voice begins to speak, and the tomograph records the corresponding activity in the brain. When someone has to hear spiteful reproaches coming out of nowhere every ten seconds, then that person needs a doctor and not a philosopher of culture. The difference between illness and "divinely inspired madness" was already well known in Plato's time.

# Sixteen Bullets
# for Brother Malcolm

$M$ALCOLM LITTLE, BORN IN OMAHA, Nebraska, in 1925, the son of a Baptist preacher, was never troubled by hallucinations, had only contempt for speaking in tongues, and underwent his religious conversion in a prison cell, without the aid of supernatural voices. Nonetheless, at the beginning of the 1960s he became, along with Martin Luther King, the best-known representative of the awakening self-consciousness of the "Negroes," as he calls them in his autobiography. He married in 1958, and on the marriage certificate, under the heading "Religion," he had written: Muslim. Malcolm X, as he later called himself, in memory of the unknown family name of his African ancestry, began his career as a "hustler" in Harlem. Malcolm led a restless existence at this time, operating in the push and shove of nightlife, constantly looking to make a quick dollar—preferably out of sight of the police—with a package of marijuana cigarettes in his pocket and in his head the telephone number of a madam who procured girls. Eventually the young man wound up behind bars for burglary. The sentence was ten years, of which Malcolm X served seven, from 1946 to 1952. The other convicts called him "Satan" because of his hostile attitude toward religion.

The metamorphosis of a nearly illiterate small-time criminal into the missionary of the Nation of Islam who succeeded in turning a sect of four hundred souls into a functioning organization with forty thousand members didn't happen with anything like the suddenness popular in heroic legends. The first step wasn't his conversion to religion, but his conquest of the written word, which began while he was in prison. To start with, he took a correspondence course in English on the advice of a veteran jailbird who recognized his fellow convict's intelligence and pointed out to him the existence of the prison library.

At first, to be sure, the books guarded their secrets. Many of the words that came before the reader's eyes were unknown to him. The dictionary that he finally managed to get hold of seemed so important to him that he copied it out word for word by way of mastering its contents. There were so many words, and he hadn't even had an inkling of their existence. Gradually the books began to speak intelligibly. Even after the light in his cell was switched off at night, the prisoner read on until three or four in the morning by the glow of the corridor light that shone through the little window in his cell door. Malcolm X later said that prison was his university.

It was also in prison that the voice of the Prophet of Mecca reached this later witness to his truth. At first it came as an unequivocal command: no pork, no cigarettes. The sender of these instructions was Reginald, one of Malcolm's brothers. "Don't eat any more pork, and don't smoke any more cigarettes. I'll show you how to get out of prison," Reginald wrote. Malcolm, hoping for freedom, obeyed.

When Reginald came to visit him, experience had already made Malcolm a little wiser. He had drawn the attention of the entire prison by his refusal to eat pork. White people thought that Negroes couldn't exist without their pork; that was the rule. I'm the exception to the rule, Malcolm told himself, and besides, he wanted Reginald to teach him the trick of getting out of prison by renouncing pork.

Reginald showed up, wearing a dark suit and a necktie, chatted about their other siblings, and gave no sign of being about to reveal the great secret he was obviously privy to. Malcolm restrained himself from pressing his brother. Then one day, almost casually, Reginald dropped for the first time the name of him who knows all things: Allah.

Malcolm listened, assuming that there was certainly more to come.

Allah has 360 degrees of knowledge, Reginald said, but the devil has only thirty-three degrees.

The devil?

*The white man is the devil,* Reginald said, and took his leave.


Thus began the theological education of Malcolm X. Soon he was receiving at least two letters a day from his brothers and sisters in Detroit, particularly Wilfred, Philbert, Reginald, and Hilda. They were already followers of The Honorable Elijah Muhammad, the founder of the Nation of Islam. Its Temple Number One had been set up in Detroit before Mr. Muhammad began serving a five-year prison sentence for draft evasion. Now Elijah Muhammad was living in Chicago, where he was busy organizing Temple Number Two, as Hilda told Malcolm while visiting him in the Norfolk Prison Colony in Massachusetts, where he had been transferred toward the end of 1948 at the instigation of their older half-sister, Ella. In Norfolk each inmate had his own cell, and the cells were rooms without bars and with flushing toilets. There was a great deal of greenery, fresh air, and a large library whose collection emphasized history and religion. Malcolm's brothers and sisters had put money together to pay for Hilda's visit.

"Would you like to hear how the white man came to this planet Earth?" Hilda asked. The answer was "Yacub's History," The Honorable Elijah Muhammad's fundamental lesson.

Hilda related the history to Malcolm. First, she explained, the moon separated from the earth. Then came the first humans. They were black, and they founded Mecca. There were twenty-four wise men, and one of them held views that deviated from those of the other wise men. He was the first of the mighty tribe of Shabazz, from which we American Negroes are descended. Then, about 6,600 years ago, Mr. Yacub was born in Mecca. His head was unusually large. He was among the dissatisfied, and at the age of eighteen he had finished all his nation's colleges and universities. He preached rebellion against Allah in the streets of Mecca, and for this he was banished with 59,999 followers to the island of Patmos. There he began the scientific breeding of successive races, brown, red, yellow, and, finally, white, each of which required two hundred years. (Meanwhile Mr. Yacub had died at the age of 152.) The whites, savage, naked devils with cold blue eyes, walked on all fours and lived in trees; six hundred years after they were created, they returned from Patmos to Mecca. There, by telling lies, the whites sowed strife among the blacks, until finally they, the whites, were expelled from the country and arrived in Europe, where for two thousand years they lived in caves. Then Allah sent them Moses to bring them out of the caves and civilize them, for it was written that the white race would rule the world for six thousand years. The Jews were the first whites to obey Moses. It was also written that some of the black people should be brought as slaves to North America so that they could learn to understand better the white devil's true nature. At last, in the year 1931, Master Wallace D. Fard appeared in Detroit, and he gave Elijah Muhammad Allah's message: the millennia of white domination would soon be over.

The Honorable Elijah Muhammad, Hilda concluded, grew up on a farm in Georgia. A small, gentle man. Write him a letter, she said, he's sure to answer you: 6116 South Michigan Avenue, Chicago.

Welcome into the true knowledge, Mr. Muhammad wrote. It is not we who are the criminals, but the whites, who keep us from getting decent jobs and drive us to crime. The letter was signed with the title of the "Messenger of Allah." That impressed his correspondent, and he was delighted with the enclosed five-dollar bill.

At the same time, Malcolm's brothers and sisters began to urge him. They wrote to him again and again: Submit to Allah; pray to the East.

That was the hardest part. Up to that point, Malcolm had bent his knee only when it was necessary to pick a lock. For a week the convict tried to force himself to kneel down in his cell, only to leap to his feet immediately, overcome by shame and wounded pride.

When he finally got himself into the praying position, he had no idea what to say to Allah.

The correct formulas were passed on to him later. What was decisive was the moment when his knees remained on the ground. Islam means submission, devotion.

The right hemisphere of the brain was completely satisfied with that.

.   .   .

The writer Alex Haley, to whom Malcolm X entrusted his memoirs, had this to say about his partner in many conversations: "The man had charisma, and he had power." Eloquence. Radiance. In biblical times, such gifts were attributed to the workings of the Holy Spirit. Twenty centuries later, the left hemisphere of the brain had become dominant, and it was that hemisphere that had to be trained in order to make Malcolm X into a speaker in demand for assemblies and an agitator suitable for radio broadcasts. But where did the power and the charisma come from?

Not from his "African instincts." Malcolm X mentions them merely in retrospect, looking back on his time as a wild dancer in Boston and New York around 1940, when Count Basie, Lionel Hampton, and Duke Ellington were playing the clubs. Malcolm could dance so well that a blonde with her own car took notice of him, apparently quite interested in African instincts.

Only once did the Other, the Taskmaster, take on bodily form. He sat on a chair next to Malcolm's bed and said not a single word. This visit took place after Reginald had been suspended from the Nation of Islam for carrying on improper relations with the secretary of the New York Temple. Malcolm was still in prison at the time, and the humiliation of his favorite brother weighed heavily on his mind. He was praying to Allah instead of sleeping, and suddenly he noticed that someone was in his cell. Dark suit, light brown skin, oily black hair, somehow Asiatic-looking.

Was that God?

In any case, Malcolm had felt no fear. After a while, the stranger disappeared as suddenly as he had come. Later Malcolm came to believe that he had had a vision of Master Fard, Allah's envoy, who had appointed The Honorable Elijah Muhammad as God's Last Messenger to the black people of North America. The line of the prophets still had not been broken.

Master Fard was the Messiah, Mr. Elijah Muhammad later recounted. This was after Malcolm's release from prison, during one of the many discussions that The Honorable Mr. Muhammad graciously conducted with the ex-convict: Master Fard left us in 1934, spoke no farewells, vanished without a trace.

During an assembly in Chicago, The Honorable Elijah Muhammad told the men and women of the Nation of Islam that Brother Malcolm had written him daily letters from prison. Now he's free, he said, and many temptations await him. I believe that he'll keep his resolve.

A few months later Brother Malcolm received his "X," a sign of his formal membership in the Nation of Islam. He was working in an automobile plant in Detroit and spending his evenings in the city's black neighborhoods, on street corners and in poolrooms, making propaganda for Temple Number One. Near the temple, which was actually a storefront, was a pork slaughterhouse. The pigs' squealing provided a background for the preacher's performance. Soon Brother Malcolm was allowed to make his first speech.

Our white slavemasters' Christian religion has brainwashed us black people, Brother Malcolm preached. We have believed that we will sprout wings when we die and fly up into heaven, while the white people already have their heaven right here on earth. Think about the screams of black women being raped, being taken in the fields, in the kitchen. Look at each other! The lighter your skin, the more white devils raped your mothers, your grandmothers.

Within a year of his release, Malcolm X was a full-time minister for the Nation of Islam, hurrying from one city to the next to found new temples. The Nation grew. When a brother had been beaten for no reason by the police, within half an hour the Nation of Islam produced fifty disciplined young black men, dressed in immaculate dark suits and ties, who appeared as though out of nowhere outside the precinct house and waited until their spokesman was allowed inside. In Harlem, where Malcolm X had his headquarters, everyone soon knew about the "Muslims."

In late 1959, all America learned who the Black Muslims were through a television documentary program broadcast on the *Mike Wallace Show* and entitled "The Hate That Hate Produced." Telephones began to ring for Malcolm X. Angry reporters wanted the minister to tell them why he was preaching hatred, why he was against racial integration.

The wolf asks the sheep, Malcolm X replied, if it feels unfriendly toward him. The rapist asks the raped if she has a problem.

Question: Mr. Malcolm X, why are your Fruit of Islam guards being trained in karate?

Answer: The white Boy Scouts take karate lessons—why shouldn't we do the same?

Question: Haven't there been many whites who have supported the blacks' cause?

Answer: I can think of only two, Hitler and Stalin. World War II produced good jobs in the armaments industry for many blacks.

Soon there weren't just two hundred brothers and sisters listening to the words of The Honorable Elijah Muhammad, but ten thousand and more—in Washington, D.C.'s Uline Arena, in Chicago's Coliseum. Police escorts for Mr. Muhammad from the airport to the rally hall. No whites admitted.

Let us separate ourselves from the whites, preached The Honorable Elijah Muhammad. We want a separate state, a separate territory, where we can take care of ourselves.

Teach us, Messenger of Allah, the crowds screamed.

Brother Malcolm, Mr. Muhammad said, I want you to become well known. Because if you are well known, it will make me better known. But you need to realize one thing. The better known you become, the more jealousy you will arouse.

A prophetic word. In November 1963, after Brother Malcolm had made some unseemly remarks on the assassination of President Kennedy, The Honorable Elijah Muhammad forbade his minister to speak for ninety days, if not longer. There were a few people sitting in offices in the Nation of Islam's headquarters who were jealous of Brother Malcolm, and furthermore his attitude toward the personal conduct of the supreme leadership seemed to them to be too unyielding. Certain incidents, certain irregularities had taken place, and Brother Malcolm knew too much.

A vacation would do him good. Invited with his family to Miami by the prizefighter Cassius Clay, Malcolm could relax for the first time since getting out of prison. But his thoughts would not relax.

I had put my entire faith in Mr. Muhammad, said Malcolm X to Alex Haley. There had been hints about illicit relationships between Mr. Muhammad and his secretaries since 1955. I refused to believe any such thing. In 1962 the rumors grew more frequent. I questioned three of Mr. Muhammad's former secretaries, and they confirmed that he had fathered their children. Then, last April, I visited him. Noah got drunk once, I said to Mr. Muhammad, but he preserved mankind from the Flood. Lot slept with his daughters, but he saved the righteous from God's judgment upon Sodom. David committed adultery, but he slew Goliath.

Yes, my son, Mr. Muhammad said, I'm Noah, I'm Lot, I'm David. All these prophecies must be fulfilled in me.

In the meantime, Malcolm X told Alex Haley, I know I've been declared fair game.

In April 1964 Malcolm X made a pilgrimage to Mecca and came back as El-Hajj Malik El-Shabazz. I was a zombie, he told a press photographer. A man's entitled to make a fool of himself if he's ready to pay the cost. My stupidity cost me twelve years of my life.

El-Hajj Malik El-Shabazz declared to the press that the trip to Mecca had opened his eyes. Racism of any kind was absurd, including the racism of blacks against whites. Of course, whites must first prove—by humane treatment of blacks—that they belonged to the human family. And incidentally, Islam was incompatible with religious sectarianism.

On Sunday, February 21, 1965, Malcolm X was scheduled to give a speech in the Audubon Ballroom, located on West 166th Street between Broadway and St. Nicholas Avenue. Shortly after he stepped onto the stage, several men in the first row stood up and opened fire on him. Sixteen bullets were found in his body.

So it came to pass as it was written in the book of the Prophet Isaiah: *He was pierced for our transgressions.*

*Sense*

*of Time*

I T WAS HIGH TIME FOR A NEW WORLD. AFTER

*the death of Frederick II of Hohenstaufen, Europe had grown weary of the Crusades.*

*Before this there had already been talk of a second Christ, who came from Assisi and bore*

*the five wounds of the Crucified on his own body. Under his authority, the human race*

*would enter upon a new world order, the world order of the Holy Spirit.*

*In a similar mood of eager expectation, the aged abbot Pietro del Morrone, who had consecrated the chief monastery of his order to the Holy Spirit, was elected to the papal throne.*

*This "angel pope," as he was called, remained in office for only five months. His abdication from the papacy, the only one of its kind, took place on December 13, 1294.*

*Thus it became clear that the old world order was still quite stable.*

*Therefore, two hundred years later, a few adventurers sailed across the Atlantic and discovered a New World in America.*

# The Third Reich

WHEN? THE CONVERSATION THAT TOOK place between Richard Lionheart and Joachim of Fiore in Messina in the beginning of the year 1191 revolved around political issues of the very highest significance. The main topic was the place of Sultan Saladin in the divine plan of salvation, and by extension the chances for the next crusade. The famous Calabrian abbot Joachim, whom the English king consulted as an expert, drew his knowledge from the last book of the Christian Bible, the Apocalypse of Saint John, and more specifically from the twelfth chapter, which describes the vision of the huge, red, seven-headed dragon. The heads of this dragon, Joachim explained, represent the persecutors of Christendom since Herod and Nero; five of them have already perished, and the sixth adversary is Saladin. On October 2, 1187, he succeeded in getting control of the city of Jerusalem, but not for long. Soon he will lose it again.

When will that be?

When seven years have passed since Jerusalem's capture.

In that case, my undertaking is premature, said Lionheart.

No. Victory over the enemy has nonetheless been granted to you, and your name will shine brighter than the renown of all other princes.

After passing on this information, the blessed abbot began to expatiate upon the dragon's seventh head, the last and most awful of the enemies of the Holy Church. His name was Antichrist, he had already been born, and he would ascend the throne of Saint Peter.

Is he the present pope?

No.

The abbot would reveal no more. In April, Richard sailed for Palestine with his knights, conquered Cyprus along the way, ordered the slaughter of three thousand Saracen prisoners after the capture of Acre because their ransom had not arrived in time, won a victory over Saladin at Jaffa in September, was forced to break off an advance on Jerusalem around the beginning of the new year, and, after several more skirmishes, finally concluded a three years' armistice with Saladin in September, 1192.

The deadline predicted by Joachim for the reconquest of Jerusalem passed without any particular incident.

Joachim's calculations in the matter of the Antichrist had also been rather faulty. The two monstrous beasts of the thirteenth chapter of the Apocalypse, the ones whom the Antichrist requires for his final victory, were only to emerge seven hundred years later, in Braunau am Inn, Austria, and in Gori, Georgia.


S oon!
*The Spirit and the Bride say: Come! And the one who bears witness says: I am indeed coming soon.*

The urgency in the final verses of Saint John's Apocalypse was sufficiently clear, and it was due to the inspiration of the Spirit (the *ruach*, the *pneuma*), which, two hundred years before the birth of Christ, had started preparing the Jews for the Last Judgment through various esoteric texts written by terrified souls for whom time passed more swiftly than for those who led comparatively comfortable lives. For these apocalyptic authors, the countdown had already begun; in the divine world the cosmic clock was ticking toward its final hour, the angels of wrath were reaching for their heavenly trumpets, and even the ancient, evil dragon himself had emerged, ready for the final struggle with the armies of the just. These apocalypses, which depicted the so-called last things (from the Greek *ta eschata*, the origin of the word *eschatology*), were filled with delight in doom, wildly, not to say insanely, visionary, and obsessed with violent destruction—a cataract of furious male fantasies, written as though under the pressure of a deadline. For the critical moment was nigh.

Joachim, the brooding monk from the Calabrian hinterland, also had a copy of Saint John's Apocalypse on his table. The monastic career of this man, the most important theologian of history since Aurelius Augustinus, began in 1171, upon his entrance into the monastery of Corazzo in Calabria, where he quickly advanced to abbot. This was no special honor, for the little settlement was rather a wretched one, most urgently in need of a patron. Therefore, in 1183, Joachim proceeded to Casamari (in Latium, ten miles east of Frosinone), where there was an abbey run by French Cistercians. There, at Easter and Pentecost, he received the decisive inspirations of his life; they were concerned with the interpretation of the Apocalypse of Saint John and with the purposes of the Most Holy Trinity in regard to the history of mankind.

Joachim wrote that his reading of the Apocalypse had stalled at the tenth verse of the first chapter, where it is written, *I was enraptured in the Spirit.*

For what does "in the Spirit" mean?

In the middle of the night before Easter Monday, Joachim continued, at the hour of Christ's resurrection from the dead, I woke with a start (*excitato a somno*).

Immediately, in the silence of his cell, the monk's thoughts began to circle around the mysteries of the Apocalypse, which would not go out of his mind. He was involved in a kind of struggle (*quasi quedam pugna gerebatur in mente mea*), when suddenly, like the opening of an internal eye, came the revelation about that verse—which he hadn't been thinking of at all—from the first chapter of the Apocalypse (*subito mihi meditanti aliquid quadam mentis oculis intelligentiae claritate percepta*), namely an insight into the complete meaning (*plenitudo*) of the Apocalypse and into the harmony between the Old Testament and the New (*tota veteris ac novi testamenti concordia*).

Then the nightly bell rang, summoning the monks to matins, and Joachim sang in chorus with his monastic brothers: *Alleluia.*

. . .

The first book that Joachim began writing after his nocturnal inspiration in Casamari is the *Liber Concordiae*, which established the abbot's renown among churchmen. Joachim wanted first of all to essay a broadly structured account of the rules by which he proposed to decipher the different levels of meaning in Holy Scripture. Then came Pentecost.

I was in the church, wrote Joachim, offering prayers to Almighty God, when there came upon me an uncertainty concerning my belief in the Trinity (*accidit in me velut hesitatio quedam de fide Trinitatis*). Frightened, I intensified my prayer, indeed I felt moved to beseech the Holy Spirit, whose feast was celebrated on that very day, to show me the holy mystery of the Trinity (*oravi valde, et conterritus vehementer compulsus sum invocare Spiritum Sanctum cuius sacra solemnitas presens erat ut ipse mihi dignaretur ostendere sacrum mysterium Trinitatis*). I began to recite the prescribed Psalms, and in the same moment there appeared in my mind the shape of a harp with ten strings, and in it the mystery of the Trinity shone so clearly that I was impelled to cry out: What God is so great as our God (*ocurrit animo modo forma Psalterii decachordi et in ipsa tam lucidum et apertum sacre mysterium Trinitatis ut protinus compellerer clamare: Quis Deus magnus sicut Deus noster*)? The experience impressed Joachim so deeply that he made a drawing of the Trinity zither. It looks as conventional as a panel painting made by a pedantic teacher. Apparently the quality of spiritual inspiration doesn't let itself be captured so easily.

Joachim was nearing the age of fifty. He remained as a guest in the abbey for another full year, finished his *Liber Concordiae*, and began work on his *Expositio in Apokalypsim* and his *Psalterium decem chordarum*. In these three books, the Calabrian abbot expounded with great diligence the intuitions that had come to him on Easter and Pentecost. As presented in these works, Joachim's conception of human history proved to be so original that his view of things has determined Western thought to this day:

First, history makes sense.

Second, the course of history proceeds in three successive periods.

Third, history obeys the law of progress.

Joachim's writings demonstrated that the terrible and meaningless accounts of the past—a tale told by an idiot, as Shakespeare says—resolve themselves, if they are examined "in the Spirit," into smaller patterns of a marvelous overall design. This was, and not only for Joachim, the solution to the riddle of the world.

Meanwhile, in May 1184, as he was still laboring over his writings in the monastery of Casamari (which still stands today), Joachim was called before the pope for an interview. The old gentleman, Lucius III by name, had diplomatic concerns about his upcoming summit conference with the Hohenstaufen Emperor Frederick Barbarossa. The conference was scheduled for November in Verona. Veroli, a summer retreat favored by popes because of its fine mountain air, lay about two hours on foot from Casamari, and it was there that the pope's conversation with Joachim took place. Apparently the monks of Casamari, with their good connections to the papal Curia, had praised the profundity of their Calabrian guest. The topic for discussion was an anonymous written prophecy that had surfaced among the effects of the recently deceased Cardinal Matthew of Angers. The brief text passed itself off as a sibylline oracle, and it held out the prospect of troubled times for the Church.

Joachim immediately identified the red-bearded Hohenstaufen as a representative of the forces of opposition, as the *Rex Babiloniae* announced in the Book of Ezekiel. Originating in the center of the negative pole, he operated on earth under different names. The negative pole, named Babylon, was at war with the positive pole, named Rome, Joachim proclaimed, using the Apocalypse of Saint John as his reference, and it was not in God's plan of salvation that any resistance should be mounted against the Babylonian king. Holy Church must suffer in patience, like Christ, and not act like a military power.

So the Holy See must not ally itself with the cities of Lombardy against the emperor?

No.

Nods of agreement. Among those close to the pope, there was a powerful faction that wanted to bring to a peaceful conclusion the hundred-year-old struggle between north and south, Germany and Italy, emperor and pope, for mastery in Europe. Pope Lucius, too, was inclined toward this view. From now on, Joachim stood in high regard with the papal Curia, and worldly monarchs also began to take notice of him.

The Calabrian abbot drew his authority from a weighty principle. He was convinced that the outline of the totality of earthly occurrences since Adam and Eve was written down in a single book, and that that book was the Bible. However, the sketch of the divine plan, as rendered in this greatest of all books, was not plain to see, not discernible to every cursory glance; it was, rather, hidden inside a variety of ciphers. Anyone who wanted to grasp the meaning of life, the meaning of the world, the meaning of history, had to conduct himself like a patient reader to whom the sense of what he is reading is not immediately apparent.

In reading the world, the biggest mistake was to take it literally.

For example, a person who spoke the name "Jerusalem" meant, first of all, the city thus named, with its houses, streets, and walls, a destination for pilgrims to the Holy Land (among them Joachim himself, before he became a monk). That was the literal meaning of this name, and it was useful if one had to ask the right way.

But the pilgrim isn't looking for houses, streets, and walls. When he finally reaches the goal of his pilgrimage, he has another Jerusalem in mind, a heavenly city of eternal peace. *Caelestis urbs Ierusalem, beata pacis visio.* The geographical term takes on an ideal significance.

Every medieval theologian had at least four such levels of meaning in his head. Along with the literal sense, three kinds of figurative meaning, their application varying from case to case, were employed in the interpretation of biblical texts. The metamorphosis of the earthly Jerusalem into the Jerusalem of the life to come fell under the "anagogic" (i.e. "upward-leading") sense; the view of Jerusalem as the epitome of the Holy Church was the "allegorical" (i.e. "speaking otherwise") sense. Finally, a "moral" interpretation was also possible, which considered the example of Jerusalem as an appeal to the conscience to live a life pleasing to God.

Acting in concert, the three figurative significances led to a Spirit-guided understanding (*intelligentia spiritualis*) of the Bible, in contrast to a reading that took the text literally (*sensus litteralis,* and also *historica interpretatio*).

Abbot Joachim moved among the different levels of significance with astonishing agility. He introduced new ways of understanding (in certain cases he found as many as fifteen meanings), he juggled with symbols and figures. It could happen that the abbot would use the Bible to prove to an emperor that he should consider himself a negative force, as was the case with Henry VI during the siege of Naples in the summer of 1197. Four years later, before his coronation in Palermo, the emperor recalled quite clearly his conversation with the abbot and certified that the latter's prognoses had contained a high degree of accuracy.

By that time, Joachim was already living 3,250 feet above sea level, in the wild mountains of La Sila, where he had founded the monastery of San Giovanni in Fiore. The name of the settlement calls to mind blooming mountain flowers as well as the gleaming future that, according to Joachim's reckoning, was going to dawn very soon, under the patronage of the third person of the Trinity; the Age of the Holy Spirit was about to begin.


Organized according to Abbot Joachim's decisive idea, the development of human history from the time of Adam and Eve onward passed through three states or conditions (*status*), which corresponded to the three divine persons of the Christian Trinity. God the Father had determined the course of things from Adam and Eve until the birth of Christ. From that point on, God the Son had been occupied with the government of the world. God the Holy Spirit, who had operated rather in the background till now, would have his turn during mankind's last days, which would begin around 1200. Quite possibly his reign would not last very long, perhaps only half a year, before the time came for the Last Judgment.

The monstrous Antichrist was already in diapers, and his appearance would signal the most awesome challenge for Christianity. His downfall would make possible an age of happiness, the Third Reich of the Holy Spirit, a brief period of time under the leadership of those spiritual persons who had discerned the higher meaning of Holy Scripture. Since the days of the pioneering monk Saint Benedict, these *viri spirituales* had begun preparing for their task in the silence of their monastic cells, and the deeper that silence, the better it was. Joachim knew that evil could be effectively encountered only "in the spirit," and therefore he had climbed into the mountains of La Sila with a handful of resolute companions in order to strengthen the positive pole of the world.

The year 1200 passed without incident. Joachim paid a visit to the six-year-old Frederick of Hohenstaufen (the future Emperor Frederick II), who was in Palermo under the guardianship of Pope Innocent III, and afterward made his testament. He was convinced that Innocent III would be the last pope.

In point of fact, the papacy never again attained the expansion of power it enjoyed under Innocent's reign. Joachim had erred merely in regard to the duration of the modern age, whose beginning he perceived. It was to end only in the year 1989, with the fall of the Berlin Wall. Since then mankind has seemed to be chiefly occupied with the operation of computers.

# *We Wanted Nothing More*

WHEN JOACHIM DIED IN MARCH 1202, a man filled with God was already in the world. His name was Giovanni Bernardone, and his father called him Francesco, "little Frenchman." His parental home was in Assisi, he had just turned twenty, and he worked for his father, who was a very successful cloth merchant. There was nothing to indicate that Francesco was to dawn like a sun over the new century.

But the Spirit (the *ruach*, the *pneuma*) came upon him, though not with the vehement prophesying frenzy that had seized the sibyls and prophets of the past, nor in the form of Pentecostal babbling or epistemological intoxication; rather the inspiration made itself felt as an overwhelming sense of peace, a feeling that overcame the young Francesco quite unexpectedly after a festive banquet with his friends, who had chosen him master of the evening's revels. The entire merry company went marching through the streets of the town, more bawling than singing, while Francesco brought up the rear, swinging a kind of ceremonial staff. Suddenly God touched him—according to the text—and such a sweet joy filled his heart that he could neither stir nor move. That sweetness (*dulcedo, dolcezza*) was all he felt, so intensely, in fact, that his ability to perceive anything else was switched off. Eventually the tipsy company noticed that their chief had been left behind. What's wrong with you? Have you got a pretty girl on your mind? Perhaps I do, the embarrassed Francesco replied, and there was general laughter.

The metamorphosis of the carefree young scion of a good family into a man for the ages required four years. Francesco heard voices and began brooding. Rumor had it that one day he had appeared in the leprosarium below Assisi and kissed the hand of every leper before giving him a coin. When I lived in sin, Francesco wrote in his Testament, the sight of lepers was a great bitterness to me. But God led me among them, and I showed them compassion. When I left them, what had previously seemed bitter to me was transformed into sweetness of body and soul [*fu convertito in dolcezza dell'anima e del corpo*].

With that the paradoxical intention, the key to Francis of Assisi's epochal personality, is expressed as though in a formula for the world. Francesco had recognized that the profound joy that he had felt at the beginning of his new life would always return when he did the opposite of what common sense suggested to him. It was not a question of some good that would be his in the next life, but of the "true and perfect joy" (*vera et perfecta laetitia*), the most important thing in human life. One day, so the story goes, Francesco and a faithful companion were traveling from Perugia to Assisi, where the "Minor Brothers" (*fratres minores*), already in existence as a group, had their lodging. It was winter, and the two men were terribly cold. Francesco called to his comrade, who was going on ahead, and said to him: Brother Leo, even if the Friars Minor give a shining example of the holy life to everyone around here and edify many people, note it well and carefully write it down, perfect joy doesn't lie in this!

After a little while, Francesco called a second time and said: Even if the Friars Minor make the blind see and the crippled straight, note it well and carefully write it down, perfect joy doesn't lie in this!

While they went on further, Francesco called once again: Even if the Friars Minor preach with angels' tongues and convert all unbelievers, if they understand the courses of the stars and the virtues of herbs, if they know the treasures of the earth and the properties of birds and fishes and all other animals, and can even grasp the nature of trees and stones, of roots and waters, note it well and carefully write it down, perfect joy doesn't lie in this!

They went on for two miles in this manner, and then Brother Leo, in great astonishment, began to speak and said: In God's name, will you finally tell me where perfect joy lies! Francesco answered: If we manage to reach our quarters, drenched with rain and stiff with cold and dirty and starving, and we knock on the door, and the porter looks out sullenly, failing to recognize us, and thinks we're tramps and closes the door and leaves us standing out there in the snow and rain, and we bear this amicably and without murmuring, then, Brother Leo, write it down, this is where perfect joy lies!

And if we should knock again and the porter comes out in a furious rage at this new disturbance and boxes our ears, and we remain quiet and patient, then, Brother Leo, write it down, this is where perfect joy lies! And if finally night has fallen and we're in tears and we knock on the door one last time, and the porter comes out with a stick and gives us a thorough thrashing, and we calmly bear even this injustice, then, Brother Leo, write it down, it's here, in this, that true and perfect joy lies!

A t first sight, this program of self-abasement falls within the traditional framework of virtuosic world-fleeing that had reached the Christian West from the yellow-clad followers of Buddha by way of the enlightened adherents of Mani. All the same, something radical had happened: the Franciscan way of life had been manifestly identified with those *minores* who occupied the lowest stratum of contemporary society and who gave Francis of Assisi's Friars Minor their name. In contrast to the better circles of society (*maiores*), the *minores* were all those disadvantaged little people in the slums of European towns, the day laborers, dogsbodies, and loafers who had drifted there from the countryside, the corpse washers and grave diggers, ragpickers and dogcatchers, washerwomen and small-time hustlers, who squatted randomly outside the city walls, filthy and unshaved, quick to pull knives, disrespectful, and always hungry, a rootless, growing underclass, malcontent and therefore dangerous for the *popolo grasso,* the fat-bellied members of the aristocracy and the propertied middle class.

From this latter group came Francesco d'Assisi.

The brusque gesture with which he bade farewell to his origins took place before the eyes of the public and in the presence of the bishop of Assisi, who was trying to reconcile the renegade son with his father. By the beginning of 1207, the father's patience with Francesco's bizarre behavior had come to an end. Meanwhile, the whole town was convinced that the young gentleman had gone mad. Old Bernardone turned to the bishop for help, and the bishop in turn set up a kind of tribunal in front of the entrance to the church of Santa Maria Maggiore. The subject of the dispute was a sum of money that Francesco had appropriated from his father's business without permission in order to pay for the restoration of an old chapel. Draped in his purple cloak and wearing his mitre, the bishop sat on a chair outside the church portal and admonished the young man before him to return the money to his father.

Not only the money, said Francesco. He disappeared briefly into the episcopal residence, and soon he was back, wearing only his underbreeches. Up until now I have called Pietro di Bernardone my father; now I am giving him back his money, along with the clothing that I have from him, and from now on I will say, Our Father who art in heaven.

Whether Francesco took off his breeches, too, as one biographer reports, can remain an open question. In any case, the Holy Spirit, under whose guidance Francesco so manifestly stood, had absolutely no objection to his chosen one's class betrayal.

One year later, children were already running behind Francesco whenever he showed himself in the streets of Assisi, and there he obtained final certitude about the nature of money and private property. To the amusement of the town, he had begun with his own hands the renovation of the little church of San Damiano. The repair of this chapel, located a short distance from Assisi, was of great importance to him. When his work there was done, he scrounged together some more stones to make two dilapidated churches in the environs of Assisi, San Pietro della Spina and Santa Maria degli Angeli, functional again. In February 1208, while he was attending holy Mass, Francesco heard the words of the Gospel that gave his life its definitive direction.

The priest read: At that time Jesus sent out the twelve, charging them as follows: Do not go among the Gentiles or enter any town of the Samaritans; go instead to the lost sheep of the House of Israel. And as you go, proclaim that the kingdom of Heaven is close at hand. Cure the sick, raise the dead, cleanse those who have leprosy, drive out devils. You have received without charge, give without charge. Provide yourselves with no gold or silver, not even with coppers for your purses, with no haversack for the journey or spare tunic or footwear or a staff. For the worker deserves his keep.

Francesco heard: No gold, no silver, no money! No sack of provisions! Only one single tunic! No shoes, no walking staff!

With that, everything was clear. The use of money, the ownership of land, a settled existence, were repugnant to the Holy Spirit. The ethos of a life without property became the basic principle of the company that Francesco gathered around himself. After the Lord gave me brothers, Francesco wrote in his Testament, there was no one to show me what I ought to do, but the Most High himself revealed to me that I ought to live according to the pattern of the Gospel. I had this written down in few and simple words, and the Lord Pope confirmed it for me. All those who then came to choose this life gave everything they owned to the poor, and they were satisfied with one tunic, patched inside and out, with a cord for a belt, and breeches. We wanted nothing more.

The history of the Franciscan movement begins with the papal permission to preach, which Francesco obtained in 1209. In the seventeen years from then until Francesco's death in 1226, the Friars Minor grew to include several thousand brothers, with settlements all over Italy, in France, Spain, Portugal, Germany, Hungary, and England. A thousand years earlier, during the age of God the Son, perhaps this movement would have become a world religion. For the coming epoch of the Holy Spirit, a somewhat less ambitious manifestation recommended itself. Francesco

wished to bring his troupe among the people anonymously and inconspicuously, like wandering street musicians whose entire repertoire consisted
of variations on a single theme—divine love. Francesco's company had
renounced the use of possessive pronouns, and with it the common notion
that happiness was bound up with the desire for possessions. For Francesco, in his famous song of praise to God and the world, extolled the
sunbeams, the moonlight, the stars, the flickering fire. In the thought of
the man from Assisi, wind and water and brightly colored flowers and
fragrant herbs became the subjects of an all-inclusive gratitude that embraced even adverse things, every imaginable sort of suffering and disease,
as well as death itself, *per lo Tuo amore*, with reference to a comprehensive
principle of love that recognized no grounds for exclusion.

For just a moment, the great bird of prey, the heraldic animal of all
authority, had disappeared from the heavens, beak, claws, and all. In the
woods where Francesco laughed and wept with his God, the noises made
by the third Innocent and the second Frederick could not be heard.

Admittedly, the long-standing discrepancy between spiritual and
worldly power could not be eliminated by flight alone. The more famous
the eccentric *Poverello* became, the more interesting he became to the leaders of the Church.

This was the reason behind the memorable sermon that Francis of
Assisi preached before the Sacred College in Rome. He had been invited
to speak by Ugolino, the cardinal of Ostia, who was well disposed toward
the Friars Minor. The Holy Father, Ugolino said, personally desired that
the man who had espoused poverty might address some edifying words to
him and to the princes of the Church; to be on the safe side, therefore, the
cardinal had prepared a carefully designed speech, and he proposed that
Francesco should learn it by heart.

When, on the appointed day, Francesco was led before the pope and
the cardinals, our source tells us that he was suddenly unable to remember
a word of the speech Ugolino had drafted for him. After the blessing had
been given and it was time to begin, Francesco, deeply embarrassed,
reached for his prayer book, opened it, and came upon the passage in the
Psalms where it is written, *All day long my disgrace is before me, and shame has
covered my face.*

Francesco translated the Latin text into the vernacular, and then he began to speak in his Umbrian dialect about the arrogance of prelates, and about the great shame they were bringing on Holy Church by their bad example. For it was reasonable to think of the prelates as the face of the Church, and what could be dearer to God than that this face should shine forth in all its beauty and not blush in shame for deplorable failures?

While Francesco was speaking in this way, we are told, he rose into such an ardor of the spirit (*cum tanto fervore spiritus loquebatur*) that his feet began to move as though in a dance, until finally, beside himself with joyous excitement, he forgot where he was and started leaping about before the august assembly.

According to our account, the lords took leave of one another pensively. For one long, precious moment, the Holy Spirit had fluttered out of the theological tomes, and done so (just this once) in Rome, before the throne of Saint Peter. Not long thereafter, the pope, Honorius III, in the papal bull *Cum dilecti*, confirmed the orthodoxy of the Friars Minor.

This was, however, rather premature. It is true that in the last years of his life the son of Pietro di Bernardone was considered an exemplarily blessed person, and that wherever he went to preach a sermon, the people flocked to hear him. But this sanctity was already carrying in its core the dynamite for the bourgeois revolutions of the coming centuries.

The "very smallest brother" (*picciolino Fra Francesco*) had expressly recommended for his movement a form of manners that did without hierarchical chains of command (*et nullus vocetur prior*) and a way of life that was free from subjection to authority (*non habeant potestatem vel dominationem inter se*), though circumscribed by the rigid institutions of feudalism. So now equality and brotherhood (*égalité, fraternité*), as these maxims were called at a later date, had attained an irrevocable position on the wish list of Europe's rising social classes. In the "catholic garden," as Dante called it, seeds that no one had cultivated began to sprout.

Every year at Pentecost, a general chapter of the Friars Minor was convened in a little forest below Assisi named Porziuncola. In the year 1221, five years before his death, Fra Francesco addressed this assembly and announced to the surprised brothers that he no longer wished to lead them. It is said that this remarkable man declared, "From now on I am dead to you." In future all the leadership positions would fall to the so-called "ministers," who would be responsible for the ongoing affairs of the Order.

For, in accordance with the will of the papal Curia, the Franciscans' association was to become an Order, with a binding rule, well-defined conditions for admission, set times for prayer, study routines, and disciplinary provisions.

None of this was what the founder had in mind. The only minister that Francesco recognized for his movement was the Holy Spirit (*generalis minister Religionis, Spiritus Sanctus*), who did not allow himself to be regimented. The century-long conflict of the Franciscans with that highly structured business, the Roman Church, was thereby programmed in advance.

By contrast, another conflict in Fra Francesco's life, namely that between earthly and heavenly love, was resolved "in the spirit." When Francesco finally dared to spend a few weeks in the company of the woman whose hair he had cut off in God's name, he was mortally ill and virtually blind. The noblewoman's name was Chiara di Offreduccio (she is known in English as Saint Clare), and she lived, wretchedly enough, with her mother, Ortolana, and her two sisters, Agnes and Beatrice, at the little church of San Damiano, which Francesco had restored with his own hands. Two other women, likewise from noble families, completed the little convent. These ladies could have returned whenever they wished to the fine houses they had fled from. The life of the spirit (*la vita dello spirito*) was apparently more important to them.

On the decisive night that marks the inception of the female branch of the Franciscan movement, Chiara, eighteen years old at the time and filled with enthusiasm by Francesco's radicalism, runs away from her parental home and down into the valley where the Friars Minor are waiting for her. The torchlit scene that follows her escape quivers with religious eroticism. Francesco steps forward and grasps the girl by the hair in order to cut it in the *sacra tonsura*, that atrocious metamorphosis of female biology into the sexlessness of the angelic life.

Thereafter they might not see one another again.

The cruelty of the separation seemed unreasonable to Chiara, at least according to a popular legend; it is set in winter, and in it the two saints take one last walk together through a silent landscape before they say their final farewells. When shall we see one another again? Chiara asks. In the summer, when the roses bloom. And suddenly, all around them the juniper bushes are covered with roses.

Near the end of his life, an exhausted Francesco settled into a shelter made of reeds on the outer wall of the little convent of San Damiano. The severe pain in his eyes seldom let him sleep, and in addition he was plagued by a host of mice that gave him no peace even when he was eating. According to one account, Francesco stayed at San Damiano for fifty days, but not a word is said about why he was drawn to San Damiano. Another text expresses Francesco's feelings more clearly; it says that Chiara was his one and only love.

The lovers were not to be reunited, not even in the age of the Holy Spirit. People whom the Spirit guided (*spirituali*) would march into the future segregated according to sex.

The last high point in the life of Francis of Assisi was reached on the mountain of La Verna, where the Friars Minor had established a hermitage. Francesco used to withdraw into this rugged wilderness every now and again. Awakened by the cry of a falcon, he would arise before daybreak, recite the Psalms with whatever comrades were present, and then, after breakfast, disappear into the forest. Later, the others could hear their solitary friend, far away, as his deep sighs and loud talk rent the silence.

In September 1224, during a stay on La Verna, Francesco received a very clear answer. Accounts of his vision speak of a beautiful, manlike figure, which bore the six wings of the Seraphim and assumed in its hovering the position of the Crucified. The apparition, it is said, gazed at Francesco kindly and lovingly, until he began to feel something on his hands and feet. Then four nail wounds took shape in his extremities, along with a further opening on the right side of his chest, and they never went away, greatly to Francesco's consternation, for he found the whole deification process rather embarrassing.

After receiving the stigmata, Francesco had only two years to live. He suffered from afflictions of the stomach, liver, and heart, and, on top of that, from dropsy, headaches, and progressive loss of sight. With this man, the image of the suffering Christ, the Franciscan brothers and sisters got what they needed—an old-new God-man showing them the way into what they hoped was a better future.

# *Surprise in Pisa*

ONE WANTS PRECISE KNOWLEDGE OF EVERY-thing that people were ever willing to die for, Elias Canetti noted.

In the early days of the Franciscan movement, readiness to die and perfect joy came close to being the same thing. The women in their cramped cloisters starved themselves nearly to death. The men wished to fall into the hands of the Saracens, like those six who attempted to travel to North Africa in order to be killed by the Muslims. One became ill and had to turn back. The other five, having arrived in Seville, immediately ran into a mosque and began to curse the Koran. They were beaten up by the enraged faithful. The next day they were seen on a minaret, shouting down that Muhammad was a con man and a devil's lackey. Expelled from the city, they continued their journey and managed to reach Morocco, where they were arrested and brought before the emir, Abu Yakub Yusuf II, in Marrakech. They declared to him that the Koran was a pack of lies, whereupon they were flogged. A Spanish diplomat intervened on their behalf, and an escort was charged with bringing them to the seacoast. But they escaped from their guards, hastened back to Marrakech, forced their way into a mosque, and began cursing the Prophet and his teachings. The emir offered them generous gifts, but in vain. Only when he threatened them with death did they seem satisfied. On January 20, 1220, Beraldo, Pietro, Adjuto, Accurso, and Otho were beheaded. Their bodies were taken to the Augustinian church in Coimbra, Portugal, and soon people were flocking there to give honor to the first martyrs from the ranks of the Franciscans.

One hundred years later, four Franciscans were publicly burned in

Marseilles because of deviation from Christian doctrine. Honoring them was not permitted. Between these two executions falls the noteworthy conflict between the Roman Church and the branch of the Friars Minor that was not prepared to make any compromises. The members of this strict Franciscan faction wished to regulate themselves solely in accordance with the directives of the Holy Spirit. Therefore they were called the "Spirituals."

For them, the meaning of life was far more important than life itself.

The antagonist of the Spirit-faction was named Elias, the first minister general of the Friars Minor after the death of Francesco d'Assisi, who, as Christ come to the West a second time to reform a corrupt Church, had preached the ideal of insignificance and demonstrated it by the example of his life.

Brother Helias Coppi, as he is named in the inscription on his tomb in Cortona, was quick to make sure that Francesco's tiny corpse became an object of the propensity to venerate that characterizes the European peoples. In a letter that was circulated far and wide under his name, Brother Elias wrote: Verily, the presence of our brother and father Francis was a light, and not only for us who were near him. Never yet has the world seen such a sign, except in the case of the Son of God, Christ the Lord. Not long before his death, our brother and father had the appearance of a man crucified. He bore on his body the five wounds that are, in truth, the stigmata of Christ.

Despite his fine words, Minister General Elias was not reelected at the general chapter of the Friars Minor that took place at Pentecost in 1227. In compensation, he received from the pope the charge of erecting in Assisi a mighty edifice to do honor to Francesco's mortal remains. This project naturally cost a great deal of money. As the visitor can still see today, two complete churches were stacked up, one on top of the other, much to the dismay of those who respected the wishes of the second (and last) Christ, their Spirit-guided *Poverello*, whose love for abandoned chapels made Brother Elias and his papal sponsor look like traitors to the Franciscan cause.

A few diehard followers went to the building site in Assisi and smashed the marble receptacles that were to hold the coins offered by the faithful, but in vain. Elias had the perpetrators whipped and expelled from the town.

Meanwhile Pope Gregory IX had decreed that Francesco's *Testament*, complete with its clear pronouncements on the subject of living without possessions, should have no binding power over the Franciscans.

After the completion of the gigantic complex of buildings—the double basilica and the attached monastery—a visitor was announced. Brother Giles, one of Francesco's first companions, had walked over from Perugia to take a look around. The brothers in Assisi took great pride in showing him the entire complex. Giles examined everything carefully and remarked upon leaving: Now all you need is women.

The Spirit-faction received its theological momentum through one of those coincidences that, like God's playful thoughts, deflect the usual course of things. Pope Gregory IX, who had known Francesco personally, canonized him in 1228. In 1241, the year of his own death, Pope Gregory and his forces were under attack by the troops of Frederick II of Hohenstaufen, which controlled the Papal States with the exception of Rome and several well-fortified cities, including Bologna. Emperor and pope reciprocally accused each other of being the Antichrist. Most Franciscans stood on the papal side, but Brother Elias had gone over to the emperor.

Then one day the Franciscans in Pisa received a guest who wanted to put some precious books in safekeeping from the emperor's followers. The newcomer, abbot of a monastery that lay in the direction of Lucca, belonged to the order of the late lamented Joachim of Fiore, author of the works that the visitor was carrying in his baggage.

The Friars Minor of Pisa had a few shining lights in their community, theologians thoroughly versed in the Bible and past masters of rhetoric. Out of curiosity—at first—they began browsing through the Florensian abbot's folios. Their reading grew into study, their study grew into addiction. For it very soon became clear that the old man from Calabria, with great clairvoyance, had discerned already in his time the outline of the figure from Assisi and assigned to it the title of *novus dux*, thus alluding to Francesco's qualifications as a leader for the march into the realm of freedom. Even the name of the *minores*, a name of which they were as proud as others might be of a noble coat of arms, emerged before its time, like an enticing signal seen through the enveloping fog of Joachim's chiaroscuro prose. The beginning of the petite bourgeoisie's triumphant progress through the centuries could be delayed no longer.

Almost exactly seven hundred years later, in 1947, eight years after the greatest war in human history had been instigated by a petty bourgeois from Austria, the philosopher of religion and ordained rabbi Jacob Taubes (1923–1987), who had been born in Vienna, published his dissertation, "Occidental Eschatology." It contains a passage in which the ardor of the Spirit of Pisa burns as hotly as it did of old. What is needed are clergymen, Taubes wrote, who can separate the masses and make them into individuals; clergymen who don't place too high a premium on study and place none at all on control; clergymen who may be capable of powerful eloquence, but are no less powerful in keeping silent and enduring; clergymen who may be capable of knowing the human heart, but are no less learned in refraining from judgments and prejudices; clergymen who know how to use authority, not through force, no, anything but that, but through their own obedience; clergymen, above all, who patiently put up with the sick person's bad habits without getting disturbed any more than a doctor is disturbed during an operation by a patient's scolding and flailing. For the human race is sick, and, from the spiritual viewpoint, sick unto death. Time has a limit, Taubes wrote. Anyone who believes he's thinking in a Christian way, and believes this without thinking about that limit, is feeble-minded.

Time has a limit. The quartet of theologians in Pisa—Fra Gerardus, Fra Salimbene, Fra Bartholomeus, and Fra Rudolphus, who became the nucleus of the new spirituality among the Friars Minor—discovered in Joachim's tractates a deadline for the dawning of the new world order of the Holy Spirit, the prophesied period of salvation. According to Joachim, the raging of the Antichrist would come to an end in the year 1260 and the new age of spiritual freedom would begin, under the leadership of those who had remained true to the Franciscan ethic. There was also no doubt that the Antichrist was identical with Emperor Frederick II, whose innermost circle included the renegade Brother Elias, much to the detriment of the cause of the second Christ from Assisi.

Then, however, a great misfortune occurred; Frederick II died on December 13, 1250, and by the Spirit-faction's reckoning that was ten years too soon.

One of the Pisan four, Fra Salimbene, heard the news in Ferrara, where Pope Innocent IV preached a sermon in September 1251. I was standing next to the pope, Salimbene reported, so close that I could have touched him. The Holy Father spoke about God's providence, which had graciously watched over him on his return journey from Lyons, whither he had taken flight from the emperor. Then the pope wished the citizens of Ferrara peace, adding that the former emperor, who had so wickedly persecuted the Church, was now indeed dead. Then, Salimbene continued, Fra Gerardinus of Pisa poked me in the side and whispered, Did you hear that? The emperor is dead! Forget about your Joachim!

Thereupon Fra Salimbene resolved to believe henceforward only what he saw with his own eyes, and he was left in peace. His fellow friar Gerardus got off less leniently. He published in Paris a work entitled "Introduction to the Eternal Gospel," which was denounced as heretical in 1256 and brought its author lifelong imprisonment in Sicily. One year later, the pope compelled John of Parma to resign his post as minister general. He was called before a theological tribunal, and afterward he disappeared into a Franciscan house in Greccio for the rest of his life. When he died in March 1289, the deadline set for the ascent of the kingdom of spiritual freedom had long since passed.

But even without a specific terminal date on the agenda, the vision of the Franciscan Spirituals remained stimulating enough. In northern Italy, southern France, and Catalonia, more and more people outside of religious orders wanted information about the new spirituality. For example, in a residence between Marseilles and Nice, notaries, physicians, and other educated people would meet in the study of the learned Brother Hugo of Digne, who owned copies of all of Abbot Joachim's writings and was known for speaking his mind. In Lyons, Brother Hugo read the riot act to the pope and the cardinals, speaking to them "as though to children at play," as Fra Salimbene noted with satisfaction. It was also this Hugo who was the first to coin the designation "Spirituals," clearly a thrust at the prelates, who were enjoying their roast meats and wine and had forgotten the poor Lord Jesus; they represented the fleshly Church, and no one was nursing any illusions about its corruption. Various tracts produced by the Franciscan Spirit-faction were in circulation, even among working-class people; these pages were copied out and passed on clandestinely, despite the growing number of edicts, special reports, and judgments of damnation against a theology that was instilling a new principle of hope based on the Third Person of God. That hope looked not to some pallid hereafter, but to fulfillment within the parameters of earthly time.

This Holy Spirit found a particularly warm welcome among the intelligent women who lived in that troubled epoch of the transition from cattle-trading to capitalism. They filled the women's refuges in Cologne and Paris, translated portions of Holy Scripture from Latin into the vernacular, and preferred to associate with Jesus Christ rather than with some stable-scented country squire.

They were called beguines, bizoches, papelardes; men threw their books into the fire, forced narrow-minded priests on them as overseers, turned them over to the Inquisition, and, when they went journeying on foot and unprotected, raped them in roadside ditches.

The inquisitor Bernard Gui wrote the following about them: "They distinguish two Churches, to wit, the fleshly Church, by which they mean the Roman, which regards the degenerate majority, and the spiritual Church, which is responsible for those persons who call themselves Spirituals and Evangelicals and live the life of Christ and his apostles. And they consider this latter Church their own."

But again, the life of Christ and his apostles, as the man from Assisi had understood it, dispensed with private property. According to the belief of the left-wing Franciscans and their steadily increasing following, it was with this renunciation that Christianity would vault into the prognosticated kingdom of the Holy Spirit.

Or not. In the year 1309, Pope Clement V summoned a commission of cardinals for the purpose of mediating the conflict in principle between a vision of possibility and a sense of realism, between the spiritual and the conventional way of life inside as well as outside the Order of the Friars Minor. Both factions were represented in the commission, and to begin with the delegations each received a questionnaire so that they would be able to enunciate their arguments as clearly as possible. The central issue was the problem of private property. The memorable "poverty quarrel," as it was later called, had begun.

At first, the Holy Spirit seemed to stand a good chance in the struggle over the fundamental priorities for Europe's march into the modern age. The Franciscans, now numbering around twenty thousand, had grown so rich since the founding of their Order that they had long been an object of public mockery in the marketplace and in literature. A good dozen papal bulls had transformed the *Poverello*'s poverty ethic into a complex system of legalistic norms. The Order itself stood, together with the Dominicans, in service to the Inquisition, had at its disposal the most modern houses of study in all the important university towns, and produced a series of authoritative professors of theology. For Ubertino of Casale, spokesman of the Spiritual faction, these were unequivocal indications, and in the answers that he submitted to the papal commission's questionnaire, after arguing that the Order had fallen away from the wishes and the legacy of the Blessed Francesco, he asked for a return to the Order's original, propertyless state.

Thereupon the pope sent out a bull that in principle acknowledged the validity of the Spirituals' complaints. The Spirit-faction in southern France was given three friaries (Narbonne, Béziers, Carcassonne), under the protection of the Holy See. This was not much more than a cease-fire. It lasted until 1317.

Meanwhile Pope Clement V had died. His successor, an undersized and choleric old gentleman, took the name of John XXII and immediately moved to attack the Spirit-faction. He summoned sixty-five leading Spirituals to the papal court in Avignon. Forty of these submitted to the dictates of the Curia, and the rest were turned over to the Inquisition. It handed down four death sentences, which were carried out on May 7, 1318, when the condemned men were burned to death in Marseilles. The other defendants were sentenced to life imprisonment. Further decrees excommunicated the beguines of France, who were suspected of heresy, and those Franciscans in Italy who opposed the pope. In 1319, three unrepentant Spirituals went to the stake in Narbonne, and two years later seventeen more Spirit-brothers were incinerated in the same town. Further executions were carried out in Carcassonne and Toulouse.

Against this background of terror, eight professors, commissioned by the pope, were working to produce a report on the most dangerous book of Spiritual theology, the *Commentary on the Apocalypse* by Pierre de Jean Olieu (Petrus Johannis Olivi), who had died in 1298. It didn't take these gentlemen long to denounce Olivi's Joachimite doctrine of the three ages of history and the coming Church of the Spirit. The only issue they had trouble with was the central question of Christ's attitude toward property, the use of money, and possessions. Olivi is right, the commission maintained, if he asserts that Saint Francis's view of poverty corresponds exactly to the life led by Christ and his apostles. Olivi errs, the report went on, if he asserts that therefore the pope has no power over this basic rule of the Franciscans because it is identical to God's Gospel, which stands, as is well known, higher than the pope.

This sort of hairsplitting made the entire report wasted paper as far as the pope was concerned. Therefore, in March 1322, he decided to take the unusual step of formulating the jackpot question in the dispute as concisely and clearly as possible and soliciting an answer to it from all interested parties, above all from the Friars Minor, but also from the theological faculties of European universities. The question was whether or not it was heretical to assert that Christ and the apostles possessed nothing, neither individually nor collectively.

To the pope's chagrin, the Franciscans pulled themselves together for a counterattack. They called a general chapter in Perugia, where the leaders of the Order drafted a circular letter, addressed to all Christians, in which the papal jackpot question was answered in the negative. The Franciscans wrote that it was sound and orthodox Catholic doctrine to assert that Christ and his apostles, having renounced all rights of ownership over any possessions, had neither personal nor collective property.

On December 8, 1322, the pope had a papal bull nailed to the door of the cathedral of Avignon, like a hammer stroke against the ethic of poverty. Could his predecessors, the pope asked ironically, really have been so stupid as to deny the Franciscans' right of ownership over every piece of cheese they consumed at their evening meal? The text went on to say that the contention of the Friars Minor, who claimed that they had formally renounced all rights to their immovable property and their houses, was a fiction, and the time had come to put an end to it.

A scant year later, the Savior of Christianity was definitively placed into monetary circulation, and the Holy Spirit disappeared once again into the lower depths of the world-soul from which he had emerged.

# On the Heights of Time

BUT NOT FOREVER. ON OCTOBER 13, 1806, the German philosopher Georg Wilhelm Friedrich Hegel wrote to his friend, the theologian Friedrich Immanuel von Niethammer: "I saw the emperor, this world-soul, riding out through the city to reconnoiter; it is indeed a marvelous sensation to see such an individual, sitting here on a horse, concentrated on a single point, and at the same time reaching out over the world and mastering it."

He was talking about Napoleon. The letter came from Jena, where the French emperor defeated the Prussians on October 14. Hegel was just then going over the galley proofs of his first important collection, *The Phenomenology of Spirit* (also translated in English as *The Phenomenology of Mind*). It was to appear in a first edition of 750 copies.

In this treatise, the death of God was already a presupposition, but that made no difference to the "Spirit" of the book's title. That Spirit had merely been required to renounce the attribute of holiness. From this time on, the Holy Spirit—at least in educated circles in Germany—was called the "World-Spirit" (*Weltgeist*) or the "Absolute Spirit" (*Absoluter Geist*). As the "Zeitgeist" or "spirit of the time," he dominated his era; in the intellectual journals he looked after the "life of the spirit" (*Geistesleben*); in higher education he was concerned with the cultivation of the "humanities" (*Geisteswissenschaften*, literally "knowledge of the spirit"); in the culture industry he strove for a general "spiritualization" (*Vergeistigung*), or simply for "the spiritual" (*das Geistige*) as opposed to the vulgar "material." The spiritual or intellectual side of life (theatergoing, reading, family music-making, educational trips) was cultivated by the middle class, as was the case, for example, in Weimar (Goethe, Schiller, Herder).

It was to Weimar, to the attention of the responsible minister, Goethe, that the part-time lecturer Hegel sent his petitions for financial aid. The philosopher had to wait until he was forty-one before he could afford to start a family, in Nuremberg, where Niethammer had procured him a post as headmaster of a secondary school.

The family. In its middle-class form, it gave the century its distinctive signature. For the bourgeois family, pompous opera houses were built in Bayreuth, Germany, and Manaus, Brazil. For the sake of the family, daguerreotype and photography were invented, to immortalize its dignified steadfastness. It was served by hygiene and gas lighting. Empire and Biedermeier styles furnished its homes. The bourgeois family was responsible for the split between the public and private spheres, for the tyranny of intimacy that was ultimately obliged to divulge its dirty little secret in the presence of a Viennese neurologist. It was in the salons of the middle class that lofty souls were wont to foster their sensibilities to the higher values of humanity, while smoke poured from factories everywhere and the riches of the colonies were transported to Europe.

Love was the ideal of the middle-class family. In love, Hegel wrote, one finds himself again in another. Not for long, however. Those who have been united divide once more, but in the child the union itself remains undivided.

With these words, the Trinity of Christian faith was brought down from heaven to earth and rendered dynamic in the triangle of father, mother, and child. Hegel sensed the silent energies that lay behind the façades of middle-class houses in Frankfurt, Jena, Nuremberg, Berlin. What went on between Mama and Daddy, that striving of two opposites toward reconciliation in a third entity, nine months after the wedding night, could bring only temporary peace; then new relationships and conflicts would arise, and these would have to be worked out in their turn before a solution could be found.

The dialectic of love, once recognized, could be encountered everywhere, wherever there was life. The world, as a whole, had a system. It needed only to be put down on paper.

In September 1806, shortly before Napoleon entered Jena, Hegel made the following statement in a lecture: "We live in an important era, in a ferment, when the Spirit has given a sudden jolt, moved beyond its previous form, and taken on a new one. A new emergence of the Spirit is preparing itself."

The jolt was the French Revolution, whose representative, Napoleon, was approaching, but not as a lover; with him came cannon. The world-soul in uniform, sitting on a horse, embodied the violence of an occurrence whose significance the philosopher clearly perceived, while the French and Prussian soldiers were chiefly afraid of getting a belly wound. The Red Cross had not yet been invented. The soldiers whom the philosopher was obliged to admit to his bachelor's rooms were not interested in the galley proofs of *The Phenomenology of Spirit.* After the Battle of Jena and its disruption of university life, Hegel was left virtually destitute and forced to take up residence in Bamberg, where he worked on the editorial staff of the local newspaper and saw his book through the press. The new emergence of the Spirit proceeded in what were for the philosopher difficult circumstances.

So the Holy Spirit's career move from the Christian credo to the helm of human history (at first, to be sure, only on the paper used by the publishing house of Joseph Anton Goebhardt, Bamberg and Würzburg) was all the more remarkable.

At first, Hegel's Spirit was but partially understood as the third member of the league formed by the Most Holy Trinity, well within the boundaries of Christian faith. Hegel had gained personal experience of that faith while a student in the theological foundation of the University of Tübingen, together with Friedrich Hölderlin and Friedrich Wilhelm Joseph von Schelling. One evening over after-dinner drinks, it was suggested that a syphilitic fellow student might leave disease germs on the liturgical vessels. Hegel felt that this hypothesis was incompatible with the Nazarene's ideal of love.

Not this idea, therefore, but rather the notion of an invisible, spiritual Church was what the three young men really had in mind, especially when they were in the open countryside and could sense the presence of the Immeasurable under the pale shimmering of the nightly stars. The pact of friendship they made did not endure very long. Hölderlin began to suffer from a disease that would later be called schizophrenia. Schelling published some ideas that Hegel felt unable to condone. What they all retained in common was their withdrawl from the faith of their fathers and their wish to abolish it from the (German) Spirit.

Within only fifteen years, from the *Essay toward a Critique of All Revelation* (Johann Gottlieb Fichte, 1792) to Hegel's own *Phenomenology*, which arrived in bookstores in April 1807, that Spirit sprang onto the philosophical stage and put "idealist" thought on the program. "In Hegel's work," a reviewer wrote, "reason shows itself at its full strength. Hegel's efforts are directed toward giving philosophy the strict form of science."

The undertaking required great coldheartedness. Hegel's Spirit had no time to spare for the contemplation of individual destinies. Dying soldiers, homeless women and children, political prisoners, all were of no interest to him. He was occupied only with himself, striding onward to ever-higher forms of cognitive clarity, from the mute existence of nature, over the less felicitous awareness that characterized past cultures, to the future self-awareness for whose sake the whole operation had been set in motion.

With Napoleon, the future had already begun. But Hegel did not want to write that quite so plainly into his *Phenomenology*. He contented himself with quietly emptying a bottle of red wine, all alone, on every anniversary of the French Revolution.

His caution was thoroughly justified. The Congress of Vienna had solidly reinstated the crowned heads of Europe for the next hundred years by the time the philosopher, having received a most prestigious appointment as professor in the University of Berlin, arrived in the Prussian capital in 1818. Napoleon was languishing in definitive exile on the island of St. Helena. The World-Spirit would not let itself be pushed.

Hegel's lectures were well attended. Weary, morose, the lecturer sat there—so wrote one of his auditors—his head sunk upon his chest, his body collapsed upon itself, talking all the time as he paged back and forth in his long folio volumes, looking high and low for something;

his constant coughing and throat-clearing destroyed any continuity in his speech; every sentence issued forth only with difficulty, in pieces, thoroughly muddled, and stood there in isolation; every word, every syllable freed itself reluctantly, as though each were the most important, and then received a wondrously painstaking utterance in broad Swabian dialect.

After the turmoil of the past three decades, Hegel was convinced that the World-Spirit had found a place of refuge in Germany, where it finally had the opportunity to reflect upon itself—especially in Berlin—and was supported by state funds. "I salute this, the sunrise of a purer Spirit," said the new professor of philosophy in his inaugural lecture on October 22, 1818. Karl Marx, born in Trier on May 5 of this same year, was still in diapers.

The theology department looked upon Hegel with distrust. The evangelical man of God, Friedrich Ernst Daniel Schleiermacher, well known because of his *Discourses on Religion, Addressed to Its Cultured Despisers,* was the rector of the university, and he had attempted to use his office to block Hegel's appointment. The philosopher avenged himself four years later with a sharp attack on Schleiermacher's definition of religion as a feeling of "absolute dependence." If religion were based merely on a feeling, Hegel wrote, then such a feeling would have but one purpose, namely to feel its dependence; and therefore the dog would be the best Christian, because he carries this feeling in himself most intensely, and in this feeling he principally lives.

Only the free spirit has religion, Hegel continued. Religion frees a person from the burden of himself; but it also frees him from the illusion that he is facing, in God, a being alien to him. Theologians take much delight in talking about the warmth of the heart. But religion is not merely a warming; rather it is the absolute fire in which the heart burns, and the spirit, out of this annihilation of something that mattered little to it, rises again to unite with God as the Holy Spirit.

What was expected of the Holy Spirit could scarcely be decreed more decisively. As long as he exercised influence over the devout consciousness, he remained a piously worshiped entity, an alien God, an incomprehensible authority from the next world. In this period of bourgeois revolutions, the view that mankind's relationship to God was a subservient one was practically a thing of the past. As the new epoch in human history began, neither the thundering voice from Mount Sinai nor the Pentecostal flames rained down upon ecstatic congregations was of much significance any-more. Now, at last, the Spirit of God would awake to full self-awareness, in the first-person pronouns of emancipated people. Man's spirit for knowing God, Hegel explained, is the Spirit of God.

From this we infer that the Holy Spirit first articulated himself with certainty in the mind of Hegel. This arrogance did not go unremarked by his colleagues. In turn, those who attended Hegel's lectures—at least in the case of his brighter students—came more and more to feel, under the influence of their master's philosophy of the Spirit, that they were dis-pensed from Sunday churchgoing. One of them was named Ludwig Feuer-bach. "I was his student for two years," Feuerbach wrote. "His attentive, undistracted, enthusiastic listener. He was the only man who made me feel and experience what a teacher is."

When Feuerbach published his principal work (*The Essence of Christian-ity*) in 1841, Hegel had already been ten years in his grave. Then every-thing started happening very fast, at least on paper, in Germany. In 1845, Karl Marx conceived his "Theses on Feuerbach." The eleventh and last of these reads as follows: "The philosophers have only interpreted the world in different ways; the point is to change it."

Vladimir Ilyich Ulyanov, alias Lenin, said scornfully that the Marxists hadn't understood Marx for fifty years. Anyone who has not made a thorough study of Hegel's *Science of Logic*, he said, will not understand Marx's *Capital*. In April 1917, Lenin traveled in a sealed railway car from Zürich to St. Petersburg; his purpose was to translate the German Spirit into Russian practice. One year later, Lenin sent a telegram to Yevgenia Bosch, chairwoman of the governing committee of the city of Penza, authorizing her to shut up "suspicious persons" in concentration camps. During the course of the next seventy years, many men and women be-came acquainted with the more unpleasant aspects of Hegel's Spirit. One such person was Alexander Solzhenitsyn (b. 1918). His novel *Cancer Ward* contains the following sentence: "Books are glorified that don't deserve to be."

The answer to the theological questions of the present day lies buried under the Siberian snow, in the graves of the prisoners in whose consciousness, according to Hegel, the Holy Spirit would be reconciled with himself.

# *Women's*
# *Friend*

DURING THE SECOND WORLD WAR, THE FRENCH

*writer Simone Weil died of malnutrition. Her medieval foremothers, who were, according*

*to circumstances, vilified as witches, honored as saints, or regarded as madwomen, experi-*

*enced their accesses of grace so intensely that they frequently forgot to eat. This sisterhood, in*

*its happiest moments, became immersed in the divine Spirit like tears in the ocean.*

# But No,
# But No, She Said

$S$HE WAS SO FAIR, SHE WAS SO FAIR. NO fairer maiden could be found, not anywhere on Polish ground. But no, but no, she said, not this; I never kiss.

In this soldiers' song about a Polish girl, male desire encounters a female refusal, and the less the young woman is prepared to change her mind, the more delightful she becomes. As they sing, the marching troops grow familiar with images that urge them to rape. Deeds that are taboo in peacetime go unpunished in war. The troops have long ago grasped the notion that relations between the sexes are equivalent to war. In this age-old order of things, the Polish girl really doesn't have a chance.

*I never kiss.* Unexpectedly, as though emerging out of fog—their outlines are still blurred—certain female forms enter the history of couples and their relations. These are girls who say no, and they're made of sterner stuff than the Polish maiden of the soldiers' fantasy. They are women whose daily bread doesn't come from the bakery. They speak, down through the centuries, with a single voice.

Like this, for example:

He came into my room and said, You poor wretch, you understand nothing. Come with me and I shall teach you some things you haven't even an inkling of. I followed him. He led me into a church. It was new and ugly. He walked me up to the altar and told me, Kneel down. I said to him, I haven't been baptized. He said, Fall on your knees with love before this place as though before the place where truth is. I obeyed. He had me leave the church and climb up to an attic room with an open window from which one could see the whole city, a few wooden scaffolds, the river where ships were unloaded. He told me to sit down. We were alone. He talked. Sometimes someone would come in, join the conversation, and then leave. It wasn't winter anymore. It wasn't yet spring. The branches of the trees were bare, without buds, and the air was cold and full of sunlight. The light brightened, grew radiant, faded, then the stars and the moon came in through the window. Then the dawn brightened again. Sometimes he stopped talking, went to the cupboard and took out a loaf of bread, and we shared it. This bread truly had the taste of bread. I've never found that taste again. He poured me and himself some wine that tasted like the sun and like the earth on which this city is built. Sometimes we stretched out on the floor of the attic room, and the sweetness of sleep descended upon me. Then I woke up again and drank the sunlight. He had promised to teach me something, but he taught me nothing. We chatted about all sorts of things, in a general way, as old friends do. One day he told me, Now go. I fell on my knees, I embraced his legs, I begged him not to send me away. But he threw me onto the stairs. I went down them without knowing anything, my heart seemed to be in pieces. I walked through the streets. Then I realized that I didn't have any idea where that house was. I never tried to find it again. I understood that he had come looking for me by mistake. My place is not in that attic room. Sometimes I can't stop myself from repeating, with fear and remorse, a little of what he told me. How can I know if I remember correctly? He isn't there to tell me so. I know well that he doesn't love me. How could he love me? And yet deep inside me something, some part of me, trembles with fear and can't stop thinking that maybe, in spite of everything, he loves me.

Simone Weil (1909–1943), a teacher in a secondary school, wanted to use the above text as the prologue to a book she was planning. As it turned out, the publication of her writings began only after her death, and since 1988 several volumes of a planned sixteen-volume collection of her works have appeared. She looks out quite cheerfully upon the world from the few photographs of her that exist. But appearances are deceiving. There were the chronic headaches, there was the chronic problem of money. And always, the sensation of hunger. A note on Simone Weil's death certificate reads: "cardial failure due to degeneration of the heart muscles due to starvation and pulmonary tuberculosis."

Self-starvation, practiced by young women until their bodies are fatally exhausted, is called anorexia nervosa, "nervous loss of appetite," by medical science, which in this case is fairly helpless. In the fall of 1906, the French neurologist Pierre Janet was invited by the Harvard Medical School to give a series of lectures, in one of which the eminent psychiatrist discussed anorexia. In the first stage, Janet observed, a girl complains about vague stomach pains and takes her medicine willingly. Next, when the medicine doesn't work and her parents are getting exasperated, she vomits whatever she has been induced to swallow. This stage can last ten years and includes hyperactivity on the part of the patient. Finally, according to Janet, the girl has little urine and is constantly constipated, her breath is foul, her skin dry and cracked; her pulse quickens; she is bedridden and now delirious. At the last minute, some girls realize what is happening to them, yield to the authority of their doctors, and recover. The others die.

Physicians treating the disease were struck by the remarkable euphoria their patients displayed during the second and longest phase of the disease. Janet compared this elevated mood with the state of consciousness reached by ecstatic saints. Anorexia, the lecturer concluded, is to be traced back to much deeper sources than was supposed.

The comparison with the female ecstatics was not chosen at random. Since 1896, ten years before his journey to America, Janet had been treating a woman who gave her name as "Scapegoat" (*le bouc*), because she had to atone for the sins of the world. In the photographs that Janet made of his patient, one could see a petite, pretty person wearing light sandals, standing on tiptoe, and lifting her skirt a little, as if to show off her shapely legs. From time to time, the stigmata of the Crucified appeared on her body, twice in 1896, five times in 1897, ten times in 1899. The wounds would be bandaged and allowed to heal, but then they would reappear in the same places, usually just before the onset of her period. Once a day, the patient had to be compelled to eat at least a small piece of bread and to drink some milk. Even this modest nourishment was skipped when the woman went into ecstasy, which lasted for two or three days.

Janet discharged his patient from the Salpêtrière sanatorium in Paris after a stay of six and a half years. She was then forty-seven years old. After her death in 1921, Janet began to write a two-volume account of her story, under the title *From Anxiety to Ecstasy.* In studying his patient, the neurologist was unable to detect very much more than a vague connection between her refusal to take nourishment and her propensity to go into ecstasies. Her ecstasies, Janet wrote, exhibit the essential characteristics of all the ecstasies of genuine mystics. Apparently Madeleine, as Janet called his patient, had come into the world at the wrong time. Her true place was in the Middle Ages. Medieval mysticism is without significance today, declared the professor.

Who knows. The refusal of women to take nourishment is not an invention of contemporary prima ballerinas and models. It can be traced to the Middle Ages, all the way back to Saint Clare of Assisi, a hunger artist of the first rank, whose reputation quickly spread far beyond Italy. In Prague, for example, the Princess Agnes founded a convent on the model of the Poor Ladies of Assisi and entered it on Pentecost Sunday, 1234. She fasted so excessively that Saint Clare felt obliged to warn her against going to extremes: "We are not made of bronze or granite, rather we are, unfortunately, quite fragile and weak," she wrote to Agnes.

That was only the beginning. In the following centuries, father confessors throughout Europe were obliged to deal with women whose deliberate self-starvation made the fasting customs of the male orders look like gluttony. Of a group of 170 Italian women whom the Vatican has declared worthy of veneration between 1200 and the present day, more than half displayed clear signs of anorexia. Whenever the most famous of them, Saint Catherine of Siena (d. 1380), tried to eat something to humor her father confessor, she vomited everything she managed to swallow, and she died from general debilitation at the age of thirty-three. In the Trecento, the scene of her visionary marriage to Christ was so popular that it was immortalized in hundreds of paintings.

There was the occasional hoax. Around the middle of the thirteenth century, in the little town of Marsal, France (northwest of Nancy), a young woman named Sybilla drew attention to herself by her particularly assiduous attendance at early Mass. She also told tales of visits from both heaven and hell and was wont to withdraw to her bed without food or drink, and so she became a frequent topic of conversation among her fellow citizens. The bishop of Metz was already thinking about building a chapel for Sybilla so that the people might better admire her miraculous way of life. Then, however, a priest became suspicious and peeped through a crack in the locked door behind which the pious woman could be heard struggling with the demons. He saw Sybilla simulating the bawling and hissing of the devilish brood while calmly making her bed. An inspection of her lodging brought to light from under her bed a supply of food that a young clergyman was providing for her at night. The incensed bishop had the false saint imprisoned and starved to death.

Men remained vigilant. The appearance of high-performance female mysticism between 1200 and 1600 engaged the father confessors in a theater of sublime eroticism about which they had not the slightest clue.

*A more!*

It's always a supernatural lover whom Clare, Catherine, Madeleine, and Simone encounter. . . . *deep inside me something . . . trembles with fear and can't stop thinking that maybe, in spite of everything, he loves me.* Clare and Catherine know that it is Christ who appears to them in the mirror of their soul. In the lunatic asylum, Madeleine hints at the incomparable pleasure that God gives her with his burning hands. Only the unbaptized Simone leaves the name of the Other unspoken.

What are friends and relatives, what are father confessors, inquisitors, neurologists supposed to say to such extravagances?

In the streets of Siena, a satirical poem was recited against the hysterical young miss from the house of Benincasa. Did Catherine consider herself holier than the apostles, who had followed Jesus' advice to eat everything that was set before them? Was she starving herself because she craved admiration? *Si lo Spirito ti mena, non cercar loda terrena.* "If the Holy Spirit guides your ways, you shouldn't look for earthly praise."

This was the question that interested the Holy Inquisition as well. Was it the Holy Spirit or the devil that spoke from the mouths of these hunger virtuosos and ecstatics? Was one dealing with saints, or with witches?

Now and then the Other could be quite direct. "Lay yourself on top of me," he commanded his maidservant, "just as the prophet Elisha lay upon the boy. Lay your hands in my hands, your eyes to my eyes, your limbs against my limbs."

Such desires from on high were dangerously reminiscent of the tricks played by the fallen angels, who slipped into the bed of many a woman and engaged in disgraceful behavior there while the husband lay snoring alongside.

The inquisitors wanted to know everything, and as precisely as possible. If nothing transpired at the hearing, they showed the suspected woman the instruments of torture. If that didn't help, then the torture itself began. This resulted in the clarity that mattered so much to the inquisitors: Yes, I was at the witches' Sabbath, and there I kissed the devil's behind.

Women who were God's lovers could be helped against the omnipresent danger of being hauled before a court as a witch. A regular father confessor, intimately familiar with their inner lives, could keep a positive character reference ready in case it was needed. Without this sort of protection, the holy woman was as helpless as a whore without a pimp. Catherine had a certain Raymond of Capua, Madeleine had her Dr. Janet.

I, who had hidden my soul so bashfully, how could I open myself to you in a way I had never yet used with anybody? This is the complaint Madeleine makes when she's in despair over the incomprehension of the man who is the only person she talks to. He will never allow himself to get too close to her. He doesn't wear a cassock, but he has remained what his predecessors were, an ear behind a grille into which unspeakable confessions are whispered.

The father confessor, for his part, had in his head that single question so superbly formulated by Sigmund Freud: What do women want?

.  .  .

The Other, too, desires to discover what wish he is to fulfill for his beloved. The answer given by the Florentine Maria Maddalena de' Pazzi (1566–1607) has become famous. *Pati non mori.* "To suffer, to suffer more and more, but not to die doing so." Three hundred years later, Madeleine Le Bouc received the name "Passionflower" in Dr. Janet's card index of patients, which he called his Herbarium. Her sufferings and her ecstasies were mutually dependent, they alternated with each other, they became virtually interchangeable. Physical pain can turn into pleasure. The yellowed label of female masochism, invented by men, does nothing to explain the riddle posed by the stories of the sufferings that Spirit-intoxicated women practicing advanced methods of self-discovery have undergone over the course of eight hundred years.

Three weeks before her death, Simone Weil wrote a letter to her parents in which she asserted that only the creatures who have fallen to the lowest depths of degradation in this world are qualified to tell the truth. All others lie.

The letter was written in godless times. As prophesied in the Apocalypse, both monstrous Antichrists had climbed up out of the depths and made themselves at home in the world. Because she was of Jewish extraction, Simone was obliged to escape from Hitler. When she arrived in England, she immediately applied to the Forces de la France Libre to be sent back to France as a partisan. Her proposals got so thoroughly on General de Gaulle's nerves that he dismissed them as madness.

Simone understood more about theology than she did about fighting for the Resistance. Faced with the godlessness of her century, she played a waiting game. "I can say," she wrote, "that I have never at any moment in my entire life been searching for God." The initiative must have come from the Other.

The Other was conspicuous by his absence.

Simone was waiting for Godot. Why didn't he come? In Sartre's opinion, Beckett makes us understand that we're too flabby to have real need of Godot; we're missing the literally insane stubbornness that would alone be capable of making us an urgent case.

Simone Weil possessed that literally insane stubbornness. She had grown up as an atheist, and this preserved her from falling into the trap of the father confessors. For Simone, atheism remained a kind of purification exercise, a talisman of great value against the blindness of self-delusion.

Then, however, when she was twenty-seven years old, in Assisi: "Something stronger than I forced me, for the first time in my life, to kneel down."

But that was as far as she went. A Dominican priest whom Simone befriended in Marseilles soon noticed the spirit of resistance in this woman, who had traveled to Spain in 1936 to help the communists against Franco. Nothing that smacked of institution or establishment, even in its Catholic form, could seduce Simone. Despite her strong desire to consume the body of Christ in the consecrated bread, she remained unbaptized. The sight of the light and slender body of God on the cross was enough to make her forget the weight of the world.

*Something stronger than I.* For Simone Weil's medieval sisters, it was the Holy Spirit who had placed his sail in their souls. He had lost his name in the disillusionment of Europe, which had become godless. But he was far from having disappeared on that account.

# *A Taste Sweeter Than Honey*

DR. JANET, WHOSE METICULOUSNESS IN observing his patient, the mystical lady hospitalized in the Salpêtrière, has remained unsurpassed, didn't believe in the Holy Spirit. Instead he recorded in detail what his Madeleine experienced in her ecstasies.

This:

I tasted everywhere the sweetness of these kisses. Pleasure in the mouth and on the lips is endless, it can be compared with nothing else, it's sweeter than honey. I sense a fresh, sweet taste, my tongue is delighted as never before. This sweetness in my mouth is intoxicating. What kind of sweet and intoxicating liqueur is this that fills my mouth? It's like honey I don't dare swallow, it's as if I were eating sugar candy.

And this:

I taste an immense sweetness on my lips and in my stomach, which contracts in truly divine spasms. Something happens to my bladder, its opening is sealed, and this inability to make water is not a torment but a pleasure. God has sealed me everywhere with his kisses, and I shall never be able to make water again.

Furthermore:

What an indescribable pleasure it is to keep moving with your feet off the ground, the imagination cannot impart the sweetness you feel when you can fly all over in this way.

For reasons of propriety, the doctor deleted "the all-too-crude expressions" from his patient's statements. All the same, one may suspect that it wasn't only in her mouth that Madeleine sensed the divine sweetness. Janet also recorded that she would ask for something sweet to drink before the approach of her ecstasies. In India, where competence in mystical experience is developed more highly than it is in Europe, this would have caused no surprise. Every child who lives there knows that the swamis have a weakness for sweet snacks. Madeleine came into the world in the wrong country.

And at the wrong time, too, as already mentioned. In that star performance of medieval divine science, the *Summa Theologica* of Thomas Aquinas (d. 1274), ecstatic sweetness still belonged to the stock of self-evident knowledge. Every experience of God (*cognitio divinae bonitatis seu voluntatis affectiva seu experimentalis*) is there described as a taste of divine sweetness (*dum quis experitur in se ipso gustum divinae dulcedinis*). A contemporary and colleague of Aquinas, the Franciscan cardinal Bonaventure gave an even briefer definition of the matter. According to this influential man, the best way of knowing God is to be found in the experience of sweetness (*optimus enim modus cognoscendi Deum est per experimentum dulcedinis*).

These two master thinkers, in contrast to too many of their present-day colleagues, were at pains to employ a rigorous and precise terminology, in keeping with the high standards upheld by the universities of the time. The two professors put the taste of divine sweetness into their tractates not as a flowery phrase but as a current technical term.

Moreover, and likewise in contrast to present-day experts on mysticism, Aquinas and Bonaventure knew what they were talking about, because piousness meant more to them than anything else. Whether they themselves at one time or another had experienced the bliss that they were writing about is irrelevant. What remains decisive is that rarefied instances of divinely inspired blissfulness were beyond question for the scientific authorities of the High Middle Ages, and that such states were linked to definite sensations of taste, to a certain sweetness that was still detectable, six hundred years later, in Dr. Janet's psychiatric clinic.

After 1300, the signs multiplied, demonstrating that it was principally women who were attaining the delights of the *dulcedo*—on the Rhine and in Tuscany, south of the Pyrenees and east of the Elbe. Many of these female virtuosos of divine intimacy voluntarily became beggars and wandered over half of Europe; others lived under the roofs of women's refuges. However, for the theologians in the universities of Paris and Bologna, Oxford and Cologne, these *mulieres religiosae* or *sanctae*, as they were called, posed a constantly growing problem, and foreheads were furrowed at the papal court as well. For, you see, if it got about that the divine sweetness tasted far better than the sacraments of Holy Mother Church, then priestly power would be seriously threatened.


On July 1, 1310, a wellborn woman was burned at the stake. Her only offense was that she had written and distributed a book. The bishop of Cambrai had publicly consigned that book to the flames in Valenciennes, in the presence of the author, and she had been warned that in the future she must keep her ideas to herself. The writer, whose name was Marguerite Porete, had sent copies of her treatise to three respected theological authorities and received positive responses. Because she persisted in disseminating her views, she was arrested and handed over to the Inquisition in Paris, where an inquisitor named William Humbert took charge of her case. The man had a great deal to do, because he was occupied with mounting a show trial on behalf of the French crown against the rich order of the Templars. He had little time to spare for the defendant from the Hainault region in northern France. At any rate, Brother William had several suspect articles excerpted from Marguerite's devotional book and then commissioned a group of twenty-one theologians from the University of Paris to examine the passages thus torn from their context. The commission decided unanimously for heresy, and the rest was routine.

Thereafter *The Mirror of Simple Annihilated Souls and Those Who Only Remain in Will and Desire of Love* circulated anonymously in the cloisters of Europe as an eagerly read travel guide to the world beyond this one. Because of its popularity, copies of the original Old French version as well as translations into Latin, Italian, and Middle English have been preserved, and shortly after the Second World War an Italian historian succeeded in identifying Marguerite Porete as the author of *The Mirror of Simple Souls.* Piquantly enough, the sensational attribution was first published in the Vatican's newspaper, *L'Osservatore Romano,* on June 16, 1946.

Apart from what is contained in the Inquisition's documents of her case, nothing is known about Marguerite Porete. The conclusion that she was highly educated is based on the contents of her work, which employs the literary and stylistic devices of her time; for example, the fictitious disputation between Love and Reason, who appear personified. Porete describes herself in her book as a miserable beggar (*mendiant créature*), which is hardly meant to be taken literally and rather refers to her belonging to the women's religious movement whose members were called "beguines," and who, because of their unregulated way of living, had been repeatedly loaded with judgments of damnation by the higher clergy. The beguines' public begging ("Bread for God") was the expression of a program that took as its model Jesus and his apostles, in contrast to the richly endowed Church. In any case, Porete was identified by the spiritual police as a conspirator, as a false nun and a liar without legal status or official papers.

Not only that, but Porete's book contained, below its surface, the elements of what the organs of orthodoxy assessed as freethinking.

"Virtues, I take my leave of you," wrote Porete. "I am parted from your dominations, in peace I rest."

In the eyes of the authorities, that was to be understood as a rejection of accepted standards of decency and a possible invitation to dissoluteness, illicit sex, and man-swapping.

It was also a conspicuous fact that Marguerite obliquely and repeatedly presented the Holy Spirit as the driving power that thrust her vessel up into the spheres of blissful liberation. And what is such a soul? says Holy Church. Most sweet Holy Spirit, teach it to us.

O Holy Church, says the Holy Spirit, I will tell you what she wills. She wills only one thing, that is, she wills nothing.

Had the Holy Spirit blown a breath from India into Christian Europe? The Soul has finished with the world, wrote Marguerite, and the world has taken leave of her. She is hidden in God, has no more will, nor any anxiety from any sin which she might have ever committed.

Porete's "annihilated souls" (*ames anienties*) had let themselves be brought by the Holy Spirit to the point of feeling neither attraction nor abhorrence in the face of the Church's innumerable sacred customs, regulations, practices. Such souls were no longer dangling from the hook of religion. Divine services, sermons, pilgrimages, confession, prayer were superfluous in the soft ecstasy of that love that gets the last word in Porete's book.

The author calls the beloved Other "Farnearness" (*loingprès*)—that is, "In-the-distance-but-so-close"—in the style of the troubadour poetry and romance literature of the time, where love was always directed toward a distant object (*amour loingtaine*), the refined (*fine*), unadulterated (*pure*), noble (*noble*), true (*vraie*), perfect (*parfaicte*), exalted (*haulte*) love of languishing and longing that left the vulgar act of sex to horse grooms and stable whores. The climb into the higher spheres is arduous. Only on the fifth rung of the soul's ladder does the lover meet her friend for the first time. He is an abductor, he seizes his prey and snatches her up into the sixth stage (*estat*). This happens often, but always only momentarily, in the famous mystical split second, the lightninglike opening (*ouverture*) followed immediately by the closing (*closure*). One is tempted to think of a flash camera. *Click!*

The name Marguerite gives to her mystical climaxes is "flash of lightning" (*esclar*), and this is not a subject for discussion. She stresses that even beguines who are well experienced in such matters can find no words to describe the spiritual ecstasy of love. After the lightning bolt, it takes a while for the brain waves to return to their normal frequency, and during this period of subsidence the soul feels pleasantly unfettered, calm, willless, peaceful, relaxed, remembering her intimate friend, who has once again withdrawn to his distant place. He will come again.

As for the seventh and last stage, it can be reached only at the moment of death. The chronicler observed that the execution of Marguerite Porete at the Place de Grève in Paris moved the great majority of witnesses to tears.

So that's what he was like, the new and free Spirit at large among the noble dames and daughters of the middle class who were too proud to go along with their parents' plans for marrying them off. There was nothing holy about this Spirit, at least not in the judgment of Saint Albert the Great (Albertus Magnus, d. 1280), who lined up the crosshairs of his theological sight on 121 "impudent assertions." The fact that there were people in the Swabian town of Nördlingen who considered themselves fit for deification must have shocked this teacher of Thomas Aquinas as much as the notion that possession by the Holy Spirit transported a person to a state beyond good and evil.

Ambitious religious writings, composed by laypeople in the vernacular languages spoken both north and south of the Alps, were circulating everywhere, at least among the literate upper classes, and the contents of these treatises absolutely failed to jibe with the concept of the divine right of throne and altar that had functioned throughout the past thousand years. There had been a crusade against the heretics in southern France in 1209, but the Holy Spirit of Constantine's Nicene Creed had quietly become the principle of a new human consciousness against which no crusade could be mobilized. The Free Spirit (*spiritus liber*), as he was called in a bull that Boniface VIII issued on August 1, 1296, eluded any sort of localization, because he was not part of any organized party (*secta*). In May 1312, therefore, the Council of Vienne preferred to publish a decree against the beguines and condemn their alleged errors regarding the attainment of perfection. Item 6 in this document includes, word for word, the farewell to virtue as formulated by Marguerite Porete.

In reality, the intention was to compel the women to give up as quickly as possible their claim of direct access to God. The items in the decree were copied immediately into the handbooks of the inquisitors, thus providing a set of questions to be asked when examining mystical females who were under suspicion. Yes or no: Is it her opinion that spiritual perfection releases one from obedience to the Church? Does she think that a human being can attain eternal bliss here on earth? Does she believe that sexual intercourse is not a sin?

Some inquisitors added one or another question of their own. In Bohemia, for example, the notorious Walter Kerlinger (a member of the Dominican order) asked one of the accused Free Spirit heretics whether Jesus Christ had performed the sexual act with Mary Magdalene after his resurrection.

The papal secret police never gained entrance to the locked gardens of female erotica. *She is a garden enclosed, my sister,* it is written in the Bible; *my promised bride is a sealed fountain.* Some few men gained admission, men such as Meister Eckhart (a Dominican, d. 1328). In the refectory of the cloister of Saint Jacques in Paris, he broke bread together with Magister Berengar, who had been active in the theological commission that ruled against Marguerite Porete. This was but one year after the burning of the God-intoxicated author, and what the two men chatted about has not come down to us. We can take it for granted, however, that Eckhart was sympathetic to Marguerite's thinking. Her "annihilation" reappears in Eckhart's texts, more radical than ever. "So let us pray to God," Eckhart preached, "that we may be free of God."

Eckhart was transferred from Paris to Strasbourg, where he soon became renowned, among the nuns in the innumerable convents of the upper Rhine valley, as a pulpit preacher of the most inspired kind, one who was adding enduring refinement to the German language. It was noted that he sometimes got carried away. "The wise Meister Eckhart wants to make nothingness accessible to us," wrote a nun, "and if someone doesn't understand that, let him complain to God." The women could tell quite clearly that this man in the black-and-white Dominican habit was no inquisitor; his speech was fluid, not obdurate; it was spiritually inspired, and it led to freedom.

"Spiritual" (from the Latin *spiritualis*) is in German *geistlich*, which is cognate with English "ghostly." This word doesn't turn up in the feminine piety of the late Middle Ages in reference to a class privilege of the clergy; rather it serves to indicate the country of origin, as it were, of a level of consciousness that the Holy Spirit had helped to raise.

The entrance examinations to the upper school of the new spirituality were stringent.

Before the soul's guest, so far away and yet so intimate, deigned to descend, the candidate must minimize her usual predilections, and this practice was much more difficult than it was in traditional monastic discipline. These women aspired to ascend, and the things they did to themselves in order to climb the first few rungs of the soul's ladder strike the average citizen of today as absolutely scandalous. "Take the bitter for the sweet," the *Poverello* from Assisi had recommended. The women who conducted their solitary struggle in convents, middle-class homes, and beguine houses took this maxim extremely literally.

Chiara of Assisi, Francesco's female counterpart, wore under her coarse woolen habit a vest made of pigskin, with the bristles on the inside. On Mondays, Wednesdays, and Fridays, she ate nothing, and very little on the other days. She spent the greater part of every night awake and in prayer. As long as her strength held out, she worked like a chambermaid and washed out the chamber pots used by her bedridden companions. The fact that she tolerated a small cat in San Damiano is a bright spot in an otherwise somber picture.

However: Chiara herself reported that she had been granted a vision in which she was bringing a pitcher of hot water and a washcloth to her spiritual partner, the blessed Francesco. Stepping lightly as though over flat terrain, she had climbed up a steep flight of stairs. At the top Francesco offered her his breast and invited her to suck it, twice, and what flowed into her mouth tasted perfectly delightful and sweet. Afterward the round tip of the nipple (*rotondità ovvero bocca de la poppa*) remained in her mouth. She took the little pellet in her hand and observed it, whereby it appeared to her like the purest gold, and in its luster she could see herself as though in a mirror.

In the year 1224, at the age of thirty-one, Chiara fell sick, and for the rest of her life, some twenty-nine years, she was nearly always confined to her bed. It is not known how often the bedclothes were changed.

On the other hand, we have confirmed testimony to the stench that emanated from Saint Margaret of Cortona because she refused to change her clothes. Before she became a penitent, she had been for several years the mistress of a nobleman from Montepulciano. After his death, she and her child found shelter in the palazzo owned by two charitable women in Cortona, where Margaret, a contrite sinner, worked as a midwife. Her beauty must have been extraordinary. She acquired a razor and requested permission from her horrified confessor to cut off her nose. She insisted on eating alone, which she did in the afternoon: tiny portions of bread, nuts, and raw vegetables. Her transports put one in mind of the events that occur on Italian stages. At Mass one Sunday she suddenly interrupted the sermon, crying out and asking where the crucified Christ had been hidden; on Good Friday she ran screaming through the streets and then lay doubled up on the ground with chattering teeth. Finally, at a peak of ecstasy, the crucified God bade her to lay her hands on his. Then Christ's breast opened, and in the bloody darkness there lay beating, with the utmost vehemence, the heart of the world.

The body of the Lord (*frôlîchnam* in medieval German) is famously edible. Its feast day (the feast of Corpus Christi, *Fronleichnam* in modern German) can be traced to the carryings-on of a visionary woman who ran a home for lepers in Liège. Margaret of Cortona wasn't the only one who would have preferred to take the host as her only nourishment. Another Italian celebrity in the field, Angela of Foligno (d. 1309), described quite precisely her sensation upon taking Communion. She felt how the host expanded in her mouth; it tasted, not like bread, but more like flesh, and yet completely different, and in any case deliciously sweet. Only because doing so was prescribed, she swallowed down the body of Christ. She would have liked to keep it in her mouth for a longer time. Similar sensations arose while she was washing a leper's feet in the local hospital of San Feliciano. The sick man's flesh was already so rotten that a piece of it peeled off into the wash basin. Angela proceeded to drink this mixture, and at once she tasted again the incomparable taste of God.

Some confessors toyed with such women, enjoying their power over them by using trivial excuses to forbid them to receive the food of the angels.

In vain. Neither burning at the stake nor terrorized consciences sufficed to keep awakening femininity in check. Its leader, the Holy Spirit, was a flatterer. During a pilgrimage to Assisi, the aforesaid Angela heard him clearly in the middle of the vineyards of Spello: My dearest love, my temple, my delight, my bride. Against this divine seducer, the father confessors were at a decided disadvantage.

# *Dead   Ends*

*I*N   THE   SECOND   THIRD   OF   MARGUERITE Porete's *Mirror*, Reason *(raison)* plays a role. Ah God! says Reason. How dare one say this? I dare not listen to it. I am fainting truly, Lady Soul, in hearing you; my heart is failing. I have no more life.

This is just fine with the Soul. For as long as I had you, Lady Reason, says this Soul, I could not freely receive my inheritance, what was and is mine.

A daring statement. In the period of the Enlightenment, Francisco de Goya wrote a caption on one of the etchings in his series *Los Caprichos:* "The Sleep of Reason Produces Monsters." A great variety of nocturnal fowl can be seen in the print. The Holy Spirit's dove is not among them. In the foreground is depicted a male figure who has fallen asleep at his desk, his head resting on his crossed arms. This figure, at least in the waking state, personifies critical thought, which shrinks in horror before the onset of the irrational. The special knowledge of lordship, which is

the province of men, considers every expansion of the limits of consciousness a female weakness and resists it.

Marguerite Porete, on the other hand, does not put reason to rest
because she wants to set the monsters of the unconscious free, but because
the interior monologue of thought must be suspended. Toward the end of
her book, in a kind of synopsis of what has been said, Marguerite begs
pardon of those of her readers who have already attained the loving nothingness of the sixth stage and to whom "human knowledge" doesn't mean
very much anymore. Necessity has no law, according to the author, and
therefore she has had to write in a rational way, has had to bow to the
conventions of discursive speech and composition, and therefore also to
the standards of "theological learning," which she doesn't think very much
of: "Everything one can say or write about God, or think about Him, God
who is greater than what is ever said, is thus more like lying than speaking
the truth."

So wrote Marguerite Porete. In the two hundred pages of her treatise,
there is only a single reference to the mystical *click*, and that one instance is
rather incidental, hidden between the lines. It isn't what's important.
Without discretion (from the Latin *discernere*, "to distinguish," "to tell
apart") it is better not to think, speak, or write about the more refined
sort of dealings with the other world.

For the terrain of the nonquotidian, with its raptures, trances, ecstasies, heavenly flights, is by no means free from danger. Shamanesses and
shamans (those that still exist) go through years of training in order to
commit to memory those roads that are more or less safe for their journey
and to learn to avoid the labyrinths, dead ends, and trapdoors that are
most certainly waiting for them as soon as the sacred frenzy begins.

In comparison with the expertise of shaman culture, Christian knowledge about experiences in the realm of the spirits seems rather modest. In
the eyes of priests, levitation and flight were witchery; visions could come
from the devil. And so it came about that the numerous European women
of the late Middle Ages for whom going to church and having children
were not enough had to undertake their adventures in the supernatural
more or less alone, without instructions and expert guidance. Whatever
reading matter came to them from their literarily ambitious fellow trav-

elers was not particularly informative. When the poor soul comes to court, wrote Mechtilde von Magdeburg, she behaves in a sensible, well-bred manner. Then the happy one looks upon her God. Ah, how lovingly is she received! Now she holds herself still and feels unbridled longing for his praise. Then he shows her, in her great yearning, his divine heart, which is like the red gold that glows in a great fire of coals. On another occasion, the soul dances around the woods with a handsome young man who is not further described. Only rarely is Mechtilde's encoded prose direct and clear, and that is when she is setting at nought the counsels of the father confessors. Mechtilde (d. 1282) lived as a beguine in Magdeburg until she entered the Cistercian convent of Helfta near Eisleben (fifty miles south of Magdeburg) in the company of Gertrude "the Great" and Mechtilde von Hackeborn, two extremely talented colleagues, experienced visionaries whose publications would soon be read all over Europe.

Only unmarried noblewomen were granted admission to Helfta. The property lay in a friendly landscape. "I sat down beside the little lake," wrote Gertrude, "and gave myself over to the charm of this place. The clarity of the streaming water, the green of the surrounding trees, the free flight of the birds, especially the doves, and above all the intimate peacefulness of this secluded retreat filled me with happiness."

But the devil doesn't sleep. Shaken by the death of her elder sister, who had headed the convent as its abbess, Mechtilde von Hackeborn became deeply disconsolate and in addition had to suffer from a raging headache that tormented her night and day for a month. Her desperate cries, calling on God to take her in her turn, echoed through the house. Then, to the amazement of her companions, immediately after early Mass she fell into a state of bliss of the most peaceful kind and remained so for several hours; her eyes were closed, and she could not be spoken to. This sequence of events was repeated many times, and it precipitated the composition of the renowned *Liber specialis gratiae*, the "Book of Special Grace," which made its fifty-year-old author famous. Gertrude the Great and another nun copied down everything that Mechtilde von Hackeborn told them. The book was in the Latin tongue, and its contents were rather sensational:

One Saturday she saw Jesus bend down from Heaven and come

toward her with outstretched arms to embrace her. Thereupon she was utterly swallowed up (*absorpta*) in God and lost consciousness (*se deficeret*), so that she had to be carried out of the church. She was filled with such indescribable happiness that she continued to feel it for an entire week.

Or: The Lord called her soul to him and laid his hands upon her hands, his so gracious eyes against her eyes, his ears against her ears, his mouth upon the mouth of the soul. Finally he united his honey-flowing heart to the soul's heart. And in this wise the union of her blissful soul with the Beloved was consummated.

It was not only nuns who sat in a circle around Mechtilde von Hackeborn when she divulged her experiences. So many curious people came to beseech her for information about the fate of their dead relatives that such visits finally had to be stopped.

Too late. The pressure of the public caused her visions to become more and more monotonous. Christ appeared to her punctually during the Mass, he held the watering can when the vineyard had to be watered, he awakened her from sleep at the prescribed hour.

Such a routine threatened to become boring. Now and then, therefore, the visions had to become ever bolder, until Mechtilde, who because of her lovely voice performed the office of choir leader, once again found herself at the foot of the throne of the Most Holy Trinity and besought the Virgin Mary to sing the psalmody in her place, which happened straightaway.

With this, however, rapture had become conventional, making free use of the images that the painters and sculptures of the time included in their repertoire. Rocking baby Jesus in his cradle became a convention too; Mechtilde, along with other visionaries, was entrusted with this task.

Mechtilde of Magdeburg kept a sharp eye out for exaltations of this kind. "That's a childish love," she wrote in her book, *The Flowing Light of Godhead,* about the weakness of her colleagues for the Christ child.

The refined psychological insight of this severe judgment is surprising. Professor Janet, several centuries later, will not get much further. What can he say, when, around Christmas, his patient's breasts grow heavy? She must nurse the child Jesus, but not only that; at intervals she herself becomes a child again, her mouth makes sucking movements as she sits motionless in her chair with her eyes closed. Like the divine child, she is sleeping on Mary's breast.

All things flow. In the visionary prose of the German female mystics, God is liquefied ("O thou flowing God") or melted ("O thou melting God"). Then the loving soul cannot insist so pedantically on her boundaries anymore; she lets the stream flow through her ("a sweet pouring"), yields like heated wax, loses her fixed shape. At such times it's not always easy, neither for the anxious witnesses nor for the affected person herself, to distinguish between mysticism and madness. This was the case with Angela of Foligno, who went through periods when she considered herself insane.

At any rate, the Holy Spirit was capable of some pretty wild behavior with his brides, and total loss of self-control on their part was a frequent result. Regaining that control was important, because otherwise the powers of the individual ego threatened to be lost. A beguine from the duchy of Brabant, the setting for the story of Lohengrin and Elsa, was especially knowledgeable in this area. The lady (who was possibly of ducal blood) was only ten years old when she found her liberator, namely the Holy Spirit (the *heyleghe gheest*). Little is known of her, neither her birth and death dates nor the circumstances of her life, and even her belonging to the high nobility can only be conjectured. Her verse, written in trouvère style, points to a private tutor in the art of the minnesingers, and only people at the highest levels of society could afford such a luxury. At her death, Hadewijch, as she was called, left behind letters to a friend, an autobiographical description of her visions, and forty-five strophic poems. Because Hadewijch mentions in her writings a certain Master Robert ("Le Bougre," a feared inquisitor), who was in Flanders between 1235 and 1238, it is possible that she lived around this time. In any case, her literary works were published circa 1350, in the Middle Dutch language. From this tongue comes the key word *orewoet*, which connotes the vehemence of feminine eroticism when subjected to high tension.

In this linguistic coinage, frenzy or fury (*woet*) is linked to wind or storm (latin *aura*, Old French *ore*) to produce the quintessential locution for a rage that is expressly associated with the pleasures and torments of love (*van minnen*).

"My heart and my veins," Hadewijch wrote,

all my limbs trembled and quaked with desire, and I had the feeling I had often had before, so excruciating and so terrible that every one of my limbs seemed to break in turn, one by one, and all my veins stirred, each one of them filled with pain. I longed to possess and to know my Beloved completely, and in pleasure to taste his human nature to the utmost . . . then he himself came to me and took me all into his arms and pressed me against him, and every one of my limbs felt his in all their ecstasy, according to my heart's desire, according to my human nature. And I was satisfied completely from without.

The *orewoet* can last for half an hour, or, in exceptional cases, for as long as three days. Afterward the habitual misery of a solitary woman returns for a whole long winter. *"Ic was in orewoete,"* Hadewijch notes, and the temptation to translate *orewoete* with "orgasm" is difficult to resist.

It would be wiser to try to find traces of a cardiac infarction, if, that is, the mortal remains of these divinely blissful women were available for an anatomical inspection. One of Hadewijch's contemporaries, the nun Beatris van Tienen (d. 1268), brings every inquiry around to that crucially important muscle in the breast. She writes: "Sometimes courtly love takes control, when it so impetuously and powerfully touches the heart, so immediately and overwhelmingly the soul, that the latter deems the heart to have suffered many a terrible wound; and those wounds are torn open afresh every day amid pain and torment."

Arrows and wounded hearts appear like a recurring theme in the literature of love, among both courtly minnesingers and visionary women, including the most prominent of them all, Saint Teresa of Avila (d. 1582), whose wounding at the hands of the smiling angel can be viewed in the church of Santa Maria della Vittoria in Rome, sculpted in marble by Gian Lorenzo Bernini. It is popularly believed that surgeons examined Teresa's heart long after her death and found that it bore a scar an inch and a half long.

However that may be, let us return to Hadewijch. In an attempt to stabilize herself, she arranged her visions in a certain order: first, second, third, and so on to the final chapter. This arrangement hints at the

possibility of progress, of maturing. The love arrows, however, are continually fired off until the very end.

Therefore it's difficult for Hadewijch to keep her sense of reality
reasonably intact in the face of the visionary world, into which she would
by far prefer to disappear. In that world, she stands at the center of events.
Sun, moon, and stars must pause in their courses, the saints in heaven
must interrupt their songs of praise, solely in order that a mighty revelation may be announced to the enraptured one by, it goes without saying,
Jesus Christ in person.

It is a tribute to this visionary's psychic health that she does not
become addicted to raptures. Her life must prove itself in the everyday, in
disconsolate godforsakenness, in the dark night of the soul, when all
certainties have disappeared and even the memory of visionary events
becomes insipid theatrical pomp, optical illusion, blindness. Then who
can be sure that the names imposed on transcendent reality are anything
more than a vocabulary of helplessness before an abyss of despair? *God was
crueler to me than any devil ever was.* This sentence is from Hadewijch's first
letter to her friend, intended for the domestic use of that friend and the
other tranquil beguines of Antwerp, where Hadewijch may have lived. The
gist of her words: Love is what matters (*minne es al*). Even in coping with
God, we might add.

W ithout the loving presence of a support group of like-minded
associates, even the most gifted visionary can wind up in difficulties. In the godlessness of the French *Belle Époque*, it was inevitable that the
poor Madeleine, alias Scapegoat, would land where the "shrinks" were
already waiting for her.

Dr. Janet, who kept a record of his patient's past life, was very discreet. One must imagine Madeleine's parental home to be somewhere in
northern France. Hers is a family of affluent industrialists. There are three
siblings. Madeleine prefers to be alone. The smallest sound, say the creak-
ing of new shoes, causes her to collapse in a faint. From the early age of
five, she falls into the deepest sadness for weeks at a time. She's told that
she is supposed to suffer pain on behalf of others. She does well in school;

during the holidays she falls in love with a boy of her own age; she takes pleasure in dancing.

This cannot be permitted. She forbids herself alcohol, snacks, music. She has a certain destiny, and therefore, after successfully completing her education as a teacher, she leaves her parents in order to serve those in need of service. She finds work in Germany as a chambermaid, but her employers spoil her too much. She flees into a convent, but little discipline prevails there. Back in France, she works as a maidservant and as a nurse, and then in a factory, until finally she finds happiness caring for a woman who is sick with cancer. This lasts for nine years. She would later tell her doctor, "I constantly felt an inner joy."

Then the decline begins. Obeying an inspiration, she spends the night on a park bench and is arrested. To avoid compromising her family, she refuses to tell the judge her name, and she is sentenced to a year in prison for vagrancy and refusal to give evidence. After six months she's released, but soon she's arrested and convicted again (vagrancy, fraud, prostitution, begging). The list of charges is dictated by that stereotyped ritual that must condemn any conspicuous behavior as an offense against the public order. After another five months, she's a branded woman.

Since her childhood, Madeleine has had visions. During her periods of homelessness, delusions mingle with things actually seen. Madeleine writes letters to parliamentarians, warning them of a conspiracy against France. Ultimately, already under police surveillance, she begins walking around Paris only on tiptoe.

This must be investigated. In the hospitals she is suspected of being a former opera dancer who wants to keep her occupation a secret. Affusions and mesmerism bring about no successful result. At last, at the age of forty, Madeleine lands in the Salpêtrière, under the care of Dr. Janet.

The last twenty years of her life pass peacefully. An anonymous benefactor provides her with a respectable place to live. Madeleine obtains a position in a school for the poor and stops walking on tiptoe. As far as Dr. Janet is concerned, her insanity has been cured.

.   .   .

A half century later, universities are less narrow-minded about what they teach. Discussions of "altered states of consciousness," of trances and ecstasies, are no longer mere recountings of case histories from European and North American mental hospitals. Ethnological research and comparative cultural studies have expanded the concept of psychic normalcy, where there is now room for the experiential wealth of Indian yogis, possessed Brazilians, Siberian shamans, Australian dreamwalkers. If the context is conducive, visions and episodes of flight can be an expression of perceptions whose cognitive value is not necessarily to be set at naught.

A Canadian psychiatrist has gone a step further. He has discovered that mystical experiences also occur among people who work at executive levels in industry, and that such experiences can be beneficial in maintaining proper psychic balance. A point in Madeleine's (and her medieval sisters') favor.

The conclusion of a more or less impartial evaluation of some exceptional women of yesteryear is that what is normal and what is not count only within definite cultural (social, societal, political) conventions and constraints. The *heyleghe gheest* in Antwerp follows these conventions as little as *lo spirito* in Siena, circa 1300. Whoever automatically declares him to be the product of madness on that account is merely sympathizing with the police.

# Sister Katrei

BLASPHEMOUS NONSENSE. THAT WAS, IN 1957, the judgment of a specialist concerning the work of an unknown male or female author of the late Middle Ages. The object of this professorial pique was an anonymously written Alemannic text, datable to around 1320, and bearing a somewhat elaborate title: *Daz ist Swester Katrei Meister Ekehartes Tohter von Strazburc* ("This is Sister Katrei of Strasbourg,

Meister Eckhart's Daughter"). The specialist's uncompromising condemnation makes one curious.

At issue is the tale of a relationship between the famous Meister Eckhart and a woman whom he directs as her confessor, a beguine named Katrei (Catherine), who soon turns out to be a freethinking personality par excellence. The first time, she comports herself entirely obsequiously, and her spiritual guide admonishes her to obey the Ten Commandments and sin no more. At their next meeting, she's cheekier, announces that she is no longer satisfied with being a follower of Christ, and contemplates the highest goal of all mysticism, union with God; the Holy Spirit shall help her achieve this. She separates herself from her family and from all material security and chooses a life of penniless wandering in foreign lands. When she returns, she is transformed. So much has she changed that the Meister no longer recognizes her and sees in her an angel. He looks for her and finds her in a church, where she confesses to him that she's still not capable of attaining the mystical union in a permanent way. This is the moment when her confessor proves himself an initiate in these matters and gives the woman the advice her situation requires. She must renounce every sort of desire. Soon Katrei sinks into the void, into the formlessness and calm of Eckhart's spirituality, and reaches her goal. *Herre, fröwent üch mitt mir, ich bin gott worden* ("Gentlemen, rejoice with me, I have become God"). She falls into a deep trance that lasts three days, and she awakens from it with the intention of living as inconspicuously as possible in the future, without excessive mortification, unassuming and ready to help. Her detachment from all desire is so radical that the choice between heaven and hell has become a matter of indifference to her. When the Meister asks her whether she has now permanently vanished "into the naked godhead," her answer is Yes.

Blasphemous nonsense? Sister Katrei's radical position had been formulated long since, at least in theory, by Shankara, or Samkaracarya, a philosopher and founder of a religious order, who renounced the world around 810 A.D. This most famous of Indian thinkers taught a rigorous monism (*advaita*), in which only the pulsating, all-pervading, self-knowing cosmic Spirit-principle is real, while everything else (stars, molecules, gods, angels, animals, men and women, plants, sacred writings, stocks, tortures, coronations, etc.) constitutes an illusion (*maya*). Even in India, people found this particular intellectual fare difficult to digest. It did away with personified (and thus adorable) deities and was thus not exactly healthy for traditional religion, but that made absolutely no difference to the yellow-clad renunciators. While Europe was still occupied with the migration of peoples, Indians were already striving toward mystical union (*samadhi*). Along the way they made use of a rich, multifarious, available store of highly elaborated methods of mystical contemplation, compared with which the pious cultures of Christianity and Islam seem decidedly undeveloped.

Mystical union with the Brahman was the practical answer to the theoretical illusionism of Shankara and his school. Anyone who wants to push on to ultimate reality must disappear into it.

This very topic, more or less unconcealed, is the subject of Sister Katrei's little book. This seems all the more amazing insofar as she had no recognizable contact with kindred spirits in India. Katrei's program is encoded in a Christian way, with *Gott* in the place of *Brahman*. But the nature of such material makes Katrei better suited to the banks of the Ganges than to Strasbourg. And the fact that the central figure in this treatise is a woman renders the whole business even more confusing. To attribute such experiences to a woman would have been unacceptable for the classical spirituality of India.

The solution to the riddle lies in the transcultural nature of authentic mysticism. India may be considered its homeland, but it also emerged among Jews, Christians, and Muslims. Because mysticism tends to consider the tenets laid down by the great established faiths as mere deception, it makes all dogmatists uncomfortable. On March 26, 922, the dervish Husayn ibn Mansur al-Hallaj was executed for having uttered, in Arabic, a shout of joy identical to the one Katrei describes. Meister Eckhart was spared a comparable fate only because of his timely demise. Sister Katrei may be a fictitious character, but that makes her program no less explosive.

The renowned religious scholar and ordained monk Agehananda Bharati (born Leopold Fischer, in Vienna, 1923; d. 1991), one of the few mysticism experts who deserve the name, proposed the expression "zero-experience" for the authentic mystical state. This state occurs, as Bharati stressed again and again, only very rarely. He himself experienced it for the first time, spontaneously and most unexpectedly, as a schoolboy—though a baptized Catholic, he was developing a strong inclination toward Indian culture. "I was falling asleep," Bharati wrote, "when the whole world turned into one entity, one indivisible certainty, of which I was at the center; for a fraction of a minute perhaps, I saw nothing, felt nothing, but was that oneness, empty of content and feeling. Then, during a five-minute phase of subsidence, the visual faculty and the ability to reflect returned, along with the inalienable knowledge that this was not the last time."

Indeed, Bharati underwent the zero-experience three more times: during the Second World War in France, then in India, where he spent eight years and was received into an order of monks, and finally in the United States, at the beginning of his university teaching career. The summary of his experience and knowledge of authentic mysticism is formulated rather laconically: the zero-experience comes to those to whom it comes, regardless of what they do; it also comes to those few who try very hard over a long period of time. To attain it permanently remains an unfulfillable wish.

Accordingly Sister Katrei's declaration that she has entered definitively into the naked godhead should be read not as a statement of fact, but as an objective or goal of the most audacious kind, originating in the circles of freethinking beguine women who lived in Strasbourg during Eckhart's time. The theological point thus made is as plain as it is risky. Only when a person engaged in a religious search stops placing the object of her adoration outside herself has she reached the goal of her learning. Then there is no more Other—not because of a burned-out godlessness that no longer recognizes the existence of anything with which it might fuse, but rather because of the joyous abolition of all opposites, which are resolved and remain in solution.

The fourteenth century, the witness to such lack of restraint, was characterized by plague, famine, and war. By the end of the century, the population of Europe had declined from 73,000,000 to 45,000,000.

The Golden Age of the female Christian mystics was one long dance of death.

The Indian alternative offered a way of escape from this depressing world. "Lord, what is thy command?" Mechtilde of Magdeburg asked her God this question and received the following answer: "Lady Soul, you must take off your clothes. You are so entirely united with me (*genaturt in mich*) that there can be nothing between us any longer."

The Holy Spirit refrained from blowing in the hidden chamber where this wedding took place. *Nirvana* can be translated as "becalmed wind." What's going on outside is insignificant. *Der mensche ist tot aller werlt und lebet in gote und got in ihm* ("Man is dead to all the world and lives in God and God in him"). Even the crucified Christ, with whom the ecstatic women so gladly fuse, is inaccessible to the world, for the simple reason that he's already dead. What then does it mean, when the pestilential corpses lie, unburied and stinking, under the cross? Only that God's ventricle, pierced by the lance thrust, is still dripping blood.


# Metabolism


*I*N OCTOBER 1942, SIMONE WEIL PUT down on paper her most urgent desire. Only God could fulfill it. She wished to be transformed into food.

"Father, in the name of Christ grant me this." This is the beginning of the incredible prayer in which Simone precisely enumerates everything that she has at her disposal—and asks that it all be given as nourishment to those who otherwise will starve in body and soul.

Simone wants to renounce bodily movement. She will be left a complete cripple who no longer feels even so much as an impulse to move her little finger.

Then it's the turn of her faculties of perception. Away with them. No colors, no sounds.

Her final offering is her ability to think. Simone doesn't want to retain the ability to make the slightest connection between two thoughts.

God the Father is entrusted with processing the offer into usable material. He is to devour Simone's vital energy and transform it into "Christ's substance," which will then be supplied to the body of mankind.

The time requested for the beginning of this chemical process? Immediately.

Six months later, Simone Weil learned that she had tuberculosis.

The physicians in the Middlesex Hospital prescribed nourishing food. Although she was weak and had lost a great deal of weight, the patient nonetheless ate but little. Her temperature was 94.4 degrees. Was there anything she particularly wanted? Yes, perhaps a couple of cherries.

In the last months of her life, Simone Weil's reading was the *Bhagavad Gita*, with the Sanskrit textbook beside her. Indian Krishna, Egyptian Osiris, Jewish Jesus—the dying woman was not alone. In addition, she was visited by a Catholic clergyman, who gave her his blessing, by Maurice Schumann, the politician, and by Guigui, one of her old trade union comrades. Smoking, her single vice, was naturally forbidden.

"Let nothing remain of me," Simone had demanded of God. This desire was not fulfilled.

It was only relatively late in her short life that Simone came upon the idea of expressing her strivings in the language of religion. She had completed her course of study at the famous École Normale Supérieure and taken up her first post at the girls' lycée in Le Puy in 1931; why should this young teacher have gone to church? There were no unions in the Middle Ages. The Red Virgin, as Simone had been called since her student days, marched with a delegation of a hundred unemployed to see the mayor and then appeared with them at a meeting of the city council, thus causing the conservative press to cry scandal. The police wanted to know whether she had indeed gone into a café with some workers, and the school inspector demanded an explanation of her behavior. "The national university administration," Weil wrote in the bulletin of the National Teachers' Union of the Haute-Loire, "lags several thousand years behind human civilization. It still lives under the caste system."

The following school year the troublesome teacher was transferred to Auxerre. Because she was disinclined to give her students tests, two thirds of them failed the final examination. Her next stop: Roanne. In early December 1932, Comrade Weil demonstrated—of course—with the miners against cuts in their wages and was allowed to carry the red flag. From the podium in the great hall of the Labor Exchange in Saint-Etienne, she shouted to the crowd: "We must arm ourselves against Fascism, and I mean that literally!"

The list of people with whom Simone Weil was politically associated reads like an almanac of the French Left. Thévenon, Guérin, Battaille, Serret. Simone saw in Rosa Luxemburg (d. 1919) a kindred soul. "Her life, her work, her letters affirm life and not death," wrote Simone. "Rosa aspired to action, not to sacrifice. In this sense, there is nothing Christian in her temperament."

There were differences with Trotsky. The revolutionary, banished from Russia, took up residence in France in July 1933 under the strict condition that he should not take part in any political gathering. This in no way prevented him from sharply attacking an article that Simone published in the August 25 issue of the journal *Révolution Prolétarienne*. Simone was of the opinion that the communist regime in the Soviet Union looked a great deal like the fascist dictatorships in Europe. Trotsky was furious. "Simone Weil speaks majestically of our 'illusions,' he wrote in *La Vérité*. "Many years will have to pass for her and her like before they free themselves of the most reactionary petty bourgeois prejudices."

Trotsky was called "Papa" among the Leftists. "Papa has done me the honor of attacking me," Simone wrote to her mother in Paris. "It's too bad I won't get a chance to meet him."

But she did. Simone had learned that Trotsky was looking for an opportunity to get together with political friends. In the building where Simone's parents, the Weils, lived, there was a vacant apartment that belonged to them. After the Christmas holidays in 1933, Trotsky appeared in the Rue Auguste-Comte for a few days' stay, accompanied by his wife and two bodyguards. To avoid being recognized, he had shaved off his goatee and mustache. Returning from a movie one evening, Papa and entourage overloaded the service elevator and got stuck between floors. After these efforts to remain inconspicuous, the secret conference began. During a break, Simone had a discussion with Trotsky. Papa was not about to let himself be criticized by a little daughter of the bourgeoisie for having signed the order to fire upon the sailors in Kronstadt in 1921, and he began shouting at her.

"This is the chair he was sitting on," Simone said quite proudly to a friend a few days later. Then the holiday season was over, and Simone had to go back to Roanne.

There, during the course of the next few months, it became clear to her that political activism was not for her, especially in view of a disaster that she saw coming more clearly than her comrades in the workers' movement. In the meantime, word had spread among members of the Left that Simone Weil had the clearest head on her shoulders since Rosa Luxemburg. Simone worked for a year on a long essay that was to be her farewell to Marxism, her Testament, as she jokingly called it. It was not printed.

"I knew her very well," Trotsky wrote in a letter of July 30, 1936, to his comrade Victor Serge. "I have had long discussions with her. For a period of time she was more or less in sympathy with our cause, but then she lost faith in the proletariat and in Marxism. It's possible that she will turn toward the left again. But is it worth the trouble to talk about this any longer?"

It was. In the midst of Europe's gathering darkness, this highly gifted, intellectual young woman took a year off from her teaching duties for purposes of study. Simone Weil began her studies on December 4, 1934, as an unskilled worker in a factory owned by the Alsthom Company, which built electrical machinery. She learned to place heavy copper bobbins in a furnace and then take them out again without burning her hands and arms too severely.

She's killing herself, her father told a friend. Simone wanted to find out how a person could get through life on the wages of a factory worker. When her parents invited her to supper, she placed on the table the money that she would have spent in a restaurant. She learned what it meant to be laid off and unable to get a new job. Her last factory employment was with Renault, where she worked as a milling-machine operator from the beginning of June to the end of August 1935. Then her sabbatical came to an end. She summarized in one word the knowledge she had gained about factory working conditions: inhuman. She also said: "This year killed my youth."

Simone Weil had reached the fourth rung on the ladder of the soul, as described by Marguerite Porete.

Three years passed before Simone reached the fifth rung, in November 1938. Once again, her headaches were ruining any possibility of clear thought. The only thing that helped her was a poem by the English poet George Herbert (d. 1633), a poem she embraced wholeheartedly. Its title was "Love."

While Simone, with her skull about to burst, was reciting this poem to herself, suddenly, from far away and yet so familiar, the Other was there, in person, amorphous, evident, tender, overwhelming. Simone gave him a name: Christ. In the same month, in Germany, six hundred Jewish synagogues were destroyed during a single night.

"On a dark night I went out unobserved," wrote the Spanish poet and mystic Juan de la Cruz (d. 1591), whose poems Simone was later to read. Juan called the road that leads out of the darkened world spiritual negation (*el camino de la negación espiritual*). Without rigorous self-negation there can be no blissful affirmation, no rapturous Yes. Simone surpassed her colleagues from Catholic Spain in logicality, because she grasped that the Church, too, must be negated spiritually, the Church with its choral singing, its Holy Mass in the Latin language, its sacred hosts.

In 1938, Simone and her mother went to Solesmes to hear the Benedictines there, who were renowned for their beautiful singing of Gregorian chants, perform the liturgy of the Easter season. Simone and Mme. Weil spent ten days at Solesmes, from Palm Sunday to Easter Tuesday. Because of her headaches, which were growing more and more severe, Simone's teaching career was by then definitively over. "Each sound hurt me like a blow," Simone later wrote, referring to the Easter services in the abbey's church. "But by an extreme effort of concentration I was able to separate myself from the pain and to find a pure and perfect joy."

In Marseilles, where Simone Weil and her parents took refuge from the advancing Germans in the fall of 1940, the final and most subtle temptation awaited the philosopher. It was provided by a Dominican priest, whose name was Jean-Marie Perrin. This ascetic man was nearly blind and spoke in a gentle voice. Simone put her trust in him at once. He had been recommended to her because she wanted to work in the country-side as an agricultural laborer. Perrin put her in contact with the commit-ted Catholic author Gustave Thibon, who had a farm in Provence. Si-mone, however, continued to return to the busy pastor and patiently waited her turn to speak to him. Before long, he brought up the question of baptism.

No. How could Indian Krishna, Egyptian Osiris, all the folk religions with which Simone felt an affinity, find a place within a Church that declared itself the only means of attaining blessedness?

The priest thought that these difficulties would lessen with the pas-sage of time.

Simone already found herself within the magnetic field of the Catho-lic Church, attracted by the Gregorian music, enchanted by the *Poverello* of Assisi. She longed to partake of the small, white, wheaten disc, the form in which Christ's body presented itself, satisfying supernatural hunger without burdening the digestive organs.

But the priests, whose anointed fingers distributed the hosts, set cer-tain conditions. Simone wanted to be clear about them, but in her studies of Catholic dogma she kept running across two little words: *Anathema sit.*

That was the formula, in use since the beginnings of Christianity, for cursing those who thought differently. They were to be excluded, handed over to the devil, excommunicated—however "anathema" was translated, it always drew a boundary, erected a wall, differentiated between within and without. If Simone considered it possible to believe that the Second Per-son of God had been realized not only in the flesh of the Nazarene but also (for example) in the figure of Krishna, then came the anathema.

Why did she want to know everything so precisely? Simone peppered the priests with questions about the condemnation of a third-century heretic whose name she remembered only vaguely from her student days. Finally one Benedictine priest lost patience. Baptism must be denied to a heretic.

Before Simone and her parents left Marseilles, she wrote a long letter to Father Perrin. Since the Albigensians were wiped out, she said, the Catholic Church had established a sort of totalitarianism in Europe. Without readiness to undergo a fundamental change, Simone wrote, the Church was unfit to operate effectively in the modern world.

On May 14, 1942, the steamship *Maréchal-Lyautey* sailed for Casablanca with the emigrants on board. As she was taking leave of her friends, Simone smiled and pointed to the sea. "If we are torpedoed, what a beautiful baptismal font!"

In the memoirs of one of Simone Weil's school friends, there is the following sentence: *She seemed to us like a saint of the Middle Ages.*

# *Freedom's*

# *Air*

O N  FEBRUARY  11,  1990,  THREE  MONTHS  AF-

*ter the fall of the Berlin Wall, Nelson Mandela was released from prison in South Africa*

*after a confinement of twenty-seven years. He said: We have waited too long for our*

*freedom. We can wait no longer.*

*With these words began a new chapter of an old tale in which happy days had only rarely interrupted the long periods of waiting, and in which there had been many setbacks, many defeats. At the beginning of the story stood the wish that the man Moses had expressed to the Egyptian Pharaoh: Let my people go.*

*The miracle that transformed a slave people into a self-assured confederation didn't take place overnight. The power that was to bring it about is called "Spirit" in the Bible.*

*The appropriate passages from the books of Moses were read with special attention whenever struggles for liberation were under way—in England, for example, during Oliver Cromwell's rule, when a crowned head of Europe had fallen to the headsman's axe for the first time.*

*From the British, who were their occupying army, black South Africans received the Bible and turned its message against their overlords. We were obliged to learn, said Mandela, that we had no other choice but to arm ourselves; our oppressors forced us to do so.*

# The Red Thread

"THE DEAD ARE COMING AGAIN." SO wrote the Marxist philosopher Ernst Bloch after the end of the First World War, when there was hope of a communist Germany. "The dead are coming again, they will be active among us once more."

This sentence was printed in 1921, in the book that Bloch wrote about Thomas Müntzer, the "theologian of revolution." By the time this book appeared, it had become an obituary to the dream that had envisioned an imminent victory for the working class. In the interval between composition and publication, the shades of the dead had vanished again until the next opportunity.

One of the revenants who found no peace in the grave was that same Thomas Müntzer, whose head, after his execution on May 27, 1525, had been stuck up "in the field" outside the town of Müllhausen. Müntzer came knocking on Bloch's door in the company of Lenin. Bloch thought that Müntzer, an implacable organizer in the German Peasants' War, was absolutely the equal of the Russian revolutionary. Bloch also believed that he himself was a witness to times pregnant with great significance, and it seemed imperative to look toward Moscow. "The last earthly revolution is being born," the philosopher wrote; "the heirs of journeyman weavers and cloth-workers' apprentices are included in the agenda, they can no longer be driven away."

*The dead are coming again.* In his masterpiece, *The Principle of Hope*, written in the United States between 1938 and 1947, Bloch passes in review a contingent of all the idealists who planned to set the world to rights, not just the warlike freedom fighters. Behind Müntzer appeared Jesus, and behind him Moses, illumined by the burning bush that would not be consumed. From that bush issued the earliest call to revolt against the whiplash and the master's house.

Martin Luther, Müntzer's contemporary and polar opposite, was not to be found among the dead whose return Bloch desired.

Because he was of Jewish extraction, Ernst Bloch (1885–1977) was forced to emigrate to the United States. After the war, in 1949, he accepted an invitation from the University of Leipzig, remained in the German Democratic Republic until the building of the Berlin Wall, and lived thereafter, from 1961 until his death, in the West German town of Tübingen. His writings can be read as a commentary on Beethoven's opera *Fidelio.* Whenever the philosopher heard the trumpet call in the second act, tears always came to his eyes.

During the sixties, Bloch's fame as a thinker quickly began to spread, and not only in the German-speaking countries. Wherever the old gentleman (white mane, thick eyeglasses, aquiline features) appeared, journalists fought each other for a chance to speak to the master. He would hold his pipe in his hand and formulate answers that didn't need retouching: *The world itself doesn't yet know whether it's coming or going. We are the last act.*

*Socialism has not yet even begun. Marxism is, so to speak, much older than Marx. An essential element of hope is that it can be disappointed. We must bring German imagination back to Marxism. And therefore Hegelian philosophy has, as it were, no room for the future. Midwifery is the tenor of every book I've written. We live in very paltry times. Evil comes unobserved. A seventeen-year-old actress was significantly more important to me than philosophy professor Lipps. In any case, a student movement is better than nothing at all.*

At the end of August 1968, just as Bloch was reading a paper before the World Congress of Philosophy in Vienna, someone slipped him a note: *Russian tanks in Prague.* Bloch launched into a tirade, and the entire contingent of philosophers from the Eastern bloc rose as one man and left the hall.

Bloch nevertheless persisted in maintaining what he had written in *The Principle of Hope:* The end of the tunnel is in sight, not from Palestine, to be sure, but from Moscow; *ubi* Lenin, *ibi* Jerusalem. Zionism leads to socialism, or it leads nowhere at all.

For the philosopher, the New Jerusalem of the Apocalypse remained bound up with the name of Lenin, with the October Revolution, with (as Bloch expressed it) the betrothal period of socialism. In Vienna, Bloch said that what the Russians had done in Prague was the opposite of Marxism.

The fact that betrothal and pregnancy had led to a miscarriage could do nothing to challenge the Spirit, to whom Bloch remained loyal. How many ships had already gone down on the voyage to the land of freedom? Even as it sank, the principle of hope nailed its banner to the mast. Setting off was more important than arriving.

The year 1968 likewise marked the appearance of a book, written by Bloch, in which the red thread that runs through Christianity was exposed. The work was provocatively titled *Atheism in Christianity,* by which Bloch meant a theological program that did without the presence in heaven of an authoritarian, paternal God. Bloch's God was kicking like a fetus in the womb of the world, and this was his slogan: What is not now can yet come to be. The philosopher countered the text of the Bible, which was used to maintain the Church's authority, with another interpretation; it went against the grain, and its logical conclusions were surprising.

For Bloch, the book that lay on Christian altars and purported to contain the word of God was a manipulated text, a smoothed-down version in which any notion of rebellion was an abomination. For example, the passage in the book of Numbers that describes the rebellion led by Korah, including God's dreadful judgment against the blasphemers, permits an alternate reading, according to which this tale, like an island in the ocean of correctness, is all that remains of a rebelliousness, of a vanished spirit of political revolt. Bloch saw such islands as the mountain peaks of a sunken country whose exploration was as exciting as a deep-sea expedition.

The philosopher drew the inspiration for his enterprise from the gypped and cheated of all history; to the unstopped ear, their grumbling was still completely audible. The Bible's heavy-laden laborers, Dostoyevsky's insulted and injured, still made up two thirds of the population of the earth, from Cairo and Delhi to Mexico City. For the most part, they lacked the words to give theological, moral, political grounds for their complaints. Bloch, therefore, read Holy Scripture as a *biblia pauperum,* as a Bible of the poor, and in it he sought out every passage that could be used against the bosses, every verse that had always been quoted when the burden became too heavy. *Let my people go.*

Among all the Marxist thinkers, Bloch was the only one for whom the Bible was not a book to be tossed aside but rather a timetable for travel to the land of freedom. "Where there is hope, there is also religion," wrote the leftist thinker, expressly in the present tense, and with a likewise express stab at his fellow Marxists, most of whom felt a hearty revulsion for all religion. For them, it was a sanctimonious leftover from the conditions of feudalism; the most one could say for religion was that a study of the history of heresy in Europe revealed a certain foreshadowing of the socialist idea.

Bloch's attitude was different. Among the heretics, dissidents, enthusiasts, and rebels of former times, he thought, there was a defiance, rooted in the Bible, that continued to work its effect up to the present and into the future. He would distill into the textbooks of Marxism—drop by drop, as it were—that irrational oil without which revolutionary prose degenerates into ideological clattering.

To the great astonishment of his fellow party philosophers, Bloch developed a special fondness for the Edenic serpent, whose counsel had had such weighty consequences. It wasn't written anywhere that the serpent had lied. One Christian sect of late antiquity considered it the reasonable antagonist of the despot God, a fact that Bloch dug up with the greatest delight, as it supported his thesis about the "subversive fractures in the Bible."

Bloch was equally pleased to give his attention to the "Exodus-light," which had shown the children of Israel, definitively and irrevocably, the way to the Promised Land.

In 1970, the Peruvian priest Gustavo Gutiérrez published his "notes for a theology of liberation." He wrote: "The poor, the wretched of the earth, are not questioning the religious world or its philosophical presuppositions; rather they are calling into question the economic, social, and political order that oppresses and marginalizes them."

And the Chilean Jesuit Gonzalo Arroyo added: "Christian humanism, whose objective is the kingdom of God, and Marxist humanism, whose objective is the classless society, must be society's inspiring force."

Bloch's philosophy of the future had got some company, but not of the atheistic kind.


After 1989, the future received a great deal of bad press. The idea of a classless society was in such disgrace that from now on it was propagated almost exclusively in Chinese, in the party-run universities of the Middle Kingdom. Elsewhere, a full dozen subsidized underground armies suddenly found themselves without contributions from Moscow. In compensation, they gained two new slogans: one about the New World Order, and the other about society in the Information Age. The question of which automatic process would see that even the poorest devil got his municipal housing unit had somehow been forgotten. Had the red thread running through human history hidden itself in the Internet?

One fine day even Ernst Bloch's *Atheism in Christianity* will be able to be called up on a computer. Then, with the press of a key, this sentence will appear on the screen: *True creativity has as its subject, pouring himself out into us— the Holy Spirit.*

# O, My Deare Lords

ON THE MORNING OF JULY 13, 1524, the preacher and caretaker of souls, Thomas Müntzer, parish priest in the church of Saint John in the Saxon town of Allstedt, put on his finest apparel. He had been summoned to the castle to give a sort of specimen sermon to the brother and co-regents of the sovereign. The Elector, Duke Johann of Saxony, had brought along his son, Crown Prince Johann Friedrich, who like his father and uncle was an adherent of the Lutheran cause and interested in theological questions.

Müntzer, an ordained Catholic priest with a master's degree in liberal arts, thirty-five years old and recently married, was not a quantity unknown to these great lords. His wedding ceremony had not been the only action of his that contravened the laws of the time. In Zwickau, where Müntzer was active from May 1520 to April 1521, the vehement man had mounted the pulpit and called for violent measures against the unworthy monks and clerics of the old faith, whereupon his listeners had stoned a clergyman named Hofer and hounded him through the streets. It was said that Müntzer was a *schwirmig geyst,* a fantast or zealot; *schwirmig* derived from the word for "swarm," as in bees, and implied in this case their readiness to sting.

Moreover, Müntzer had made an unfavorable impression with his sharp attacks on a little pilgrimage church that stood outside the gates of Allstedt. Subsequently a few men had set fire to this shrine, on Maundy Thursday, no less, and the result was the lodging of a complaint in the chancellery of the crown prince.

As the preacher made his way to the castle, it must have been clear to him that the burning of the chapel had been a point in his disfavor. He planned, therefore, to draw attention to the mollycoddled clerics of an obdurate Christianity and its idolatrous worship of miraculous images instead of daily Bible study with singing, readings, and instructive sermons.

Half a dozen grave gentlemen, draped in fine cloth, were awaiting Müntzer; they were the two princes and their escort, which included Brück, the chancellor of Electoral Saxony. Hans Zeiss, the senior civil servant of Allstedt, was also present. To begin with, the second chapter of the Book of the Prophet Daniel was read to these lords, first in Latin and then in German. This was the text that Müntzer intended to interpret for the princes: the story of the mighty Nebuchadnezzar, king and lord of Babylon, whose vivid dreams gave him no peace until Daniel revealed to him the significance of the stone that shattered the kingdoms of the earth.

There could be no clearer formulation of the basic rule that governed the relationship between God's messengers and the powerful of this world, the "big fellowes," as Müntzer was pleased to call them. Their only chance to avoid annihilation lay in their preparedness to take their stance resolutely on Christ. "O, my deare lords," said Müntzer, "how prettily will God with His rod of iron dash the olde pots in pieces, as it is written in the second Psalm. Therefore, my most deare, my most esteemed lords, learn your judgement aright, from the mouth of God. The poore laity and the villeins do see more sharply than you."

This "Sermon to the Princes" (which soon found its way into print) probably lasted about two hours. Its main section treats of the "holy ghost," whom the scribes have made into a mockery, as Müntzer expressed it.

In Müntzer's view, the scribes were sitting not only in Rome, but also in Wittenberg, Luther's headquarters. There was no room in Wittenberg for bizarre characters whose current was always switched on and who spewed out their inspirations on street corners. The cloth-maker Nicolaus Storch of Zwickau, for example, was a fervent funnel of God's word and had attracted a following, but Luther sent the wretch packing, calling him a rabble-rouser and a counterfeit prophet, while Müntzer declared of him, "He hath the holy ghost."

In his sermon before the most esteemed rulers, Müntzer took care not to mention Storch's name. People in high places still remembered the riot that Müntzer and Storch had incited among the cloth-workers' apprentices of Zwickau with audacious speeches denouncing the spiritual authorities. The laity must become our prelates and our priests, Müntzer had asserted, and yielded the pulpit of Saint Catherine's to Storch, who was only too happy to proclaim the arrival of the Pentecostal fire among the ordinary people, here and now, in the last days before the violent birth pangs would cease and all values be overturned.

That had happened three years previously. Now Müntzer had the opportunity to expound his Spirit-theology to those who made the decisions about the course of the Reformation in Saxony, and also about the future of the troublesome man they were listening to. He laid his finger on the Gospel according to Saint John, chapter six, verse sixty-three, where it is written that it is the spirit that gives life. Müntzer carried on, saying that his "deare brothers" had to be prepared daily for God's revelation, whereby they might experience "the noble puissance, the oncoming of the holy ghost, who is our Maister in the feare of God."

That sounded quite edifying. For refined ears, however, this doctrine of the presence of the Spirit contained the presumptuousness and aversion to proper order that gave the lowest gutter whore hope of becoming a landing pad for the heavenly dove and slighted the self-important university professors and privy councillors who stuck to prescribed regulations and treated suspect prophets and their visions, dreams, and raptures with the greatest reserve.

Müntzer went on to say, quoting the Book of Daniel, that a dream of revelation had been sent even to a heathen despot, to that same Nebuchadnezzar, a message of the greatest prophetic power that outlined the five ages of history, and the sages and soothsayers whom the king consulted had remained baffled.

So how could one distinguish false or imaginary visions and inspirations from those that were true and sent from God? Müntzer refused to accept the common opinion that the Holy Spirit had ceased all activity after the days of the Lord Jesus and his apostles.

Quite calmly, as if Müntzer had to deal with a spiritual question and not with an explosive political issue in which Martin Luther was his opponent, the "Sermon to the Princes" took up the teaching of the German Friends of God, who demanded the strictest detachment from all the comforts of the flesh as the prerequisite for the arrival of the clear word of God in the depths of the soul: "Perchance now you will ask how it cometh into the hearte. It cometh down from God above in a great astonishment. And if there be one who hath not become aware of this and responsive to it through the living witnesse of God, then can he have nothing of substance to say about God, though he had gorged himself on a hundred thousand bibles."

That was plain enough. Obviously the preacher was distancing himself from Luther's insistence on the written word, from appeals to the reliability of the Bible, and claiming for himself an inspired authority that made him a new Daniel and his audience descendants of the Babylonian king whose kingdom stood on feet of clay. Müntzer was speaking one year after the revolt of the knights under Franz von Sickingen and a few months before the German Peasants' War. He could speak openly and frankly to his audience only with express reference to the Spirit of God, which, he said, is revealing at this time to many unworldly, pious men that a full and invincible reformation must needs be carried out, and that ere long. With the power of the sword, Müntzer added, making sure there was no misunderstanding about the Holy Spirit's intentions. Such a statement was thoroughly consonant with the preacher's desire to provoke great astonishment in his illustrious listeners.

Any further objections? "And here will our learned men reprove me, holding up the kindnesse of Christ," Müntzer went on, with a sidelong glance at Brother Soft Life in Wittenberg, who shrank from spilling blood to defend the Gospel. Must the Holy Spirit expressly remind the princely lords of the significance of the sword that they always carried at their side, their right hand resting on the pommel? They were armed in order that they might not let the idolatrous live any longer, as it was written in Exodus 22. Whosoever let his sword rust would have it taken from him.

War, therefore. To separate the godless from the elect. A clean-up operation. "Otherwise will the Christian church not return to its source. We must teare out the tares from God's vineyard in the time of harvest, for then will the fair red wheat gain firm roots and growe aright. But the Angels, who sharpen their sickles to this end, are God's earnest servants who carry out the wrath of godly wisdom. And this shall our esteemed fathers, the princes, do, that they may roote out the godless. Do but be bold! And may he, to whom all power is given in heaven and on earth, as it is written in Matthew his last chapter, bless and keep ye, my dearest ones, for ever."

Our sources do not reveal the reactions of the illustrious audience. All that is mentioned is a discussion between Müntzer and the chancellor, Brück, who cautioned the parish priest or preacher not to have anything printed without the prior permission of the sovereign prince's representatives.

During the night of August 7, the Allstedt priest bade farewell to his young wife, climbed over the city walls, and set off in a westerly direction. He wrote the town council a letter, stating that his cause had made it necessary for him to take to the road.

The cause in question led him to Mühlhausen, where the political barometer was already indicating a storm.

Luther, when he learned of this change of location, immediately sent a letter addressed to the reverend and wise lord mayor, the council, and the entire municipality of Mühlhausen. "Since it hath been noised abroad"—wrote Luther—"how a certain Maister Thomas Müntzer doth intend to betake himself to you in your towne, we wish hereby to give you true counsel and warn you from his teachings. May it please you therefore to prepare yourselves against this false prophet and spirit, who goeth about in sheep's clothing but is within a ravening wolf."

Luther had previously (in July) prepared a longer text against Müntzer and dispatched it as an open letter to the dukes of Saxony, bidding them to be on their guard against the revolutionary spirit. "The outcast Satan," Luther declared, "has settled in Your Princely Grace's principality and made for himself a nest in Allstedt. And spouts forth his words most courageously, as though he were filled with three holy spirits. He must be a wicked spirit, who cannot otherwise shew himself than by smashing of churches and burning of holy images."

In November, Müntzer struck back with a pamphlet that was printed in Nuremberg and immediately confiscated: "A highly provoked Defense and Answer against the spiritlesse softliving Flesh in Wittenberg, that with Perversion and Robbery of Holy Writ hath so grievously besmirched our piteous Christendom."

The controversy between Luther and Müntzer revolved around the single question of whether or not the Holy Spirit was a revolutionary force.

The earliest description of revolutionary politics can be found in the Book of the Departure (Exodus) in the Bible, written during the millennium before the birth of Christ. It depicts the enslavement of the children of Israel in Egypt, the calling of Moses, the ten plagues, the departure and march to the Red Sea, the journey through the desert and the making of the covenant with the Ten Commandments, the incident of the golden calf and the erection of the Tent of God. The narrative was amplified and extended in the Book of Numbers with the account of the Israelites' arrival in the land of Canaan, later known as Palestine.

Academic historical research has long since moved away from interpreting the stories about Israel's departure from Egypt as narratives of fact. The oldest biblical texts concerning Moses and the Exodus were set down in writing only some three hundred years after the events they describe, and another five hundred years passed before the definitive version was produced. It contains numerous inconsistencies and contradictions. So far no one has succeeded in making even so much as a halfway reliable reconstruction of what may have taken place in the region between the Nile and the Jordan around the year 1200 B.C.

This does no damage whatsoever to the cause for which Müntzer took to the road. When the priest from Allstedt stepped before the princes in order to read them the riot act, he was playing a role that had been performed often before, among other places in the Book of Daniel, in which the prophet, armed with the might of the Spirit, faces the Babylonian king. Such a role was as topical in 1524 as it had been at the time of Ramses II. In the original version, the all-powerful Pharaoh, lord of life and death, is confronted with the man Moses and his political demand that a definitive end be put to the oppression of his people. This is the script that Müntzer was following when he said, "The poore laity and the villeins do see more sharply than you." Whether the original performance of this drama was played out exactly as the Bible describes it is relatively unimportant. What counts is the script of the meeting between master and servant, with the liberating trumpet call in the background.

The script expressly states that Moses did not confront Pharaoh single-handedly. Moses constantly protests to the disembodied voice that urges him on, saying that he is utterly unsuited for the task that is being assigned to him. Only reluctantly, as though under compulsion, does he finally obey. Because it announces so outrageous a project, the imperious voice from the burning bush leaves no doubt about its subversive nature. It calls into question something that belongs to the world as naturally as the weather—the difference between the free person and the slave. Such tact-lessness would not even have occurred to the gods. The voice comes from somewhere out of their jurisdiction. It gives itself a new name and strictly punishes its use so that it won't degenerate into small change in the religion business.

The process set in motion by the voice is progressive. It doesn't ordain an ultimate return to a familiar home after long wandering, as in the case of Odysseus, but a march into the unknown. The goal is certainly de-picted in friendly colors, but it can be reached only after all those who have come out of Egypt are dead.

This script made habitual emigrants of the Jews. The oath they have sworn never allows them to settle down completely in the land that they ultimately reach. Every year during the first full moon of spring, wherever they are, they must celebrate departure. At that time the youngest member of the family circle asks why this night is different from all other nights, and the head of the household replies, We were slaves in Egypt, and the Eternal led us forth from there with his mighty hand and his outstretched arm; otherwise we would have remained in bondage. Whoever tells the story of the departure, he is worthy of praise.

This was because almost nothing that had been promised actually came to pass in Canaan. At the height of their power, David and Solomon acted like despots, and then the priests of Baal held the advantage until the kingdom in the Promised Land was obliterated by two great powers, Assyria and Babylon. Autonomy was out of the question; in its stead came deportation and emigration, until further notice.

In these circumstances, the hope for an ultimate Anointed One, for the Messiah and his peaceable kingdom, where the infant plays near the viper's hiding place and the nasty phase of human history comes to an end—that hope became all the more extravagant. Of course, such yearning is the subject of another script, wherein the concrete liberation politics of Exodus is transformed into a grandiose, apocalyptic scenario of the sort that cost Müntzer his head.


The story of the Exodus refers to the spirit whom Müntzer recognized as his moving force only in the form of hints and still without the attribute "Holy." The spirit "is on" the man Moses (Numbers 11, 17) and then is "put" on the seventy elders, the leaders of the people, thus sending them into prophetic ecstasy (Numbers 11, 25), whereupon Moses expresses the wish that all the people might be seized by this spirit (Numbers 11, 29). This wish went unfulfilled.

Another text grants to the seventy worthies nothing less than the sight of God (Exodus 24, 9–11), which was otherwise forbidden under penalty of death. The vision takes place on the famous mountain that is sometimes called Mount Sinai and sometimes Mount Horeb, the place where the Ten Commandments were handed down amid thunder and lightning. It is not noted whether the seventy always had this ready access.

Otherwise the stories of the Exodus, despite the proximity of God and the high miracle rate, read like the chronicle of a laborious undertaking with many setbacks. The emigrants grumble again and again about Moses and his telegrams from far-off Headquarters, they doubt that all this endless shifting about amid the detritus of a hostile world makes much sense, and they dance around the golden calf. Revolts against Moses must be cruelly suppressed. The revolutionary avant-garde (Moses and the seventy elders) can see farther than the rest. They know that the slave mentality must be driven out of the people before the Promised Land can come into sight. Moses himself can view it only from a distance, almost like a fata morgana. After the portrayal of the original exuberance of freedom, the theme of the Exodus stories is the arduous work of moving people around who are either thinking back on the Egyptian fleshpots or wildly impatient to reach the land, awash with milk and honey, that has been promised them. They are "coarse," as Müntzer expressed it; they must be "uncoarsened."

The Exodus stories allow forty years of desert wandering for a transformation of this sort; our revolutionary theologian's time allotment was much tighter. In August 1524, Müntzer delivered to the printer Hans Hut in Bibra a work meant for publication and intended to reveal to miserable, pitiful Christianity both the error of its ways and a succinct program, to be implemented at once, for bringing about a general and complete change in its thinking. Nine months later, imprisoned in the fortress of Heldrungen, the author dictated his last letter, addressed to the people of Mühlhausen, in which he pleads with them not to be angered by his death. The people, he says, did not understand him properly, for they sought only their own interests. Not even the Holy Spirit had been capable of "uncoarsening" human self-interest. By contrast, the princes' answer to the sermon by the Allstedt preacher had been formulated very effectively— with artillery.

# *Sworders and Staffers*

AT THE END OF APRIL 1525, MÜNTZER wrote to his parishioners in Allstedt: "The whole of Germany, France, and Italy is awake. The maister desireth to begin the game. The miscreants must be undone. At Fulda, during Easter-week, were four abbeys laid waste. The peasants in Klegau, Hegau, and the Blacke Forest are up, three thousand strong, and the number of their host groweth apace. Now to it, to it, to it! The time is at hand, we can no longer slumber. Let not your swords grow cold! Hammer the anvils of Nimrod til they ring, cast down their tower to the earth! They can say nothing of God to ye so long as they rule over ye."

The last sentence could have been written by Baron Holbach or Karl Marx. Müntzer sees religion clearly and rejects it as an element in a political system based on oppression. The key term for its elimination did not emerge until 150 years after Müntzer, during the "Glorious Revolution" in England. The concept of "revolution" fails to occur in Müntzer's writings, but the restless man had certainly never taken his eye off his cause. What he lacked was a competent field marshal and two dozen cannon.

The military actions that Müntzer participated in strike us as unprofessional, lacking in discipline, muddleheaded. We are told of a band of some four hundred men. Provided with a white banner that bears the image of a rainbow, they march from Mühlhausen to Langensalza. There they palaver for a while and finish off two barrels of beer. Early in the morning, on the way back, they descend on the monastery at Volkenroda, where "they do knock out all the windowes in the cloister, despoil the library entirely, destroy every dwelling-place most piteously, take away wine, grain, beer, barley, oats, and meat, and drive off a goodly number of beasts."

With troops like this, could a war be won? Several most noble lords mobilized against the rebel movement in the region between Lake Constance, Thuringia, and the Rhine. Georg, Duke of Saxony, Philipp, Landgrave of Hesse, and Heinrich, Duke of Braunschweig, together with their vassals, recruited a disciplined, well-led host of cavalry and infantry and brought with them a sufficient number of guns.

So on May 15 a battle was fought that was really no such thing. Right up to the last moment, Müntzer had sought to bolster the courage of his troops, but as soon as their attackers opened fire on their defenses the peasants ran off in all directions, and several thousand of them were cut down by the princes' soldiers. Müntzer was caught, imprisoned, interrogated, put to the torture. His execution was delayed until Mühlhausen capitulated. Müntzer's last words to come down to us were spoken in the presence of the headsman and addressed to the princes, who were spectators at his execution on May 27, 1525: "You should read the *Libros Regum.*"

In the biblical Books of the Kings, the prophet Elijah goes up against the idolatrous King Ahab. Müntzer had already alluded to this story in his sermon to the princes. Ahab tried to kill the prophet, but in the end the dogs licked up the king's blood.

Thus the confirmation of Christianity was going ahead rather slowly. Confirmation (Latin *confirmatio:* "strengthening," "support")—which the early Christians thought of as a kind of sealing of baptism through the Holy Spirit—was considered a "sacrament," whose effectiveness in bestowing grace was bound up with definite ritual formulas, and also with such actions as the laying on of hands and anointing with oil. It was in this way that there arose a distinction between the form and the matter of the sacraments. Without water, no baptism; without oil, no confirmation.

Without weapons, no revolution, taught Müntzer. His Spirit-theology looked toward a kind of collective confirmation, not as a liturgical act, but as the overthrow of humiliating relationships. Such a revolution required the exhalations of the Holy Spirit, but also a knowledge of military science.

That was, at least, the theory.

That this theory could work in practice had been demonstrated for the first time in Bohemia. At the age of sixty years, the knight Jan Žižka (d. 1424) became a successful and indispensable leader of the military resistance against emperor and pope. He called himself a "brother of the Chalice" (*bratr z Kalichu*) because of his demand that the consecrated wine be offered to all Christian people. The crystals of dissatisfaction bonded together in this appellation, especially after the execution of the rector of the University of Prague, John Hus (d. 1415), sentenced to burn at the stake by the Council of Constance.

Žižka won his first engagement on July 14, 1420, against the troops of King Sigismund, who, with the blessing of the Church—which had declared his undertaking a crusade against the Hussite heresy—was advancing to besiege Prague. The Czechs were eventually to succeed in fending off no fewer than five such crusades; then, for almost two hundred years, they were left in relative peace.

Žižka had put together his peasant army in the town of Tabor in southern Bohemia. This place, named after the mount of Christ's Transfiguration, was a new settlement. It had sprung from the belief in the imminent return of the Lord Jesus, whom the people gathered together to greet, and at first it was only a campground under the stars. It was from these people that Žižka recruited his infantry soldiers.

The battle song of the Taborites has come down to us, a mighty expression of unified will sung by several thousand male voices, with every note like a hammer blow. These are God's fighters, they sang. (The Czech words for "God" and "fight" begin with the same syllable, *bo*, and intensify each other.)

Žižka brought armored wagons as well as guns into action. His "Military Ordinance," a rigorous military constitution that assigns every man his proper place according to a kind of Swiss principle of community and class, set an example for military systems throughout Europe. Consequently Žižka's troops were clearly superior to the crusading armies fielded by his opponents, which tended to operate somewhat chaotically.

The Bohemians, one chronicler wrote, now became so strong and mighty, and so arrogant, that they were feared on all sides. After Žižka's death, God's fighters crossed the borders of Bohemia and marched to Leipzig, Bamberg, Nuremberg. In the writings that provide some information about their mentality, the Holy Spirit receives hardly a mention. Apparently they preferred to rely on their cannon. They were *Schwertler* ("sworders," men of the sword), as people would say a hundred years later in Nikolsburg (Mikulov), in contrast to the peace-loving *Stäbler* ("staffers," men of the staff).

The sworders' skill in making lightning-swift belly thrusts with their halberds during hand-to-hand combat did not square very well with their proneness to hearing the clear words of the Holy Spirit in the depths of their souls. But this very combination was what Müntzer had called for; his pedagogy of "uncoarsening" led directly to a union of warlike readiness to strike and inner composure that resembled the practices of martial arts masters in China and Japan. Nowhere in Europe, however, could one find a training program that offered a combination of meditation and weapons drill, and the contrast between spirituality and experience in arms remained correspondingly stark. The Holy Spirit was more likely to side with the staffers.

In September 1524, a humanist from the patrician class of Zurich named Konrad Grebel, in collaboration with several like-minded people who were satisfied neither with Zwingli nor with Luther, wrote a letter to Thomas Müntzer. "We are marvelously well pleased," the letter said, "to have found a man who dares proclaim to the evangelical preachers their manifest errors . . . One should not protect the Gospel and its followers with the sword, nor should they do so themselves. As we have heard, this is your opinion and bearing as well. Rightly-believing Christians are sheep in the midst of wolves, sheep marked for slaughter; they must be baptized in fear and distress and prove themselves in the fire, not seek to attain the fatherland of eternal peace by throttling their bodily enemies."

In January 1525, Grebel was one of the first who, quaking and hesitant, dared to commit an enormity: as a protest against the baptism of children, he and a few others ladled water from a basin over one another's head. Two years later the Zurich city council condemned one of these men to death for this offense and had him drowned in the Limmat river.

Of course, Grebel and his comrades had been mistaken about Müntzer, who was (at least theoretically) a man of the sword. The Zurich Anabaptists, on the other hand, were convinced staffers who would rather turn the other cheek than strike back. Their teachings, as Sebastian Franck noted in 1531, soon "crept into" German, Austrian, Bohemian, and Dutch Christianity, only to be most rudely suppressed. As early as the imperial diet held in Speyer in 1529, the penalty of death was decreed for the "now newly risen secte and aberration of Rebaptysers." Some were so strained and so stretched, we read in a chronicle of the Moravian Anabaptists, that the sun could shine through them, some were torn asunder and killed with torture, some burned to ashes and dust as heretics, some rent with red-hot tongs, some hanged from trees, some put to death by the sword.

For the victims, such Spiritless measures were a confirmation of their conviction that any arbitrary bodily injury, whether ordered by government officials or carried out by rebellious mobs, belonged to the carnal sphere. One of the fundamental declarations of the Anabaptists asserted that the authorities ruled according to the flesh, and the Christians according to the Spirit.

Once again the latter was urging his chosen ones (this time in Swiss dialect) to make an exodus. They took their departure by way of a formal resignation. What they left behind was all churchly faith, whether old-fashioned Catholic or newfangled Reformed, that resided in the minsters and cathedrals and catered to those in the front pews, and moreover they abandoned infant baptism and all other palpations that were part of churchly dealings with God. In the Anabaptist view, all this extravagance was nothing but a backslide into Egyptian bondage. Of course, they placed themselves outside the law by holding such opinions, which were more revolutionary and more dangerous than threshing flails.

The differences between staffers and sworders nevertheless remained unreconciled, especially in Nikolsburg in southern Moravia, where Anabaptist groups from southern Germany and the Tirol had sought refuge. Both factions had their loyal supporters there. One party, hardened veterans of the German Peasants' War, had brought their spears along with them, while the others carried only walking staffs. Among the conscientious objectors, however, there was an agitator, a man from the Tirol named Jakob Hutter. He had read his Bible carefully, and he preached the community of property practiced by the original Christians. They owned everything in common, as it is written in the Acts of the Apostles.

The idea of spiritual communism was a success. The Hutterians organized their lives around *Bruderhöfe* (communities of large, multifamily households) and owned no private property. Numerous communes, each composed of two hundred to three hundred persons and self-sufficient in agricultural production, settled in Moravia, where they adhered to the same principles that would be practiced (though not quite so meekly) four hundred years later in the kibbutzim of Israel.

To this day the Hutterian Brethren are still staffers, noncombatants by definition. In 1917, those Hutterite groups who had emigrated to America sent a petition to the president of the United States. "Our community was driven from one country to another," they wrote, "until at last we came here from Russia in 1874. Our young men cannot take part in military service without violating our principles."

The U.S. government complied with their request, and the Hutterites performed alternative service as game wardens for the National Park Service until universal conscription was abolished in 1973. The *Bruderhöfe* are flourishing in South Dakota and Montana, as well as in the Canadian province of Alberta. The 25,000 Hutterites still dress as they did in the sixteenth century. They see themselves as a divine corporation founded by the Holy Spirit. When it comes to tractors, the Holy Spirit has no objections. Television, on the other hand, is abhorrent to him.

.  .  .

The Anabaptists of the sworder persuasion suffered their most terrible defeat in the Westphalian town of Münster in 1535. Today three iron cages are still hanging from the tower of the Lambertikirche (Saint Lambert's church) in Münster. In these cages the bodies of the three most prominent of the radical Christians were exhibited "as a warning to all restless spirits." The first of these men was named Jan Bockelson, a journeyman tailor from Leyden in the Netherlands. When he was led to his execution, the chronicler simply referred to him as "the King." After him the cloth merchant Bernd Knipperdolling, mayor of the town and the king's "sword-bearer," was slowly tortured to death. And finally Bernd Krechting, one of the king's senior counselors, perished under the glowing tongs.

"The great, penetrant, endlessly resourceful Spirit would not have planned things so foolishly and grossly," declared Luther about the events in Münster. "It must be obvious to all that the devil in person keeps his household there, indeed, one devil sits on top of another, like toads."

The adherents of the old faith likewise entertained no doubts about the demonic origins of the Anabaptist madness. This was the view of the victors after the fifteen-month siege of the revolutionary town. The leader of the besieging troops was the prince-bishop Franz von Waldeck, who wanted to preserve his rule and was supported in his effort by Luther and his followers. A report to the magistrate of Frankfurt states that the town has been defeated by the special grace of God alone and not by any skill on the part of the attacking forces.

It was defeated also by treachery—which further complicates an impartial judgment about the sacred experiment in Münster.

The story begins quite innocently. Thirty years after the catastrophe, a disillusioned Anabaptist wrote about it. "Dear friends," he said, "we were all untried, simple, innocent, without any malice or guile, and we knew nothing of any false visions or prophecies or revelations. And in our simplicity we believed that it behooved us but to be on guard against Papists, Lutherans, and Zwinglians, and all would be well, nor would we have any cause for care."

It had been prophesied that in the year 1532 the New Jerusalem would descend upon Strasbourg, bringing to the world, with the power of the Spirit, a definitive, divine government for the last days before the

Second Coming of Christ. But the deadline passed, and so a baker from Haarlem named Jan Matthys rose up, abandoned his wife, and replaced her with a brewer's daughter, a beautiful girl well versed in the Bible, luring her away from her parents with holy words. He took her secretly to Amsterdam, pretending that he was being relentlessly driven by the Holy Spirit, and from there he sent out pairs of emissaries to various towns. One of those sent to Münster was Jan Bockelson of Leyden. In his wake he drew other rebaptized Frisian and Dutch Christians to Münster, where a priest named Rothmann had won over the city with his sermons. Bockelson's band, by now several hundred souls, declared that they had come in peace and were admitted into the town.

By the beginning of January there were already fourteen hundred Anabaptists in Münster. They wished to establish there the New Zion, completely free from authority and constraint, but at the end of February the prince-bishop, accompanied by a troop of two hundred horse, set up his headquarters in Telgte, a few miles away, and so things became serious.

"God knows," the defenders now said, "that the deepest purpose of our baptisms was to suffer for Christ's sake whatever might be done unto us; but it hath pleased the Lord otherwise, and doth please Him yet, not only that we and all true Christians at this time do fend off the godless with the sword, but moreover He will give the sword into the hands of His people, that they may take revenge for everything that is unjust."

Therefore, early in the morning of February 27, armed Anabaptists ran through the streets, battering doors open with their halberds and shouting: "Come out, ye godless!" All those who refused baptism were driven out of the town, in the rain and snow, without possessions or provisions. Then, for three days, baptisms were performed in the market square.

It should not be overlooked that many a lout took advantage of the hurly-burly by breaking into cloisters and churches and causing havoc. Some terrorized the nuns in the convent of Niesing, others attacked the brothers of Springborn, stealing clothing, money, household implements, sacred garments, chalices. They smashed the precious cathedral clock with hammers and axes, tore out the pipes of the organ, smeared valuable books with excrement.

Meanwhile some people were jumping up and down, trying to fly the way Georg the tailor showed them to do. The carpenter's wife roamed the streets, crying out for repentance. Knipperdolling spoke to the walls in his house. Many people, including children, were filled with joy and prophesied.

In March it became clear that the town of Münster was completely surrounded by the prince-bishop's troops. In the meantime, the eloquent Jan Matthys had presented himself, together with his Bible-studying brewer's daughter. He announced categorically that Münster was the New Jerusalem and set Easter as the deadline for the end of the world. Actually he had predicted his own death, for he fell in a firefight and was hacked to pieces by the enemy, so that the brothers needed a basket to collect his corpse. Thereafter Jan Bockelson of Leyden became the chief prophet, took the deceased Matthys's widow as his wife, and proclaimed to the whole citizenry that a new constitution had been revealed to him and was to go into force immediately. It provided for a council of twelve mature men, to be named by himself. They were to have the power to make decisions in all public, private, spiritual, and worldly matters, particularly in regard to the defense of the town.

Its fortifications, which were already in excellent condition, were speedily prepared for war and their defense put in the hands of fifteen hundred able-bodied men, divided into battalions and companies under the command of captains and sergeants. Knipperdolling saw to it that every man knew where he had to stand as soon as the fire bell began to ring. The smallest breach of discipline was punishable by death.

In May and August, the besieging troops of the prince-bishop, their ranks swelled by some eight thousand mercenaries, suffered severe defeats. These so strengthened Bockelson's position that nothing more stood in the way of his being proclaimed king.

The women whom he took into his court—there were more than a dozen of them—all had to be young and pleasing to the eye. They were lodged near the cathedral, in the provost's house, right next to the curia of the cathedral cellar, where the king resided. The Dutch Anabaptists who had arrived in Münster also lived together with several wives, in accordance with the biblical injunction: *increase and multiply.*

In November the Lutheran preacher Dietrich Fabricius, sent as an envoy by the landgrave of Hesse, appeared before the town gates, gained admission, and was received by Bockelson. Fabricius wrote in his report that after he had been led into the town hall a magnificent procession entered. First there came about twenty bodyguards and six lackeys, clad in silks and satins and wearing neck bands of gold. They were followed by two small boys, one carrying a golden sword and the other a book. Then came the king himself in a black velvet frock coat, over which he wore a cloak of white damask; around his neck was a double chain of gold, and from it hung an emblem like a coat of arms displaying a black imperial orb encircled horizontally and vertically by two golden rings and pierced by two golden swords; above the orb was a golden cross. Following the king came Marshal Knipperdolling, the other members of the council, the courtiers, and the servants, a total of approximately two hundred persons.

In January 1535, Münster began to run out of food. A tally revealed that there were only two hundred and twenty cows and ninety-six horses still alive. People resorted to roasting cats and mice. Supplies of rye and barley were almost exhausted. A deserter wrote a letter to those he had left behind: "Dear people of Münster, because it hath come to pass that God hath opened my eyes and I have seen how false and poisonous a business it is that now goeth forward in Münster, it is my humble prayer that you but look upon your business and see that it is clearly against God. You poor, foolish people, who cannot discover that you are altogether deceived and led astray in what you do."

Bockelson announced that Easter would bring deliverance, for then a hundred thousand Dutch co-religionists would come to their aid. When Easter arrived, but no deliverance, the people began to say that everything had been a lie. "Now, dear brothers and sisters," was the king's reply, "have you construed my sense so narrowly? First you must be cleansed of your sins, and then God will surely deliver us." But the armed host of Dutch and Frisian Anabaptists that Bockelson had pinned his hopes on had already been smashed and scattered by the imperial forces, and the people's hunger grew. When sermons were preached in the market square, the king sat in the royal chair, full of dread, with his head in his hands, for he surely realized that things would end badly.

In April many women and children left the city because there was no more food.

In May, in an attempt to keep the people obedient amid the increasing distress, Bockelson appointed twelve princes and divided the town into as many districts, which the princes were ordered to oversee, along with the town gates; treason was to be made impossible. Nevertheless, Haensken von der Langenstraten and Heinrich Gresbeck managed to escape. They were captured by the besiegers and bought their lives by giving a precise description of the town's defenses.

In June, a report was sent to Frankfurt from the prince-bishop's camp. Our soldiers can run up to the town walls without fear, it said. There are still two hundred cows in Münster, now the people are slaughtering them. They still have wine and several ditches filled with fish. Peas, beans, and cabbage are planted in the squares. They don't shoot from the walls anymore without very good cause.

On the night of June 24, the traitor Gresbeck swam across the outermost moat with a rope around his waist, reached one of the outer gates, and pulled down the bridge. Sixteen hand-picked men crossed over it, climbed the rampart, and stabbed the sleeping sentinels to death in their huts. Then they stood before the unlocked little door in the city gate that Gresbeck had indicated to them, notified the four assault groups that were awaiting their signal, and the battle was won.

News of the disaster in Münster quickly spread among the Dutch Anabaptists: several hundred brothers and sisters in the faith slaughtered or beheaded. It was said that Bockelson had played a knavish game, that he was baseborn, unpredictable, a verse-maker and an actor, a tavernkeeper and a pimp, randy as a goat, rapacious, brutal. Furthermore, he had ferreted out all the money in the town, down to the last coin, under the pretext that it was not seemly for a Christian to possess silver or gold; and then hard florins had been minted, allegedly as currency for this liberated Christianity. There was talk of unseasonable love with tender little girls after the introduction of polygamy; all his prophecies had been false and mendacious; and so forth.

Thus did the land subside into silence. To be sure, there were still a few incorrigible sword-swingers stirring about, but they were given to understand that God and his saints would not come before their due time to take revenge on the godless. David Joris, Obbe Philips, and Menno

Simons were of this mind. It was owing to them that the Anabaptist legacy was passed on. "Our weapons," Simons wrote, "are not weapons for ravaging towns and countries, dashing walls and gates to pieces, and spilling human blood like water, but they are weapons for overcoming stoney hearts with remorse."

That this would have to happen without compulsion, and certainly not from one day to the next, was the lesson of Münster.

This lesson was learned again and again—by Mahatma Gandhi, for example. As a rule, of course, it was the sworders who were the determinant factors when a revolution was on the agenda. The more professional—and thus the colder—the revolutionaries became, the more distant their relationship to the Holy Spirit turned out to be. He was a living presence in Thomas Müntzer's heart; a Robespierre, who spread terror in the name of freedom, would have had no idea what to do with him.

# *Sunbeams Wrapped in Newsprint*

*T*HE DECAPITATION OF CITIZEN LOUIS Capet, formerly King Louis XVI, on January 21, 1793, in Paris had a negative effect on the reputation of the supreme Lord and heavenly Father. Our breast is full of terrible pity, wrote Heinrich Heine (1797–1856). It's old Jehovah himself who's getting ready to die. We've known him so well, from his cradle on, in Egypt, where he was raised among divine calves and crocodiles, sacred onions, ibises, and cats. We know how he became a little god-king in Palestine among a poor, insignificant pastoral people. We saw him emigrate to Rome, where he intrigued a long time until he came to power and ruled the city and the world from the Capitol. We saw how he spiritualized himself still more, how he tenderly whimpered, how he became a loving father, a friend to all mankind, a bringer of happiness to the world, a philanthropist—and none of it did him any good. Do you hear the little bell ringing? Kneel down, they're bringing the sacraments to a dying god.

In the German and Austrian *Vormärz* (the period between 1815 and the March revolution of 1848), under the watchful eye of Prince Metternich, the famous poet's theological mockery must have seemed exceedingly provocative, detrimental to law and order. Every police informer knew that freethinking had become more or less taken for granted among the educated classes in the age of the bourgeois revolutions—just as it had once been among the students of medieval Paris. Such a change in mentality, because of its undermining effect upon the unity of throne and altar, was inimical to the state chancelleries of the monarchistic restoration. A resolution of the German Parliament on December 10, 1835, illustrates this: "Since a literary school has been formed whose efforts in poetry and fiction are openly directed at attacking the Christian religion in the most impudent way, be it resolved that all the governments in Germany shall assume the obligation of applying with the utmost rigor the laws and penalties of their respective countries against the authors, publishers, printers, and distributors of this literary school, known under the name of 'Young Germany' or 'Young Literature,' to which school belong the following named, to wit, Heinrich Heine, Karl Gutzkow, Heinrich Laube, Ludwig Wienbarg, and Theodor Mundt; and the said governments shall prevent the distribution of such writings with every means that the law puts at their disposal."

Heine had been living as an emigrant in Paris since 1831. A year before his departure from Germany, he read in the newspapers the reports concerning the July revolution in Paris. "It was sunbeams," Heine wrote, "wrapped in newsprint." When it became obvious that Germany was still in the dark, the poet crossed the border to France.

In spite of the omnipresent censorship, yearly book production in Germany was rising meteorically, from 4,181 titles in 1805 to 14,039 titles in 1843. In later years, publishers could only dream of such rates of increase in their business. These were the decades in which many a pen was whetted on revolutionary ideas. "If there's anything that can help in our time," the medical student Georg Büchner (1813–1837) wrote from Strasbourg to his parents in Darmstadt, "it is violence. We know what we can expect from our princes. Everything they have conceded has been forced from them by necessity. Our young people have been reproached for using violence. But isn't violence our eternal condition? Because we've been born and raised in a dungeon, we no longer notice that we're stuck in a hole, chained hand and foot, with a gag in our mouth."

Despite his intention to avoid getting mixed up in any childish revolutionary pranks, in March 1834 Büchner wrote a pamphlet addressed to the rural inhabitants of the Grand Duchy of Hesse. This was the pamphlet's slogan: "Peace to the cottages! War on the palaces!"

The clandestine distribution of this work began in July, but a police informer had already got wind of it. In early August a certain Minnigerode was picked up by the police with 139 copies of the illegal text. In it one could read: "For centuries in Germany, justice has been the whore of the German princes. The graven images of our native tyrants sparkle with gold and precious jewels, with medals and decorations, but inside them their worm dieth not, and they have feet of clay. God will give you the strength to shatter their feet. Resurrection day will not tarry. Germany is now a corpse-field; soon it will be a paradise."

Revolutionary writers usually had an educated audience in mind, but "The Hessian Messenger," young Büchner's first published work, was addressed to the humble people in the rural villages. In the midst of the period of religious criticism that followed the Enlightenment, an angry intellectual, like an intermediary between Müntzer and Bloch, helped himself most uninhibitedly to the biblical stockpile of criticism against the ruling class. The authorities appeared to be highly alarmed. A Hessian court councillor averred that the religion of peace was mingled in the pamphlet with the firebrand of revolutionary overthrow, and the consultant of the Federal-Central Authority added that the publication misused the words of the Bible, portrayed the difference between the landed and the non-landed classes as injustice, and preached rebellion as though it were a sacred work. A highly treasonous, undoubtedly revolutionary product of the most impudent, most unrestrained republicanism—the official classifications of the printed work mobilized a whole series of solemn paragraphs directed against the youthful agitators to whom Büchner had delivered this example of his prose.

Meanwhile the brazen young man of letters dedicated his efforts to the "Society of Human Rights," a group that he had founded in Darmstadt, continued his study of the French Revolution, and pondered the question of how he was going to earn his living. To this end he began writing his drama *Danton's Death* in the middle of January 1835, sent it to a publisher at the end of February, and in early March evaded a summons to appear in court by fleeing to Strasbourg. In the middle of June, the *Frankfurter Journal* and the *Grossherzoglich Hessischen Zeitung* published a personal description of Georg Büchner, who was wanted by the police: age twenty-one years; height five feet nine inches; student in medicine; has eluded judicial investigation of his alleged participation in treasonous activity by leaving the country. Particular features: shortsightedness.

In Strasbourg the wanted man supported himself by doing translations. At the same time, he was preparing a scientific treatise on the nervous system of the barbel, a type of European freshwater fish. This work was accepted and published by the *Société d'histoire naturelle* in Strasbourg; the author was admitted to the society as a corresponding member, and soon afterward the University of Zurich awarded him a doctorate. In November 1836, Büchner delivered a "trial lecture" on cranial nerves in Zurich and was thereupon appointed a *Privatdozent* or outside lecturer. His first course of the winter semester ("Demonstrations of Comparative Anatomy") was also his last. Typhus. An obituary stated that he had been obliged to leave his native country, but Genius is everywhere at home.

"Aristocraticism is the most shameful contempt for the Holy Spirit in men and women." With this pointed theological statement, Büchner denounced any form of condescension, even if religious in origin, as stupid and spiritless. In his revolutionary thinking, God the Father and God the Son, the two male beings enthroned in the clouds, turned out to be an exalted projection of vulgar power structures. After many centuries of civil rebelliousness against barons and priests, only the Holy Spirit showed himself to be truly divine.

But that was not enough. In order to be rid of the lovely but superficial aura with which pious tradition had surrounded him, the Holy Spirit emancipated himself, in the age of the revolutions that he himself had instigated, even from the attributes of his divine nature, made himself an anonymous force—the creative inspiration of artists and writers—and became Genius. From now on, anyone who wished to know him better had to study, not theology, but psychology, or perhaps, like Büchner, cranial nerves.

# *The Reinstatement of the Flesh*

*T*HUS, WHILE THE HUMAN RACE WAS gathering steam, the prognosis of a fifth-century Syrian monk was fulfilled. His name was Stephen bar Sadaili, he was born around 480 A.D. in Edessa (today Urfa, Turkey), and he is believed to have been the author of a tractate that has survived the passage of time under the title of the "Book of Hierotheus." In it occurs the following passage:

> Corporal punishment, my son, will come to an end, he who is charged with scourging will scourge no longer, the judge will not judge anymore, those who are imprisoned will be set free. Demons and men will be pardoned, the angels will conclude their divine service, the Seraphim will cease their songs of praise, the Thrones will no longer guard their ruler. Supernatural hierarchies, like natural distinctions, will disappear, and all things shall be one. God will pass away, Christ will dissolve, the Spirit will no longer be called the Spirit. Names will pass away, but not essences.

In fact, by the beginning of the year 1844, at least in the writings of German authors, the criticism of religion had essentially been completed, as Karl Marx said. "The criticism of religion," the revolutionary author declared, "is the premise of all criticism. Man, who sought a superman in the fantastic reality of heaven and found there only his own reflection, will no longer be inclined to find only the semblance of himself, only the inhuman, where he seeks and must seek his true reality."

Heinrich Heine expressed the matter still more concisely, and with a touch of mordant disdain: "Let's leave heaven to the angels and the sparrows."

Marx and Heine were hauling on the same rope. The power at its other end wasn't going to let itself be yanked off the stage easily. The biblical God whom these two warriors of the spirit were attacking could not be their adversary. He had brought their forefathers out of the land of bondage. The real enemy of mankind had to have another name. When Marx met Heine (who was his senior by twenty years) in Paris at the end of 1843, the poet had just returned from a trip to Germany and was planning to describe his impressions in verse. In Heine's view, "philosophy" rhymed with "inanity." Marx, too, had realized that he wouldn't be able to get anywhere by going up in the hot-air balloons of German idealism, and so he began to study economics. Amid his notes from the year 1844, the name of the opponent with whom he was to fight a running battle until his death appeared for the first time: capital.

What Heine brought before the footlights was far more vivid. A naked woman, like a marble monument, rolled out of the wings.

The young German literati, defamed by their enemies as the "Jewish School," longed to see the revolutionary spark set fire to the relationships between man and woman; they wanted a "reinstatement of the flesh." It was incumbent upon every progressive writer to pay a visit to George Sand, the female evangelist of the new sexual mores, at her Parisian home. "Chopin prepared her coffee in the fireplace," Heinrich Laube reported for the *Augsburger Zeitung* in 1840. "As she drank it, she gave us a warm and cheerful welcome. Heine seemed to be a favorite of hers; she stroked his hair and scolded him because he had not visited her for a long time."

According to Sand, as soon as a woman gives herself to a man, she becomes either enslaved or guilty. "I can't advise anyone to enter a marriage that is based on civil law and thus endorses the dependence, inferiority, and social invalidity of the woman," she said. "I've arrived at the conviction that complete, ideal happiness in love is absolutely impossible if one sex is unequal to and dependent upon the other. Men have succeeded in forcing women into a state of servitude and stultification that is made out to be the eternal ordination of divine providence."

"I'm very sad," Heine wrote to George Sand. "You don't know my utter unhappiness. I love you very much, with all my heart, with every fiber of my heart. If you're free, enjoy your freedom. Never weep—tears weaken the eyesight. How beautiful your eyes are. And you have the most beautiful hair I've ever seen."

Heinrich Heine's utter unhappiness was that he could feel real love only for the dead and for statues. Perhaps Sigmund Freud might have helped him, but Freud wasn't born until the year of Heine's death. The poet was left to reach out for beautiful women and the sunbeams of revolution. In May 1848, just when they were beginning to shine again, Heine left his apartment for the last time, already stricken by the spinal disease that was to chain him to his bed until he died. "I dragged myself to the Louvre," Heine wrote, "and I almost collapsed as I entered the lofty hall where the most blessed goddess of beauty, our dear lady of Milo, stands on her pedestal. I lay at her feet for a long time, and I wept so bitterly that even a stone would have had to take pity on me. The goddess, too, looked down on me compassionately, but at the same time hopelessly, as if she wanted to say, Don't you see? I have no arms; therefore, I can't help you."

George Sand, née Dupin, ex-wife of the baron Dudevant, needed no neurosis to become a celebrated author. At the age of twenty-five, when she was a young mother (a son and a daughter) and a bored wife, she began to write. Having stubbornly insisted on a separation, she established herself in Paris, and by way of augmenting her scanty income she worked for *Figaro* and other magazines. "I had a confident step with my little steel-capped heels," she wrote later, describing how she got the idea of going about in men's clothing. When she was twenty-eight, she entered into a contract with the *Revue des Deux Mondes:* for an annual salary of 4,000 francs, she obligated herself to deliver the equivalent of 122 printed pages every six weeks. Her novel *Lélia* caused a scandal. The author received a note from Alfred de Musset, and the most famous liaison of the French Romantic period was under way. "She was walking like a soldier," Musset recalled, "swinging her arms and singing at the top of her voice. All at once she turned around, ran up to me, and threw her arms around me."

Equally famous was the slip of paper that someone handed to Frédéric Chopin in a Parisian salon one spring evening in 1838. It read: *On vous adore—George.*

As the very type of the artist, the object of her adoration embodied the divine in humanity. Intimate association with an incarnation of the Holy Spirit brought with it certain problems. Sand confessed to one of Chopin's friends: "Like some pious puritan, he seemed to have contempt for gross human desires and to be afraid of soiling our love through excessive arousal. This way of considering the ultimate union of love has always repelled me. If the consummate embrace is not as sacred and holy a thing as all the rest, then there's no virtue in abstaining from it. Contempt for the flesh can, at best, be wise and useful with persons who are nothing but flesh."

Thus, from a female point of view, the Christian antithesis between flesh and spirit was recognized as a male obsession. "Yes, there are angels in disguise," Sand said, "who pretend to be human beings and dwell for a time on earth in order to give comfort to poor, tired, despairing souls and lift them up with themselves into heaven." In November 1838, George Sand went on a holiday with her disguised angel to Palma de Mallorca, seeking relief for his sick lungs. When the angel coughed, one was even allowed to kiss him.

George Sand had to fulfill her weekly quota of twenty pages on Mallorca, too. Writing came easily to her, and she delighted in it, in stark contrast to colleagues like Flaubert, who might spend an entire day in search of the right word. She was indifferent to posterity. In compensation, she had a château in the country and an elegant apartment in Paris, merry guests, romantic adventures to an advanced age, and always enough cigars.

Flaubert guessed the secret of this successful life in a letter that he wrote to George Sand: "Despite your great sphinx eyes, you've always seen the world in golden colors. They came from the sun in your heart. What you lack is hate."

# Soul's Salvation

CHILDREN IN SCHOOL STILL LEARN THAT

*the so-called modern age began two hundred years ago, a product of the interaction among*

*economic growth, population increases, the scientific method, the spirit of invention, the right*

*to vote, hygiene, and compulsory school attendance, under the radiant sun of the enlightened*

*reason. Such lessons suppress any mention of the blissful forms into which the common belief in progress frequently organizes itself, among clairvoyants, Spiritualists, Theosophists, spirit healers, esoterics, and occultists. Out of this milieu, there arose the notion that a truly modern age is just now coming into being, under the astrological sign of Aquarius.*

*Viewed in this way, the last two hundred years are nothing but a somewhat insignificant episode in the life of humanity and its gods. If this is the case, then fresh syllabuses will have to be written for the next generation of schoolchildren, or for the one after that.*

# The Business Associate in the Sweet By-and-By

IN 1901, AT THE UNIVERSITY OF EDINBURGH, William James (1842–1910) gave the series of lectures on religion that shortly thereafter appeared in print under the title *The Varieties of Religious Experience* and was on its way to becoming a classic. At the end of his course, the scholar admitted that, as a scientist, he did not feel competent to dispute the reality of the supernatural sphere. In this connection he hit upon a formulation that could occur only to an American: We and God have business with each other, stated James. He went on to say that God is real since he produces real effects.

In the new world of the United States, there was no state church as in old Europe. The immigrants from England, Holland, and Germany had seen to that, all the Quakers, Pietists, Puritans, Baptists, Methodists, and various other believers, for whom the hand of king and prince had grown too heavy in matters of religion. Dozens, hundreds, thousands of religious groups, large and small, old and new, battled between New York and San

Francisco for a share in the market of immortal souls. The title of James's essay on the psychology of religion alluded to the multiplicity of American religious possibilities and promised a sort of variety show of the forms of piety. All forms could take part, provided that they sought salvation not in dogmatic stipulations but in the experience of being seized by a higher power.

What counted for James was religious *experience,* even if it manifested itself in wild behavior, effusive exaltations, or the extravagances of autodidacticism, even if it did without the scholar's cap or the bishop's staff, even if it was self-opinionated, credulous, eccentric, or psychopathic. The psychologist wasn't interested in secondhand believers, in those who merely carried on the traditions into which they were born, the unimaginative plebes in the institutions of mass salvation, whether Christian, Buddhist, or Islamic. The professor's eye was trained on the trendsetters of divine worship, the virtuoso mystics, the religious geniuses. Often enough, his clinical examination of such people detected nervous ill temper, abnormal psychic states, neurotic compulsions. And why not? According to James, George Fox, the founder of the Quakers, presents a clear case of mental illness, but anyone who considers the religion he founded is filled with admiration. James thought that a consistently and genuinely religious life disposes a person to deviate from the everyday modalities of consciousness.

This notion did not apply exclusively to those exceptional people who were adept at achieving intimacy with God, even though the guest from Harvard quoted extensively from the writings of such people. James also referred to records assembled by his colleague, Professor Starbuck, in which inconspicuous contemporaries reported extraordinary experiences of a mystical or otherwise supernatural kind. Although he did not say so expressly, Professor James was on the trail of the Holy Spirit. In the United States, the Holy Spirit was involved in—among other things—the business of health care.

In one of his lectures, Professor James discussed, most respectfully, the so-called "mind-cure movement." The *American Journal of Psychology* for 1899 had published a paper on "faith cures" whose genuineness was beyond question. The author of this study concluded that the human mind apparently had at its disposal health-promoting powers comparable to those officially recognized in medicine as cures by suggestion.

One of the new schools of spiritual healing mentioned in the article was called "Christian Science." One hundred years later, this movement has become a respectable Church, with three thousand congregations throughout the world.

The soul of the enterprise was a farmer's daughter named Mary Baker Eddy (1821–1910), a woman of considerable energy. A housewife's painfully infected finger, for example, which her doctors had pronounced to be in need of immediate amputation, posed no problem for Mrs. Eddy. She touched the bandaged finger, lightly and fleetingly, and by the next morning the "putrefaction" had disappeared.

The future religious founder had had her decisive encounter with a higher power when she was forty-one years old. Since the birth of her child, she had suffered from recurring cramps, stomach and gallbladder illnesses, and spinal problems. When no physician could help her, she chanced to hear of a healer, the learned watchmaker Phineas Parkhurst Quimby. She sought him out, and after eight days of treatment she felt as though she had been reborn.

Quimby's practice was unconventional. He bade his patients to sit down, took a seat facing them, and silently took them by the hand. After a while he told them what it was that their "inner man" was suffering from; this identification of their tribulations amounted to diagnosis by telepathy. Then, after a level of trust had been established, it was time to eliminate the error that was causing the illness. This was accomplished by informing the patients of the hidden nature of their malady, which had its origin in an erroneous "state of mind." After the psychosomatic core of the complaint was exposed, the inner man had to be fortified, and this process, too, took place in silence. "The truth is the healing," Quimby used to say.

After her recovery, Mrs. Eddy studied the master's "science of life and happiness" in his miscellaneous manuscript writings and remained in contact with him by post until his death four years later. Her own book, the fruit of long labor, appeared in print in 1875 under the title *Science and Health*.

The real author of this vast work, which went through its fiftieth edition in 1891 and was revised again and again, was God. He had finally made Mrs. Eddy healthy.

The most important passage in *Science and Health* has traditionally been read as a kind of credo during the Sunday service in Christian Scientist churches. Mrs. Eddy called this text the "scientific statement of Being," and it reads as follows: "There is no life, truth, intelligence, nor substance in matter. All is infinite Mind and its infinite manifestation, for God is All-in-all. Spirit is immortal Truth; matter is mortal error. Spirit is God, and man is His image and likeness. Therefore man is not material; he is spiritual."

This solemn declaration was not in any way meant to be understood as religious poetry or theological speculation. Like the chemists, astronomers, and physicists in the universities, though with greater penetration of knowledge, Jesus Christ was to be conceived of as a "scientist." Mrs. Eddy had recognized that the real must not be confused with the material. The real, a dance of invisible energies, remained hidden to sensory awareness. What was real was—Spirit.

Later, in popular scientific presentations of the quantum theory, similar trains of thought could be found. Respected physicists (Planck, Einstein, Born, Eddington, Bohr, Heisenberg, Schrödinger, Pauli, Jordan, Bohm) speculated about the religious aura that surrounds their view of the world. James Jeans wrote that we can think of the laws of nature as the laws of thought of a universal mind.

In late summer of 1969, a physicist named Fritjof Capra was sitting by the ocean. "I was watching the waves rolling in," Capra later wrote, "and feeling the rhythm of my breathing, when I suddenly became aware of my whole environment as being engaged in a gigantic cosmic dance. Being a physicist, I knew that the sand, rocks, water and air around me were made of vibrating molecules and atoms, and that these consisted of particles which interacted with one another by creating and destroying other particles. I knew also that the Earth's atmosphere was continually bombarded by showers of 'cosmic rays,' particles of high energy undergoing multiple collisions as they penetrated the air. All this was familiar to me from my research in high-energy physics, but until that moment I had only experienced it through graphs, diagrams and mathematical theories. As I sat on that beach my former experiences came to life; I 'saw' cascades of energy coming down from outer space, in which particles were created and destroyed in rhythmic pulses; I 'saw' the atoms of the elements and those of my body participating in this cosmic dance of energy, I felt its rhythm and I 'heard' its sound, and at that moment I *knew* that this was the Dance of Shiva, the Lord of Dancers worshipped by the Hindus."

Phineas Quimby and Mary Baker Eddy would hardly have objected to this piece of prose. In contrast to them, however, the physicist did not become a mind healer. His divine business partner had other plans for him.

P rofessor James's ideas, too, were very much in line with those of Mrs. Eddy. At the conclusion of his series of lectures, he summarized the important features of all these extravagant forms of religious experience into two stages. First, James says, there comes a certain uneasiness. We sense that there is something wrong about us. This is followed by the second stage, in which we are saved from the wrongness by making proper connection with the higher powers. The better part of ourselves makes contact with a related something that is at work in the universe.

Professor James had certain difficulties with defining this superior force in terms of its content. A Christian explanation of the divine would be offensive to Hindus, a Hindu explanation to Muslims, a Muslim explanation to Buddhists, a Buddhist explanation to Jews, a Jewish explanation to Eskimos. The old battle of the theologians would begin afresh, without doing anything to further the psychological discussion of religious experience.

Therefore the professor risked a bold leap into the "subconscious self" of the individual. William James asserted that religious experience is the subconscious continuation of our conscious life.

Thus James set off down the road that was to be the highway of psychological treatment for the next hundred years. He didn't know that Dr. Freud's *The Interpretation of Dreams,* the work that set the standard for all future psychiatry, had been published in Vienna a short time before. Unlike James, Freud had no interest whatsoever in a business relationship with God. But such differences of opinion could do nothing at all to halt the triumphant march of psychotherapy.

All the same, the spiritual healing of a septic finger continued to be a phenomenon reserved to people outside the academic world. In the universities of the twentieth century, the Holy Spirit still fell within the jurisdiction of the faculties of theology. This did no harm to his effectiveness in the New World, among humble people who couldn't even afford to buy a railroad ticket.

There was something wrong with them; as children they were not well loved. Out there in the universe, in there in the subconscious, there had to be a firm that kept the right medicine in stock. Unfortunately, the firm's address had been lost. Mrs. Eddy declared that she knew where it was, and many believed her. Others stuck with their parish priests, even though they had no experience in healing. Still others sat in darkened rooms and listened to messages from the dead. Anyone who had enough money could pay for a voyage on the submarine of psychoanalysis. Along the way, one was required to talk endlessly, mostly about dreams. Now and then the dreams came from God.

# *Voluble Spirits*

IMMANUEL KANT PUBLISHED HIS *DREAMS of a Spirit-Seer, Illustrated by Dreams of Metaphysics* in 1766. The man whom he criticized in this work (and wanted placed in a madhouse) had the same first name as himself: Emanuel von Swedenborg (1688–1772). The name means "God with us."

The scorn of the philosopher from Königsberg was directed at a Swedish contemporary, an assessor of the Royal College of Mines, engineer, inventor, and author of scientific treatises, who had made a name for himself throughout Europe even before 1747, the year he was nominated for president of the Royal College of Mines in Sweden and responded by submitting a letter of resignation.

Swedenborg later wrote to the landgrave of Hessen-Darmstadt: "Because the Lord had prepared me for this from childhood, he revealed himself in person to me, his servant, and ordered me to perform this work. This happened in the year 1743, and afterward he showed me the face of my spirit and thus led me into the world of the spirits and allowed me to see heaven and its wonders, and at the same time to see hell as well, and also to speak with angels and spirits, and this has gone on continually now for twenty-seven years."

The story of how it came to this may be understood as an exemplary tale of convalescence, in which the newfangled science of engineering was inspired and transposed by the old-time Holy Spirit, to the advantage of the individual concerned.

When Swedenborg was forty-five years old, the signs that something was up as far as he was concerned began to multiply. "When I woke up this morning," the scientist noted on October 27, 1743, "such a dizziness or *deliquium* (a swooning away) overcame me that I felt close to death."

This happened in Amsterdam, where Swedenborg was busy with the composition of a work about the economy of the animal kingdom. Soon afterward he began to have vivid dreams. Naturally, he wrote them all down. The sleeper was standing next to the wheel of a machine, got caught in its spokes, and was yanked upward. He ran down some steps to a ladder that went down into a deep hole. He went walking in a park and noticed that the place was full of vermin that had to be collected and destroyed. He had injured himself and was waiting for some medicine to arrive. He found himself in a new house without a single item of furniture. His dead father appeared to him repeatedly, praised the one theological work that his son had thus far written, led him to a chamber where someone lay sleeping, admonished him to take up a spiritual vocation. Vicious dogs turned up frequently, also ghastly corpses that appeared lifeless but then suddenly began to move in their chains.

Swedenborg spent his life as a bachelor, though it can be assumed that he did not always practice abstinence. Then, suddenly—overnight, as it were—his passion for women was spent. He preferred to go to bed with the Bible.

On Easter Sunday, 1744, while still in Holland, Swedenborg, though he had gone to church and received Communion, fell into a state of intense anxiety. He felt that he was in hell, and at the mercy of Satan. "I went to bed around nine," he wrote in his diary, "but the temptation and the shivering that accompanied it lasted until ten thirty. Then I fell into a sleep in which my entire temptation passed before my eyes."

Sometime during the night, things took a turn; there was a radical change, "wonderful and indescribable," as Swedenborg expressed it. "I woke up in ecstasy. I was in heaven and heard words whose life and glory and bliss no tongue can tell. It was clear to me that there is such life and such glory in every single thing that I cannot describe it at all. I rose between nine and ten, and so had been abed twelve or thirteen hours. Praise, honor, and reverence to the Most High. I had in my spirit and body the feeling of such an indescribable bliss that it would have destroyed me had it been any stronger. This lasted the whole day."

Swedenborg had yet to hear any unearthly voice, but then, the next night (Easter Monday), Christ asked the astonished visionary, loudly and clearly, whether he had a health certificate.

The allusion was to a near disaster that had occurred in 1710. Because the English authorities believed that plague had broken out in Sweden, the ship that was taking the young Swedenborg to England to continue his studies was obliged to wait offshore for six weeks before passengers and crew could obtain permission to disembark. Swedenborg defied this prohibition and went ashore anyway, whereupon he was apprehended and very nearly hanged.

Swedenborg's diary entry for the night of Easter Monday, 1744, goes on: "I thought, what can this signify? Was it Christ whom I had seen? It's sinful of me to doubt it. But the injunction to test spirits obliged me to consider everything, and so I recognized from the events of the previous night that I had been purified, cared for, protected, and prepared by the Holy Spirit."

In May 1744, Swedenborg, still unsure what heaven wished of him, traveled on from Holland to England. In a dream two ladies, one younger and one older, had followed him; he had kissed their hands without knowing to which of them he should give precedence. It was possible that the older lady personified the works of scientific research he had thus far produced, the *Observations and Discoveries concerning Iron and Fire, together with a New Way of Constructing Ovens* of 1721, the *New Method of Determining the Degree of Longitude of Places, on Land or at Sea, by Observation of the Moon*, the *New Mechanical Plan for Constructing Docks and Dikes and the Method of Mechanically Testing the Powers and Properties of Vessels*, and *Miscellaneous Observations of the Natural World, Chiefly Minerals, Fire, and the Stratification of Mountains* of 1722, and so forth and so on, up to and including the third volume of his work, *The Animal Kingdom*, which he wanted to bring out in London.

But who was the younger lady?

In the middle of April 1745, Swedenborg was eating his midday meal when he was surprised by an angel who admonished him to keep a tighter rein on his appetite. The terrified scholar left the reserved room in the eating house where he took his meals. That night was a rocky one for him. The Lord God, draped in royal purple and majestically radiant, appeared in person next to mine assessor Swedenborg's bed and informed him that he had been chosen to unlock the spiritual meaning of the Bible for mankind. The actual calling, Swedenborg later related without particular emphasis, required about a quarter of an hour. During that same night, the spirit-world, hell and heaven, had been opened to him, he claimed, and he had seen several deceased acquaintances. "From then on," Swedenborg continued, "I renounced all worldly intellectual labors and worked only in the spirit."

The understanding king of Sweden graciously complied with his subject's request, and the assessor was pensioned on half salary.

His Majesty had surely acted wisely. The rest of Swedenborg's life— and he was to live on for nearly thirty years—was uncommonly fruitful. He produced about twenty thousand pages of print, remained alert and healthy to an advanced age, and was a convivial, charming companion. When a great fire broke out in Stockholm in 1759, Swedenborg was in Gothenburg, three hundred miles away from the catastrophe. He described it in detail to the people he was with, and a few days later, when a messenger arrived on horseback from Stockholm, Swedenborg's description was thoroughly confirmed.

Along with the gift of second sight, this remarkable man, like an

Indian yogi, had the ability to slow down his breathing considerably. From childhood on, it had sometimes happened that Swedenborg's breathing would become quite shallow, so that his chest hardly expanded at all. At first, this occurred during his daily prayers. Later, when he was engaged in intense reflection upon some scientific problem, he would forget to breathe for long periods of time, and of course when he was dealing with angels and spirits his breathing was practically suspended. "I became so completely accustomed to this type of respiration," Swedenborg remarked, "that I sometimes passed an entire hour without taking a breath. I had breathed in only enough air so that I could think."

Again and again, the visionary recorded what happened to him under such conditions. For example: "One day I was in the process of reflecting upon the creation of the universe. This was noticed by the angels who were on my right above me, where some were located who had reflected upon this subject a few times themselves. One climbed down and invited me to join them. I came in the spirit and accompanied him. After I had entered, I was led to the Prince, in whose court I found an assembly of about a hundred, with the Prince in their midst. When I was taking my leave, sparks of light from the sun of that place fell down through the angels' heaven into their eyes, and through these into the dwelling-place of their spirit. Thus were they illuminated, and they applauded my performance and followed me into the forecourt. But then my former escort followed me to the house where I was, and from there he climbed back up to rejoin his company."

The learned academy to which Swedenborg is translated has nothing obscurantist or sanctimonious in its makeup. The guest takes part in a disputation among enlightened spirits, and what he has to say is gladly accepted. On another occasion, famous philosophers present their cosmological theories, are convicted of their errors by angels, and cry out: "We were crazy!"

Swedenborg did not at all like to be interrupted during his absences. He was, however, caught in the act during a trip to Holland. Becalmed and unmoving, his ship lay before Helsingör, and a general of his acquaintance took advantage of this opportunity to row out and pay him a visit. The general opened the door of Swedenborg's cabin unannounced and found the famous man sitting on a table in his dressing gown, with his face in his hands and his open eyes turned upward. Some time passed before Swedenborg slowly began to come to, stood up in confusion, made a few faltering steps in the direction of his visitor, and recognized him at last.

Occasionally the spirit-seer also conversed with prominent figures, including Abraham, Moses, Solomon, and the apostles. Such encounters always proceeded discursively, in the tone of excited conversation, and both angels and evil spirits proved to be uncommonly eager to engage in debate. Eventually the debates were not about some theological subtlety, but about the most important project of modern European thought: the reconciliation of faith and knowledge.

This was the reason for Swedenborg's father's repeated appearances in his son's visionary states. The old gentleman had served the Swedish church as a bishop, feared by the royal court because of his intrepid sermons against abuse of high position and dissoluteness, famous among the people because of his powers as an exorciser of devils and a healer. Bishop Jesper had never been completely satisfied with his son Emanuel and his scientific leanings, always kept him short of cash, and feared that the younger man's learning would be injurious to his piety.

The son knew that such reservations were not to be gainsaid, even after the successful opening of the heavenly perspectives. What he learned there contradicted Christian dogma. "It's a fact worth knowing," Swedenborg wrote a few years before his death, "that some months ago the Lord called together his twelve apostles—they are now angels—and sent them out into the entire spiritual world with the mission of preaching the Gospel afresh, because the Church founded by the Lord through his apostles is presently so broken down that only a few remnants of it are still in existence. It has come to this because the divine Trinity has been divided into three Persons, each of whom is supposed to be God and Lord. From this beginning there has spread something like lunacy over all of theology and over the Church itself. Lunacy, I say, because this fundamental error has sent human minds into such madness that people do not even know anymore whether God is one God or three Gods."

By the end of his life, it had become clear to the elderly gentleman that such bizarreries belonged to a vanished past, or, more precisely, to the last of the four ages the world had passed through thus far, declining from

Adam's gold through Noah's silver and Moses' copper to the iron of Christianity. Starting in 1757—Swedenborg was quite categorical on this point—heaven had begun to take its leave of Christianity. A fifth, last, new era was already in the offing; it would entail a transformation of heavenly things, and this change would then have an effect upon people on earth.

Swedenborg called the future era the "New Church" and the "New Jerusalem." From there it was but a short step to the "New Age" of the English artist and poet William Blake (1757–1827). Phineas Parkhurst Quimby and Mary Baker Eddy also received stimulation from Swedenborg's thought. In the United States, there was the "General Convention of the New Jerusalem," established in 1817 in the spirit of the Swedish master. His writings were read with interest in the New World, for example by Ralph Waldo Emerson (1803–1882), New England's leading Romantic author.

Swedenborg's continuing influence took a more sensational form among American Spiritualists, who were interested in establishing communication with the spirits of the dead. The first propagandist of this ardent movement, Andrew Jackson Davis (1826–1910), said that even though he had never read a line of the Swedish mystic's work, Swedenborg was his first mentor from the next world. Starting in March 1848, when the Fox family home in Hydesville, New York, was afflicted by the famous rapping sounds, the dead began to make their presence known, with the greatest persistence, in the midst of the Industrial Age. A certain W. C. Brownell addressed this subject in *Scribner's Magazine:* "The influence of the Holy Spirit is a matter of actual experience, as solid a reality as that of electromagnetism."

Spirit-communication leaped like lightning from America to Europe and made tables dance all over the continent. "You laugh at us Yankees," a German immigrant wrote in 1853 to his sister in Bremen, "but there are things happening here that you in Europe don't even let yourselves dream about, and they're not as ridiculous as you might think. Have you ever in your life seen a heavy mahogany table, weighing sixty, eighty pounds, start to move, without being shoved or pushed by hands or feet or mechanical means, without being set in motion by any external, visible cause? Not once, but ten times have I seen this remarkable spectacle with my own eyes. I know a hundred people who've repeated it, everybody here is familiar with it."

It worked in Bremen, too. The woman who received the letter invited a few friends to her salon, as though to some sort of parlor game. Following the American brother's instructions precisely, the ladies and gentlemen sat around a table and formed a chain by clasping hands—and straightaway the table began to move. Soon afterward there appeared in Berlin a concise set of instructions for "producing in company this remarkable phenomenon of a newly discovered, human, elemental force."

At the same time, a hundred mediums were already working in New York, intermediaries between the spirit world and the public. This situation gave rise to a great deal of swindling, because a successful medium stood to make many dollars.

The most famous intermediary of this kind, a native-born Scot named Daniel Dunglas Home (1833–1886), never accepted money in return for demonstrating his incredible powers. He had been sent as a child to live with an aunt and her husband in America. From 1850 on, it was clear that the young man was a medium of the first order. In the presence of a committee from Harvard University, and in broad daylight, the table around which the gentlemen were sitting rose up on two legs like a rearing horse, while Home kept urging those present to hold tightly on to his arms and legs in order to ascertain that no tricks were being employed.

That was only the beginning. In 1855, Home went to London and stayed at Cox's Hotel in Jermyn Street, where the proprietor was interested in spirit-communication. Soon people from the best society were queueing up to arrange séances with Home. Dignified gentlemen like Sir David Brewster found themselves crawling under heavy tables to verify the phenomenon of levitation, and Mr. and Mrs. Robert Browning, freshly arrived from Florence for a holiday in their homeland, were pleased to accept an invitation to attend one of Home's evening sessions. The Brownings' poetry had made them famous, and accordingly their reaction to Home aroused considerable attention. The evening was a disappointment to Robert Browning, but Elizabeth reacted with enthusiasm. Charles Dickens refused to set eyes on Home. As far as the renowned author was concerned, "spirits" uttered nothing but nonsense. The socialist Robert Owen, on the other hand, delighted in their company.

Before Home retired in 1872, he traveled extensively, sojourning in Italy, France, and Russia, always welcome as a guest in the Tuileries or at the czar's court, invited by the Dutch queen Sophia, received by the pope. Home would allow no more than eight persons to attend his séances. He appeared before larger audiences only as a speaker; the talks he gave are said to have been quite humorous. He kept his distance from Spiritualist societies, wrote a book about his life, and worked as a correspondent for the *San Francisco Chronicle* during the Franco-Prussian War, which he covered from Prussian headquarters at Versailles. Home was twice married; he dressed like a snob, and because of the tuberculosis he suffered from all his life, he liked to make long stays on the Riviera. Sir Arthur Conan Doyle (1859–1930), a convinced Spiritualist who created in Sherlock Holmes the epitome of the sharp-witted investigator, thought that Home would be canonized some day.

During all his twenty years of activity as a medium, Home was never caught in a single deception. What took place in his presence is recorded in hundreds of eyewitness reports. One of these comes from the American author Nathaniel Hawthorne, who was present in Florence on an occasion when Home made the tables dance. A grand piano rose into the air while the Countess Orsini was playing on it; the ghost of twenty-seven dead monks manifested themselves collectively and tore a lady's skirt. All this was too much for Hawthorne. The incredibilities were so numerous, he said, that he had forgotten most of them. He did not doubt the "hundred percent" actuality of the events, but they were repeated so often that he grew bored. "I cannot force my mind to take any interest in them," Hawthorne concluded.

Much more concentration was brought to bear on this subject by Sir William Crookes, who had made a name for himself in 1861, when, at the age of twenty-nine, he discovered the chemical element thallium. In London, with the aid of special apparatus that he himself had made, Crookes investigated Home's paranormal abilities quite conscientiously and published the results between 1870 and 1874 in the *Quarterly Journal of Science*. The list of thirteen groups of individually performed exploits that

Crookes had observed contained, among others, levitation phenomena (in which human bodies floated freely in the air), luminous appearances, percussive sounds, and the materialization of disembodied hands and faces.

On July 17, 1882, four years before Home's death, Henry Sidgwick, professor in moral philosophy at Cambridge University, delivered an inaugural address before the members of the newly founded Society for Psychical Research. "The present state of affairs," Sidgwick said, "is a scandal for the enlightened age in which we live. It is utterly impossible to exaggerate the scientific significance of these amazing phenomena, even if only a tenth of what is asserted by generally reliable witnesses could be proved to be true. It is a scandal that the dispute about the reality of these phenomena is still going on."

A hundred years later, after the Society had published a total of forty thousand printed pages, the dispute wasn't over yet.


The problem of the century turned out to be so complicated because the spirits, loquacious though they might be, hardly ever said anything that went beyond simple understanding. The otherworldly realm that they told of matched the imaginative power of chambermaids; their reports to those they'd left behind didn't move past banalities. The greatest illusionist of all time, the unsurpassed Harry Houdini, who knew every trick and thought no undertaking too dangerous, was obliged to learn about spirits, much to his chagrin. During the 1920s his feats included jumping from one airplane to another, high in the air; hanging upside down from a skyscraper while wearing a straitjacket and escaping from it; being buried for forty-five minutes six feet underground in a coffin and stepping out of it unscathed. Obviously, it posed no problem for Houdini to go onto a public stage and make a few tables sail through the air or some spirit-hands appear. Nevertheless, to enter into contact with his deeply beloved mother, who had gone before him into eternity, remained his fondest wish.

During a European tour, Houdini made the acquaintance of Sir Arthur Conan Doyle, and the two world-famous men struck up a friendship.

In June 1922, they and their wives spent a few days on holiday together in the seaside resort of Atlantic City. One afternoon, as Houdini was playing with the Doyles' children on the beach, Sir Arthur appeared with the news that Lady Doyle felt moved to hold a séance. Houdini's mother was on the other end of the line.

In the hotel room, soon after they prayed together, Lady Doyle went into a trance. Her hands began to tremble a great deal, and with a quavering voice she asked the spirit that had seized her for a message. It was June seventeenth. The Doyles could not know that the séance was taking place on Houdini's mother's birthday. Soon Lady Doyle began to write, in English. *Oh my darling, thank God, thank God, at last I'm through.*

Never, the writing continued, had a mother such a son. He should not grieve; she was indescribably happy. There, where she was living now, everything was much more beautiful, filled with joy. Her only shadow was that her beloved one hadn't known how often she had been with him, all the while, all the while.

It would be appropriate, Sir Arthur opined, if Houdini should ask his mother a question, for example, whether or not she could read his mind. Why not, Houdini thought.

At once Lady Doyle's hand went flying over her writing pad again.

*I always read my beloved son's mind.* But, she went on, she still had so much to say. *God bless you, Sir Arthur. For what you are doing for us over here, who so need to get in touch with our beloved ones on the earth plane. Good-bye. I brought you and my darling son together. I felt you were the man who might help us to pierce the veil. Tell my dear son I am with him. Good-bye again. God's blessing be on you all.*

"My sainted mother spoke only broken English," Houdini said. He remained skeptical. What bothered him most was that there was a cross at the top of the writing pad. "My mother would never have made a cross," said Houdini. "She was a devout Hungarian Jewess. And why didn't she mention that today was her birthday?"

Sir Arthur became furious. Later, he wrote to Houdini: *The Cross is put by my wife above the first page of all she writes, as we guard against lower influences. I don't propose to discuss the subject any more with you.*

The great magician, however, was so disappointed that in the future he let slip no opportunity to catch mediums in the act. Sir Arthur called him a "medium-baiter," the sensitives' pest. Houdini himself was quite a distinguished medium, Conan Doyle added.

Perhaps. As mentioned, the controversy that Houdini and Doyle engaged in continues to this day. What's at stake are final certainties. The spirits give signs, but the signs are fleeting. That the Holy Spirit, the epitome of everything spiritual, is able to express himself only through hints is a bitter lesson that neither Doyle nor Houdini was able to accept. Doyle wanted to construct certain knowledge out of questionable communications; Houdini felt he'd been made a fool of. Once again skepticism and faith stood opposed to each other, unreconciled and unreconcilable. The Holy Spirit didn't get his messages through very well; apparently there was some little fault in the line. Too much noise.

# *Psychoanalyzing*

NO ONE COULD GUESS THAT THE HOLY Spirit, mobilized by means of good travel connections, was contriving the triumphal march of modern psychiatry, beginning with Swedenborg's spirits, who went to America, multiplied wondrously, and then returned in full force to Europe. Are the much despised "Spiritualism" and the "Society for Psychical Research," asked William James, to be the chosen instruments for a new era of faith?

Not necessarily. For the time being, the new era belonged to psychotherapy. The investigators of the psyche, having only recently attained a position of some respectability, flung themselves greedily upon the Spiritualistic bait. They could learn what the soul was capable of from mediums, and especially from the females among them.

In elegant Geneva, it was an attractive saleslady who aroused the interest of a professor of psychology named Théodore Flournoy. The young woman, Catherine-Elise Müller, was a dedicated spirit-medium and never accepted money for her séances. Flournoy was invited to one of her sittings for the first time in December 1894, and he was amazed to hear Mlle. Müller give detailed descriptions of events that had occurred long ago in his own family.

Thus began a relationship in which (as is so often the case) the woman was the giving one, while the man thought only about the book that was going to make him famous. For five years, Flournoy regularly attended the young lady's séances, and he was richly rewarded. The trances that the object of his investigations fell into grew steadily deeper; new speech patterns emerged, sounding like unintelligible gibberish.

In order to prevent prejudices from limiting his ability to make accurate observations, Flournoy proceeded according to a rule that he called the "Hamlet principle": Everything is possible. The Hamlet principle was qualified in turn by another maxim: The more unlikely an occurrence was, the weightier should be the proofs that spoke for it.

First of all, Flournoy found out that his parents knew the parents of Mlle. Müller. The medium, Flournoy concluded, could have heard those stories about the Flournoy family as a child, and then the same tales had come back to her in her trance. Because doctors love foreign words, Flournoy called this phenomenon of unconscious memories "cryptomnesia." It wasn't spirits that were at work, but childhood impressions.

Did the young woman have any idea how coldly she was being contemplated? In any case, she presented Flournoy and her other guests with an increasingly rich repertory of variegated, mysterious worlds, full of strange beauty, in stark contrast to the monstrous black-and-white everyday life of a minor employee in a department store.

Catherine (or Helen Smith, as she was known later on, when she became an international celebrity) had been a fifteenth-century Indian princess in one previous life and Marie-Antoinette in another. She consorted with Martians and spoke their language.

Flournoy wondered where all the details came from. He was delighted when he came across some books that Catherine had read as a child—*A History of India*, for example. Thus he could show the origin of the material the young woman used to embellish her revelations—or, to put it better, he could show the workings of the spirit that spoke through her when she was in a trance. The spirit's name was Leopold, and Flournoy interpreted him as an unconscious subpersonality of the medium. Even the idiom of the Martians gave up its secrets. A great part of the vocabulary was composed of distorted Hungarian words borrowed from the mother tongue of Catherine's father.

These disclosures dealt a heavy blow to Mlle. Müller's feelings. She broke with Flournoy, withdrew from the spiritist circle in which she had celebrated her triumphs, and quit her job. A wealthy American woman gave her a fortune. From then on Helen Smith lived in seclusion and occupied herself with painting religious pictures while in a state of trance. After her death, these paintings were exhibited in Geneva and Paris.

*Possibly schizophrenic.* In 1907, a Swiss psychiatrist named Jung gave this opinion about Helen Smith. She had entered the psychiatric literature, immortalized as a clinical case by Professor Flournoy. The twentieth century had begun. It was to bring forth any number of neurotics, some among them quite prominent, for example, Hitler. In peacetime neurotics underwent psychotherapy; in wartime they ran the government.

Carl Gustav Jung (1875–1961), son of a Protestant minister, heard about the mediumistic abilities of his fifteen-year-old cousin, Hélène Preiswerk, while he was a medical student in Basel. Later he was present when Helly gave edifying sermons in the deep voice of her grandfather, Pastor Samuel Preiswerk; chatted as the fifteenth-century Countess of Thierfelsenburg or the thirteenth-century Madame de Valours, who had been burned as a witch; and even became the mouthpiece of a Christian martyr from the time of Nero in Rome, not using Swiss dialect, which she usually spoke, but High German.

Jung was prepared for their first meeting. He was familiar with Spiritualist literature and had read with great interest seven volumes of Swedenborg's writings. The world gained depth and background. In his family home, an unflawed bread knife suddenly exploded into four pieces after the four o'clock coffee. Then came Helly.

Starting in the summer of 1899, during the sittings that Jung arranged for her with a small group of relatives, Helly described the canals on the planet Mars. Rapping sounds came from the walls of the room, and she told of her seduction (in a former life) by Goethe. She described the structure of the mystical world in terms of seven circles, but after some time she sensed that her audience was starting to get bored. Eventually she was caught out while attempting to "materialize" little "gifts from the spirits," which were in fact various odds and ends that she had secretly brought with her to the sessions.

At any rate, Jung now had a subject for his dissertation. In 1902, Oswald Muntze in Leipzig published Jung's *Zur Psychologie und Pathologie sogenannter occulter Phänomene* ("On the Psychology and Pathology of So-called Occult Phenomena"), in which Helly appears as a hysteric under the pseudonym "S.W."; Professor Flournoy gave the essay an enthusiastic review. When Jung visited Helly a year later in Paris, where she was an apprentice dressmaker, she was unable to remember anything about her mediumistic activity. It was only later that Jung realized that she had fallen in love with him.

L ike his older colleague Sigmund Freud (1856–1939), with whom he worked for a few years, Jung was an extreme psychopath. At the age of forty he went through an intense psychological crisis, in which he was haunted by the voices of the dead. During the First World War, Jung's villa on the Lake of Zurich began to be haunted. A white figure was wandering about, the front doorbell rang frantically, but no one was there. Jung heard the spirits' voices. They cried out in chorus: *We have come back from Jerusalem where we found not what we sought.*

Jung no longer had any business teaching at the University of Zurich, where he had been a *Privatdozent,* or outside lecturer. He gave up his academic career and stopped reading the specialist literature in his field. Every morning he sketched in a notebook a circular figure that corresponded to his mental condition. After the midday meal, he would walk along the shore of the lake, gathering small stones like a child and building things with them: little houses, a whole village. His psychiatric practice, at fifty francs an hour, was doing well; his family was in no danger of going hungry. What was going on inside him was nobody's business, at first. "I stood helpless before an alien world," Jung later recalled. "I was living in a constant state of tension; often I felt as if gigantic blocks of stone were crashing down on me. My enduring these storms was a question of brute strength. Others have been shattered by them."

At first the Holy Spirit came to him in a dream, in the shape of a friendly white dove that alighted on a table made of green stone where Jung and his children were sitting, somewhere in Italy. Then the bird metamorphosed into a little girl with golden-blond hair who ran off to play with the children. She came back and tenderly placed her arms around Jung's neck, then suddenly became the graceful dove again and said: "Only in the first hours of the night can I transform myself into a human being, while the male dove is busy with the twelve dead."

Jung had no idea how to interpret this dream. During the years when his principal occupation was his own inner life, Jung occasionally traveled to Geneva to see his colleague Flournoy; the two men discussed Spiritualism and the psychology of religion.

Physician, heal thyself. Jung's patients profited from this turning point in their psychoanalyst's life, because it opened for him the divine world into which he allowed himself to fall, just as he required them to do. The hackneyed catchwords (*individuation, archetype, collective unconscious*) that stand like petrifying slogans under Jung's name in every encyclopedia mark the points of reference in a wilderness whose laws the psychologist, by experimenting upon himself, was able to work out only very slowly. "I had an unswerving conviction," said Jung, "that I was obeying a higher will, and that feeling continued to support me until I had mastered the task."

After the war, in 1919, Jung gave a talk at the Society for Psychical Research in London. His subject was belief in spirits, which he interpreted as projections of the split parts of the unconscious. As a punishment for this impudence, in 1920 the local ghost appeared to him in an English haunted house.

With the localization of gods and spirits in the unconscious, the theorists of depth psychology found themselves caught in an epistemological cleft stick. Meaningful (and therefore scientifically useful) propositions presuppose consciousness. Strictly speaking, statements about subject matter that is beyond consciousness are not possible. "What we cannot speak about we must pass over in silence," declared Ludwig Wittgenstein in his famous logical-philosophical treatise. The depth psychologists had no intention of adhering to such a maxim. Like the spirits, they loved to chatter.

In order to keep from appearing scientifically absurd, Jung sought and found in the history of religion documentation for the confused world that he had encountered in his own dreams and in the stories of his patients. He read, for example, a four-volume work from 1812, *Symbolik und Mythologie der alten Völker, besonders der Griechen* (*"The Symbolism and Mythology of Ancient Peoples, Particularly the Greeks"*), by Georg Friedrich Creuzer. What Jung found conspicuous was that all the centaurs, nymphs, and other hybrid beings from Creuzer's collection of curios were strongly suggestive of the chaotic fantasies of the mentally disturbed. More and more, Jung's prose was enriched by learned quotations from the Bible, the Epic of Gilgamesh, the Upanishads. The psychiatrist was transformed into a scholar of comparative religion, collected an impressive library of rare alchemical treatises from the Baroque period, corresponded with sinologists and Indologists, wrote a commentary on *The Tibetan Book of the Dead*, and after 1933 was the central figure in the summer gatherings known as the Eranos Lectures, annual conferences held on the lake estate of Casa Gabriella, near Ascona on Lago Maggiore, where renowned theologians and religious scholars from all over the world delivered their learned papers.

Naturally Jung was called upon to answer the question of whether he believed in God. "I do not believe, I know," Jung answered on British television, two years before his death. His remark provoked many letters, to which Jung replied with a letter to the editor of the *Listener*. "Insofar as I know of the clash with a higher will in my own psychic system," Jung wrote, "I know about God."

The celebrated man expressed himself so decisively only in his old age, when he had already become an icon and no longer needed to fear the judgment of the psychiatric guild, which had long since stricken the Good Lord from its professional vocabulary.

In May 1986, Ronald David Laing (1927–1989), psychiatrist and critic of psychiatry, asked: What does God have to do with the manual of American psychiatry?

Nothing, he wrote. He was the David who took on a Goliath in the form of *DSM III (The Diagnostic and Statistical Manual of the American Psychiatric Association, Third Edition)*. Psychiatrists all over the world followed *DSM III*, which provided a complete inventory of all forms of "mental disorders," such as, for example, magical thinking, superstition, telepathy, and clairvoyance. In *DSM III*, Laing continued, anyone who resists the authority of his parents and teachers is suffering from a mental disturbance. *DSM III* censures everything that doesn't jibe with the psychiatrists' notion of normalcy, including very many concepts that at all times and places have been deemed ordinary manifestations of ordinary human minds, speech, and conduct in human civilizations, for example, God. I hate this manual, Laing concluded, and I fear it. I recognize myself, torn into items, strewn over almost every page of *DSM III.*

# *Of Low Estate*

THE PSYCHIATRISTS DIDN'T KNOW WHAT to do with God the Holy Spirit because they had become accomplices in the official surveillance of the citizenry. Whatever deviated from the norm was necessarily an object of suspicion to them. The Holy Spirit had never let himself be appropriated by those in high places—in contrast to God the Father and God the Son, who were glad to be brought in to help with royal coronations, during oath-taking in courtrooms, and in the event of war. The Holy Spirit preferred to linger among half-crazed nuns, eyeball-rolling prophets, desert dwellers, forest people, at the edge of the world, not in the centers of power. He was inclined to recruit his mediums from the bottom levels of society, from the low-income groups of every period, starting with the carpenter's son and his following of Galilean fishermen and continuing through Phineas Quimby, Mary Baker Eddy, and Daniel Dunglas Home. Once or twice such play resulted in a world religion, but much more often produced some fringe group, or nothing at all.

.   .   .

In America that same Andrew Jackson Davis who had claimed Swedenborg as his otherworldly mentor insisted on a combination of Spiritualism and socialism, with good success among tradesmen and workers. In 1858, at a convention of Spiritualist societies held in Plymouth, Massachusetts, delegates from all over the country adopted a program that called for education reform, women's emancipation, the abolition of slavery, and social reforms based on the principle of universal brotherhood. Out of a population of 28,000,000 in the country at the time, one million Americans were involved in the Spiritualist movement.

Davis was from Poughkeepsie, New York, on the Hudson River. He never went to school, but he learned the shoemaker's trade from his father. When he was seventeen years old, he attended a series of lectures on hypnotism, allowed himself to be put into a trance, and in this way discovered that he was a gifted clairvoyant. By the age of twenty-one, Davis was already a successful author and much in demand as a lecturer who accurately predicted the imminent manifestations of spirits from the next world. Beginning in 1848, Davis worked on the composition of his five-volume *Great Harmonia,* which was influenced by the ideas of the French utopian thinker Charles Fourier (1772–1837) and advocated the abolition of alcoholism, prostitution, slavery, racial discrimination, social oppression, the death penalty, and war. Davis had little use for the Christian consciousness of sin and was thus able to concentrate all the more intensely on the harmonious higher development of mankind, under the beneficent *influx* of the departed. These latter lived in "Summerland," into which Davis was permitted the occasional peek.

What he saw there inspired him to conceive a pedagogical program whose details he took from the writings of the German educational reformer Friedrich Fröbel (1782–1852), which were read and appreciated in America. Advanced ideas about schooling were translated into the "Children's Progressive Lyceums," schools for children three years and older that did away as much as possible with classroom-bound, teacher-centered instruction and recommended a great deal of movement in fresh air and cheerful singing. It goes without saying that it was humble provincial folk and not the Vanderbilts who sent their children to Lyceum schools.


Similarly, back in England, Spiritualism blossomed not among members of the House of Lords, but in the "Workmen's Hall" in Keighley, a town that lay to the west of the industrial center of Leeds, amid the factories of one of the most economically important region of the country. Beginning in 1853, a health fanatic named David Richmond preached Spiritualism there, with marked success among the working people of Yorkshire and Lancashire. Of course, the workmen couldn't spare a great deal of time for Spiritualism. They worked sixteen hours a day.

In England, proletarian Spiritualism and radical engagement in the class struggle got along famously. Shortly before his death, the old socialist leader Robert Owen (1771–1858) wrote *Footfalls on the Boundary of Another World*. Halting steps on the margins of a different reality were not conceived as warrants of the next life, but rather as anticipations of a spiritually enlivened socialist future.

In addition, all sorts of alternative healing methods were taught in Spiritualist circles, and this saved many workers' families from running up doctors' bills. Along the same lines, it wasn't rare for mediums to replace pastors on Sunday mornings, in an atmosphere of freethinking piety without dogmatic constraints. The spirits in the coal-mining districts had decidedly anticlerical leanings.

Apparently they preferred to express themselves in English. They spoke German only in the better circles of society between Hamburg and Vienna, while the working classes there preferred to read the *Communist Manifesto* of Engels and Marx. The revolution-friendly intelligentsia of Germany and Austria would have been glad to shake things up thoroughly in 1848. To their disappointment, all that happened was that the tables began to dance. The English had their Glorious Revolution behind them; revolution had never worked in Austria and Germany. The spiritual telegraph system in those countries functioned principally on the right side of the political spectrum; social democracy combated Spiritualism as a new version of the old sanctimonious swindle of the parsons, and only in one single case did the Holy Spirit take part in the building of a New Jerusalem for ordinary people. This story begins in 1921 in the state of Brandenburg, south of Berlin, between the towns of Trebbin and Beelitz.

There, despite inflation and the worldwide economic crisis, a garden city arose, with spacious houses for families, a school, a farm that was an agricultural model, a large community laundry, an old people's home with health spa facilities, an assembly hall, a church, a restaurant with a terrace café, and a museum. By 1934 five hundred people were living in the settlement, which was located in the midst of a delightful landscape on the slopes of the Glauer Mountains. Above the stage in the assembly hall, under an imposing crucifix, hung the picture of a stocky, white-haired man with an impressive girth and the look of a respectable innkeeper. Dark eyes, large mustache. This was Joseph Weissenberg, born in 1855, founder and leader of the *Evangelisch-Johannische Kirche* (the Evangelical Church of the Revelation of Saint John the Divine, also known as the *Johannische Kirche* or Church of Saint John) and the driving force behind the idea of the *Friedenstadt*, the City of Peace, large enough for twenty thousand inhabitants and situated on German soil. To this day the *Johannische* Christians say the following prayer: "I believe in God the Father, I believe in God the Son, I believe in the Holy Spirit and in God's revelations through Moses, Jesus Christ, and Joseph Weissenberg."

On January 17, 1935, the German state police office for the Berlin police district banned the Church of Saint John, declared it dissolved, and confiscated its property. The *Friedenstadt* was placed under compulsory public administration. The weekly newspaper *Deutsche Wochenschau* wrote: "Through the initiative of Hermann Göring, an end has been put to the Weissenberg nuisance once and for all." On March 1, Weissenberg wrote to Hitler: "My Führer! Give a German his religious freedom back. I know that my heavenly Father is your Father, too." On May 18, the eighty-year-old Weissenberg was arrested, charged with sex crimes, and sentenced to eighteen months in prison. In 1938 he was temporarily released, then committed to an insane asylum, and finally handed over to the care of his family in Bad Obernigk, Silesia, where he died in 1941. However, several years later, in the Glauer Mountains above the *Friedenstadt*, a Soviet officer spotted him, walking with a dog but otherwise alone.

The Master—as Weissenberg's congregation still likes to call him— had to suffer in more ways than those devised for him by the National

Socialist authorities. Before 1933, the medical profession brought numerous suits against him for quackery. He was also a thorn in the side of
Prussia's Protestant clergy, because (among other reasons) he taught the
transmigration of souls and claimed to be the incarnation of the Holy
Spirit. Politics, medicine, and religion dealt quite ungraciously with this
intruder into their domains.

On a higher plane, attitudes were different. "The power to heal the
sick by the simple act of laying hands on them or stroking them manifested itself in me when I was still a child," Weissenberg wrote. "The gifts
I was given were magnetic healing power, second sight, keenness of hearing, sensitivity of feeling. I have seen things in many, many forms, including spirits."

They spoke to the boy as he watched his flock in the Silesian countryside, where he grew up in the care of a shepherd after the deaths of his
parents. Later he learned bricklaying, then got called up for military
service. After that was over, he struggled along, working as a domestic
servant, cab driver, waiter, and street vendor during the winter months
when no building jobs were to be had. Marriage with Auguste Lautner,
birth of a daughter, a move to Berlin, launching of a career as a hypnotic
healer in 1903, separation from his wife in 1907, beginning of cohabita-
tion with Grete Müller in 1909, two more daughters. Weissenberg, who
had been baptized as a Catholic, converted to Protestantism in 1904; he
founded the *Johannische Kirche* in 1926.

In 1903, Weissenberg wrote to Kaiser Wilhelm II: "I see Your Majesty in fifteen years, leaving Germany and carrying a beggar's staff."

This prediction proved to be completely correct.

People began to talk about the Master's healing practice on the north
side of Berlin at 42 Gleimstrasse, among the rented barracks of the workers' district, consultations daily except Wednesday and Saturday from 10
A.M. to 4 P.M. In order to answer the great demand for his services, the
busy healer instructed a series of female assistants in the art of hypnotic
treatment. The patients would take a seat; the apprentice would kneel on a
stool facing them. Then she would stroke them with her hands, along the
arms and down over the hips, for five minutes. At this point the Master
would appear and prescribe, depending on the patient, salted curd cheese,
yarrow tea, ablutions with urine, gruel, two Our Fathers.

Many of those who were healed remained devoted followers. They attended the weekly assemblies of the "Christian Association of Serious Explorers from This Life to the Next," which Weissenberg registered with the authorities. These gatherings took place in rented halls and featured the messages of the "spirit-friends," delivered through the mouths of various mediums, chief among them the Master's companion. Otto von Bismarck spoke with particular frequency from the land of the dead, but Luther, Frederick the Great, and Baron von Richthofen also made themselves heard. The denizens of the next world railed against Freemasons, Bolsheviks, Jews. From time to time while this was going on, one or another of the young mediums might become overwrought and begin to scream, which behavior, under certain circumstances, could earn her a box on the ear from the Master.

For the most part, however, Weissenberg's command was enough: *I'm switching off!* Then that spirit stopped talking, and the Master switched on another one. "Throughout the hall dozens of hysterical women jump out of their seats," wrote the *Journal for Public Education against Quackery and Healing Fraud.* "Waving arms. Distorted faces. Wild, nerve-shattering, hooting shrieks, the excruciating animal sounds of women in painful childbirth, the muffled, fearful, voluptuous groans of women being raped. One woman marches up and down the center aisle, throwing out her legs like a marionette and strenuously calling for the Lord Jesus. But the Master shoos his raving female admirers into silence like a flock of cackling hens; in the midst of this rapturous screaming, this blasphemous and pathological adoration, he stands unmoving, as though he expects nothing less."

Weissenberg's faithful defended themselves against such malevolent accounts of their worship by distributing apologias. "It is the pure and simple Word of God that is preached among us," they wrote, "from spirit-friends of the light to new tongues. Our goal is the reconciliation of all churches and the return of the fragmented communities of faith to Christ's original Church. The Church of St. John has the third doctrine, the doctrine of the Holy Spirit."

By the end of the 1920s, the Master was welcoming as many as a thousand visitors to the halls where services were held. At the entrances to the halls, magazines and health teas were on sale and membership fees were collected. "Without exception, the public came from the lower middle class," an observer wrote; "women are in the majority, but the number of male participants is by no means small. There was a strikingly large number of children and young girls. Most of the women wore brooches with portraits of the Master."

By that time, the Church of Saint John counted forty thousand members in Berlin alone, with an equal number in the surrounding area, all the way to Saxony, divided into four hundred congregations. Their name referred to the Apocalypse of Saint John, and they prophesied every imaginable future event, perhaps including the world economic crisis of 1929 and Hitler's seizure of power a few years later.

At any rate, *Der Weisse Berg* (*"The White Mountain"*), the magazine of the *Johannische Kirche*, carried the following headline: "Isolating the Powers of Darkness through the Might of the Holy Spirit in National Socialism!"

In this regard, the Master, like the famous Professor Martin Heidegger, was mistaken. Whether Spiritualistic or philosophical in origin, attempts to distinguish among spirits were fraught with perils. Hitler's *Heil* proved to be a salute to the impostures of the Antichrist, enacted amid the laughter of hell.

After the war, Weissenberg's daughter, Frieda Müller, her father's designated successor, gathered the faithful together again and made a fresh start. In 1976, she received the Order of the Federal Republic of Germany, First Class, for the social work of her organization. Twenty years later, after the *Friedenstadt* had been restored to the possession of the Church of Saint John, the still sprightly old lady wrote a prayer on the occasion of a groundbreaking ceremony for a new cow barn.

# *First*

# *Beginning*

IN THE YEARS BETWEEN THE TWO MOST AMBI-

*tious armed struggles of human history, the leading minds of the literary world had but two*

*wishes. They wanted to become immortal, and to look upon the face of God. Some were*

*granted the first wish by being awarded the Nobel Prize. But even those chosen ones fared*

*as did Moses, who was permitted to glimpse God only from behind.*

# The Struggle for God

*T*HE DESERT GROWS. THE RESPECTABLE professor of classical philology Friedrich Nietzsche (1844–1900) had taken early retirement at the age of thirty-five because of ill health, and now, three years later, he was having more and more difficulty coping. "Pain vanquishes life and will," he wrote, describing his migraine attacks (which lasted for days) to his most constant friend, the critical theologian Franz Overbeck. For a time another friend, the musician Heinrich Köse-litz, had to lead the sufferer around Venice like a blind man because of his ailing eyes. The cheap rooms that were all Nietzsche could afford on his meager pension offered him no sort of comfort. He had broken with Richard Wagner, the most significant person in his life during his most hopeful years, in 1878. Only a few copies of the works that Nietzsche had thus far published had been sold. *The desert grows. Woe to him who conceals deserts.*

The God of the Lord's Prayer and of the Lutheran pastor's house into which Nietzsche was born had disappeared. Where has God gone, Nietz-sche wondered in his notebooks, what have we done? Have we drunk the ocean dry? How have we managed to wipe away that eternally fixed line according to which all master builders of life have built until now? Are we ourselves still standing on our own feet? Aren't we incessantly falling? Haven't we wrapped infinite space around us like a cloak of icy air? We still fail to see our own death, our own dust, and this deceives us and makes us believe that we ourselves are light and life—but it's only life as it once was, the old life in the light, bygone humanity with its bygone God, whose rays and heat still reach us. How much brightness do we have, compared with bygone generations?

The young lady whom Nietzsche met in April 1882 had similar problems. She was Louise von Salomé (1861–1937), a native of St. Petersburg, the only daughter of a Russian general of French Huguenot descent. She had been living in Rome with her mother since the beginning of the year, and she was interested in the new ideas that were swirling around in the intellectual world. Respectable ladies in the capital city of the czarist empire still recalled the general's daughter's clandestine visits to the pastor at the Dutch embassy and her refusal to be confirmed in her family's faith. The extravagant girl thought as little of convention as she did of the physical circumstances attendant upon eroticism. The sickly German scholar, who had agreed to meet the young Russian for the first time in Saint Peter's Basilica, of all places, could not hide his fascination.

Before long a drama began to unfold whose script was much the same as the one that had determined the relationship between the general's daughter and the Dutch pastor. Lou, as Nietzsche was soon permitted to call her, felt strongly drawn to intellectual men, who for their part mistook her affection for a declaration of love. This time the scenario called for a triangle. Nietzsche's friend Paul Rée, who had instigated the meeting in Rome, remained thoroughly present in this complicated force field, which was later immortalized, almost as a joke and at Nietzsche's insistence, in a photographer's studio in Lucerne, Switzerland. The picture shows the two men standing on either side of the shaft of a two-wheeled farm cart, in which Lou kneels with a little whip in her hand.

The story ended, naturally, with a farewell forever, after six months. Lou moved to Berlin with Rée; Nietzsche remained alone, working on his book *Thus Spoke Zarathustra.*

Lou recognized the constant in her relationship with Nietzsche immediately and accurately, identifying this difficult man as a "God-seeker" and attributing to him a "religious nature." She expatiated upon her meaning in her first novel, *Im Kampf um Gott ("The Struggle for God"),* published under the pseudonym Henri Lou in 1885. The novel records the memoirs of an old man named Kuno, like Nietzsche a parson's son, who loses his faith early in life and then becomes entangled in three insoluble love affairs, each of which ends fatally for the woman involved. Ultimately he comes to the conclusion that the best life, for natures born to struggle like his own, is characterized by moving from god to god. The book was favorably received. Nietzsche read it too, and found its contents—apart from its schoolgirlish style—not bad at all.

The philosopher was less lenient in his judgment of *Parsifal*, the work of Richard Wagner's old age, which had its premiere in the Bayreuth Festival Theater in 1882. This work, too, dealt with religion, but it did so in a manner that Nietzsche was obliged to reject, like an obscene arrangement. After Wagner died in 1883, the composer's former friend and admirer felt released from all scruples of consideration and publicly attacked the maestro in a pamphlet entitled "The Wagner Case." Through Wagner, Nietzsche wrote, modernity speaks its most intimate language. It hides neither its good nor its evil, it has lost all sense of shame.

Nietzsche was at loggerheads with the modern anyway. Anti-Semitism and German hyper-patriotism were as repugnant to him as socialist ideas and belief in progress. He perceived his time as the feeble final joke in a long comedy that, under the direction of Christianity, had become increasingly dull over the course of the last two millennia. And it was the aforesaid Christianity that had persuaded mankind to make its salvation dependent on works of mercy, the care of festering wounds, kindness to stinking beggars. The servants of the man who died on the cross did not preach successful development, health, and cheerfulness, but rather consciousness of sin, humility, and willingness to suffer. Sick shepherds, sick flocks was Nietzsche's description of the priests of the Church. Their morbidity had infected the body of European society, whose excretions Nietzsche, influenced by the French cultural critic Paul Bourget, denounced under the code word *décadence*. "I am, as well as Wagner," Nietzsche wrote, "the child of this time, I mean a *décadent*; the difference is that I understood this, I defended myself against it . . . My greatest experience was a convalescence. Wagner belongs to my diseases."

Nietzsche thought of the disappearance of God as a moment within a general process of cultural decline. Instead of requiring his audience to face that fact, Wagner had become pious in his old age and devised a festival production for a consecrated stage. What does it mean, Nietzsche wrote, when an artist like Wagner pays homage to chastity? Parsifal, that poor devil of a nature boy whom Wagner by such awkward means makes a Catholic at last—what does Parsifal really matter to him?

Wagner had tried to forestall such embarrassing questions with a little joke. He had dedicated a copy of his libretto for Parsifal to "his dear friend Friedrich Nietzsche" and signed it "Member of the Church Council"—but in vain. Wagner and Nietzsche never spoke to each other again.

The conflict between these two epochal men admittedly concerned more than Good Friday magic tricks for distinguished magnates and superior daughters. The brightness of contemporary "culture" was at stake, compared with the uplifting achievements of bygone generations—the Gothic cathedrals, the *Divine Comedy*, Michelangelo's "David," Raphael's *Stanze* in the Vatican, the Masses of Palestrina, the cantatas of Johann Sebastian Bach. All these things owed their existence to a religious faith whose truth had faded away long since, according to Nietzsche, who admitted to himself, "not without deep pain," that the artists of every age, in their finest creations, had elevated into heavenly transfiguration those very same images "which we now recognize as false."

The eagle eye of the cultural critic and philosopher registered with great precision his famous friend's weakness, his inability to endure such pain. Wagner's entire oeuvre was an attempt to conjure up the past, decked out on historicist principles like the neo-Gothic city halls and churches of the Industrial Age. Nietzsche decreed that Wagner was to be understood, not as a seer into the future, but as an interpreter and transfigurer of the past. He had made this assessment, ironically enough, in his tribute, "Richard Wagner in Bayreuth," written to commemorate the opening of the Bayreuth Festival Theater in 1876.

There was more. The maestro was "backward," not only in the selection and shaping of his material, but also in his music, the soul of the enterprise, which Nietzsche felt obliged to characterize as "dying away," "too late in coming," and "swansong."

After "everything was clear, but everything was over" between Wagner and Nietzsche, as the latter described the situation in a letter to Lou, Wagner had a bad dream. A crowd of people forced their way into his house. The last of them was Nietzsche, who sang the maestro a mocking song set to the melody of the "Pilgrims' Chorus" from *Tannhäuser.*

During the next hundred years, the marriage between philosophy and music went blithely on. Wagner was played, Nietzsche was read. Hitler admired both of them, and God had disappeared—not only from Germany.

# *Inaccessible*
# *to Your Steps*

*L*OU, HOWEVER, WANDERED FROM GOD to god. Whether it was Rainer Maria Rilke (1875–1926) or another man who kissed her awake cannot be determined with absolute certainty. It was not the Orientalist Friedrich Carl Andreas, whom Lou married in 1887; she had agreed to the marriage only under the condition that they were not to consummate it. Another candidate for sharing Lou's first night of love was Friedrich Pineles, a Viennese physician seven years younger than Lou, who in the meanwhile had reached her middle thirties. There is no mention of him, however, in *Lebensrückblick* (*"Looking Back at Life"*), Lou's memoirs.

When the twenty-two-year-old René Rilke was introduced to her in May 1897, Lou Andreas-Salomé was already a noted writer, the author of studies of Ibsen and Nietzsche. After meeting this beautiful woman, Rilke wrote her a letter telling her that he had experienced her essay "Jesus the Jew" as a revelation. Though his gratitude could not be expressed with others present, perhaps he might hope to read her some of his poems on another occasion.

This request, and more, was granted. Within four weeks René had been renamed Rainer and was wandering barefoot with Lou through the dewy meadows around the little town of Wolfratshausen, near Munich, where a small farmhouse had been rented. "Oh you, my June night with a thousand paths," Rilke wrote, "whereon no initiate has trod before me." Lou's husband arrived, but his presence didn't cause any complications. They agreed to take Rilke with them to Berlin, where Lou lived with her husband on the outskirts of the city. Lodgings for Rainer were found in a nearby village. He helped Lou with cooking and chopping firewood. His favorite dishes were Russian gruel and borscht.

Although punctuated by long intervals of separation, the relationship between the authoress and the poet lasted until Rilke's death. Happiness and harmony prevailed during the two trips to Russia that Lou and Rainer took together, in 1899 and 1900, the first with Lou's husband, and the second without him. Later she wrote that Rainer had adopted the Russian God, which lets himself be pressed to the bosom like a little dove. In Rilke's *Book of Hours,* he expresses the view that man has to place God under his care.

And vice versa. This sense of complete security, Lou thought, leads to confidence in one's surroundings, whatever they may be. Besides, she wasn't ready to play the role of the little God-dove in Rilke's life. She sent her sensitive friend to the artists' community in Worpswede, near Bremen, where he checked the galley proofs of his *Stories of God* and made the acquaintance of the painter Clara Westhoff, whom he married a year and a half later, when she was already expecting a child. Lou was pregnant, too, and keeping company with Pineles, her physician friend from Vienna, but her pregnancy lasted only a few months. She must give up the idea of being a mother, she wrote to Rilke. And she told him: "Go on, follow your dark God! He can do what I can no longer do for you."

This challenge to keep moving reflects the need for travel that was part of the makeup of this extraordinary woman. After she left St. Petersburg, she never lasted more than several months in the same place. The half year of her association with Nietzsche was passed in Rome and Milan, on Lake Orta in northern Italy, in Lucerne, in Tautenburg in Thuringia, in Leipzig. In between these places, Lou, happy as a little bird, made stops in Zurich, Hamburg, Berlin, the west Prussian town of Stibbe, and Bayreuth. To be sure, it wasn't long before Mama traveled back to St. Petersburg and paid no more hotel bills, but she sent a monthly allowance of 250 marks, which was enough for Lou to get by. From Berlin, where she set up her first base of operations, Lou made long sojourns in Merano (southern Tirol) and near the Tegernsee (southern Bavaria), as well as in

Paris, Vienna, and Munich. Later she went to the Balkans and Turkey, to the Sudeten Mountains, to Spain, Sweden, and Switzerland, to visit relatives in St. Petersburg, to the Harz Mountains, to Venice.

Rilke, too, was a restless vagabond, with a certain inclination toward elegant surroundings in noble houses, constantly on the lookout for places conducive to poetic inspiration. When the Princess Marie von Thurn und Taxis took him along for a drive in her automobile, he was as delighted as a child.

Nietzsche, on the other hand, was driven by his neuralgia from place to place, to Italy in winter, in summer to Sils-Maria in the Engadine valley in southeastern Switzerland, where things were cheaper than in St. Moritz. Naumburg, Bolzano, Riva, Venice, Carinthia, Tirol, Marienbad—all in the first six months of 1880. Schedules, luggage, customs formalities, searches for lodgings. Back again to Naumburg, then in October stops in Frankfurt and Heidelberg, followed by Basel, Locarno, and Stresa, where Nietzsche wanted to spend several weeks; winter, however, was already in the air; he thought perhaps he'd try Castellamare, near Naples, and finally settled in Genoa to wait for spring.

*I*n a distant land, inaccessible to your steps. Wagner, likewise a driven man, keeps the place of redemption unreachable. *A castle lies, its name is Monsalvat.* The divine service that is celebrated there is only vaguely reminiscent of the Christian liturgy. Each year a dove from heaven draws nigh, and the purpose of its coming is to strengthen the miraculous power of the Holy Grail.

In *Parsifal,* with a sure touch, the Holy Spirit was taken out of his usual jurisdiction and placed inside the reigning divine darkness. It cannot touch him, but in exchange for this immunity he renounces the right to make denominational determinations. The Holy Grail, the vessel of miraculous blessings, merely alluded to the Christian Last Supper and to the Communion cup used during Sunday services in Germany's churches. Had the Holy Spirit degenerated into a character in an opera?

Not unconditionally. Wagner's consciousness of himself as an artistic personality took no account of the "amusement" of the public. The Maestro of Bayreuth introduced the practice of turning off the house lights during the overture, of forbidding entrance to the auditorium when the curtain is up, of limiting applause to the end of each act. All this gave evidence of seriousness and concentration; it showed that something out of the ordinary was going on. Wagner wanted his *Parsifal,* in which Grail and dove both appear, to be performed only in Bayreuth, thus preserving the worshipful quality of the work from diminishment by repertory performances on one or another little provincial stage.

Church-minded people might criticize Wagner's ambitions as ersatz religion, artificial religion. In the light of the history of religiousness, however, the maestro was holding several very high trumps. Hadn't the drama of ancient Athens arisen out of cultic performances in honor of the god Dionysus? Didn't every sort of divine worship—this was especially evident in the rites practiced in Byzantium and in ancient Rome—have its entrances, its antiphonal singing, its performances, comparable with the *Gesamtkunstwerk,* the synthesis of all the arts, that Wagner was striving for? Weren't masks and costumes as much a part of religion as they were of the theater?

In his theoretical writings, Wagner insisted that in the end there was a difference between "veritable religiosity" and "religion" as regulated by a state-sponsored Church. One of these two types was meant when the curtain rose in Bayreuth, and there was no need to emphasize which one it was.

In the light of theology as well, Wagner's concern with bringing the Holy Spirit to the stage was by no means a blunder. Had God the Father or God the Son been personified by actors and given human traits, such a representation would have clashed with the fundamental unrepresentability of the eternal and would have been constantly in danger of seeming blasphemous or even ridiculous. The dove, on the other hand, suspended between heaven and earth, was an emblem of the Spirit-intellect of God, the descent of a creative energy that would thwart and transfigure the unholy reality of the world.

The Holy Spirit's revenge on Wagner's intrusiveness was subtle. In spite of all the efforts that were made, when the white dove came down from the bright temple's vaulted dome and hovered over Parsifal, it looked like a stuffed bird. Nevertheless, Wagner was satisfied. Writing from the Palazzo Vendramin-Calergi in Venice three months before his death, he declared that what took place inside his Festival Theater had an effect that was like a consecration.

In spite of this, the problem wasn't solved. It stood in the center of the action on the stage, like a reprise of the conflict between Wagner and Nietzsche, in Arnold Schoenberg's opera *Moses and Aaron* (first performed in 1957 in Zurich). "Begone," Moses commands, "you likeness of impossibility! The Infinite cannot be captured in an image!"

He is referring to the Golden Calf, the epitome of all the sensory means of representing the divine, in religion, art, and music.

But Aaron, the spokesman for beautiful appearances, has the orchestra on his side. He sings, while Moses is only permitted to declaim.

The opera remained unfinished.

And so, as though under a neurotic compulsion, godless Europe reiterated its forefathers' brooding questions about the nature of the enthroned glory of the Most High, praised be his holy name. For earthly eyes, this glory was unbearable, the Bible said, and therefore unrepresentable. But my face you cannot see, Moses hears his divine Yahweh say to him. No human being can see me and survive. When my glory passes by, I shall put you in a cleft of the rock and shield you with my hand until I have gone past. Then I shall take my hand away and you will see my back. In this passage, God has a face ( *panim* ) and a mightiness ( *kabod* ). The latter word is often translated "glory," but this translation conceals the allusion to the male genitalia that comes into play in the Hebrew. The divine Yahweh has hands, too, with which he shields Moses' eyes; one is compelled to wonder from what, for a few lines earlier in the text, we read that the divine Yahweh "would talk to Moses face to face, as a man talks to his friend." And another passage recounts how the divine Yahweh showed himself on the mountain to Moses, Aaron, and seventy "elders." They saw the God of Israel, the text expressly states, and under his feet there was what looked like a sapphire pavement pure as the heavens. God did no harm to the Israelite notables, the passage goes on to explain; he did not "raise his hand" against them, and they were able to look upon him.

This was, therefore, something of an exception to the rule that threatens death to all who would look at God.

*No one has ever seen God.* The Gospel of Saint John states the case in this fashion, which is more typically Jewish, and so the matter will remain, even after the divine Word, the *logos*, has made him known (*exēgēsato*) by conveying the correct interpretation.

The last word on God's fundamental inaccessibility was formulated in the Vatican, twelve years before the premiere performance of *Parsifal*, by an assembly of Catholic bishops. They declared that God was distinct from the world (*a mundo distinctus*) and inexpressibly exalted (*ineffabiliter excelsus*) above everything that is other than himself (*praeter ipsum*) and can be imagined.

Neither Jewish nor Muslim theologians could have expressed the facts of the case more clearly and concisely. On paper, this conclusion looks quite brusque in comparison with the practice of divine worship that Wagner was toying with. Such practice had its origins in Egypt, the very place that the Israelites had left, with its golden calves, its incense-shrouded celebrations, its priestly orisons. The idea that gods have faces was as self-evident in ancient Egypt as it would later be in Lourdes. Russian icons and carved Gothic altars clashed obstinately with the biblical prohibition against portraying God.

It was during the time of Wagner and Nietzsche that the prayer corners that were part of many European homes first began to fall out of fashion, especially in the fast-growing metropolitan areas, where the new opera houses invited visitors inside. God became as abstract as he could wish, and thereby disappeared from human consciousness. Only the Holy Spirit—as Wagner had correctly sensed—remained untouched by this process of de-realization, because from the start he had been as faceless as the wind. When the Bible speaks of the face of God, it means the Holy Spirit. This was the determination of the praiseworthy Cyril of Alexandria (d. 444), who based his view on Psalm 139, where the "presence" (or "countenance") of the divine Yahweh is equated with his Spirit. Opera directors, incidentally, have long since abandoned the practice of deploying a dove in the final scene of *Parsifal*.

# *Superman*

WAGNER'S "MUSIC OF THE FUTURE," as it was already being called, made no particular impression on the unmusical Miss Salomé in Bayreuth at the end of July 1882. Instead she enjoyed the soirees in Villa "Wahnfried," was visited by Cosima Wagner, and flirted with the Russian painter Joukowsky, who had designed the scenery for *Parsifal.* Maestro Wagner in person, borne along on a sea of guests from all the lands of the earth, was (as Lou later wrote) constantly overshadowed because of his small stature and so only momentarily visible. Speaking to him about Nietzsche was not permitted. It was better for the striking Russian girl not to mention that she was on her way to meet the apostate.

August 1882 was the month that Nietzsche had chosen for Lou's initiation into the great mystery whose guardian he imagined himself to be. His sister Elisabeth took on the role of chaperone in the vicarage in Tautenburg, where the ladies had rented rooms; Nietzsche was staying in a private house in the same village. For three weeks, the philosopher dedicated himself exclusively to his novice, both on walks in the Thuringian forest (which Nietzsche had selected because of his sensitive eyes) and in Lou's room, where the two would sit together until midnight with the lamp turned down low.

Of Nietzsche's writings, Lou was familiar with *Dawn* and *The Gay Science.* Moreover, she was no fool, having spent the winter semester of 1880–1881 at the University of Zurich, immersed in her studies (theology, philosophy, art history). Nietzsche examined her writings, suggested corrections, drew up a list of ten pointers to improve his pupil's style. "In Nietzsche's character," Lou wrote, "there lies an heroic trait that is the essential part of him. It leaves its mark on all his properties and urges, and it gives them the unity that holds them together. We shall live to see him become the herald of a new religion, and it will be one that recruits heroes as its disciples."

The shy man felt himself understood. The girlish child, sharp-eyed as an eagle and courageous as a lion, would share his deepest secret.

In a soft, halting voice, Nietzsche told his new but intimate friend what had happened to him one year previously, up there in the Engadine valley, while he was out hiking around midday with the mountains rising up before him: Oh noon of life! Solemn time! Oh summer garden! The noonday friend. No, ask not who it is. It was midday, then one became two. I became another, and a stranger to myself. Escaped from myself. A wrestler, who overcame himself. Does anyone here at the end of the nineteenth century have a clear idea of what poets in strong times called "Inspiration"? I shall describe it. Given the tiniest remnant of superstition, one would scarcely know how to reject the idea that he is merely an incarnation, merely a mouthpiece, merely a medium of superior forces. The idea of a revelation, in the sense that suddenly, with unspeakable certainty and subtlety, something becomes visible, audible, something that shakes one to his depths and overthrows him. One hears, one does not seek. One takes, one does not ask who gives. A thought flashes like lightning, necessarily, without delay. An ecstasy, whose enormous tension now and then dissolves into a flood of tears. Involuntarily, one runs sometimes, as though attacking, and at other times one walks slowly. A sense of being utterly beside oneself, with the distinct consciousness of innumerable subtle shivers and of tingling all the way down to the toes. A depth of happiness, in which what is most painful and gloomiest strikes us, not as antithetical, but as called for, a necessary color within such a superfluity of light. An instinct for rhythmic relationships. The need for a broad, tense rhythm is practically the measure of the inspiration's force, a kind of compensation for its pressure and its tension. Everything happens involuntarily in the highest degree, but as though in a tempest stirred up by a sense of freedom, by unconditionality, by power, by divinity. It really seems as if things drew near of themselves and offered themselves as similes. That is my experience of inspiration. I do not doubt that one has to go back thousands of years to find anyone with the right to say to me, "It is mine, too." 6,000 feet beyond man and time. That day I walked through the woods that lie along the lake of Silvaplana. I made a stop not far from Surlei, at a mighty, towering block shaped like a pyramid. There this thought came to me. More correctly, it assaulted me. Should anyone wish to learn from the experience of his very own adventures how a conqueror or a discoverer feels, or an artist, a saint, a lawmaker, a sage, a scholar, a pious man, or one who is divinely remote in the old way, one thing above all else is necessary for him: he must have that great thing, health. Whereby I sang and spoke nonsense, lit up by a new glance, which gives me an advantage over everyone else. Perhaps someday the time will come when even the eagles shyly look up to me, as though up to that picture of Saint John that we loved so much when we were children. Let us beware lest we teach such a teaching like a sudden religion. It must seep in slowly, entire generations must work on it and make it fruitful, so that it becomes a great tree that will overshadow all mankind to come. What are the few millennia in which Christianity has preserved itself? Many millennia are needed for the most powerful idea, long and long must it lie small and powerless. I bear the destiny of mankind on my shoulders. My dear Lou. Pardon me.

From time to time, the nameless noonday friend laid a radiance around the philosopher. Writing from Marienbad, Nietzsche said that in 1880 a gentleman in the woods had stared at him quite fixedly, and that thereupon it had dawned on him that he had been wearing an expression of the most glorious happiness on his face for hours. When Moses came down from the mountain, he did not know that the skin of his face was radiant. When the Israelites saw Moses, they were afraid to go near him.

In Basel, Nietzsche's friend Overbeck read with concern what Nietzsche wrote to him in 1881 from the Engadine: "Now and then the thought occurs to me that I really live an extremely dangerous life, for I belong to the machines that can crack apart. The intensities of my feelings make me shudder and laugh. A few times so far, I've been unable to leave my room, for the ridiculous reason that my eyes were inflamed. I'd cried too much every time I went out on my walks of the day before—not sentimental tears, but tears of jubilation."

Was the noonday friend nudging the philosopher into the insane asylum? In retrospect, after Nietzsche's collapse, Lou remembered that her mystagogue's intellectual life included a "characteristic pathological trait" that made him vacillate between excessively good health and attacks of debilitating illness. Once again, the Holy Spirit, whose description corresponded suspiciously to that of Nietzsche's noonday friend, had got into a psychiatric context.

A fixed point in posterity's guessing game concerning the philosopher's fogbound state from January 1889 until his death was provided by a Dr. Binswanger, a medical expert in Jena, where Nietzsche was interned for a year. The doctor's diagnosis was "progressive paralysis." That indicated tertiary syphilis, with involvement of the central nervous system. Other authorities confirmed Binswanger's diagnosis, among them the psychiatrist and philosopher Karl Jaspers. This left it an open queston whether (as was likewise suspected) a manic-depressive condition had also played a role.

As far as Nietzsche's posthumous fame was concerned, his derangement was most beneficial. It brought a tragic-demonic cast to renderings of him, his life, and his thought, as in Edvard Munch's 1906 painting. Lou Salomé, with her fine nose for intellectual VIP's, gave the first impulse to the worldwide recognition of her teacher by calling him to the attention of the Danish critic Georg Brandes. In the spring of 1888, in fact, Brandes read a series of lectures on the *tyske filosof* to large audiences at the University of Copenhagen. As a result, Nietzsche had himself measured for an elegant suit in Turin.

Too late. By the time that Lou Salomé, now Mrs. Andreas, published her first articles about Nietzsche in the *Vossische Zeitung* and the *Freie Bühne* in 1891, the philosopher had already been released from the psychiatric clinic into the care of his mother at home and was incommunicado.

In the year of Nietzsche's death, the poet Stefan George, addressing the deceased as the "unhappiest redeemer," made a prophecy: "Then you shall stand, a beacon for all time."

For all this, however, the question about the content of the revelation that took place in the Engadine was still unanswered.

Yet Nietzsche had taken precautions to forestall all and any misunder-standings. "Anticipating, as I do, that before long I must confront man-kind with the most difficult challenge it has ever faced, it seems to me imperative that I should say who I am." This is the first sentence of *Ecce Homo*, written, as though in great haste, in a mere three weeks during the late autumn of 1888. Nietzsche sent the manuscript to his publisher for printing, then requested that it be sent back. Nietzsche's sister, the guard-ian and propagandist of his extensive literary estate, then saw to the publication of *Ecce Homo* some twenty years later. Its subject is the self-revelation of the only thinker since Plato who, according to his own assessment, had something new to say.

Nietzsche's noonday friend had ordained him for this task on that holy spot where the first lightning bolt of the Zarathustra idea had flashed upon him, not far from Surlei, at the time of the liturgical re-currence of Christ's Transfiguration. *Now, certain of united victory, let us cel-ebrate the feast of feasts. Friend Zarathustra came, the guest of guests!* The funda-mental conception of the work, the idea of the eternal return, the absolutely highest formula of affirmation that can be attained, belongs in August 1881.

Nietzsche was recalling the day when he conceived the idea of the book that he thought would finally make him world-famous and of which, four years later, a mere seventy copies had been sold, "to Wagnerians and anti-Semites," according to information supplied by the publisher. The disappointed author resolved to have the last part of *Thus Spoke Zarathustra* privately printed and sent as gifts to the few people with whom he still exchanged letters.

Setbacks of this sort made no impression at all on the noonday friend. He had more on his mind than four hundred pages in a book. Under a bright sky, he spoke inside the solitary wanderer's head, and his words were ready for publication. Sometimes they were as dramatic as those of the Bible, at other times they issued in sparkling aphorisms. He dictated merciless reckonings with the collections of entire libraries, had no respect even for Socrates, and mocked the apostle Paul with blinding formula-tions. On another occasion, tender poems of great suggestive power might come, or dark, riddling hints, or moving lamentations. "Is it not folly to go on living? Ah, my friends, it is the evening that asks such a thing through me. Forgive me my sadness! Evening has fallen. Forgive me that evening has fallen."

Later Nietzsche, pleased and astonished, read what was there on the page. *I teach you the superman. Man is something that is to be overcome. What have you done to overcome him?*

No explanations, Nietzsche said to himself, no backsliding into the professorial style. Wooden definitions, elaborate conceptual clarifications, linguistic elucidations would drive away the noonday friend. Nietzsche preferred to use dashes and exclamation points, and to emphasize certain phrases by using italics or spacing out words: "I implore you, my brothers, *remain faithful to the earth,* and do not believe those who talk to you of unearthly hopes!"

*Has anyone understood me?* Nietzsche repeatedly addressed this anxious question to the imaginary readers of his last hopes, in November 1888, two months before his spirit-machine came to a halt. *Has anyone understood me?*

Perhaps. The Italian philosopher and Nietzsche authority Giorgio Colli, writing a hundred years later, calls Nietzsche's highest teaching a mystical enlightenment, a vision that liberates from all suffering, from all desire, from the process of individuation itself. Since Colli was granted this insight, all Nietzsche's ideas, discussions, and teachings are nothing more than a comedy of seriousness. His voice drowns out every other contemporary voice; the clarity of his thought makes all other thought seem indistinct. For the person who has freed himself from his own chains and acknowledges no tyrant in the arena of knowledge and life, he alone counts.

Anglo-Saxon authors reacted to Zarathustra's sayings less effusively, but to greater mass effect. They moved Nietzsche's supermen into the realm of science fiction. In his novel *Odd John* (1936), Olaf Stapledon described an entire colony of supermen who live on an island in the Pacific and commit collective suicide at the end of the book. Two years later, Jerry Siegel conceived his Superman for "Action Comics." As drawn by Joe Shuster, Superman had no difficulty bringing fast-moving railroad trains to a screeching halt left-handed, as it were, and so became famous. When he wasn't in action, Superman made an inconspicuous living as a somewhat Left-leaning newspaper reporter.

This ingenious arrangement quite accurately reflects the double existence of the mustachioed philosopher, who silently spoons his ice cream on a piazza in Turin or Genoa or Rome while secretly busy with the overthrow of the papacy and the detonation of Saint Peter's Basilica.

# *What's Calling?*

RILKE LACKED SUCH VIOLENT TENDENCIES. He wanted to become famous, too, but not through the revaluation of all values. Inside he was, for the most part, without form and void, as in the beginning of the Bible, and unfortunately the Holy Spirit was not moving upon the face of the waters. Rilke was waiting for him. The morning of creation could dawn at any moment, but mostly a great deal of time went by before the miracle of beginning took place and the first verse of a new poem descended. Lou Andreas-Salomé summarized the process: Whatever wanted to be made into art gathered itself in increasing fullness and clarity; however, the weeks or months that passed between raptures emptied themselves till they were nothing but waiting with a suffering conscience. The impossibility of summoning even the tiniest inspiration on one's own authority, no matter how powerfully one unites the forces of his understanding and his will, ultimately fills the empty waiting with doubt and disbelief as to whether what has vanished will ever really return. The consequences are self-contempt, helplessness, tormented arrogance, disgust with life, yes, even despair.

When Lou was fifty years old, she came under the influence of Sigmund Freud. She took part in the Weimar Congress of the International Psychoanalytical Association in September 1911, and a year later she requested permission to join the doctor's Wednesday-evening seminars in Vienna; permission was gladly granted. After her six-month stay in Vienna, her photograph had a place of honor in Freud's study. On his recommendation, Lou soon became a practicing psychotherapist, published probing essays in *Imago*, a journal that was under Freud's aegis, and eventually received as a gift one of the very few rings that Freud ordered for his most faithful collaborators. Throughout all this, the psyche expert remained baffled by the mystery of why a mature woman, and an established author to boot, would venture so deeply into the labyrinth of the unconscious, there to wash other people's dirty laundry.

The Swedish psychiatrist Poul Bjerre, with whom Lou was linked for a time and who had introduced her to Freud, said that she needed a new name for her gallery. She longed for deliverance from her strong personality.

Maybe he was right. But she loved Rilke most of all, as she loved no other man in her life, even after their separation from bed and board. When she was seventy, she wrote a text for her memoirs in which she addressed the dead Rilke with the familiar *Du:* "And so we were like brother and sister—but as in prehistoric times, before incest became a sacrilege. If for years I was your wife, it was because you were the first real thing for me. Every time we met, we lived in an eternal present." Rainer was there, totally, again, and they sat hand in hand, like people who are inexpressibly secure.

Unfortunately, Rainer while alive was prone to bouts of despair, to fits of depression that amounted to virtual derangement. Then he would cry out for help in letters: It seemed as though I wouldn't recognize anyone who came to see me, and as though I was a stranger to everyone as well, like a man who had died in a strange land. Something so dreadful came, then came and came again, and hasn't altogether left me.

It was probably a touch of the flu, Lou wrote back, somewhat helplessly. She was dealing with a typical hysteric, but she didn't learn that until ten years later, after she had gone to Freud's school.

Dr. Freud, for his part, had quite a few reservations about the cultural avant-garde to which Rilke belonged. He considered the Expressionist painters fools. Every writer who came after Goethe—Dostoyevsky, for example—put him in mind of his patients. Not even the leaders of the Modern movement in Vienna (Loos, Kokoschka, Schoenberg, Hofmannsthal) were able to charm or inspire him.

Lou Andreas-Salomé put up an obstinate resistance against this sort of blanket dismissal, but Freud gallantly countered her, intimating that it was she who was the expert in matters artistic.

At the final tally in this zero-sum game, there was nothing left for Rainer. Should he undergo psychoanalysis? Lou, having discussed the question with Baron von Gebsattel, a practicing analyst who knew Rilke personally, brought Rilke and Freud together. But there was nothing to be done. Since artistic talent and productivity are intimately connected to sublimation, Freud thought, we must admit that the nature of artistic ability is psychoanalytically inaccessible to us.

With regard to the psychoanalysis of living, working artists, Lou wrote, "I should think that one would be obliged to distinguish between two kinds of possible effects, one artistically liberating, and the other artistically perilous, insofar as it can invade the darkness where the fruit lies germinating."

Better to skip it, therefore. The Holy Spirit was a rare bird, and moreover a very shy one.

On January 20, 1912, he finally appeared, as fresh and imperious as he had been in his best days, when he beguiled the three swindlers of mankind. As always, he merely hinted at what he wanted to say. It was the old problem between transmitter and receiver, between the divine and the human spheres. All the most renowned divine antennae had picked up something, but who could be sure that the messages were getting through undistorted? Between God and man (*inter creatorem et creaturam*) the dissimilarity (*dissimilitudo*) is greater than the likeness (*similitudo*), decreed the Fourth Lateran Council (1215), during a bright moment in the history of the jejune hairsplitting so dear to learned theology. So, Herr Rilke, be cautious. Don't take everything literally.

Caution was the last thing on Rilke's mind at Duino castle, where at the end of 1911 his friend, Princess Marie von Thurn und Taxis, had arranged winter quarters for him, overlooking the sea, with a view of Trieste and Grado. A factotum named Carlo served the vegetarian meals Rilke requested; at nine in the evening, the poet went to bed. He passed a silent Christmas night; once again he drew up a balance sheet of his life for Lou. Nearly two wasted, wretched years. Everything that Rilke touched turned to ashes. Dear Lou, things are bad with me if I wait for people, need people, look around for people. That drives me deeper down, into greater gloom, and makes me guilty. Every morning I wake up and my shoulder is cold, there, where the hand should grab me and shake me awake. How is it possible that now I'm left with no calling, superfluous? And I'm descending into a drought that won't become anything else.

A strong *bora* was blowing outside on that January morning, Marie von Thurn und Taxis reported. The sun was shining, the sea was a radiant, gleaming, silvery blue. Rilke had gone down the narrow path that connects the castle's two bastions and from which the cliffs fall two hundred feet to the sea. In the roaring of the storm, a voice called: *Who, from among the ranks of the angels, would hear me if I cried out?*

What is that? What is it, what's coming?

Out with the notebook. That evening the whole "First Elegy" is written down, as though from dictation. *Every single angel is terrible.*

The *Duino Elegies*, however, were finished only ten years later, in the little Château de Muzot, the place Rilke had rented near Sierre, Switzerland, in the canton of Valais. February 2, 1922. The poet was standing at his high desk, busy with his correspondence, and suddenly, to his own surprise, he must write down sonnets. Once again, the poems came to him as though by dictation, twenty-five of them in three days, all sonnets and all addressed to Orpheus. We're told that he groaned during those days and nights, as he had done ten years before in Duino. The as-yet-unfinished *Elegies* were likewise trying to push their way out. "Joy and wonder, I'm over the mountain, Lou, dear Lou, on Saturday the 11th of February I lay down my pen, after the last, completed Elegy, the tenth. Just think! I've been allowed to survive this long. Through everything. Wonder. Grace. Everything in a few days. It was a hurricane."

Enough complaining. The approving angels stepped next to the terrible ones. It's glorious to be alive.

# *Yes*

IT WAS ANOTHER LITTÉRATEUR, HOWEVER, who succeeded in making the decisive breakthrough into a spirituality that combined the old and the new. While Rilke was listening to the voice that came from the roaring wind of the *bora*, James Joyce (1882–1941) was living in Trieste, a stone's throw (as it were) from Duino. But not even Lou Salomé, for all her hustling about on the literary scene, had heard anything about the idiosyncratic Irishman, who had published nothing worth mentioning besides a collection of poems and an essay. He was able, with some difficulty, to put food on the table for himself, his longtime companion, and their two children by giving private lessons in English; he smoked Austrian cigars made from Virginia tobacco; and he contemplated writing an unprecedented novel. The grand literary entrepreneur wanted his work to keep literary scholars thoroughly busy for the next few hundred years.

At the age of twenty, Joyce had already known what he wanted. On February 1, 1902, before the Literary and Historical Society of Dublin, he read a paper: "As long as human fear and cruelty are in league to make life ignoble and sullen and to speak evil of death the time is come wherein a man of timid courage seizes the keys of hell and of death, and flings them far out into the abyss, proclaiming the praise of life, which the abiding splendor of truth may sanctify, and of death, the most beautiful form of life. All those who have written nobly have not written in vain. Shall not such as these have part, because of that high original purpose, in the continual affirmation of the spirit?"

The young Joyce's intuitive confidence that sensational, overwhelming experiences were not necessary for the illumination of existence articulated itself early. As a student he began to write short prose pieces that he called "epiphanies," alluding to the Feast of the Epiphany of Our Lord (*in Epiphania Domini*) on January 6. The liturgy celebrated on this day is intended to recall three manifestations of the divine nature of Christ: the worship of the three Magi, the baptism in the Jordan, and the wedding at Cana.

Joyce wasn't aiming so high as that. He was gathering snapshots of things that had made an impression on him in daily life—fragments of a conversation, the memory of a girlish shape on the seashore, dreams. A trivial occurrence could turn into a sudden spiritual manifestation through a sort of profane enlightenment that must not be encoded either religiously or aesthetically and from which artistic inspiration drew its nourishment. It was for the man of letters to record these epiphanies with extreme care, seeing that they themselves are the most delicate and evanescent of moments.

With that, Joyce, Irish Catholic though he was, bade farewell to religion and all the help it could give in making up for the inconspicuousness of the Holy Spirit with hovering angels, heavenly lights, voices of thunder, leaping cripples. What remained to Joyce was a completely ordinary baby that was held up with a request for a few pennies to the astrologers who chanced to be passing by, or a man who like a thousand others was wading in the shallow waters of a little river to wash his sins away. Instead of the four Evangelists, Joyce had his fellow authors, those who carefully recorded the tender, fleeting moments that inspired the good news, the gospel that "in those days" the world was not held together by human fear and cruelty.

Joyce did all he could to keep from being taken for an evangelist. His blasphemies turned Jesus into a joke-figure and a Gregorian chorale into a melody fit for a brothel. Otherwise, the tender and fleeting moments of spiritually profane enlightenment could not have been rescued from expropriation by the Jesuits.

In Trieste, Joyce had to fill out an employment form for the Scuola Superiore di Commercio Revoltella, where he had been hired as an English teacher. In response to the question, "Religion?" Joyce wrote, *Senza* ("Without").

During the First World War, when Joyce was starting to write his book of the century, the competition he faced was disheartening. It wasn't only Homer and Dante who must be overtaken. Marcel Proust was already well along on his *Remembrance of Things Past,* and Thomas Mann and Robert Musil were writing no less ambitiously. Gide, Kafka, Shaw, and Hamsun were likewise not to be underestimated. But Joyce would outstrip them, and all the rest of the field, by taking a completely ordinary Jew on a completely ordinary day and expanding him until he became a ventriloquist of the World-Spirit—in dreary Dublin to boot, a town full of loquacious tipplers and easy girls—and producing thereby eight hundred pages of text without a single didactic sentence, richly spiced with strong language and obscenities, and furnished with an ambitious name: *Ulysses.*

In this epic a woman has the last word, in a monologue that goes for a full forty-five unpunctuated pages, until finally the end is in sight and then *he asked me would I yes to say yes my mountain flower and first I put my arms around him yes and drew him down to me so he could feel my breasts all perfume yes and his heart was going like mad and yes I said yes I will Yes.*

A fter the book had appeared, a minister in the new Irish Free State government visited Joyce in Paris. The minister said he was about to propose that Ireland nominate Joyce for the Nobel Prize.

No chance. With his justification of the banal and everyday, bowel movements included, Joyce had thoroughly deconsecrated everything that operated on the higher levels of literature. Undaunted, a few well-meaning literary critics looked for epiphanies in the rubble heap of words that had been piling up since Adam and Eve and which Joyce now presented to the confused public without pomposity or superior airs. A rude noise from the hindquarters of his protagonist counted for as much or as little as a quotation from the *Summa Theologica* of Saint Thomas Aquinas.

Only hesitatingly did Joyce reveal the design of his work, which is as grandiose and complicated as the illustrations in the famous illuminated manuscripts of the Gospels made in the Middle Ages. Joyce thought *The Book of Kells* was the purest Irish work of all. "In all the places I have been to," Joyce said, "Rome, Zurich, Trieste, I have taken it about with me, and have pored over its workmanship for hours. Some of the big initial letters which swing right across a page have the essential quality of a chapter of *Ulysses*. You can compare much of my work to the intricate illuminations."

As a stylist, Joyce could easily bear comparison with the greatest in the world. Nonetheless, he never let himself be tempted into the usual high-flown exhibitionism of the literary enterprise. He placed his art at the service of commonness and planted his feet solidly on the ground, the proper theological locus for the workings of the Holy Spirit, as it was in the beginning, is now, and ever shall be. "Don't you think," he remarked slyly to his brother Stanislaus, "that there is a certain resemblance between the mystery of the Mass and what I am trying to do? I mean that I am trying to give people some kind of intellectual pleasure or spiritual enjoy-ment by converting the bread of everyday life into something that has a permanent artistic life of its own."

For their mental, moral, and spiritual uplift, he added ironically. Such nonchalance was a cover for his benevolent project of bringing heaven down to earth. How often in the course of a lifetime is the third eye, our organ for detecting the hidden luster of the front door key, capable of opening? Up to now, this has not been investigated. And why should it be? One single time is enough, and then all the cold shark eyes of the world start to look a touch friendlier.

Time is irrelevant in these matters. Joyce and the monastic brethren who painted their manuscript ornaments a thousand years ago were working on the same project. There was a pattern to be abstracted from the confused mesh of tangled lines that was the reality of the world, a pattern that would have staying power, a pattern to which one could say Yes. Every now and then a work succeeded in accomplishing such a task, and the heavens opened once more.

On February 2, 1922, for example, while Rilke was in the Valais receiving the inspiration he had yearned for for so long, Joyce was in Paris and could know nothing of this. It was his birthday, and he had resolved to celebrate it with the appearance of the first copy of his *Ulysses*. Fresh from the press, the book lay on the table in Ferrari's Italian restaurant. There was a toast to the book and its author, and Joyce was quite moved. On this occasion the Holy Spirit had elected to abstain from a personal appearance. And there was evening, and there was morning. A good day.

# Source Notes

*The numbers in the margin refer to the respective pages in the text where material from sources appears. The italicized quotations from the text indicate the referenced passages. Full bibliographical information is provided in the initial reference to each work. When a work is cited more than once, references subsequent to the first reference are given in abbreviated form. Articles in specialized encyclopedias and lexica are cited only in exceptional cases. The translation of biblical passages generally follows that of the* New Jerusalem Bible, *with occasional reference to the* New International Version *and the* Revised Standard Version.

| | |
|---|---|
| p. 3 | *The first decently reliable news:* Mt. 3:16f. and parallels; Jn. 1:32. In this connection see Norman Golb, *Who Wrote the Dead Sea Scrolls? The Search for the Secret of Qumran* (New York: Scribner, 1995), p. 373f. |
| p. 3 | *the question suggests itself:* See Rudolf Pesch, *Das Markusevangelium, 1. Teil* (Freiburg: Herder, 1976), pp. 91f. Another view is in Heinz Schürman, *Das Lukasevangelium, 1. Teil* (Freiburg: Herder, 1969), p. 192. According to Schürman, the probability that the Hebrews considered the dove "a symbol of the Spirit of God" can be demonstrated "only within certain very narrow limits." See also H. Strack and P. Billerbeck, *Kommentar zum Neuen Testament aus Talmud und Midrasch,* Vol. I (München: n.p., 1956), p. 123. |
| p. 4 | *Yahu (Yahweh):* On the proper name of God in the Hebrew Bible, see Jack Miles, *God: A Biography* (New York: Knopf, 1995), pp. 419–20. |
| p. 4 | *"filled" with the Holy Spirit:* Lk. 4:1. |
| p. 5 | *Angels looked after him:* Mk. 1:13. |
| p. 5 | *with the Nazarene's first entrance:* Mk. 1:21–27 and parallels. |
| p. 5 | *as though on the stage:* See Victor Turner, *From Ritual to Theatre* (New York: PAJ Publications, 1992). |
| p. 5 | *Matthew and Luke have information:* Mt. 12:43–45; Lk. 11:24–26. |
| p. 5 | *the island of Bali:* See Clifford Geertz, *Dichte Beschreibung* (Frankfurt am Main: Suhrkamp, 1991), pp. 212–14. |
| p. 6 | *"from above":* Jn. 3:3–7. |
| p. 6 | *Do not cling to me:* Jn. 20:17. |
| p. 6 | *written letters kill:* 2 Cor. 3:6. |
| p. 7 | *pneuma blows wherever it pleases:* Jn. 3:8. |
| p. 8 | *the staccato pulse of the ruach:* Mk. 1:10, 12, 18, 21, 23; 15:1. |
| p. 9 | *a terrifying figure:* Rev. 1:13–16. |
| p. 9 | *The author affirms:* Rev. 1:9f. |
| p. 9 | *seven Christian societies:* Rev. 1:4 (Ephesus, Smyrna, Pergamum, Thyatira, Sardis, Philadelphia, Laodicea). |
| p. 9 | *the speech habits of dragons:* Rev. 13:11. |
| p. 9 | *the number 666:* Rev. 13:18 (this probably referred to the Emperor Nero). |

| | |
|---|---|
| p. 9 | *He who has an ear:* Rev. 2:7, 11, 17, 29; 3:6, 13, 22. |
| p. 9 | *the faithful witness:* Rev. 1:5; 19:10. |
| p. 10 | *inspired ears:* See Ulrich H. J. Körtner, *Der inspirierte Leser* (Göttingen: Vandenhoeck & Ruprecht, 1994), p. 86. |
| p. 10 | *this medium is the message:* Marshall McLuhan, *Understanding Media* (New York: Signet Books, 1966), p. 23. |
| p. 10 | *The nonfavored:* Rev. 22:15. |
| p. 10 | *the Lamb's mighty wrath:* Rev. 6:16–17. |
| p. 10 | *And they were given authority:* Rev. 6:8. |
| p. 10 | *an extensive web:* C. G. Jung, *Antwort auf Hiob,* in *Gesammelte Werke,* Vol. II (Zürich: Rascher, 1963), pp. 470–90. English translation by R.F.C. Hull: C. G. Jung, *Answer to Job,* in *The Collected Works of C. G. Jung,* Vol II (New York: Pantheon Books, 1958), pp. 432–52. |
| p. 10 | *copied out word for word:* Ezek. 1:15–21 (cf. Rev. 4:6–11). |
| p. 11 | *Emanuel Swedenborg:* See Ernst Benz, *Die Vision. Erfahrungsformen und Bilderwelt* (Stuttgart: Klett, 1969), pp. 453–55. |
| p. 11 | *While Christians wrangle:* C. G. Jung, *Vorwort zu V. White: Gott und das Unbewusste,* in op. cit., pp. 329–31. (English translation by R.F.C. Hull: "Foreword" to V. White's *God and the Unconscious,* in Jung's *Collected Works,* Vol. 11, pp. 299–302.) |
| p. 11 | *one of Jung's colleagues:* Stanislav Grof, *Beyond the Brain: Birth, Death, and Transcendence in Psychotherapy* (Albany: SUNY Press, 1985), pp. 46–48, 102–27, 304–15. |
| p. 12 | *all heathenish abominations:* Rev. 18:1–24. |
| p. 12 | *the time is near:* Rev. 1:3. |
| p. 12 | I am indeed coming soon: Rev. 22:20. |
| p. 13 | *if the Gospels . . . are to be trusted:* See Hans Kessler, Die theologische Bedeutung des Todes Jesu (Düsseldorf: Patmos, 1970), pp. 228–96. |
| p. 13 | *Sometimes it is a stranger:* Lk. 24:13–35; Jn. 20:11–18. |
| p. 13 | *Another time:* Lk. 24:36–44; Jn. 20:19–23. |
| p. 13 | *a young man, clad in white:* Mk. 1–8. |
| p. 13 | *For another witness:* Jn. 20:3–10. |
| p. 13 | *the doubtful Thomas:* Jn. 20:24–29. |
| p. 13 | *Christ's ascension:* Lk. 24:50–52; Acts 1:9–11; Mk. 16:19; Mt. 28:16–20; I Cor. 15:5–8. |
| p. 13 | *the firestorm of Pentecost:* Acts 2:1–13. |
| p. 14 | *"Receive the Holy Spirit":* Jn. 20:22. |
| p. 14 | *"We are well aware":* I Jn. 3:14. |
| p. 14 | *Peter tells:* Acts 11:15. |
| p. 14 | *a kind of outpouring:* Acts 2:33. |
| p. 14 | *We're informed:* Acts 1:12–14. |
| p. 14 | *So you had not the strength:* Mt. 26:40. |
| p. 15 | Maranatha: I Cor. 16:22. |
| p. 16 | *calls all cats black:* Ernst Bloch, *Atheismus im Christentum* (Frankfurt am Main: Suhrkamp, 1968), pp. 64–72. |
| p. 16 | Not a single stone: Mk. 13:2. |
| p. 17 | *armies that will surround Jerusalem:* Lk. 21:20. |

p. 17      *The rejected Gospels:* See Wilhelm Schneemelcher (editor), *Neutestamentliche Apokryphen in deutscher Übersetzung,* Vol. I (Tübingen: J.C.B. Mohr, 1987).

pp. 17–18      *If a person all his life:* Gerhard Wehr (editor), *Thomas Müntzer Schriften und Briefe* (Frankfurt am Main: Fischer Taschenbuch Verlag, 1973), p. 104.

p. 18      *Martin Luther then reacted:* Ibid., p. 197.

p. 18      *A person who knows nothing:* Ibid., p. 89.

p. 18      *the figure of the solitary:* Ernst Bloch, *Thomas Müntzer* (Frankfurt am Main: Suhrkamp, 1976), p. 171.

p. 20      *the fire came down:* See Walter J. Hollenweger, *The Pentecostals,* tr. R. A. Wilson (Peabody, Massachusetts: Hendrickson Publishers, 1988), pp. 22–23.

p. 20      *"When Pentecost day . . .":* Acts 2:1–4.

p. 21      *these signs:* Mk. 16:17–18.

p. 21      *Paul bears witness:* I Cor. 12:30.

p. 21      *the immediate descent:* Acts 10:46 and 19:6.

p. 21      *"as the Spirit gave them . . .":* Acts 2:4–11.

p. 22      *Charles Grandison Finney:* Garth M. Rosell and Richard A. G. Dupuis, editors, *The Memoirs of Charles G. Finney* (Grand Rapids: Academie Books, 1989), pp. 23–24.

p. 23      *"The vein of sensitivity . . .":* Georg Büchner, *Complete Works and Letters,* tr. Henry J. Schmidt (New York: Continuum, 1986), p. 147.

p. 24      *"Blessed are you . . .":* Lk. 6:21.

p. 24      *For ten years the servant of God:* Hollenweger, *The Pentecostals,* pp. 48–49.

p. 24      *persists to this day:* See Malise Ruthven, *The Divine Supermarket: Shopping for God in America* (New York: W. Morrow, 1989), pp. 287–92. An overview of the current religious situation in America is offered in Otto Kallscheuer, *Gottes Wort und Volkes Stimme* (Frankfurt am Main: S. Fischer, 1994), pp. 112–48.

p. 24      *Whoever believes:* Mk. 16:16.

p. 24      *Like this, for example:* Felicitas D. Goodman, *Speaking in Tongues: A Cross-Cultural Study of Glossolalia* (Chicago: University of Chicago Press, 1972), pp. 105–23. (Professor Goodman, according to a personal letter to the author dated Nov. 11, 1996, is currently working on a longitudinal study of the Pentecostal congregations that she has observed.)

p. 25      *A Norwegian minister:* Hollenweger, *The Pentecostals,* p. 63.

p. 25      *Daniel Berg . . . visited his homeland:* Ibid., pp. 75–78.

p. 25      *millions of people:* The *Evangelische Zentralstelle für Weltanschauungsfragen* in Stuttgart (*Orientierungen und Berichte* No. 20/94) gives a figure of 100,000,000; the *World Christian Encyclopedia* (Oxford University Press, 1990) counts 193,000,000 Pentecostals. The sociologist of religion Peter L. Berger considers evangelical Protestantism and conservative Islam the only two truly global and enormously vital religious movements in the world today. (See David Martin, *Tongues of Fire,* Oxford: Blackwell, 1990, p. vii.) For more on this subject, see Martin E. Marty and R. Scott Appleby, editors, *Fundamentalism Observed* (Chicago: University Press, 1991).

p. 25      *the Scriptures tell us:* Mt. 21:16 (Psa. 8:3; Wisd. 10:21).

p. 25      *Unless you become:* Mt. 18:3.

p. 26      *In her publications:* After her first study (see above, *Speaking in Tongues*), Prof. Goodman published a detailed report in Felicitas D. Goodman, Jeanette H. Henney, and Esther Pressel, *Trance, Healing, and Hallucination: Three Field Studies* in *Religious Experience* (New York: John Wiley, 1974), pp. 277–379. In the following description of the events that took place in the years 1969 and 1970, I have not given detailed references to the corresponding passages in the two abovementioned works by Prof. Goodman.

p. 29       What I say to you: Jn. 14:10, 26.

p. 29       *But you will see me:* Jn. 14:19.

pp. 29–30   *No one can enter:* Jn. 3:5.

p. 30       Alas for you: Lk. 6:24.

p. 30       And Jesus, filled with joy: Lk. 10:21.

p. 32       I, Jesus, have sent: Rev. 22:16, 17, 20.

p. 33       *If they do not return:* Rev. 2:4.

p. 37       *Mrs. Goodman thinks:* Private communication, March 1992.

p. 37       *a decidedly inconsistent fellow:* Felicitas D. Goodman, *Der Hauch im Spiegel,* in Adolf Holl, editor, *Die zweite Wirklichkeit* (Wien: Ueberreuter, 1987), p. 110.

p. 37       *The very first Pentecostal congregation:* See Wayne A. Meeks, *The First Urban Christians* (New Haven: Yale University Press, 1983), p. 41.

p. 37       *"I thank God . . .":* I Cor. 14:18.

p. 37       *the road to Damascus:* Acts 9:1–9.

p. 37       *"I went off to Arabia . . .":* Gal. 1:17–19 (Cephas = Peter).

p. 38       *Jesus was buried . . . :* I Cor. 15:4–8.

p. 38       *No eye has seen . . . :* I Cor. 2:9.

p. 38       *Not in the words of human wisdom . . . :* I Cor. 2:13.

p. 38       *Heard words said . . . :* 2 Cor. 12:2–4.

p. 38       *When Paul was in the right mood:* Acts 19:6.

p. 38       *It wasn't exactly the best:* Meeks, op. cit., pp. 51–73.

p. 39       *the seven Epistles:* Romans, First and Second Corinthians, Galatians, Philippians, First Thessalonians, Philemon. These were all written between 50 and 60 A.D. Modern experts deny the authenticity of the remaining Pauline Epistles in the Christian Bible.

p. 39       *Only once does Paul:* Paul quotes the so-called "words of institution," spoken by Jesus at the Last Supper, in I Cor. 11:23–27. In this connection see Howard Clark Kee, *Christian Origins in Sociological Perspective* (Philadelphia: The Westminster Press, 1980), p. 134. See also Rodney Stark, *The Rise of Christianity: A Sociologist Reconsiders History* (Princeton: University Press, 1966).

p. 39       *he hammered into their heads:* See F. S. Jones, *"Freiheit" in den Briefen des Apostels Paulus. Eine historische, exegetische und religionsgeschichtliche Studie* (Göttingen: n.p., 1987).

p. 39       *a somber background:* Rom. 1:18–3:20.

p. 40       *the immeasurable shard heap:* Rom. 9:21–23.

p. 40       *Abraham had two sons:* Gal. 4:22–31.

p. 40       *abundantly clear:* Gal. 3:18; I Cor. 12:13; Rom. 10:12. See also Meeks, *Urban Christians,* pp. 20f., 161.

p. 40       *the water of baptism:* Ibid., pp. 150–57.

p. 40       *occurs the outbreak:* I Cor. 12:1–11.

p. 40       *collectively known:* There is no obvious historical model for Paul's discussion of the charismatic gifts. See Hubert Cancik, Burkhard Gladigow, and Matthias Laubscher, editors, *Handbuch religionswissenschaftlicher Grundbegriffe,* Vol. 2 (Stuttgart: Kohlhammer, 1990), p. 195.

p. 40      *As soon as the Christian crowd:* I Cor. 12:1–11; Rom. 12:6–8. See also Meeks, *Urban Christians,* pp. 119–22.

p. 41      *Paul intervened:* Kee, *Christian Origins,* p. 96.

p. 41      *Rather five words:* I Cor. 14:19.

p. 41      *Everybody wait their turn:* I Cor. 14:27.

p. 41      *Just suppose:* I Cor. 14:23.

p. 41      *the women's head covering:* I Cor. 11:2–16.

p. 41      *The host evidently found nothing:* I Cor. 11:17–34. See Meeks, op. cit., pp. 68, 159.

p. 41      *the Holy Spirit's noblest gift:* I Cor. 13:1–13.

p. 41      *the Pauline Epistles:* The noun *agapē* appears only twice in the Gospels according to Matthew, Mark, and Luke, whereas it occurs seventy-eight times in the Pauline writings.

p. 42      *always patient:* I Cor. 13:4–7.

p. 42      *like a baby:* Heb. 5:12–14.

p. 42      *"poured into our hearts . . .":* Rom. 5:5.

p. 42      *Do not stifle the Spirit:* I Thess. 5:19–20.

p. 42      *burning, glowing:* Rom. 12:11.

p. 42      *at least ten thousand miles:* Meeks, op. cit., p. 16.

p. 43      *"Where the Spirit of the Lord . . .":* 2 Cor. 3:17.

p. 43      *The whole creation:* Rom. 8:18–27. See also Heinrich Schlier, *Der Römerbrief* (Freiburg: Herder, 1957), pp. 256–59, and Otto Kuss, *Der Römerbrief, 3. Lieferung* (Regensburg: Pustet, 1978), pp. 637–44.

p. 46      *In the gray dawn:* See Robin Lane Fox, *Pagans and Christians* (London: Viking, 1983), pp. 609–27. Also Hubert Jedin and John Dolan, editors, *A History of the Church,* Vol. 1: *From the Apostolic Community to Constantine,* by Karl Baus, with a General Introduction to Church History by Hubert Jedin (New York: Herder & Herder, 1965), pp. 405–32.

p. 47      *on the imperial coinage:* See Rudolf Leeb, *Konstantin und Christus* (Berlin: Walter de Gruyter, 1992).

p. 48      *this supernatural intervention:* See Eric Robertson Dodds, *Pagan and Christian in an Age of Anxiety* (Cambridge: University Press, 1965), pp. 46–47.

p. 48      *as in the case of another, later emperor:* See Joseph Bidez, *Kaiser Julian* (Reinbek: Rowohlt, 1957). In the original French, this book is called *La Vie de l'Empereur Julien* (Paris: Société d'édition "Les belles lettres," 1930).

p. 48      *glorious Helius:* See Franz Altheim, *Der unbesiegte Gott* (Reinbek: Rowohlt, 1957).

p. 50      *a disquieting incident:* Plutarch, *De defectu oraculorum* 51, 438c.

p. 50      *the wise Heraclitus:* Heraclitus, *Fragments,* translated with a commentary by T. M. Robinson (Toronto: University of Toronto Press, 1987), pp. 56–57.

p. 51      *Plato, no less:* Plato, *Phaidrus,* 244a.

p. 51      *Socrates goes on:* Ibid., 265a, b.

p. 52      *Consultations took place at night:* Robin Lane Fox, *Pagans and Christians,* pp. 171–76.

p. 53      *But he had come too late:* Bidez, *Kaiser Julian,* pp. 180–207.

p. 55      *We have an early hint:* Lane Fox, op. cit., pp. 257f., 190.

p. 56      *fifty million inhabitants:* Ibid., p. 201.

p. 57      *a long tradition:* See Siegfried Morentz, *Ägypten,* in Kurt Galling, editor, *Die*

*Religion in Geschichte und Gegenwart*, Vol. I (Tübingen: J.C.B. Mohr, 1986), pp. 121–24.

p. 58    *He ordered Hosius:* Lane Fox, op. cit., pp. 638, 654. See Jedin and Dolan, editors, *History of the Church*, Vol. 2, Part I: *The Imperial Church from Constantine to the Early Middle Ages*, by Karl Baus and Eugen Ewig, pp. 17–23.

p. 59    *under the discreet direction of Hosius:* Ibid. The Greek text of the Nicene Creed is printed in Henricus Denziger and Adolfus Schönmetzer, *Enchiridion Symbolorum* (Barcelona: Herder, 1973), no. 125.

p. 59    *committed to the devil:* The Greek verb *anathematizein*, which indicates exclusion from the community of the Church, may be translated in this way.

p. 60    *bore witness:* The words martyr and martyrdom derive from the Greek word *martys*, which means "witness."

p. 60    *Filled with the Holy Spirit:* Acts 7:55–58.

p. 61    *"Cappadocian fathers":* St. Basil the Great (329/31–379): his brother, St. Gregory of Nyssa (334–394); and St. Gregory Nazianzen (330–390).

p. 61    *"His dastardliness":* Quoted in Bidez, *Kaiser Julian*, p. 79.

p. 61    *"Just open it":* Ibid., p. 167.

p. 62    *Basil produced his treatise:* Migne, *Patrologia Graeca* 32, 67–217.

p. 62    *Gregory observed:* See the Fifth Oration in *Faith Gives Fullness to Reasoning: The Five Theological Orations of Gregory Nazianzen*, introduction and commentary by Frederick W. Norris, translated by Lionel Wickham and Frederick Williams (New York: E. J. Brill, 1991).

p. 62    *one God in three Persons:* See Karen Armstrong, *A History of God: The 4000-Year Quest of Judaism, Christianity, and Islam* (New York: Alfred A. Knopf, 1994), pp. 107–31.

p. 63    *"I have not yet conceived of the One":* Bibliothek der Kirchenväter, Vol. 40 (Kempten: Kösel, 1869ff.), p. 85.

p. 63    *this metaphysics of light:* See Michael Polemis, *Zum Begriff der Trinität* (Wien: Passagen Verlag, 1993), pp. 111–29.

p. 63    *to occupy the center:* Leeb, *Konstantin und Christus*, pp. 93–106.

p. 64    *those who enjoyed the most prestige:* See Karl Rahner and Joseph Ratzinger, *Episkopat und Primat* (Freiburg: Herder, 1961).

p. 65    *the staid, middle-aged men:* Fox, *Pagans and Christians*, pp. 493–545.

p. 66    *their spiritual father:* See Peter Brown, *Society and the Holy in Late Antiquity* (Berkeley: University of California Press, 1989), p. 150.

p. 66    *when he admonished the priests of Jupiter:* Bidez, *Kaiser Julian*, pp. 173–77.

p. 68    *a follower of these Enthusiasts:* See Hans-Georg Beck, *Vom Umgang mit Ketzern* (München: C. H. Beck, 1993), p. 107.

p. 68    *to be taught by women:* Ibid., p. 49.

p. 68    *a plague upon the land:* Ibid., pp. 102–5; Peter Brown, *The Body and Society: Men, Women, and Sexual Renunciation in Early Christianity* (New York: Columbia University Press, 1988), pp. 332f.

p. 68    *one of the thousand falsehoods:* This was the so-called Messalianism, whose name was derived from the Syriac *metsalleyane* ("one who is in prayer").

p. 69    *The sacred Mount Athos:* See Erich Feigl, *Athos. Vorhölle zum Paradies* (Wien: Zsolnay, 1982).

p. 70    *who shared its reservations about Evropi:* See Remi Brague, *Europe, la voie romaine* (Paris: Criterion, 1992), p. 21.

p. 70    *The Holy Spirit will come upon you:* Lk. 1:35.

p. 70    *will penetrate into you:* The Hebrew rendering of the Greek word *episkiasei* ("he will throw a shade upon," "he will overshadow") connotes the sexual act. (I am grateful to Günther Schwarz for this and other information that contributed to the considerations presented in this section.)

p. 71    *Joseph was the father of Jesus:* Mt. 1:16 in the Sinaitic Syriac version. (In all probability, the version of Mt. 1:16 presented in current editions of the Bible goes back to a forgery.) On the ancient idea of the so-called virgin birth, see Uta Ranke-Heinemann, *Nein und Amen* (Hamburg: Hoffmann und Campe, 1992), pp. 45–68. There is an English translation of this book by Peter Heinegg: *Putting Away Childish Things: the Virgin Birth, the Empty Tomb, and Other Fairy Tales You Don't Need to Believe to Have a Living Faith* (San Francisco: Harper San Francisco, 1994).

p. 74    *"Only a god . . .":* Der Spiegel, 23/1976.

p. 75    *the reasons for his support:* See Karl Löwith, *Mein Leben in Deutschland vor und nach 1933* (Stuttgart: Metzler, 1992), pp. 45–68.

p. 75    *"inner truth and greatness":* Martin Heidegger, *Einführung in die Metaphysik* (Tübingen: Max Niemeyer, 1953). (Translated into English by Ralph Manheim: *An Introduction to Metaphysics* [New Haven, Yale University Press, 1959], p. 199.) This later version of Heidegger's 1935 lecture includes a suggestion that qualifies, but does not expressly retract, his reference to National Socialism. See also the previously cited issue of *Der Spiegel.*

p. 75    *a "peculiar analogy":* Hans Jonas, *Gnosis und spätantiker Geist, Erster Teil* (Göttingen: Vandenhoeck & Ruprecht, 1964), p. 107.

p. 76    *he expressly stated:* Ibid., pp. 90f.

p. 76    *The site of the discovery:* See Kurt Rudolph, *Gnosis*, edited by Robert McLachlan Wilson, translated by Wilson, et al. (San Francisco: Harper & Row, 1983), pp. 34–52, and Giovanni Filoramo, *A History of Gnosticism*, translated by Anthony Alcock (Oxford: Basil Blackwell, 1990), pp. 1–19.

p. 77    *the Spirit blows where it pleases:* Jn. 3:8.

p. 77    *In the papyrus pages:* There are 53 texts, bound into 13 codices; the majority of these texts are Gnostic in content. See Filoramo, op. cit., pp. 15–19, and Rudolph, op. cit., pp. 40–58.

p. 77    *the joys of parenthood:* Filoramo, op. cit., pp. 181, 187.

p. 78    *Ordure and stench:* See Elias Canetti, *Masse und Macht* (Hamburg: Claasen, 1960), p. 239. (An English translation of this book, *Crowds and Power*, was published in 1962.)

p. 78    *for the Christian cliques:* Scholars are divided as to whether the phenomenon of Gnosticism is to be described as Christian in origin or as a movement that arose independently of Christianity. The latter view is presented in Filoramo, op. cit., p. 19, in Jonas, op. cit., pp. 81f., and in Arno Borst, *Die Katharer* (Freiburg: Herder, 1991), p. 58. Gnosticism is described as a special sort of Christian teaching in Martin Hengel, *The Johannine Question*, translated by John Bowden (Philadelphia: Trinity Press International, 1989), pp. 113f., and by Barbara Aland, *Was ist Gnosis*, in Jacob Taubes, editor, *Gnosis und Politik* (München/Paderborn: Fink/Schöningh, 1984), p. 59. Rudolph, in *Gnosis*, pp. 277 and 282, detects in Gnosticism "a critical self-dissolution on the fringes of Judaism." Micha Brumlik, *Die*

*Gnostiker* (Frankfurt am Main: Eichborn, 1992), intended for a nonspecialist audience, is worth reading. There is a two-volume selection of Gnostic texts in Peter Sloterdijk and Thomas Macho, editors, *Weltrevolution der Seele* (Zürich: Artemis & Winkler, 1991).

p. 79    *interrupted by a woman:* See Elaine Pagels, *The Gnostic Gospels* (New York: Random House, 1979), pp. 64f.

p. 80    *the best part:* Lk. 10:42 (Vulgate).

p. 80    *in the various Epistles:* First and Second Timothy, Colossians, Ephesians.

p. 80    *For Adam was formed first:* I Timothy 2:13f.

p. 80    *a man named Aberkius:* The inscription was rediscovered by W. Ramsey in 1883.

p. 81    *How impudent and audacious:* Quoted in Pagels, op. cit., p. 60.

p. 81    *The disputatious Bishop:* See Rudolph, *Gnosis*, pp. 18–20, 205, 247–50, 257. The *Panarion* was compiled around 370 A.D.

p. 81    *a seducer named Marcus:* See Rudolph, op. cit., pp. 11–12, 241, 251, and Pagels, op. cit., pp. 59f.

p. 82    *Women were a decided majority:* See Lane Fox, *Pagans and Christians*, pp. 310f.

p. 82    *The leaders of the schools:* See Rudolph, op. cit., pp. 308–26, and Filoramo, op. cit., pp. 157–69.

p. 83    *innumerable variations:* Examples in Pagels, op. cit., pp. 53–56; Filoramo, op. cit., pp. 67–77; and Jonas, op. cit., pp. 351–62. See in addition Thomas Buske, *Heiliger Geist und Weisheit Gottes*, 1991.

p. 83    *"Look upon me . . .":* See Filoramo, op. cit., pp. 68f., and Rudolph, op. cit., pp. 81–82.

p. 83    *Marcellina:* See Rudolph, op. cit., p. 211; Filoramo, op. cit., p. 161; and Pagels, op. cit., p. 60.

p. 84    *Flora:* See Rudolph, op. cit., pp. 268–70, and the grave inscription on p. 211.

p. 84    *another version:* Jn. 21:24. On the so-called Johannine question, which deals with the authorship of the Gospel according to St. John, see Martin Hengel, *The Johannine Question* (cited above), as well as Rudolph Schnackenburg, *The Gospel According to St. John* (New York: Herder and Herder, 1968), especially Vol. 1 (translated by Kevin Smyth), pp. 75–104, and Vol. 3 (translated by David Smith and G. A. Kon), pp. 375–88.

p. 85    *the beloved disciple slips into the text:* Jn. 13:23–26.

p. 85    *under the cross:* Jn. 19:26f.

p. 85    *On Easter morning:* Jn. 20:3–10.

p. 85    *Finally, at the end:* Jn. 21:7, 20, 24.

p. 85    *another hidden allusion:* Jn. 18:15f.

p. 85    *writes the author:* Rev. 1:9f.

p. 86    *"We are writing this . . .":* I Jn. 1:4f.

p. 86    *The hour is coming:* Jn. 4:21–24.

p. 86    *What is born of flesh:* Jn. 3:6.

p. 86    *It is the Spirit that gives life:* Jn. 6:63.

p. 86    *The Holy Spirit will teach you:* Jn. 14:26.

p. 86    *"I shall ask the Father":* Jn. 14:16f.

p. 87    *Children, I shall be with you:* The following passage is a montage taken from Jn. 13:33; 14:2f. and 27; 15:9; 16:7, 13, and 20.

p. 87    *when the doors were locked, he had come:* Jn. 20:19–23.

p. 87    *Paul too had sojourned:* Acts 19:6.

p. 87    *flowing water:* Jn. 7:37–39.

p. 88    *the lance-thrust:* Jn. 19:34.

p. 88    *Whoever believes in me:* Jn. 11:26.

p. 88    *The light shines in darkness:* Jn. 1:5, 9.

p. 88    Whoever does the truth: Jn. 3:21.

p. 88    *people prefer darkness:* Jn. 3:19f.

p. 89    *"My kingdom is not of this world":* Jn. 18:36.

p. 89    *Father, the hour has come:* Jn. 17:1, 6, 9, 11, 14.

p. 89    *like a district attorney:* Jn. 16:8–11.

p. 90    *Mani asserted:* See Karl Matthäus Woschitz, Manfred Hutter, and Karl Prenner, *Das manichäische Urdrama des Lichtes* (Wien: Herder, 1989), pp. 40f. (My text is a montage taken from these pages.)

p. 90    *handicapped from birth:* See Georg Widengren, editor, *Der Manichäismus* (Darmstadt: Wissenschaftliche Buchgesellschaft, 1977), pp. 483–85.

p. 91    *a world religion:* See Rudolph, *Gnosis*, pp. 326–54.

p. 91    *put into the world like retorts:* See Ernst Bloch, *The Principle of Hope*, translated by Neville Plaice, Stephen Plaice, and Paul Knight (Cambridge: MIT Press, 1986), p. 1,246.

p. 92    *the Lord Gautama:* See Hans Wolfgang Schumann, *Buddhismus* (Olten: Walter, 1978).

p. 93    *two-toned leg coverings:* See Widengren, op. cit., pp. 482f.

p. 93    *clothes of gleaming white:* Ibid., p. 390.

p. 93    *a certain Addas:* Ibid., pp. 387–92.

p. 94    *a notorious prostitute:* Lk. 7:36–50.

p. 94    *in the house of Lazarus:* Jn. 11:5.

p. 95    *The Comforter will lead you:* Jn. 16:13.

p. 95    *the "angelic life":* See Brown, *The Body and Society*.

p. 95    *two dozen elect:* See Widengren, op. cit., p. 482.

p. 95    *The first disciples of Mani:* Ibid., pp. 396–99.

p. 96    *the First Council at Constantinople:* Ibid., p. 396.

p. 96    *profound hopelessness:* See Hans Peter Duerr, *Sedna oder Die Liebe zum Leben* (Frankfurt am Main: Suhrkamp, 1984), pp. 229–61.

p. 96    *to use perfumes:* See Widengren, op. cit., p. 486.

p. 97    *Wittgenstein reflected:* Quoted in Ray Monk, *Ludwig Wittgenstein: The Duty of Genius* (New York: Penguin Books, 1991), p. 492.

p. 97    *The solution of the problem:* Ludwig Wittgenstein, *Tractatus Logico-Philosophicus*, translated by D. F. Pears and B. F. McGuinness (London: Routledge & Kegan Paul, 1961), p. 149.

p. 97    *"If you wish to be perfect . . .":* Mt. 19:21. On St. Anthony, see Aline Rousselle, *Porneia: De la maîtrise du corps à la privation sensorielle* (Paris: Presses Universitaires de France, 1983). This book has been translated into English by Felicia Pheasant as *Porneia: On Desire and the Body in Antiquity* (Oxford/New York: Basil Blackwell, 1988). See also Jacques Lacarrière, *Les hommes ivres de Dieu* (Paris: Fayard, 1975), pp. 51–70. For general depictions of Christian monasticism, see Otto Zöckler, *Askese und Mönchtum* (Frankfurt:

n.p., 1897) and Bernhard Lohse, *Askese und Mönchtum in der antike und in der alten Kirche* (München: n.p., 1969).

p. 98    *aretalogy:* See Kee, *Christian Origins,* pp. 61–62, 109.

p. 99    *the call of the desert:* Mk. 1:3.

p. 99    *the anchorites:* From anachōrētēs ("those who have withdrawn").

p. 99    *but one daily meal:* See Rousselle, *Porneia.*

p. 99    *Palamon:* See Lacarrière, *Les hommes ivres,* pp. 97–181.

p. 100    *obeyed the supernatural voice:* See Zöckler, *Askese und Mönchtum,* pp. 183–211.

p. 101    *Jesus appears as a guest:* Lk. 10:38–42.

p. 101    *Pachomius' death:* 347 A.D.

p. 102    *chasing after the wind:* Eccles. 1:14.

p. 102    *Many are called:* Mt. 22:14.

p. 102    *Two ways:* Eusebius, *Demonstratio Evangelica* 1, 8.

p. 104    *the Order of Preachers in Toulouse:* See Jean Duvernoy, *L'histoire des Cathares* (Toulouse: n.p., 1979), p. 274.

p. 104    *as though from nowhere:* Borst, *Die Katharer,* pp. 64–69.

p. 104    *Everwin von Steinfeld:* See Jeffrey B. Russell, editor, *Religious Dissent in the Middle Ages* (New York: John Wiley, 1971), pp. 60–63.

p. 105    *allowed no middle course:* Ibid., pp. 74f. See also Edina Bozóky, *Le Livre secret des Cathares* (Paris: Beauchesne, 1980).

p. 105    *the Comforter's consecration:* Borst, op. cit., pp. 145f.

p. 106    *stigmatized the new Spirit movement:* See R. I. Moore, *The Origins of European Dissent* (London: Penguin Books, 1977), pp. 175–82.

p. 106    *reminiscent of cats:* See Jean Duvernoy, *Le Catharisme* (Toulouse: n.p., 1976), pp. 302–4.

p. 107    *the apostles refer to two swords:* Lk. 22:35–38. In this connection, see Walter Ullmann, *Medieval Political Thought* (Harmondsworth: Penguin Books, 1975), p. 110.

p. 107    *In May 1167:* See Borst, op. cit., pp. 79–81.

p. 108    *They are swept together:* Jn. 15:6.

p. 108    *Heretics everywhere:* Borst, op. cit., p. 85.

p. 108    *"Rise up, ye soldiers . . .":* Quoted from Luther Baier, *Die grosse Ketzerei* (Berlin: Wagenbach, 1984), p. 113.

p. 109    *the Friday before Pentecost:* Ibid., p. 172.

p. 109    Do not be afraid . . . : Lk. 12:4.

p. 109    Anyone who wants to save his life . . . : Mk. 8:35.

p. 109    No one can take away . . . : Jn. 16:22.

p. 109    *"At the present time":* Nicolaus Lenau, *Savonarola* (Leipzig: Reclam, n.d.), p. 12.

p. 112    *Read!:* The Koran, Sura 96:1. Quotations from the Koran are taken from *Al-Qur'ān,* translated by Ahmed Ali (Princeton: Princeton University Press, 1988). See Ibn Ishaq, *The Life of Mohammed* (London: Oxford University Press, 1955).

p. 112    *There he stood on high:* The Koran, Sura 53:6–12.

p. 112    *We sent down the Koran:* Sura 97.

p. 113    *who promised a Comforter:* Jn. 16:7.

p. 113    *You believers:* Sura 5:51, 73.

p. 113    *he shivered:* See Emile Dermenghem, *Mohammed* (Reinbek: Rowohlt, 1960), p. 30.

p. 113     *We have whispered:* Sura 4:163.

p. 113     *Those are they to whom we gave the book:* Sura 6:89.

p. 113     *people of the book:* Sura 3:65, 67.

p. 113     *Today I have perfected:* Sura 5:3.

p. 114     *spoke through the prophets:* Denzinger, *Enchiridion*, no. 150.

p. 114     *the most entertaining example:* See Richard Benz, editor, *Die Legenda aurea des Jacobus de Voragine* (Heidelberg: Lambert Schneider, 1984), p. 964.

p. 115     *the story of a heretical monk:* Ibid., p. 966.

p. 115     *the three swindlers of mankind:* This expression goes back to freethinking Islamic circles of the 10th century. See L. Massignan, "La légende 'De tribus impostoribus' " in *Revue de l'histoire des religions* 82 (1920), pp. 74–78.

p. 115     *the Parable of the Rings:* See Ernst Bloch, *Das Materialismusproblem, seine Geschichte und Substanz* (Frankfurt am Main: Suhrkamp, 1972), p. 487.

p. 116     *couriers and messengers:* See Klaus Koch, *Die Propheten*, Vols. 1 and 2 (Stuttgart: Kohlhammer, 1980 and 1995).

p. 116     *I take no pleasure:* Amos 5:21–22.

p. 117     *"Mercy is what pleases me . . .":* Hos. 6:6 (compare Mt. 9:13 and 12:7).

p. 117     *an Islamic estimate:* See Abu-l-Ala Maudoodi, *Weltanschauung und Leben im Islam* (Damascus: The Holy Koran Publishing House, 1977), p. 113.

p. 117     *the "calling":* The Hebrew word for "prophet," *nabi*, comes from the verb that means "to call."

p. 117     *an old Bible story:* 1 Sam. 3:1–21.

p. 118     *makes King Saul into a proverbial figure:* 1 Sam. 19:18–24.

p. 119     *in another version:* 1 Sam. 10:6, 10.

p. 119     *the foot of Mount Carmel:* 1 Kings 18:40.

p. 119     *heavily bleeding wounds:* 1 Kings 18:28.

p. 119     *In stark contrast:* 1 Kings 19:1–18.

p. 120     *asks the author:* Heb. 11:32–38 (shortened).

p. 120     *the story of Jonah:* Jon. 1:1–3; 3:1–10.

p. 120     *pleading his tender age:* Jer. 1:6f.

p. 121     *his relationship with God:* Jer. 20:7–9, 14.

p. 121     *A great prophet has risen up:* Lk. 7:16.

p. 121     *Elijah is come back:* Mt. 16:14.

p. 121     *a theological committee:* Mk. 3:22–30.

p. 122     *Wait! And see:* Mt. 27:49.

p. 122     *the Nazarene had made his provisions:* Mk. 9:2–13.

p. 123     *like a sigh:* Mk. 7:34; see also 6:41.

p. 123     *like a snorting noise:* Jn. 11:33, 38.

p. 123     *profound distress:* Jn. 11:33.

p. 123     *some strong words:* Mk. 8:12.

p. 123     *And sometimes he exults:* Lk. 10:21.

p. 123     *they shall drive out devils:* Mk. 16:17f.; Mt. 10:8; Lk. 10:9, 17.

p. 123     *the gift of prophecy:* 1 Cor. 14:3.

p. 123     *congregation in Antioch:* Acts 13:1, as well as 11:28; 15:32; and 21:9f. See also Ferdinand Hahn, *Frühchristliche Prophetie. Von den Anfängen bis zum Montanismus* (Stuttgart: Kohlhammer, 1995).

p. 124     *In the Greek-influenced everyday culture:* See Lane Fox, *Pagans and Christians*, pp. 204–15; E. R. Dodds, *Pagan and Christian in an Age of Anxiety*, pp. 53–57.

p. 125    *an Egyptian miracle man:* Josephus Flavius, *The Jewish War*, II, 13, 5; see Acts 21:38.

p. 125    *when cries are heard:* Mk. 13:21–23 and parallels.

p. 125    *"to tell them by their fruits":* Mt. 7:16.

p. 125    *They prophesied in wild confusion:* I Cor. 14:29–34.

p. 125    *"distinguishing among spirits":* I Cor. 12:10.

p. 125    *For the sisters:* Joel 3:1; Acts 2:17.

p. 126    *The trumpet is going to sound:* I Cor. 15:52.

p. 126    *Not every spirit is to be trusted:* I Jn. 4:1–3.

p. 126    *Montanus:* See Lane Fox, op. cit., pp. 405–10, and Dodds, op. cit., pp. 63–68.

p. 126    *the voice of the Comforter:* Jn. 14:26.

p. 127    *the mountain Christians:* From the Latin *montanus*, "dwelling in the mountains."

p. 128    *the people of the Book:* The Koran, Sura 29:46.

p. 129    *"Withdrawn from Catholicism . . .":* Jean-Paul Sartre, *Les Mots* (Paris: Gallimard, 1964), pp. 201–2.

p. 129    *The Holy Spirit had become an author:* See Hermann Timm, *Das ästhetische Jahrzent* (Gütersloh: Gerd Mohn, 1990), p. 173.

p. 129    *"I have changed":* Sartre, *Les mots*, pp. 204–5.

p. 131    *so invisible and omnipresent:* Hans Urs von Balthasar, editor, *Geist und Feuer* (Salzburg: Otto Müller, 1938), p. 12.

p. 131    *all this rubbish!:* See Rudolph, *Gnosis*, pp. 312–17.

p. 132    *a passage in the Book of Genesis:* Urs von Balthasar, op. cit., pp. 46–53.

p. 132    *Origen was arrogant enough:* It is obvious that Origen's thought was close to Gnosticism, even though he polemicized against it.

p. 134    *a fundamental deficiency symptom:* See Rudolf Wolfgang Müller, *Geld und Geist. Zur Entstehungsgeschichte von Identitätsbewubtsein und Rationalität seit der Antike* (Frankfurt am Main: Campus, 1977); Julian Jaynes, *The Origin of Consciousness in the Breakdown of the Bicameral Mind* (Boston: Houghton Mifflin, 1976); and Bruno Snell, *Die Entdeckung des Geistes: Studien zur Entstehung des europäischen Denkens bei den Griechen* (Göttingen: Vandenhoeck & Ruprecht, 1975 (4th edition, newly revised).

p. 134    *just in the touchiest moment:* Iliad, Bk. I, 199f. See also Müller, *Geld und Geist*, p. 264, and Jaynes, *Origin of Consciousness*, p. 72.

p. 134    *even more detailed:* Iliad, Bk. XXIV, 120f. See Müller, op. cit., pp. 280f.

p. 135    *the finding of Julian Jaynes:* Jaynes, op. cit., p. 72.

p. 135    *"hallucinatory area":* Ibid., pp. 100–8.

p. 136    *writes the professor:* Ibid., pp. 104–5.

p. 136    *"I am suggesting":* Ibid., pp. 142f.

p. 136    *reduced to electrical processes:* Ibid., pp. 444–46.

p. 136    *religion turns out to be:* Ibid., p. 297.

p. 136    *Archilochus:* See Müller, op. cit., pp. 273–79, and Jaynes, op. cit., p. 283.

p. 137    *Achilles' "kinship":* Jaynes, ibid., p. 431.

p. 137    *a somewhat flamboyant theory:* Ibid.

p. 137    *We have made a mistake:* Jaynes, ibid., p. 437.

p. 137    *Patients who hear voices:* Nature, 378 (Nov. 9, 1995), pp. 176–79.

p. 138    *in his autobiography:* Malcolm X with Alex Haley, *The Autobiography of Malcolm X* (New York: Ballantine, 1992).

p. 138    *a sect of four hundred souls:* Ibid., p. 448.

p. 139    *Reginald showed up:* Ibid., pp. 172f.

p. 140    *as Hilda told Malcolm:* Ibid., pp. 179–83.

p. 142    *had this to say about his partner:* Ibid., p. 440.

p. 142    *merely in retrospect:* Ibid., pp. 65–78, 121–23.

p. 142    *Only once did the Other:* Ibid., pp. 203–5.

p. 142    *Master Fard was the Messiah:* Ibid., pp. 225–27.

p. 142    *During an assembly:* Ibid., p. 215.

p. 143    *slavemasters' Christian religion:* Ibid., pp. 218–20.

p. 143    *within half an hour:* Ibid., pp. 254f.

p. 143    *In late 1959:* Ibid., pp. 257–66.

p. 144    *Brother Malcolm, Mr. Muhammad said:* Ibid., p. 209.

p. 144    *In November 1963:* Ibid., pp. 328–31.

p. 144    *a few people sitting in offices:* Ibid., pp. 317–22.

p. 144    *Certain incidents:* Ibid., pp. 322–28.

p. 144    *my entire faith:* Ibid., p. 215.

p. 145    *a pilgrimage to Mecca:* Ibid., pp. 348–73.

p. 145    *I was a zombie:* Ibid., p. 473.

p. 145    *declared to the press:* Ibid., p. 420.

p. 145    He was pierced: Isa. 53:5.

p. 148    *The conversation . . . between Richard and Joachim:* See Bernard McGinn, *The Calabrian Abbot: Joachim of Fiore in the History of Western Thought* (New York: Macmillan, 1985), p. 26.

p. 149    *Antichrist:* The idea of the Antichrist can be traced back to the second century after Christ. See Bernard McGinn, *Antichrist: Two Thousand Years of the Human Fascination with Evil* (San Francisco: Harper, 1994).

p. 149    *In April, Richard sailed:* See Hans Eberhard Mayer, *Geschichte der Kreuzzüge* (Stuttgart: Kohlhammer, 1965), pp. 138–41.

p. 149    *The Spirit and the Bride:* Rev. 22:17,20. (See above, pp. 18–24.)

p. 150    *the critical moment:* Rev. 22:10.

p. 150    *The monastic career:* McGinn, *The Calabrian Abbot*, pp. 19–21.

p. 150    *since Aurelius Augustinus:* In *De civitate Dei*, St. Augustine (354–430 A.D.) presented a view of world history that divided it into six ages, the last of which was the Age of Christianity. See Peter Brown, *Augustine of Hippo: A Biography* (London: Faber & Faber, 1967), pp. 295–312.

p. 150    *Joachim wrote:* McGinn, *The Calabrian Abbot*, pp. 21f.

p. 151    Liber Concordiae: Ibid., pp. 31f., 130f.

p. 151    *I was in the church:* Ibid., p. 22.

p. 151    Expositio in Apokalypsim: A commentary upon the Apocalypse. See McGinn, ibid., pp. 32f.

p. 151    Psalterium decem chordarum: "The Ten-Stringed Harp." See McGinn, ibid., p. 33.

p. 152    *a tale told by an idiot:* Shakespeare, *Macbeth*, Act V, scene 5.

p. 152    *called before the pope:* McGinn, ibid., pp. 11, 22–24.

p. 152    *the Book of Ezekiel:* Ezek. 26:7 (Vulgate).

p. 153    *Caelestis urbs:* A hymn from the *Commune Dedicationis Ecclesiae* in the Roman liturgy.

p. 153      *at least four such levels:* Körtner, *Der inspirierte Leser,* pp. 62–77. (See above, pp. 180–87.)

p. 153      *new ways of understanding:* See McGinn, *The Calabrian Abbot,* p. 129.

p. 154      *the siege of Naples:* Ibid., pp. 26f.

p. 154      *Joachim's decisive idea:* See Gert Wendelborn, *Gott und Geschichte. Joachim von Fiore und die Hoffnung der Christenheit* (Wien: Böhlau, 1974), pp. 17–43.

p. 154      *perhaps only half a year:* See Robert E. Lerner, "Joachim von Fiore," in *Theologische Realenzyklopädie,* Vol. 18 (Berlin: Gruyter, 1988), p. 88.

p. 155      *the last pope:* McGinn, *The Calabrian Abbot,* p. 29.

p. 155      *only in the year 1989:* See Francis Fukuyama, *The End of History and the Last Man* (New York: Free Press, 1992), and Romano Guardini, *The End of the Modern World,* translated by Joseph Theman and Herbert Burke, edited with an Introduction by Frederick D. Wilhelmsen (New York: Sheed & Ward, 1956).

p. 155      *"little Frenchman":* Francis's mother came from France. See Helmut Feld, *Franziskus von Assisi und seine Bewegung* (Darmstadt: Wissenschaftliche Buchgesellschaft, 1994), pp. 258–62.

p. 155      *like a sun:* Dante, *Commedia,* Paradiso XI, 50.

p. 155      *after a festive banquet:* See Adolf Holl, *The Last Christian,* translated by Peter Heinegg (Garden City: Doubleday, 1980), pp. 34–37.

p. 156      *according to the text:* See Feld, op. cit., p. 113.

p. 156      *Francesco wrote in his Testament:* Quoted in Otto Karrer, editor, *Franz von Assisi: Legenden und Laude* (Zurich: Manesse, 1945), p. 567.

p. 156      *so the story goes:* See Holl, op. cit., pp. 177–78, and Feld, op. cit., pp. 207f.

p. 158      *The brusque gesture:* See Holl, op. cit., pp. 29f., and Feld, op. cit., pp. 130–33.

p. 159      *The priest read:* See Holl, op. cit., pp. 61–63, and Feld, op. cit., pp. 141f.

p. 159      *After the Lord gave me brothers:* See Karrer, op. cit., p. 569, and Feld, op. cit., p. 42.

p. 160      *song of praise to God and the world:* See Karrer, op. cit., pp. 520–23.

p. 160      Poverello: *Povero* means "poor" in Italian; *poverello* is an affectionate diminutive, approximately "little poor one."

p. 160      *the memorable sermon:* See Holl, op. cit., pp. 121–22, and Feld, op. cit., p. 199.

p. 161      *The "very smallest brother":* Quoted in Karrer, op. cit., p. 572.

p. 161      *without hierarchical chains:* See Feld, op. cit., p. 307.

p. 161      *the "catholic garden":* Dante, *Commedia,* Paradiso XII, 104.

p. 161      *five years before his death:* See Holl, op. cit., pp. 157–58; a different date is given in Feld, op. cit., pp. 302–4.

p. 162      *The only minister:* Quoted in Feld, op. cit., p. 308.

p. 162      *another conflict:* See Holl, op. cit., pp. 91–105, and Feld, op. cit., pp. 401–23.

p. 162      *The life of the spirit:* Quoted in Feld, op. cit., p. 420.

p. 163      *a popular legend:* Quoted in Karrer, op. cit., pp. 138f.

p. 163      *Near the end of his life:* See Holl, op. cit., pp. 212f., and Feld, op. cit., pp. 421f.

p. 163      *expresses Francesco's feelings:* See Feld, p. 419.

p. 163      *The last high point:* See Holl, op. cit., pp. 192–99, and Feld, op. cit., pp. 256–77, 361.

p. 164      *One wants precise knowledge:* Elias Canetti, *Die Provinz des Menschen. Aufzeichnungen*

*1942–1972* (München: Hanser, 1973), p. 76. There is an English translation of this work by Joachim Neugroschel: *The Human Province* (New York:
Seabury Press, 1978).

p. 164  women . . . starved themselves: See Rudolph M. Bell, *Holy Anorexia* (Chicago:
University Press, 1985), pp. 123–27.

p. 164  like those six: See Holl, *The Last Christian*, pp. 130f., and Feld, *Franziskus*, pp.
196f.

p. 165  Brother Helias Coppi: See Feld, op. cit., pp. 353–400.

p. 165  Francesco's tiny corpse: In 1978, an examination of St. Francis's bones revealed
that he was five feet tall. See Feld, op. cit., p. 280.

p. 166  received a guest: See Ernst Benz, *Ecclesia Spiritualis* (Stuttgart: Kohlhammer,
1964), pp. 175–81; Holl, op. cit., pp. 220–24; and Feld, op. cit., pp.
486–90.

p. 166  it very soon became clear: Benz, op. cit., pp. 4–58.

p. 167  Taubes wrote: Jacob Taubes, *Abendländische Eschatologie* (München: Matthes &
Seitz, 1991), p. 190 (slightly edited).

p. 167  a deadline: See Benz, op. cit., pp. 205–25.

p. 168  One of the Pisan four: Ibid., pp. 208f. See also Johannes Haller, *Das Papsttum.
Idee und Wirklichkeit*, Vol. 5 (Reinbek: Rowohlt, 1965), p. 183.

p. 168  Fra Salimbene resolved: Benz, *Ecclesia Spiritualis*, p. 211.

p. 168  in a residence: Ibid., p. 179.

p. 169  "They distinguish two Churches": Quoted in Arno Borst, *Lebensformen in Mittelalter*
(Frankfurt am Main: Ullstein, 1979), p. 594.

p. 169  a commission of cardinals: See Holl, *The Last Christian*, pp. 228–30.

p. 170  immediately moved to attack: See ibid., pp. 230–34, and Feld, *Franziskus*, pp.
494–99.

p. 171  the most dangerous book: See Benz, *Ecclesia Spiritualis*, pp. 256–332; also Michael
Wolff, *Geschichte der Impetustheorie* (Frankfurt am Main: Suhrkamp, 1978), pp.
174–84.

p. 172  into the lower depths: See Heinz Robert Schlette, *Weltseele. Geschichte und
Hermeneutik* (Frankfurt am Main: Knecht, 1993), pp. 132–45.

p. 172  Hegel wrote to his friend: Quoted in Schlette, *Weltseele*, p. 181.

p. 173  In its middle-class form: See Philippe Ariès and Georges Duby, editors, *A
History of Private Life*, Vol. 4, translated by Arthur Goldhammer (Cambridge:
Harvard University Press, 1990).

p. 173  responsible for the split: See Richard Sennett, *The Fall of Public Man* (New York:
Knopf, 1977).

p. 173  the ideal of the middle-class family: See Manfred Schneider, *Die kranke schöne Seele
der Revolution* (Frankfurt am Main: Syndikat, 1980), p. 11.

p. 173  In love, Hegel wrote: Georg Friedrich Wilhelm Hegel, *Der Geist des Christentums
und sein Schicksal* (Gütersloh: Gerd Mohn, 1970), p. 72.

p. 173  Those who have been united: Quoted in Hermann Timm, *Fallhöhe des Geistes. Das
religiöse Denken des jungen Hegel* (Frankfurt am Main: Syndikat, n.d.), p. 107.

p. 174  "We live in an important era . . .": Johannes Hoffmeister, editor, *Dokumente zu
egels Entwicklung* (Stuttgart: n.p., 1936), p. 35.

p. 174  disease germs: See Timm, op. cit., p. 55.

p. 175  the pale shimmering: Ibid., pp. 96f.

p. 175  "reason shows itself": Georg Friedrich Wilhelm Hegel, *Phänomenologie des*

*Geistes* (Hamburg: Felix Meiner, 1952), XL f. The text cited is the sixth edition, edited by Johannes Hoffmeister. (English versions of Hegel's work include *The Phenomenology of Mind*, translated by J. B. Baillie, and *Hegel's Phenomenology of Spirit*, translated by A. V. Miller.) See further Joseph Möller, *Der Geist und das Absolute* (Paderborn: Schöningh, 1951); Erwin Discherl, *Der Heilige Geist und das menschliche Bewusstsein* (Würzburg: Echter, 1989), pp. 587–642; and Bernd Jochen Hilberath, *Pneumatologie* (Düsseldorf: Patmos, 1994), pp. 155f.

p. 175     *Weary, morose:* Quoted in Franz Wiedmann, *Hegel* (Reinbek: Rowohlt, 1993), p. 105 (shortened).

p. 176     *"I salute this . . .":* Quoted in Wiedmann, op. cit., p. 69.

p. 176     *based merely on a feeling:* Ibid., p. 74.

p. 176     *Only the free spirit:* Ibid., p. 75.

p. 177     *Man's spirit for knowing God:* Ibid., p. 128.

p. 177     *"I was his student . . .":* Ibid., p. 145.

p. 177     *"Theses on Feuerbach":* Karl Marx and Friedrich Engels, *Ausgewählte Schriften*, Vol. 2 (Berlin: Dietz, 1970), pp. 370–72.

p. 177     *Lenin sent a telegram:* Quoted in Rudi Dutschke and Manfred Wilke, *Die Sowjetunion, Solschenizyn und die westliche Linke* (Reinbek: Rowohlt, 1975), p. 127.

p. 178     *"Books are glorified":* Alexander Solzhenitsyn, *Cancer Ward*, translated by Rebecca Frank (New York: The Dial Press, 1968), p. 336.

p. 180     *"He came into my room":* Simone Weil, *La connaissance surnaturelle* (Paris: Gallimard, 1950), pp. 9–10. This passage has been slightly abridged.

p. 182     *death certificate:* Quoted from Angelica Krogman, *Simone Weil* (Reinbek: Rowohlt, 1979), p. 176.

p. 182     *Janet observed:* Bell, *Holy Anorexia*, pp. 11–13.

p. 182     *a petite, pretty person:* See Catherine Clément and Sudhir Kakar, *Der Heilige und die Verrückte. Religiöse Ekstase und psychische Grenzerfahrung* (München: C. H. Beck, 1993), p. 22.

p. 182     *the stigmata of the Crucified:* Ibid., pp. 37–39.

p. 183     *a small piece of bread:* Ibid., p. 39.

p. 183     From Anxiety to Ecstasy: Pierre Janet, *De l'Angoisse à l'Extase* (Paris: n.p., 1926 & 1928). See also Henri F. Ellenberger, *The Discovery of the Unconscious* (New York: Basic Books, 1970), pp. 395f.

p. 183     *Her ecstasies,* Janet wrote: Clément and Kakar, op. cit., p. 23.

p. 183     *Saint Clare of Assisi:* See above, pp. 228f.

p. 183     *"We are not made of bronze . . .":* Quoted from the *Fonti Francescane* (Padua: n.p., 1980), p. 2292.

p. 183     *more than half:* See Bell, *Holy Anorexia*, p. x. Bell considered the 261 Italian women canonized by the Catholic Church between 1200 and the present day. In a third of the cases, the biographical data were too meager to allow conclusions to be drawn about the presence of clear signs of anorexia.

p. 184     *a young woman named Sybilla:* See Peter Dinzelbacher, *Mittelalterliche Frauenmystik* (Paderborn: Schöningh, 1993), pp. 290f.

p. 184     *a satirical poem:* Quoted from Bell, *Holy Anorexia*, p. 27.

p. 185     *"Lay yourself on top of me":* Quoted from Dinzelbacher, op. cit., p. 294.

p. 185     *a certain Raymond of Capua:* Raymond of Capua (1330–1399), Master General of the Dominican Order, wrote an account of the life of St. Catherine of Siena.

p. 185     *I, who had hidden my soul:* Quoted from Clement and Kakar, op. cit., p. 66.

p. 186     *his Herbarium:* See ibid., pp. 238–41.

p. 186     *Simone Weil wrote a letter:* Simone Weil, *Écrits de Londres et dernières lettres* (Paris: Gallimard, 1957), pp. 255f.

p. 186     *"I can say," she wrote:* Simone Weil, *Attente de Dieu* (Paris: La Colombe, 1948), p. 32.

p. 186     *In Sartre's opinion:* Jean-Paul Sartre. *L'Idiot de la famille* (Paris: Gallimard, 1971), Vol. I, p. 544.

p. 187     Something stronger than I . . . : Weil, *Attente de Dieu*, p. 37.

p. 187     *who had placed his sail:* Marguerite Porete, *The Mirror of Simple Souls*, translated and introduced by Ellen L. Babinsky (New York: Paulist Press, 1993), p. 80.

p. 187     *"I tasted everywhere":* Quoted from Clement and Kakar, op. cit., pp. 51–54.

p. 188     *Every experience of God:* St. Thomas Aquinas, *Summa Theologica*, 2 II, 97, 2, 2.

pp. 188–89     *the best way of knowing God:* St. Bonaventure, *Commentary on the Sentences* III, 35, I, 5 (vol. 3, p. 775 in Quadracchi's edition of the *Opera omnia* of St. Bonaventure).

p. 189     *principally women:* The 14th century is considered the high point of female mysticism in Europe. See Evelyn Underhill, *Mysticism* (Cleveland: World Publishing Company, 1955), p. 459.

p. 189     *as they were called:* "Devout women" or "holy women." See Dinzelbacher, *Frauenmystik*, p. 292.

p. 189     *a wellborn woman:* See Robert E. Lerner, *The Heresy of the Free Spirit in the Later Middle Ages* (Berkeley: University of California Press, 1972), pp. 71f, and Kurt Ruh, *Geschichte der abendländische Mystik* (München: C. H. Beck, 1993), vol. 2, p. 343.

p. 190     *circulated anonymously:* Porete, *Mirror*, p. 65.

p. 190     *succeeded in identifying:* See Romana Guarneri, *Il movimento del Libero Spirito*, in *Archivio Italiano per la storia della pietà*, vol. 4 (Roma: n.p., 1965), pp. 351–708.

p. 190     *"beguines":* See E. W. McDonnell, *The Beguines and Beghards in Medieval Culture* (New Brunswick: Rutgers University Press, 1954).

p. 191     *"Virtues, I take my leave . . .":* Porete, *Mirror*, p. 84.

p. 191     *Most sweet Holy Spirit:* Ibid., p. 121.

p. 191     *finished with the world:* Ibid., p. 124.

p. 191     *nor any anxiety:* Ibid., p. 120.

p. 191     *in the style of the troubadour poetry:* Ibid., pp. 138, 155, 218. See Ruh, *Geschichte der abendländischen Mystik*, pp. 351–58.

p. 192     *The chronicler observed:* See ibid., p. 343.

p. 192     *the new and free Spirit:* See Marjorie Reeves, *The Influence of Prophecy in the Later Middle Ages* (Oxford: Oxford University Press, 1969), p. 177.

p. 192     *"impudent assertions":* See Ruh, op. cit., p. 358; Lerner, *The Heresy of the Free Spirit*, pp. 13–19.

p. 192     *were circulating everywhere:* See Malcolm D. Lambert, *Medieval Heresy: Popular Movements from Bogomil to Hus* (New York: Holmes & Meier Publishers, 1977), pp. 175–76.

p. 192     *in a bull:* See Denzinger, *Enchiridion*, no. 866.

p. 192    *the Council of Vienne:* Ibid., nos. 891–99.

p. 193    *the notorious Walter Kerlinger:* See Lerner, *Free Spirit,* p. 134.

p. 193    She is a garden enclosed: SS. 4:12.

p. 193    *In the refectory:* See Lerner, op. cit., p. I.

p. 193    *"So let us pray to God":* Meister Eckhart, *Deutsche Predigten und Traktate,* edited by Josef Quint (München: Hanser, 1963), p. 305. See also Peter Dinzelbacher, *Christliche Mystik im Abendland* (Paderborn: Schöningh, 1994), pp. 281–92.

p. 193    *"The wise Meister Eckhart . . .":* Quoted from Kurt Ruh, *Meister Eckhart* (München: C. H. Beck, 1989), p. 12.

p. 194    geistlich: See Franz Wöhrer, *The Cloud of Unknowing (um 1380). Ein Beispiel angewandter Mystagogie aus dem englischen Spätmittelalter,* Manuskript 1993, in *Studies in Spirituality,* Vol. VII (1997).

p. 194    *a vest made of pigskin:* See Feld, *Franziskus,* pp. 424–28.

p. 194    *Chiara herself:* Ibid., pp. 421–23.

p. 195    *confirmed testimony:* See Bell, *Holy Anorexia,* pp. 92–102; Ruh, *Mystik,* pp. 501–9.

p. 195    *a visionary woman:* Juliane of Cornillon (d. 1250).

p. 195    *her sensation:* See Caroline Walker Bynum, *Holy Feast and Holy Fast: The Religious Significance of Food to Medieval Women* (Berkeley: University of California Press, 1987), p. 141f.

p. 195    *Similar sensations arose:* See Bell, op. cit., p. 108.

p. 196    *heard him clearly:* See Ruh, op. cit., p. 516.

p. 196    *Ah God! says Reason:* Porete, *Mirror,* p. 163.

p. 196    *The special knowledge of lordship:* See Hans Peter Duerr, *Traumzeit* (Frankfurt am Main: Syndicat, 1978).

p. 197    *the interior monologue:* Porete, *Mirror,* p. 182.

p. 197    *Toward the end of her book:* Ibid., pp. 194f.; see Ruh, op. cit., p. 345.

p. 198    *When the poor soul comes to court:* Quoted from Ruh, op. cit., p. 263.

p. 198    *On another occasion:* Ibid., pp. 265f.

p. 198    *"I sat down beside the little lake":* Ibid., p. 299.

p. 198    *the devil doesn't sleep:* Ibid., pp. 300–5.

p. 198    *One Saturday:* Ibid., p. 308.

p. 199    *The Lord called:* Ibid., p. 309 (abridged).

p. 199    *sat in a circle:* See Dinzelbacher, *Christliche Mystik,* p. 229.

p. 199    *he held the watering can:* Ruh, op. cit., p. 306.

p. 199    *at the foot of the throne:* Ibid., pp. 313f.

p. 199    *Rocking baby Jesus:* See Dinzelbacher, *Christliche Mystik,* p. 230.

p. 199    *"a childish love":* Ruh, op. cit., p. 266.

p. 199    *She must nurse the child Jesus:* See Clément and Kakar, op. cit., pp. 50f.

p. 200    *In the visionary prose:* See Ruh, op. cit., p. 283.

p. 200    *she considered herself insane:* See Bell, *Holy Anorexia,* p. 106.

p. 200    *A beguine:* See Ruh, *Mystik,* pp. 158–225, and Dinzelbacher, *Christliche Mystik,* pp. 203–8.

p. 200    *this linguistic coinage:* See Ruh, op. cit., pp. 151, 178–82. See also Bynum, *Holy Feast,* pp. 161–63, where orewoet is translated "insanity."

p. 200    *"My heart and my veins":* Quoted from Dinzelbacher, *Christliche Mystik,* p. 205.

p. 201    *half an hour:* See Ruh, op. cit., pp. 201f.

p. 201     *Hadewijch notes:* Ibid., pp. 193.

p. 201     *"Sometimes courtly love . . .":* Ibid., pp. 150f.

p. 201     *Teresa's heart:* See Vita Sackville-West, *The Eagle and the Dove* (Garden City: Doubleday, 1944), p. 93. Ernst Benz, in *Die Vision*, pp. 395–410, gives an overview of the theme of the love-arrow.

p. 202     *Sun, moon, and stars:* Ruh, op. cit., pp. 199f.

p. 202     God was crueler to me: Ibid., p. 168.

p. 202     *Antwerp:* Ibid., p. 152.

p. 202     *Love is what matters:* Ibid., p. 169.

p. 202     *Madeleine's parental home:* See Clément and Kakar, op. cit., pp. 26–34.

p. 204     *A half century later:* See Colleen A. Ward, editor, *Altered States of Consciousness and Mental Health: A Cross-Cultural Perspective* (Newbury Park: Sage Publications, 1989).

p. 204     *A Canadian psychiatrist:* Ibid., pp. 149–66. In this connection see also Alister Hardy, *The Spiritual Nature of Man: A Study of Contemporary Religious Experience* (Oxford: Clarendon Press, 1979). While at Oxford in 1969, Sir Alister, a marine biologist, founded an institute for research into religious experiences. Shortly before his death, he was awarded the prestigious Templeton Foundation prize, in the amount of $185,000, for his achievements in the religious field. See *Time*, November 3, 1985.

p. 204     *Blasphemous nonsense:* James M. Clark, *Meister Eckhart* (London: Faber and Faber, 1957), p. 124.

p. 204     *Alemannic text:* See Lerner, *Free Spirit*, pp. 215–21; and Dinzelbacher, *Christliche Mystik*, pp. 294f.

p. 205     *reaches her goal:* Quoted from Dinzelbacher, ibid., p. 294.

p. 206     *a shout of joy:* See Annemarie Schimmel, *Mystical Dimensions of Islam* (Chapel Hill: University of North Carolina Press, 1975), pp. 62–77. The utterance in question was *ana'l-Haqq*, which may be translated as "I am absolute Truth (God)."

pp. 206–7     *"zero-experience":* See Agehananda Bharati, *The Light at the Center* (Santa Barbara: Ross-Erikson, 1976), pp. 48–86.

p. 207     *for the first time:* Ibid., pp. 39f.

p. 207     *three more times:* Ibid., pp. 40–44.

p. 207     *The summary of his experience:* Ibid., pp. 65, 94.

p. 208     *"what is thy command?":* Ruh, *Mystik*, p. 267.

p. 208     Nirvana: Duerr, *Sedna*, p. 242.

p. 208     *insignificant:* Ibid., p. 261. The following quotation from Meister Eckhart can be found in A. M. Haas, *Sermo mysticus* (Fribourg: n.p., 1979), p. 451.

p. 208     *her most urgent desire:* See Simone Pétrement, *Simone Weil: A Life*, translated by Raymond Rosenthal (New York: Pantheon Books, 1976), pp. 486f. (In May 1942, Simone Weil emigrated from Marseilles by way of Casablanca to New York, where she remained until November. At the end of November, she arrived in Liverpool, and thereafter was active in the "Forces de la France libre" in London.)

p. 209     *she had tuberculosis:* Ibid., p. 520.

p. 209     *In the last months of her life:* Ibid., pp. 520–39.

p. 209     *The Red Virgin:* Ibid., pp. 73, 93–97.

p. 210     *Comrade Weil demonstrated:* Ibid., pp. 185f.

p. 210    *a kindred soul:* Ibid., p. 184.

p. 210    *Trotsky was furious:* Ibid., p. 178.

p. 210    *"Papa has done me the honor . . .":* Ibid., p. 187.

p. 210    *But she did:* Ibid., pp. 188–91.

p. 211    *the order to fire:* See Emma Goldman, *Living My Life*, Vol. 2 (New York: Dover, 1970), pp. 872–87.

p. 211    *her farewell to Marxism:* Simone Weil, *Oppression et Liberté* (Paris: Editions Gallimard, 1955). For an English translation of this work, see Simone Weil, *Oppression and Liberty*, translated by Arthur Wills and John Petrie (Amherst: University of Massachusetts Press, 1973).

p. 211    *"I knew her very well":* Quoted from Krogman, *Simone Weil*, p. 178.

p. 211    *in a factory:* See Pétrement, op. cit., p. 230.

p. 211    *She's killing herself:* Ibid., p. 228.

p. 211    *inhuman:* Ibid., p. 231.

p. 211    *"This year killed my youth":* Ibid., p. 215.

p. 212    *in November 1938:* Ibid., p. 340.

p. 212    *"On a dark night . . .":* "Canción II: La noche oscura" by San Juan de la Cruz (St. John of the Cross).

p. 212    *spiritual negation:* Ibid.

p. 212    *"Each sound hurt me . . .":* Pétrement, op. cit., p. 329.

p. 212    *This ascetic man:* Ibid., pp. 411f.

p. 213    *Baptism must be denied:* Ibid., pp. 458f.

p. 213    *a long letter:* Ibid., pp. 465f.

p. 214    *"a beautiful baptismal font":* Ibid., p. 466.

p. 214    She seemed to us like a saint: Ibid., p. 458.

p. 216    Let my people go: This song ("Go Down, Moses") of the American Negro slaves dates from the first half of the 19th century and quotes the Book of Exodus, 5:1.

p. 216    We were obliged to learn: Nelson Mandela, *Long Walk to Freedom* (Boston: Little, Brown, 1995), p. 146.

p. 216    *"The dead are coming again":* Ernst Bloch, *Thomas Müntzer*, p. 9.

p. 217    *absolutely the equal:* Ibid., p. 110.

p. 217    *"The last earthly revolution . . .":* Ibid.

p. 217    *formulate answers:* Rainer Traub and Harald Wieser, editors, *Gespräche mit Ernst Bloch* (Frankfurt am Main: Suhrkamp, 1975), pp. 12, 17, 18, 21, 24, 30, 194, 206, 218, 235, 250, 256.

p. 218    *a tirade:* I owe this information to Burghardt Schmidt.

p. 218    *The end of the tunnel:* Bloch, *Principle of Hope*, Vol. 2, Section 36, III.

p. 218    *Zionism leads:* Ibid.

p. 218    *the betrothal period:* Traub and Wieser, Gespräche, p. 129.

p. 218    *what the Russians had done:* Ibid., pp. 127f.

p. 219    *the rebellion led by Korah:* Num. 16. See Bloch, *Atheismus im Christentum*, pp. 108–11.

p. 219    *"Where there is hope . . .":* Ibid., p. 23.

p. 219    *a certain foreshadowing:* See Karl Kautsky, *Vorläufer des neueren Sozialismus* (Berlin: J. H. W. Dietz, 1976).

p. 220    *it supported his thesis:* Bloch, *Atheismus*, pp. 231–37.

p. 220    *"the wretched of the earth . . .":* See Gustavo Gutiérrez, *The Power of the Poor in*

*History*, translated by Robert R. Barr (Maryknoll, New York: Orbis Books, 1983), p. 191. (The original Spanish title of this book is *La fuerza histórica de los pobres*, published in 1979.)

p. 220     *"Christian humanism . . .":* Quoted from Hildegard Lüning, editor, *Mit Maschinengewehr und Kreuz* (Reinbek: Rowohlt, 1971), p. 41.

p. 220     *with the press of a key:* Bloch, *Atheismus*, p. 293.

p. 221     *On the morning of July 13:* See Walter Elliger, *Thomas Müntzer. Leben und Werk* (Göttingen: Vandenhoeck & Ruprecht, 1975), pp. 443–63.

p. 221     *the vehement man:* Ibid., pp. 111–15.

p. 221     *a fantast or zealot:* Ibid., p. 165.

p. 221     *a little pilgrimage church:* Ibid., pp. 417–43.

p. 222     *"O, my deare lords":* Ibid., pp. 453f.

p. 222     *Nicolaus Storch:* Ibid., pp. 122–26.

p. 223     *The laity must become:* Ibid., p. 123.

p. 224     *after the revolt of the knights:* See Leo Sievers, *Revolution in Deutschland* (Stuttgart: Deutsche Verlags-Anstalt, 1978), pp. 166–207.

p. 225     *All that is mentioned is a discussion:* Elliger, op. cit., p. 463.

p. 225     *wrote Luther:* Quoted in Gerhard Wehr, *Thomas Müntzer* (Reinbek: Rowohlt, 1972), pp. 97f.

p. 225     *"The outcast Satan":* The following passage is a montage drawn from texts quoted in Gerald Wehr, editor, *Thomas Müntzers Schriften und Briefe* (Frankfurt am Main: Fischer Taschenbuch Verlag, 1973), pp. 196–205.

p. 226     *The earliest description:* See Michael Walzer, *Exodus and Revolution* (New York: Basic Books, 1985), p. 134.

p. 226     *the all-powerful Pharaoh:* In Ex. 1:11 there is a historically valuable reference to the building of the cities of Pithom and Rameses, which took place during the reign of Rameses II (1292–1225 B.C.).

p. 228     *another script:* See Walzer, op. cit., pp. 117–22.

p. 228     *the famous mountain:* Tradition identifies it with what is today Gebel Musa (7500 feet above sea level) in the southern portion of the Sinai Peninsula. Some researchers prefer to locate the mountain of revelation west of the Gulf of Aqaba.

p. 229     *his last letter:* Elliger, op. cit., pp. 798–805; Wehr, *Schriften*, pp. 185–87.

p. 229     *"The whole of Germany . . .":* Elliger, op. cit., pp. 700–3; Wehr, *Schriften*, pp. 179–81.

p. 229     *"the anvils of Nimrod . . .":* An allusion to the biblical figure of the same name (Gen. 10:8), "the first potentate on earth."

p. 229     *Baron Holbach:* French philosopher (1723–89).

pp. 229–30     *never taken his eye off his cause:* See Hans-Jürgen Goertz, *Thomas Müntzer* (München: C. H. Beck, 1989), pp. 167–72.

p. 230     *some four hundred men:* Elliger, op. cit., pp. 698–706.

p. 230     *"read the Libros Regum":* Ibid., p. 821.

p. 230     *the prophet Elijah:* I Kings 18 and 22.

p. 231     *"brother of the Chalice":* See Ferdinand Seibt, *Hussitica. Zur Struktur einer Revolution* (Köln: Böhlau, 1990), p. 162. See also F. G. Heymann, *John Zizka and the Hussite Revolution* (Princeton: Princeton University Press, 1955).

p. 231     *his first engagement:* Seibt, op. cit., pp. 185–201.

pp. 231–32     *The Czech words:* Bóh (God) and boj (fighter, warrior).

p. 232     *a rigorous military constitution:* See Seibt, op. cit., pp. 162–66.

p. 232     *one chronicler wrote:* Quoted in Norman Cohn, *The Pursuit of the Millennium* (New York: Oxford University Press, 1970), p. 221.

p. 232     *In the writings:* See Robert Kalivoda, *Revolution und Ideologie. Der Hussitismus* (Köln, Böhlau, 1976), pp. 113–210.

p. 232     *"sworders":* See Hans-Jürgen Goertz, *Die Täufer, Geschichte und Deutung* (München: C. H. Beck, 1980), pp. 26f.

p. 232     *"We are marvelously well pleased":* Ibid., pp. 186 and 199.

p. 233     *as Sebastian Franck noted:* Quoted in Goertz, ibid., p. 39.

p. 233     *so strained and so stretched:* Quoted in Rudolf Wolkan, editor, *Das Geschichtsbuch der Hutterischen Brüder* (Wien: n.p., 1923), p. 184.

p. 233     *the authorities ruled:* Goertz, *Die Täufer,* p. 103.

p. 233     *a formal resignation:* Ibid., p. 126.

p. 234     *a man from the Tirol:* Ibid., p. 27.

p. 234     *They owned everything in common:* Acts 2:44.

p. 234     *sent a petition:* See Michael Holzach, *Das vergessene Volk* (München: Deutscher Taschenbuch Verlag, 1982), pp. 263–66.

p. 235     *their most terrible defeat:* See Richard van Dülmen, editor, *Das Täuferreich zu Münster* (München: Deutscher Taschenbuch Verlag, 1974). See in addition Otthein Rammstedt, *Sekte und soziale Bewegung* (Köln: Westdeutscher Verlag, 1966).

p. 235     *declared Luther:* Quoted in van Dülmen, op. cit., p. 286.

p. 235     *A report to the magistrate:* Ibid., p. 261.

p. 235     *"Dear friends":* Ibid., p. 42.

p. 235     *It had been prophesied:* The following montage is put together from van Dülmen, *Täuferreich,* and Rammstedt, *Sekte und soziale Bewegung,* passim.

p. 240     *"Our weapons":* Quoted in Goertz, *Täufer,* p. 200.

p. 240     *Our breast is full:* Quoted in Hedwig Walwei-Wiegelmann, editor, *Gesellschaftkritik im Werk Heinrich Heines. Ein Heine-Lesebuch* (Paderborn: Schöningh, 1974), p. 123 (abridged).

p. 241     *A resolution:* Quoted in Walwei-Wiegelmann, op. cit., p. 126.

p. 241     *"It was sunbeams":* Quoted in Dieter Heilbbronn, editor, *Heinrich Heine. Ein Land im Winter* (Berlin: Wagenbach, 1978), p. 74.

p. 241     *yearly book production:* See Horst Albrecht Glaser, editor, *Deutsche Literatur. Eine Sozialgeschichte,* Vol. 6 (Reinbek: Rowohlt, 1980), p. 44.

p. 241     *"If there's anything that can help . . .":* Georg Büchner, *Werke und Briefe* (München: Deutscher Taschenbuch Verlag, 1992), p. 178.

p. 242     *"For centuries in Germany . . .":* Büchner, *Werke,* pp. 44, 58, 62, 64 (montage).

p. 243     *obliged to leave:* Ibid., p. 395.

p. 243     *"Aristocraticism . . .":* Ibid., p. 286.

p. 244     *"Corporal punishment":* Quoted in Antoine Guillaumont, *Les "Kephalia Gnostica" d'Évagre le Pontique et l'histoire de l'Origénisme chez les Grecs et chez les Syriens* (Paris: Éditions du Seuil, 1962), p. 316.

p. 244     *the criticism of religion:* Karl Marx and Friedrich Engels, *Über Religion* (Berlin: Dietz, 1976), p. 98. English version: Marx and Engels, *On Religion* (New York: Schocken Books, 1964), p. 41.

p. 245     *"Let's leave heaven . . .":* Quoted in Karl-Heinz Käfer, *Versöhnt ohne Opfer. Zum geschichtstheologischen Rahmen der Schriften Heinrich Heines 1824–1844* (Meisenheim: Anton Hain, 1978), p. 227.

p. 245    *planning to describe his impressions:* Heine's *Deutschland. Ein Wintermärchen (Germany: A Winter's Tale)* appeared in 1844.

p. 245    *Marx, too, had realized:* See Richard Friedenthal, *Karl Marx. Sein Leben und seine Zeit* (München: Piper, 1981), pp. 207–17.

p. 245    *Amid his notes:* Karl Marx, *Ökonomisch-philosophische Manuskripte* (Leipzig: Philipp Reclam, 1974). English version: Marx, *Economic and Philosophic Manuscripts of 1844,* translated by Martin Milligan (New York: International Publishers, 1964).

p. 245    *"reinstatement of the flesh":* See Schneider, *Kranke schöne Seele,* pp. 180–83.

p. 245    *"Chopin prepared her coffee":* Quoted in Gisela Schlientz, *George Sand* (Frankfurt am Main: Insel, 1987), p. 133.

p. 246    *According to Sand:* Ibid., p. 124.

p. 246    *"Men have succeeded . . .":* Ibid., p. 98.

p. 246    *"I'm very sad," Heine wrote:* Ibid., p. 110.

p. 246    *Heine's utter unhappiness:* See Schneider, op. cit., p. 31.

p. 246    *"I dragged myself . . .":* Quoted in Schneider, op. cit., pp. 28f.

pp. 246–47  *"my little steel-capped heels":* Quoted in Schlientz, op. cit., p. 61.

p. 247    *entered into a contract:* Ibid., p. 69.

p. 247    *"walking like a soldier":* Ibid., p. 77.

p. 247    *the slip of paper:* Ibid., p. 111.

p. 247    *"Like some pious puritan . . .":* Ibid., pp. 122f.

p. 247    *"angels in disguise":* Ibid., p. 113.

p. 247    *went on a holiday:* See George Sand, *Winter in Majorca,* translated by Robert Graves (London: Cassell, 1956).

p. 248    *the secret of this successful life:* For an opposing view, see Hans Mayer, *Outsiders,* translated by Denis M. Sweet (Cambridge: MIT Press, 1982), p. 95: "A brilliant attempt at women's emancipation within an especially auspicious historical constellation proved to be a failure."

p. 248    *"in golden colors . . .":* Quoted in Schlientz, op. cit., p. 319.

p. 250    *a formulation:* William James, *The Varieties of Religious Experience* (New York: New American Library, 1958), p. 389.

p. 251    *The professor's eye:* Ibid., pp. 24f.

p. 251    *In one of his lectures:* Ibid., pp. 87–111.

p. 252    *infected finger:* See Robert Peel, *Mary Baker Eddy: The Years of Trial* (New York: Holt, Rinehart and Winston, 1971), p. 3.

p. 252    *Quimby's practice:* See Hans-Dieter Reimer and Oswald Eggenberger, *Neben den Kirchen* (Konstanz: Christliche Verlagsanstalt, 1979), pp. 315f.

p. 252    *The real author:* Peel, op. cit., p. 279.

p. 253    *The most important passage:* Quoted in Peel, op. cit., p. 333.

p. 253    *Respected physicists:* See Hans-Peter Dürr, editor, *Physik und Transzendenz* (Bern: Scherz, 1986).

p. 253    *James Jeans wrote:* In *The Mysterious Universe* (New York: Macmillan, 1932), p. 175.

p. 253    *a physicist:* Fritjof Capra, *The Tao of Physics: An Exploration of the Parallels Between Modern Physics and Eastern Mysticism,* Third Edition (Boston: Shambhala,

1991). Capra's "Preface to the First Edition," included in this third edition, contains the quoted passage.

p. 254     *At the conclusion of his series:* James, *Varieties,* pp. 383–86.

p. 254     *the "subconscious self":* Ibid., pp. 385f.

p. 255     *not well loved:* See Sartre, *L'Idiot de la famille,* Vol. I, p. 135. The expression Sartre uses is *mal aimé.*

p. 255     *the dreams came from God:* See Friedrich Schiller, *Die Räuber,* Act 5, scene I.

p. 255     *in a madhouse:* Immanuel Kant, *Träume eines Geistersehers, erläutert durch Träume der Metaphysik* (Stuttgart: Reclam, 1976), pp. 66f. An English version can be found in Kant, *Dreams of a Spirit-Seer, Illustrated by Dreams of Metaphysics,* translated by Emanuel F. Goerwitz (New York: Macmillan, 1900).

p. 256     *Swedenborg later wrote:* Quoted in Ernst Benz, *Emanuel Swedenborg. Naturforscher und Seher* (Zurich: Swedenborg Verlag, 1969), p. 224.

p. 256     *"When I woke up this morning . . .":* Ibid., pp. 165f.

p. 256     *vivid dreams:* Ibid., pp. 173–78.

p. 257     *his passion for women:* Ibid., p. 176.

p. 257     *On Easter Sunday:* Ibid., pp. 178f.

p. 257     *loudly and clearly:* Ibid., p. 181.

p. 257     *a near disaster:* Ibid., pp. 28f.

p. 257     *"what can this signify?":* Ibid., pp. 183f.

p. 257     *two ladies:* Ibid., p. 187.

p. 258     *works of scientific research:* Ibid., pp. 108f.

p. 258     *middle of April 1745:* Ibid., pp. 204–8.

p. 259     *slow down his breathing:* Ibid., pp. 166–69.

p. 259     *"in the process of reflecting . . .":* Quoted ibid., pp. 322f.

p. 259     *famous philosophers:* Ibid., p. 323.

p. 259     *caught in the act:* Ibid., pp. 238f.

p. 260     *"It's a fact worth knowing":* Quoted in Christoph Bochinger, *"New Age" und moderne Religion* (Gütersloh: Jaiser, 1995), p. 273.

p. 261     *to take its leave of Christianity:* See ibid., p. 261.

p. 261     *a short step to the "New Age":* Ibid., p. 280.

p. 261     *received stimulation:* Ibid., p. 270.

p. 261     *his first mentor:* Ibid., pp. 268f.

p. 261     *the Fox family home:* See Ruth Brandon, *The Spiritualists: The Passion for the Occult in the Nineteenth and Twentieth Centuries* (New York: Knopf, 1983).

p. 261     *"The influence of the Holy Spirit . . .":* Quoted in James, *Varieties,* p. 388.

p. 261     *"You laugh at us Yankees":* Quoted in Ulrich Linse, *Geisterseher und Wunderwirker. Heilsuche im Industriezeitalter* (Frankfurt am Main: Fischer Taschenbuch Verlag, 1996), pp. 55f.

p. 262     *In the presence of a committee:* See Colin Wilson, *The Occult* (New York: Random House, 1971), pp. 463f.

p. 263     *thought that Home would be canonized:* Quoted in Brandon, op. cit., p. 167.

p. 263     *A grand piano:* Quoted in Wilson, op. cit., p. 466.

p. 263     *Much more concentration:* See Brandon, op. cit., pp. 78–87.

p. 263     *The list of thirteen:* Ibid., p. 82.

p. 264     *"The present state of affairs":* Quoted in Eberhard Bauer and Walter von Lacadou, editors, *Psi—was verbirgt sich dahinter* (Freiburg: Herder, 1984), p. 62.

pp. 264–65    *on holiday together:* See Brandon, op. cit., pp. 169–73.

p. 266    *the signs are fleeting:* See Joseph Agassi, *"Flüchtige Funken in der Welt des Blabla,"* in Hans Peter Duerr, editor, *Der Wissentschaftler und das Irrationale,* Vol. I (Frankfurt am Main: Syndikat, 1981), pp. 351–76.

p. 266    *asked William James:* Quoted in Brandon, op. cit., p. 77.

p. 266    *In elegant Geneva:* See Ellenberger, *The Discovery of the Unconscious,* pp. 315–18.

p. 268    *a Swiss psychiatrist:* See Carl Gustav Jung, "The Psychology of Dementia Praecox," translated by R. F. C. Hull, in *The Psychogenesis of Mental Disease,* Vol. 3 in *The Collected Works of C. G. Jung* (New York: Pantheon Books, 1960), p. 81.

p. 268    *heard about the mediumistic abilities:* See Ellenberger, op. cit., pp. 687–91. Also Stefanie Zumstein-Preiswerk, *C. G. Jungs Medium. Die Geschichte der Helly Preiswerk* (München: Kindler, 1975).

p. 268    *The world gained depth:* Carl Gustav Jung, *Memories, Dreams, Reflections,* translated by Richard and Clara Winston (New York: Vintage Books, 1989), p. 99.

p. 268    *an unflawed bread knife:* Ibid., pp. 105f.

p. 269    *During the First World War:* Ibid., pp. 190–91.

p. 269    *"I stood helpless . . .":* Ibid., p. 177.

p. 270    *the Holy Spirit came to him:* Ibid., pp. 171–72.

p. 270    *traveled to Geneva:* Carl Gustav Jung, *Erinnerungen, Träume, Gedanken* (Olten: Walter, 1984), pp. 378f. (This reference is to a section of the Appendix to *Memories, Dreams, Reflections* that does not appear in the English translation cited above.)

p. 270    *"an unswerving conviction . . .":* Jung, *Memories,* etc., p. 177.

p. 270    *the local ghost:* See Ellenberger, op. cit., pp. 673–74.

p. 270    *"What we cannot speak about . . .":* Wittgenstein, *Tractatus Logico-Philosophicus,* p. 151.

p. 271    *Ronald David Laing:* Times Literary Supplement, May 23, 1986. See in addition John Clay, *R. D. Laing: a Divided Self* (London: Hodder & Stoughton, 1996), pp. 242f.

p. 273    *a combination of Spiritualism and socialism:* See Linse, op. cit., p. 58.

p. 273    *a convention of Spiritualist societies:* Ibid., p. 57.

p. 273    *a population of 28,000,000:* See Howard Kerr and Charles L. Crow, editors, *The Occult in America* (Urbana: University of Illinois Press, 1983), p. 95.

p. 273    *a series of lectures:* See Brandon, *Spiritualists,* p. 12. (On the development of hynosis from Franz Anton Mesmer's "animal magnetism," see Ellenberger, op. cit., pp. 57–83.)

p. 273    *Davis worked on the composition:* See Linse, op. cit., pp. 57f.

p. 273    *a pedagogical program:* Ibid., pp. 64–66.

p. 274    *among the working people:* Ibid., pp. 58–61.

p. 274    Footfalls on the Boundary of Another World: The book appeared posthumously in 1860. See Linse, op. cit., p. 235, note 89.

p. 274    *alternative healing methods:* Ibid., p. 63.

p. 274    *decidedly anticlerical:* Ibid., pp. 61f.

p. 274    *only in the better circles:* Ibid., pp. 66–72.

p. 275    *a garden city arose:* See ibid., pp. 120–25.

p. 275    *the* Johannische *Christians:* According to a letter (dated January 7, 1994) from the Berlin office of the Church of St. John to the author, the number of registered members of the Church is currently given as 3,300.

p. 275          *"I believe in God the Father . . .":* See *Johannische Kirche: Kurzdarstellung,* published by the Verlag der Johannischen Kirche (Berlin: 1983), p. 3.

p. 275          *the German state police office:* See Linse, op. cit., p. 166.

p. 275          *a Soviet officer:* See *Weg und Ziel,* the weekly newspaper of the Church of St. John, Vol. 46, no. 51/52 (Dec. 22, 1993), p. 3.

p. 276          *numerous suits:* See Linse, op. cit., p. III.

p. 276          *Prussia's Protestant clergy:* Ibid., pp. 132–35.

p. 276          *"The power to heal the sick . . .":* Linse, op. cit., pp. 94, 96.

p. 276          *"I see Your Majesty . . .":* Ibid., p. 114.

p. 276          *the Master's healing practice:* Ibid., pp. 98–113.

p. 277          *the weekly assemblies:* Ibid., pp. 115 and 149f.

p. 277          *"Throughout the hall":* Ibid., pp. 140f.

p. 277          *apologias:* Ibid., p. 125.

pp. 277–78      *"the lower middle class":* Ibid., pp. 136f.

p. 278          *"Isolating the Powers of Darkness . . .":* Ibid., p. 156.

p. 278          *the Order of the Federal Republic:* Ibid., p. 176. The *Friedenstadt* was restored to the ownership of the Church in 1994.

p. 278          *a groundbreaking ceremony:* See *Weg und Ziel,* Vol. 49, no. 37 (September 11, 1996).

p. 280          *The desert grows:* Friedrich Nietzsche, *Kritische Studienausgabe,* edited by Giorgio Colli and Mazzino Montinari, Vol. 6 (München: Deutscher Taschenbuch Verlag, 1988), p. 387. All future references to volumes in this edition of Nietzsche's works will be given as KSA.

p. 280          *Where has God gone . . . ?:* Quoted in Werner Ross, *Der ängstliche Adler* (München: Deutscher Taschenbuch Verlag, 1994), pp. 584f.

p. 281          *The young lady:* See H. E. Peters, *My Sister, My Spouse: A Biography of Lou Andreas-Salomé* (New York: Norton, 1962), and Linde Salber, *Lou Andreas-Salomé* (Reinbek: Rowohlt, 1995).

p. 281          *Nietzsche's friend:* See Hubert Treiber, *Paul Rée—ein Freund Nietzsches,* in *Bündner Jahrbuch 1987* (Chur, 1986).

p. 281          *as a "God-seeker":* Lou Andreas-Salomé, *Lebensrückblick,* edited from previously unpublished material by Ernst Pfeiffer (Frankfurt am Main: Insel, 1974), p. 84.

p. 282          *Nietzsche read it too:* Ibid., p. 248.

p. 282          *obliged to reject:* See Dieter Borchmeyer and Jörg Salaquarda, editors, *Nietzsche und Wagner. Stationen einer epochalen Begegnung* (Frankfurt am Main: Insel, 1994), pp. 1337–40.

p. 282          *Through Wagner, Nietzsche wrote:* Nietzsche, KSA 6, p. 12.

p. 282          *"I am, as well as Wagner . . .":* Nietzsche, KSA 5, pp. 340f.

pp. 282–83      *with a little joke:* Borchmeyer and Salaquarda, op. cit., p. 296.

p. 283          *according to Nietzsche:* The corresponding aphorisms 109 and 220 in *Menschliches, Allzumenschliches (Human, All Too Human)* were written at a time when the break between Nietzsche and Wagner was not yet complete. See Borchmeyer and Salaquarda, op. cit., pp. 1323f.

p. 283          *There was more:* Ibid., pp. 1325–27.

p. 283          *"everything was clear . . .":* Quoted in Borchmeyer and Salaquarda, op. cit., p. 1318.

p. 283  *Wagner had a bad dream:* Ibid., pp. 1321f. (The dream was written down in September 1878.)

p. 284  *Rilke wrote her a letter:* Donald Prater, *A Ringing Glass: The Life of Rainer Maria Rilke* (Oxford: Clarendon Press, 1986), p. 37.

p. 285  *adopted the Russian God:* Salomé, *Lebensrückblick*, p. 120.

p. 285  *This sense of complete security:* See Lou Andreas-Salomé, *Rainer Maria Rilke* (Frankfurt am Main: Insel, 1988), p. 27.

p. 285  *"follow your dark God!":* See Prater, op. cit., p. 78.

p. 286  In a distant land, inaccessible to your steps: Richard Wagner, *Lohengrin*, Act 3, scene 3.

p. 286  *Wagner's consciousness of himself:* See Hans Mayer, *Richard Wagner* (Reinbek: Rowohlt, 1980), p. 114.

p. 287  *there was a difference:* Ibid., p. 113.

p. 288  *"Begone," Moses commands:* Arnold Schoenberg, *Moses und Aron*, Act 2, scene 4.

p. 288  *But my face you cannot see:* Ex. 33:20–23.

p. 288  *the allusion to the male genitalia:* See Miles, *God*, pp. 124f.

p. 288  *a few lines earlier:* Ex. 33:11.

p. 288  *another passage:* Ex. 24:9–11.

p. 289  No one has ever seen God: Jn. 1:18. In this connection see Schnackenburg, *The Gospel According to St. John*, Vol. I, pp. 277–81.

p. 289  *The last word:* Denzinger, *Enchiridion*, no. 3001.

p. 289  *When the Bible speaks of the face of God:* Migne, *Patrologia Graeca* 75, 577b.

p. 290  *Maestro Wagner in person:* Salomé, *Lebensrückblick*, p. 82.

p. 290  *"In Nietzsche's character":* Quoted in Ross, *Der ängstliche Adler*, p. 635.

p. 291  *In a soft, halting voice:* Quoted in Jörg Salaquarda, *Dionysos gegen den Gekreuzigten*, in Jörg Salaquarda, editor, *Nietzsche* (Darmstadt: Wissentschaftliche Buchgesellschaft, 1996), p. 311.

p. 291  *Oh noon of life!* Nietzsche, KSA 5, pp. 241–43 (montage).

p. 291  *Does anyone here:* Nietzsche, KSA 6, pp. 335–40 (abridged and rearranged).

p. 292  *Whereby I sang:* Quoted in Ross, op. cit., p. 576.

p. 292  *Let us beware:* Quoted in Salaquarda, *Nietzsche*, p. 312.

p. 292  *I bear the destiny:* Nietzsche, KSA 6, p. 364.

p. 292  *a gentleman in the woods:* Quoted in Ross, op. cit., p. 574.

p. 292  *When Moses came down:* Ex. 34:29.

p. 292  *"Now and then the thought occurs . . .":* Quoted in Ross, op. cit., p. 576.

p. 293  *Lou remembered:* Lou Andreas-Salomé, *Friedrich Nietzsche in seinen Werken* (Frankfurt am Main: Insel, 1994), p. 116.

p. 293  *a medical expert:* See Ross, op. cit., pp. 784–96.

p. 293  *Other authorities:* See Salaquarda, *Nietzsche*, p. 51.

p. 293  *Edvard Munch's 1906 painting:* Munch's portrait of Nietzsche hangs in the Munchmuseet in Oslo.

p. 293  *a series of lectures:* See Ross, op. cit., pp. 744–48.

p. 293  *her first articles:* See Peters, *My Sister, My Spouse*, p. 148.

p. 293  *the poet Stefan George:* Quoted in Ross, op. cit., p. 689.

p. 294  *"Anticipating, as I do . . .":* Nietzsche, KSA 6, p. 257.

p. 294  *on that holy spot:* Nietzsche, KSA 6, p. 341.

p. 294  *Christ's Transfiguration:* The Feast of the Transfiguration falls on August 6 in the Christian calendar.

p. 294     let us celebrate: Nietzsche, KSA 5, p. 243.

p. 294     *The fundamental conception:* Nietzsche, KSA 6, p. 335.

p. 294     *"Is it not folly . . . ?":* Nietzsche, KSA 4, p. 141.

p. 295     I teach you the superman: Nietzsche, KSA 4, p. 14.

p. 295     *"I implore you, my brothers":* Nietzsche, KSA 4, p. 15.

p. 295     Has anyone understood me?: Nietzsche, KSA 6, pp. 371–74.

p. 295     *Nietzsche's highest teaching:* Giorgio Colli, *Nach Nietzsche* (Frankfurt am Main:
           Europäische Verlagsanstalt, 1983), pp. 211f.

p. 295     *In his novel* Odd John: Olaf Stapledon, *Odd John & Sirius* (New York: Dover
           Publications, 1972). See Eike Barmeyer, *Science Fiction. Theorie und Geschichte*
           (München: Fink, 1972), pp. 286f.

p. 296     *Whatever wanted to be made:* Salomé, *Lebensrückblick,* p. 116. See also Salber, *Lou
           Andreas-Salomé,* p. 90.

p. 296     *under the influence of Sigmund Freud:* Lou Andreas-Salomé, *In der Schule bei Freud*
           (Frankfurt am Main: Ullstein, 1983); Peters, *My Sister, My Spouse,* pp. 268–
           90; Salber, *Lou Andreas-Salomé,* pp. 103–26.

p. 297     *The Swedish psychiatrist:* See Peters, op. cit., pp. 270f.

p. 297     *When she was seventy:* Salomé, *Lebensrückblick,* pp. 138–50 (montage).

p. 297     *It seemed as though I wouldn't recognize:* See Prater, *A Ringing Glass,* p. 98.

p. 297     *a typical hysteric:* Salomé, *In der Schule,* p. 149.

p. 297     *He considered the Expressionist painters fools:* See Marthe Robert, *Die Revolution der
           Psychoanalyse* (Frankfurt am Main: Fischer, 1986), pp. 252f. This book was
           originally published in French: Marthe Robert, *La révolution psychanalytique: la
           vie et l'oeuvre de Sigmund Freud* (Paris: Payot, 1964).

p. 298     *an obstinate resistance:* See Peters, op. cit.

p. 298     *having discussed the question:* Salomé, *In der Schule,* pp. 181f. See also Prater, op.
           cit., p. 200.

p. 298     *brought Rilke and Freud together:* Salomé, *In der Schule,* p. 191.

p. 298     *Since artistic talent:* Sigmund Freud, *Studienausgabe,* Vol. 10 (Frankfurt am
           Main: S. Fischer, 1969), p. 157.

p. 298     *With regard to the psychoanalysis:* Quoted in Salomé, *In der Schule,* pp. 268f.

p. 298     *Between God and man:* Denzinger, *Enchiridion,* no. 806.

p. 298     *things are bad:* Quoted in Prater, op. cit., pp. 201f.; see also Salomé, *Rainer
           Maria Rilke,* p. 56.

p. 299     *A strong bora was blowing outside:* Prater, op. cit., pp. 204f.

p. 299     *The* Duino Elegies, *however, were finished:* See ibid., pp. 346–50; see also
           Salomé, *Rilke,* pp. 100f.

p. 300     *a collection of poems and an essay:* Chamber Music (1907) and "The Day of the
           Rabblement" (1901).

p. 300     *to keep literary scholars thoroughly busy:* See Richard Ellmann, *James Joyce* (New
           York: Oxford University Press, 1959), p. 535.

p. 300     *"As long as human fear . . .":* Quoted in Ellmann, *Joyce,* p. 99.

p. 301     *short prose pieces:* James Joyce, *Epiphanies,* edited by O. A. Silverman (University
           of Buffalo, 1956). On this subject see Willy Erzgräber, *Von Thomas Hardy bis
           Ted Hughes. Studien zur modernen englischen und anglo-irischen Literatur* (Freiburg im
           Breisgau: Rombach, 1995), pp. 11–117; Morris Beja, *Epiphany in the Modern
           Novel* (London: Peter Owen, 1971), pp. 71–111; Eveline Kilian, *Momente
           innerweltlicher Transzendenz. Die Augenblickserfahrung in Dorothy Richards Romanzyklus*

Pilgrimage *und ihr ideengeschichtlicher Kontext* Tübingen: Max Niemeyer, 1997), pp. 108–19.

p. 301  *a sudden spiritual manifestation:* James Joyce, *Stephen Hero* (New York: New Directions, 1955), p. 211.

p. 301  *It was for the man of letters:* Ibid.

p. 301  *His blasphemies:* James Joyce, *Ulysses* (New York: Random House, 1961), pp. 19, 428.

p. 301  *an employment form:* See Ellmann, *Joyce*, p. 350.

p. 302  *and then he asked me . . . :* Joyce, *Ulysses*, p. 783.

p. 302  *a minister . . . visited Joyce:* See Ellmann, *Joyce*, p. 546.

pp. 302–3  *"In all the places I have been to":* Ibid., pp. 558–59.

p. 303  *he remarked slyly:* Quoted in Beja, *Epiphany*, p. 71.

p. 303  *detecting the hidden luster:* See Peter Strasser, *Geborgenheit im Schlechten* (Wien: Deuticke, 1993), pp. 126–46.

p. 303  *It was his birthday:* See Ellmann, *Joyce*, p. 539.

p. 304  *And there was evening:* Gen. 1:5,8,13,19,23, 31.

# Index